Using Microsoft® Works 2.0

Using Microsoft® Works 2.0

GLENN T. SMITH

James Madison University
Harrisonburg, Virginia

RICHARD T. CHRISTOPH

James Madison University
Harrisonburg, Virginia

PRENTICE HALL
Englewood Cliffs, New Jersey 07632

Library of Congress Cataloging-in-Publication Data

Smith, Glenn T.
    Using Microsoft Works 2.0 / Glenn T. Smith, Richard T. Christoph.
        p.   cm.
    Includes index.
    ISBN 0-13-950551-2
    1. Integrated software. 2. Microsoft Works (Computer program)
I. Christoph, Richard T. II. Title.
QA76.76.I57S63 1991
005.369--dc20   90-46121
                                                        CIP

Cover design: Richard Pruder Design
Manufacturing buyer: Trudy Pisciotti/Bob Anderson

Microsoft® is a registered trademark of Microsoft Corporation.

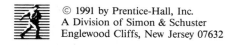
© 1991 by Prentice-Hall, Inc.
A Division of Simon & Schuster
Englewood Cliffs, New Jersey 07632

Printed in the United States of America
10 9 8 7 6 5 4

ISBN 0-13-950551-2 01

Prentice-Hall International (UK) Limited, *London*
Prentice-Hall of Australia Pty. Limited, *Sydney*
Prentice-Hall Canada Inc., *Toronto*
Prentice-Hall Hispanoamericana, S.A., *Mexico*
Prentice-Hall of India Private Limited, *New Delhi*
Prentice-Hall of Japan, Inc., *Tokyo*
Simon & Schuster Asia Pte. Ltd., *Singapore*
Editora Prentice-Hall do Brasil, Ltda., *Rio de Janeiro*

Contents

Chapter 5:   Working With Documents *87*

Chapter 6: Advanced Word Processing Features   *111*

Chapter 9: Using Advanced Spreadsheet Concepts **193**

Preface

Microcomputer usage has increased from an interesting novelty a few years ago to the point that it is a vital component of everyday life. This powerful tool has the ability to enhance the performance of the user; however, the computer also made a number of new and potentially complicated demands on the user. Perhaps the most critical of these demands is that knowledge of, and proficient use of, the computer is a required skill for everyone. In order to survive in today's world, you must be able to use the microcomputer as a tool to improve your productivity. This text is designed to help you obtain this skill.

Development of the Text

There are two basic premises that underline the development of this text. The first premise is that the user is not computer proficient. The text starts from the beginning, introducing basic concepts and terminology, and moves to advanced topics that many experienced users are not aware exist. This allows users at all levels to use this text. The second premise that underlines the text is that a new user needs more than information on what the program can do. They need guided experience on how to make the program do these functions. It was with these two premises in mind that the text was developed. We feel we have held to these premises throughout the text.

Microsoft Works 2.0

Microsoft Works 2.0 is an upgrade to the original Microsoft Works program. This upgrade was released in the Fall of 1989. The Microsoft Works program provides the user with an easy to learn set of modules that will allow him or her to perform the common tasks required by an individual or small business. These functions include word processing, electronic spreadsheets, charting, database, and telecommunications. The key element in the Works program is its ability to integrate data from any of its modules with data from any of its other modules. This provides a new user with a program that can be easily learned and mastered by a nonprofessional.

Enhancements made by Works 2.0

Some of the new features in the word processing module include reorganized menus to give the program a more intuitive feel, a redesigned approach to setting tabs, the ability to set borders around paragraphs, *Bookmarks* to easily find a location in a document, inclusion of *Footnotes* in a document, a *Thesaurus* for finding synonyms of words, and a *Print Preview* to allow you to see how your document will print before you print it.

Changes to the spreadsheet module include the ability to set borders on cells, the ability to change fonts and styles for individual cells, a *Fill Series* option, and the ability to sort rows within the spreadsheet. Enhancements have also been made to the charting routine.

Improvements to the database module provide a much easier approach to forms design and report design along with a more flexible report design module.

Improvements for all modules include a set of *File Management* utilities, a built in calculator and alarm clock feature, the *Page Preview* option, an easy approach at recording *macros*, and the ability to size, move, and arrange multiple windows.

Structure of the Text

Using Microsoft Works can be used to fill the void between concepts and applications. The first chapter introduces general microcomputer concepts. These concepts are essential for understanding the terminology of microcomputers and how to use the microcomputer. The second chapter introduces the essential MS-DOS commands to accomplish common tasks. These chapters should only be skipped if the users are proficient with using a microcomputer and are using the book only to learn the Microsoft Works program.

The remaining chapters are aimed at the Microsoft Works program. Each chapter begins with a narrative introduction to the terminology and concepts covered in the chapter. This section of the chapter explains how Microsoft Works accomplishes certain tasks and what the user should do to get Microsoft Works to accomplish a task. It familiarizes the user with the terms, techniques, and menus he or she will need when using Works. This is terminated by a short answer *self-test* to see if the reader has understood and retained the information in the chapter.

The second section of the chapter is a self-paced, step-by-step tutorial that guides the user through the development of a document, a spreadsheet, or a database. The concepts and principles covered in the first section of the chapter are implemented in the second section. This allows the user to bring together the concepts and the application.

Features of the Text

Each chapter is written with a minimal amount of computer *jargon* that often times interferes with the understanding of the material presented. Each chapter also presents several aids to assist the user in applying concepts with hints on when certain approaches should be used.

Self-paced, hands on tutorials are included that guide the user through an application of the material presented in the chapter. These applications are as *real world* oriented as possible. This allows the user to gain an understanding of not only how to accomplish a task but also what the new material may be used for. There is also an element of business principles built into all of the chapters. A collection of tutorial files allows the user to work with larger real world problems without spending endless hours of typing rather than learning the approaches.

Each subject offers special hands on practice exercises in which the user can use the computer to solve problems independently. These computer based exercises allow the user to apply techniques learned in the chapters to new problems without the guided assistance of the textbook.

The text offers a detailed Table of Contents and Index that allow topics to be found quickly and easily. The Table of Contents lists topics as presented in the narrative section of each chapter and the tutorial section of each chapter. This allows the user to examine the application of a technique as well as reading how it should be applied.

The text presents material in a narrative style and conceptual point of view, like most texts, then it follows this narrative style with a detailed tutorial. This allows the user to both understand what he or she should do and how to do it. These tutorials include many screen displays so the user can check his or her progress through the tutorial. These screen displays also help the user see if he or she is on track and has completed a task successfully.

The greatest benefit of the text is consistency. In an educational environment, where students have different instructors with different teaching styles, different expectations, different priorities, and different approaches, the student can learn a topic even if it is skipped in the classroom. The instructor can become a learning aid rather than a teaching machine. The instructor is free to cover topics in more detail or additional topics while the student can learn the basics at their own pace. This, in essence, means that all students that use the text will have been exposed to and used the same material.

To the Student

As you progress through this course and this text it is extremely important that you remember that the subject matter learned does not exist in a vacuum. This material is a foundation for a skill that is required by virtually every employer and every professional in today's world. The material learned in this course can, and should be used in every course for the remainder of your formal education and for the remainder of your professional career. For this reason, the goal of the course is not to *memorize* the material to pass a test. The goal is to learn the material so that it becomes second nature. If you learn the material with this goal in mind, passing a test and making a good grade will be a matter of routine. This learned skill will help in all your remaining courses.

To the Instructor

It is also important for an instructor to remember that this is a skill that will be used in other courses. The student relies heavily on the material learned here for their other course assignments. It is important that each student demonstrate a competency with the material that will allow them to compete in other courses and in their chosen career. It is also important to remember that this course is only one part of a larger whole and that a chain is no stronger than its weakest link. For this reason, and this reason alone, a sincere effort to meet all requirements of the course is a necessity. If any element is missed or covered too lightly, you will have placed your students at a disadvantage.

The text also has an accompanying instructor's guide. This guide has a chapter outline, answers to each chapter self test, objective quiz questions for the chapter, and transparency masters for many of the diagrams in the text. Additional comprehensive exercises for the word processing, spreadsheet, and database modules are also provided. The instructor's guide is available in printed form and also on diskette in Microsoft Works 2.0 format.

Acknowledgments

It would be impossible to acknowledge every individual that contributed to the development of this text; however, we would like to mention several groups of people and several individuals. First we would like to express our thanks and appreciation to the many suggestions we have received from those individuals that use the Microsoft Works package. We also would like to express our sincere thanks to Dr. Charles Bilbrey for his support and encouragement during the development of this project. Without his support and understanding this project would have never been completed.

A special word of thanks is given for the guidance and direction provided by our editor, Ted Werthman, of Prentice Hall. His help and guidance on content and style has been invaluable. Another special thanks goes to Nancy DeWolfe, our production editor. Without her help, guidance, and understanding, the text would not have been completed on schedule.

We would also like to thank the Microsoft Corporation for producing a product like Microsoft Works. Combined, we have over twenty-five years of experience teaching computer information systems courses. After many years of looking for a software package that will allow a student to concentrate on using the computer as a tool rather than being a technical expert in order to use the computer, we finally found Microsoft Works. Thanks again Microsoft Corporation for solving our problem.

We would also like to thank the thousands of students we have come to know and respect over the past years. We are called the professors and the teachers but we have received much more than we have been able to give. You have given us thousands of ideas, techniques, and challenges over the years but more importantly, you have taught us how to teach. Without you we would still be beginners.

We would like to thank our wives, Terri and Orinda, for their unselfish patience and understanding. No man stands alone and without your support, this project would still be only an idea. Finally, we would like to thank our children - Wesley, Jacob, George, and Erica. We know that you do not always understand why we disappear to basements and bedrooms for hours (and sometimes days) on end, but you still love us when we come out. We love all of you.

Using Microsoft® Works 2.0

1

Microcomputer Concepts

This book will introduce you to the fun and power of the personal computer and some of the software programs that make the microcomputer a productive tool. You will learn to produce professional-looking documents using a word processor as well as to create electronic spreadsheets to help prepare budgets and accounting information. You will also discover how easy it is to express this numeric information in many different graphic forms. Information about inventories and personnel-related items can be accurately maintained through the use of the database, and the fascinating world of telecommunications will also be explored, allowing you to connect one computer with another. Finally, you will find out how to combine documents created by the word processor with various spreadsheets and charts that you have created. You can even prepare form letters by combining these documents with names and addresses in a database.

While these topics may seem foreign at first, each topic will be presented one step at a time and will become second nature to you as you develop skills using the computer. Perhaps the real key to success is to experiment and have fun. Don't try to learn everything at once (at best a difficult task), and you will find that learning about the computer will be fun and will pay many dividends in numerous areas of life, including your career.

There are also many things that you will not learn from this text. You will not learn how to play games on the microcomputer. You will not learn how to build a microcomputer. You will not even learn how to select the equipment you need to set up your own microcomputer system. This information is left to other references. Rather, this book is designed for **users** of microcomputers, not builders of microcomputers. The intent of the book is to make you comfortable with the operation of the microcomputer and some of its software, so that you will use it as a tool to make your life easier.

Before you can begin to learn how to use any new tool, there are some concepts and terminology that must be covered, and the microcomputer is certainly no exception to this rule. Let's start with the actual equipment or "hardware."

Computer Hardware Concepts

Computer hardware refers to the actual equipment, machines, and physical devices of a computer system. A typical personal computer system is illustrated in Figure 1.1.

Figure 1.1

These are the various hardware components of a personal computer.

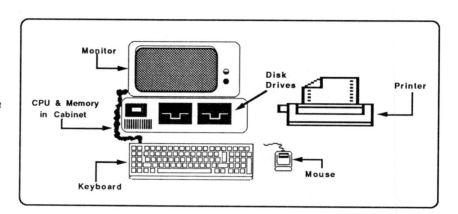

> ## ➤ *The Central Processing Unit*

The *Central Processing Unit* (normally referred to as the CPU) is a small electronic chip usually located in the cabinet beneath the video display tube of the computer system. The CPU is the heart of the computer system and is the device that allows the machine to perform many different complex mathematic and logic functions. While it is not important for us to know how the CPU works in order to be able to use the microcomputer, it is important to know that it is a major part of the machine.

The *Random Access Memory* (RAM) consists of memory that is stored using electronic chips and is located in the same cabinet as the CPU and disk drives. The function of RAM is to store programs and information inside the computer and have the information ready to be used by the CPU.

There are two important things to remember when using Random Access Memory and, therefore, the computer. The first is that the amount of RAM is limited with a computer having a specific amount of this memory installed. The amount of memory available in the system is measured in *bytes*. For our purposes, consider a byte as being the same as one character. Therefore, if your computer has 640,000 bytes of memory, think of this as saying that your computer can store 640,000 typed characters. In computer jargon, you would say your machine has about 640K bytes of RAM. One technical note: a K equals 1024 bytes, so 640K bytes will really equal 655,360 bytes.

The second important point to remember about memory is that it is *volatile*. This means that if the machine loses its power, anything that is stored in the memory is lost or destroyed. Because the memory is volatile, you should save your work to some type of non-volatile device (such as a floppy disk) periodically.

➢ *The Keyboard*

The keyboard is the standard device used to enter information into the computer's memory. It looks and operates much like a standard typewriter keyboard and includes the standard 26 letters of the alphabet, the 10 digits used for numbers, and some special characters such as the @ # $ % & * ( ) ?. In addition to these standard keys, the keyboard has a number of special sets of keys. On the right-hand side of the keyboard is the *numeric keypad* that can be used when entering large sets of numbers. Note that some of the keys on the numeric keypad also have other names such as Home, End, PgUp, and PgDn. The use of these dual function keys will be covered later. Special keys that you will use quite often include:

Function keys - These special keys labeled F1, F2, F3, . . . F12, are referred to as *Function keys*. Function keys may be located in two vertical rows on the left side of the keyboard or, on other models, in a horizontal row across the top of the keyboard. These keys perform special functions and are not used to enter information into the computer.

Shift - The shift key (sometimes labeled with an outlined up arrow) is used to select a second set of characters. When the key is pressed, uppercase letters are typed, or if the key shows two characters, the one on the top half of the key is typed. This key works like the familiar shift key on a typewriter.

ALT - This is the "Alternate" key and works in the same manner as an additional shift key. Like the shift key, this key is normally used with at least one other key. When it is pressed, an alternate or different set of characters for each key can be used. Therefore, if you have 26 standard character keys (A...Z), using the ALT key with the standard keys could double the number of characters, giving you 52 different characters. Typically, the ALT key is used to allow you to send a special command to the program that you are using in the computer. Often, when you use the ALT key, you will use it in conjunction with a second key. In this book, when using the ALT key with another key, it will be printed as ALT/x where "x" will be a second key. To enter an alternate key, press the ALT key and, while holding this key down, press the second key. For example, to enter ALT/P:

Hold down the ALT key and press the P key.

Ctrl - This is the Control (Ctrl) key. Its function is similar to that of the ALT key. It causes a second key to execute some special function. Like the ALT key, it is always used with some other key. In this book, when you are asked to enter a control key, it will be printed as Ctrl/x where x will be the second key.

Esc - The Escape (Esc) key, as its name implies, is used to escape or leave some function that has been selected. The Escape key is always used by itself.

ENTER - The Enter key may be labeled with an arrow symbol (◄┘) or simply be called Enter or Return. Usually, the Enter key is pressed to signal the computer that the last instruction you are using is completed and should be :Entered" into the system.

➤ Using Auto Repeat Keys

All the keys on the keyboard are auto-repeat keys. This means that if you hold the key down, the character or function that the key performs will be repeated as long as the key is held down. This idea is especially important when you use ALT or Ctrl keys. Since these keys usually perform a function, if you hold these keys down for several seconds, you will perform the function several times. As an example, suppose the ALT/P caused the computer system to print a document. If you held the ALT/P key down for several seconds, you could be telling the system to print the document several times.

➤ The Video Monitor

The video monitor normally sits on top of the computer system and looks much like a TV screen. It is sometimes called a Cathode Ray Tube (CRT), or Video Display Terminal (VDT), or simply a monitor and serves as the standard output device for the computer system. In practice, there are two different types of monitors: a monochrome monitor and a full color monitor. If the monitor is monochrome , it can display one color and black. These monochrome monitors are usually available in amber and black or green and black. Most of these monochrome systems can also display different shades of either the amber or green when you display different colors, much like a black-and-white television. If you want to display actual color, you will need an full color monitor.

Floppy Disk
Hard Disk

➤ The Disk Drives

The disk drives are used to hold small magnetic disks. The disks are used to store information that would normally be lost when the machine is turned off. Most computers will be equipped with multiple drives with each drive being identified with a letter designation. The first drive is named drive A:, the second is named B:, the third drive is C:, etc. This is the normal naming convention. There may be one exception to this. If the machine has only one drive that accepts a floppy disk and has an internal fixed disk (disks are discussed later), the floppy disk will be named A: and the internal fixed disk will be named C:. In this case, there would be no B: disk drive.

As mentioned earlier, the internal memory of the computer is volatile. When the machine is turned off, the information stored in the machine is lost. The disk drive is used to record information that you do not want lost when the machine is turned off. This information is recorded onto a diskette of some type for future use.

➤ The Dot Matrix Printer

The printer is used to produce a "hard" or printed copy of the information stored in the computer system. While there are many types of printers, the most common is the *dot matrix* printer. This versatile printer prints letters, numbers, and other characters by arranging a series of dots on the page to represent the character. One important point to note about these and other printers is that there will be some characters that a given printer cannot print. For example, in some instances a program may be able to display certain characters on your screen, such as italic characters, but your printer may not be able to print these characters. When the computer sends these characters to the printer to be printed, the printer cannot find the character in its list of printable characters, so the character will usually be printed in standard form.

A second important point about printers is how they determine when to underline, print in bold, and use other types of highlighting for characters. When you try to print a series of characters that are underlined, the underline itself is not sent to the printer. A special control character to start underlining is sent to the printer. This sets the printer in underline mode. Then all characters that are sent to the printer are underlined until another special control character is sent to turn the underlining off. When you think of printing special forms of text, remember that you must turn the special highlighting on, specify your text, then turn the highlighting off.

➤ **The Laser Printer**

The newest type of printer is the **laser** printer, which not only provides superb quality print but also allows you to print any character that you want. While these printers are more expensive than dot matrix printers, their quiet, high-quality print provides the best output possible, especially when you are printing charts or other types of graphics. These are the printers that you would like to use when you want the best print quality possible.

➤ **The Mouse**

A *mouse* is a special desktop device that is used to move the cursor around on the display screen and to select options from screen menus. On the bottom of the mouse is a small ball that rolls when the mouse is moved. As the ball rolls, it causes a signal to be sent to the computer, which moves the cursor in the direction that the mouse is moved. The mouse usually has two buttons. By pressing one of these buttons, you can instruct the computer to perform some action where the cursor is resting.

Computer Software Concepts

The term *software* refers to the programs that make the computer perform sophisticated tasks. There are basically two different types of programs that the computer uses and that you need to be aware of: operating system programs and application programs.

➤ **Operating Systems**

An operating system is a set of programs that control the resources and components of the computer. It consists of a number of specialized programs, each of which performs a specific task. One such task controlled by the operating system is the allocation of the computer's random access memory (RAM), which is used by application programs. The operating system is also responsible for the synchronization of other hardware components such as the monitor, printer, and disk drive(s). Most personal computers use a disk-based operating system called the **D**isk **O**perating **S**ystem, and commands executed within the operating system are often called DOS commands. Specific coverage of some of these commands is provided in Chapter 2.

➤ *Application Programs*

Application programs are written to perform a specific function for the user and might include word processing, accounting programs, or programs that handle business inventory. Historically, many application programs have been specific with regard to function; however, many newer programs now seek to combine many operations in one program. Such programs, called *integrated programs*, provide word processing capabilities, electronic worksheet and graphing capabilities, database management capabilities, and communication capabilities. The Microsoft Works program that you will be using is an excellent example of this type of program.

Disk Concepts

Computers have the ability to process and manage vast amounts of information quickly and easily, but to do so, they must have the ability to store information so that it can be retrieved when needed. Today, the *magnetic disk* is the most popular device used to store information. Information stored on disks is contained in *files* this allows the computer to find needed information at any time.

➤ *Disk Concepts*

Since the computer's internal memory is volatile and is erased when the computer is turned off, a more permanent storage device is needed to keep data for long periods. Currently, the most common long-term storage device is the diskette or floppy disk. Diskettes are available in two different sizes as illustrated in Figure 1.2.

The diskette shown on the left side of Figure 1.2 contains a round, floppy disk that is housed in a flexible, square case. The diskette is $5\frac{1}{4}$ inches in diameter and can store approximately 360,000 typed characters of data when it is used in the standard density format. This is equivalent to almost 100 single-spaced, typed pages. The $5\frac{1}{4}$ inch diskette is also available in a "high" density version that can store 1,200,000 characters of information. These high-density diskettes require the use of high-density diskette drives and are usually used for making copies of internal hard disks.

The smaller diskette in Figure 1.2 is $3\frac{1}{2}$ inches in diameter and is relatively new. These diskettes have a plastic case and a small cover that protects the actual magnetic disk inside. Because these smaller disks take up less space and are more durable, they are becoming standard equipment on many new computers. Most of these diskettes can store approximately 730,000 characters of information or about 200 single-spaced, typed pages. Note that the second diskette is much smaller than the first diskette; however, it stores twice as much information. There are also high-density $3\frac{1}{2}$ inch diskettes that will store over 1.4 million characters or about 400 typed pages.

Figure 1.2

These are the different sizes of diskettes. The new 3^1/$_2$ inch diskette usually holds over 730,000 typed characters.

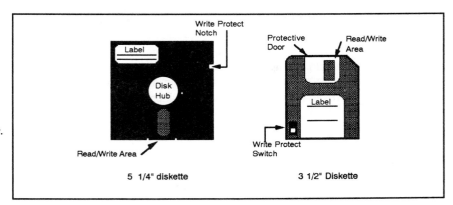

When something is *written* to the diskette, the information is recorded magnetically around the diskette on concentric circles called tracks which are further divided into sectors as illustrated in Figure 1.3. Tracks and sectors must be created by the computer before the diskette can be used, since they are not on the disk when it is purchased. This process of creating the tracks and sectors is called **formatting**. The format process prepares the disk for use by the computer when data is later stored on the diskette. This actual process of formatting is covered in the next chapter under DOS commands.

Figure 1.3

You must prepare a diskette to hold information by formatting it before you use it.

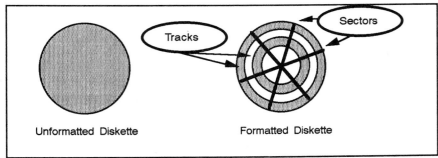

➢ **Hard or Fixed Disks**

There are also disks referred to as fixed or hard disks. The principle behind the operation of a fixed disk is similar to the diskette; however, there are some significant advantages offered by the fixed disk. The two most important advantages are that fixed disks offer much higher speed and greater storage capacity than standard diskettes. A major drawback of hard disks is that they cannot easily be removed from the computer for backup or safe keeping. For this reason, it is a good idea to use diskettes to make a copy of important data stored on the fixed disk. This procedure is called backing up the fixed disk.

➢ **Purchasing Diskettes**

You will need to purchase several diskettes, but to be sure that you get the correct diskettes, you will need to understand how diskettes are labeled. Some disks can only store information on one side of the disk. These disks will be labeled either SS (single sided) or 1S (one sided). Disks that can store information on both sides are labeled DS (double sided) or 2S (two sided).

The next thing you need to know about disk labels concerns the density of the disk, which represents how close together information can be stored on the diskette. Typical density ratings for diskettes include SD for single density, DD for double density, and HD for high density. Usually, to store the data closer together on a diskette (which would mean higher density), the diskette must be of a higher quality. Finally, be aware that all diskette drives are not capable of reading all diskette densities, so be sure to check your drive specifications before buying diskettes. Once you identify the specifications, you will find that the diskettes will be labeled in the following ways:

SS/SD or 1S/SD	Single sided / single density
SS/DD or 1S/DD	Single sided / double density
DS/SD or 2S/SD	Double sided / single density
DS/DD or 2S/DD	Double sided / double density
SS/HD or 1S/HD	Single sided / high density
DS/HD or 2S/HD	Double sided / high density

➤ *Care of Diskettes*

The diskettes that you buy today are very reliable; however, they are not indestructible. You must use reasonable care to ensure that the diskette does not become damaged, which would mean that data stored on the diskette could be lost.

To appreciate the care that you must take to protect your diskettes, you should understand that the diskette is coated with an iron oxide material. The information stored on the diskette is recorded as magnetized spots that are recorded next to each other. When the data is transferred from the diskette to the memory of the machine, the reading device must be able to interpret groups of spots as a character. If it encounters a spot that cannot be interpreted, the reading device gives an error and and stops reading. Depending upon where the error is, you may lose all the information on the diskette or you may only lose a small portion of the information. In either case, you have lost part of your work.

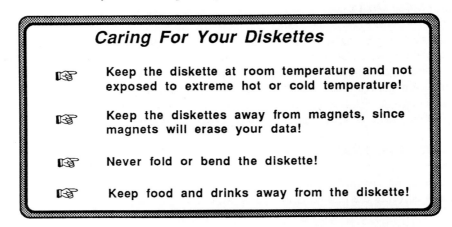

Caring For Your Diskettes

☞   Keep the diskette at room temperature and not exposed to extreme hot or cold temperature!

☞   Keep the diskettes away from magnets, since magnets will erase your data!

☞   Never fold or bend the diskette!

☞   Keep food and drinks away from the diskette!

In general, use the same care for a diskette as you would for your best stereo tapes or records. They are constructed in similar fashion and store their data in somewhat the same way. The biggest difference is that if you destroy a record, you can buy a new one. If you destroy a diskette that contains important information, you may need to manually re-create the information.

File Concepts

When information is stored on a diskette, it is stored as a *file*. A file on a diskette serves much the same purpose as a report cover that holds information under the name of the report. The disk file is similar since the file is a specific area on a diskette that is named and contains information about a specific subject. For example, if you created a resume using a word processor and stored the resume on a diskette, the resume would be referred to as the Resume file. The same would be true of a worksheet or a database.

➤ The File Name

A diskette, and especially a fixed disk, may contain many (sometimes several hundred) files. Therefore, each file must have a different name from any other file on the same disk. The file name consists of two parts: the name and an extension such as **EMPLOY.WPS**, which might be the name of the employee file. The name is used to identify the file, while the extension is used to identify the type of information in the file. These file-naming conventions are covered in the next chapter.

➤ Loading the File

You cannot directly see or change the information that is stored in a file on a disk. Rather, you can only see and change data that is loaded from the disk into memory and then displayed on the CRT screen. Therefore, before you can examine or change data, you must first load the file into memory, which creates a second copy of the file in random access memory. The copy that is on the diskette remains there and is not changed until you save your work. This is seen in Figure 1.4.

When changes are made to the copy of the file displayed on the screen, only the copy of the file in memory is altered, not the copy of the file on the disk. **No** changes are made to the copy of the file on the diskette until you instruct the computer to *save* the changed copy of the file in memory to the diskette. Then, the new copy of the file that is still in the computer's memory replaces the copy that is on the diskette. Occasionally, this process can save you some effort. Assume that you have decided to make some changes to a file and load it into memory to work on it. After making the changes, you determine that you would prefer the original version. If this is the case, do not save the file in memory to the disk, but rather reload the original file. Again, when you save a file, the new version replaces the original.

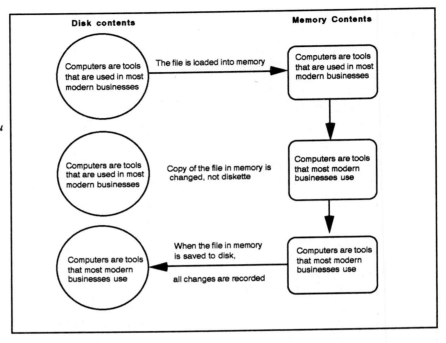

Figure 1.4

When you alter a file, you first change the copy of the file stored in the computer's memory. Then, when the file is saved to disk, the new, changed copy from memory replaces the old copy on the disk.

Directories

Because the average user may store many files on a disk, a logical method is needed to organize the different files. You can get an idea of the problem by imagining yourself looking through a catalog where the items are inserted randomly and where there is no grouping of item types. If you were trying to purchase a telephone, you would find that telephones may be on the same page with shirts and tires and that different telephones would be spread throughout the catalog. Selecting a telephone under these conditions would be an enormous task indeed!

The same problem would exist if the disks were not organized into *directories* and *subdirectories* of files which group similar files together. For example, suppose that you wanted to organize your computer work according to the subjects you are interested in: namely History, English, and Microcomputer Applications. You would set up directories for each subject area so that you could quickly find the information you where looking for. Similarly, if you wanted to keep your microcomputer work together, you might set up directories for files used for word processing, spreadsheet, and database applications.

This type of disk organization will let you search for files that are related under some common topic or area. Directories are also helpful when different kinds of application programs are stored on the same disk: one subdirectory might be used for Microsoft Works, another for a graphics program, and yet another for the MS-DOS operating system.

You might organize your directories as shown in Figure 1.5.

Figure 1.5:

The disk subdirectory system lets you group various files according to the file contents or subject.

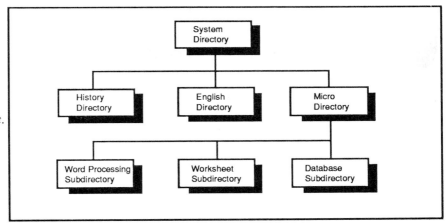

Conclusion

This chapter has introduced some of the hardware, software, and disk concepts that you will need to understand to use the computer effectively. If you feel a bit uncomfortable with some of these new topics, don't worry, since you will find that you will gain confidence as you use these new skills. To test how well you understand the material, complete the following chapter self-test.

Chapter 1 Self Test

1.   List the six hardware components of a typical microcomputer system.

2.   What is the function of RAM memory?

3.   What does the term <u>volatile</u> mean?

4.   How do you enter an Alternate or Control keystroke?

5.   What is the Esc key used for?

6.   If you have a machine with one floppy disk drive and one internal fixed disk drive, what will the names of the drives be?

7.   How does a printer determine when to start and stop underlining?

8.   What is a mouse used for?

9.   What is the function of the Operating System?

10.   What happens when you format a diskette?

11.   What is a DS/DD diskette?

12.   List four things that you should not do to a diskette.

13.   What are the two parts of a file name, and what does each part do?

14.   When you load a file from a diskette into memory and make changes, what happens to the file on the diskette?

15.   What are directories used for?

2

Introduction to MS-DOS

The personal computer is one of the most powerful tools available to help individuals with a variety of tasks which include word processing, financial analysis, and the storage of information in databases. In order to perform these tasks, the **hardware** of the computer must be teamed with programs or **software**. These programs are the instructions that tell your personal computer what to do and how to respond to your commands.

One of the most important software components of the computer is the operating system The operating system is a collection of programs that controls all of the functions of the computer, including the presentation of information on the computer screen, printing it on the printer, and storing it on disks. The operating system that is currently the most popular is called MS-DOS, that has been developed for the IBM family of computers and compatible systems that mimic the IBM. MS-DOS stands for Microsoft Disk Operating System and is named after the Microsoft Corporation that developed it.

Programs are usually numbered by the company that develops them as a way of keeping track of the software version (like editions of a book). Typically, the numbers start at 1.0, with higher numbers associated with later versions of the programs (2.1, 3.0, etc.). The later versions include enhancements that have been made to the original software. Generally, higher-version numbers include extra features and should be preferred over lower-version numbers. The MS-DOS operating system follows this numbering convention with the original set of programs for the operating system being numbered 1.0. As minor changes were made, versions 1.1, 1.2, 1.3, etc., were released. When major changes to the operating system were released, the first digit of the number changed, which results in versions 2.0, 2.1, 3.0, 3.1, 3.2, etc. The latest version, as of this writing, is MS-DOS 4.0.

One important point to remember when moving from one version of the operating system to another is that you can upgrade to a newer version of DOS with no problems. That is, you can normally move from 2.0 to 3.0 with no problem; however, the reverse may not hold true.

Booting Your Computer System

When the computer is first turned on, the operating system, MS-DOS, must be loaded into the computer's memory. This process is called booting the system. The booting procedure can vary from system to system, depending on the kind of computer being used. For example, a computer with two floppy disk drives will have a different procedure than a computer equipped with a hard or fixed disk.

➤ Booting Dual Floppy Disk Drive Systems

The general directions to follow when booting a dual floppy system are:

❑ **Insert the DOS or startup disk in drive A and close the drive door.**

❑ **Turn on the computer and the monitor.**

❑ **Enter the date and time when prompted or asked for by the system.**

Figure 2.1

This is what the computer screen should look like after you "boot" the machine.

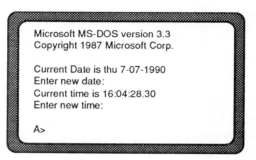

```
Microsoft MS-DOS version 3.3
Copyright 1987 Microsoft Corp.

Current Date is thu 7-07-1990
Enter new date:
Current time is 16:04:28.30
Enter new time:

A>
```

➤ The Default or Active Disk Drive

When this booting process is completed, you will see what is called the "A>" prompt on your screen. This prompt means that the A drive will be used as the default or active disk drive, and whenever a command is entered, DOS will look to the diskette in the default drive (the A drive in this case) for the command or requested operation. To change the default drive, simply enter the drive letter followed by a colon (:). For example, to change the default to drive B, you would enter **B:**. The system would then display the "B>" prompt, indicating that the B drive is now the default drive.

➤ Booting Fixed Disk Systems

Frequently, you will encounter personal computers that have fixed or hard disks built into them. These large-capacity disk drives do not need a separate DOS or startup disk, since the DOS programs are already stored on the hard disk. Therefore, all you need to do is turn the machine on. When using a hard disk equipped system, the booting process consists of these steps:

    ❑   **Turn on the computer and the monitor.**

    ❑   **Enter the date and time if requested.**

When the booting process is complete, you will see the "C>" prompt, which shows that drive C:, the hard disk, is ready for operation and will be used by MS-DOS for any commands. Should you want to use the floppy disk (perhaps to save information on it), you need to change the default disk from drive C: to the floppy disk drive A:. To activate drive A as the default drive, type **A:** and press enter. The "A>" prompt should now appear.

Introduction to the MS-DOS File System

MS-DOS stores information as a collection of files on the disk. Conceptually, these files are much like cardboard file folders that you might use to store related documents or information concerning one topic. By storing related characters, programs, or data in files, DOS can easily locate needed information from the disk. Each file must be given a unique name (like the name you might write on the file folder), called a file name, so that it can be located later on.

      File: A file is any named collection of characters that is stored on an area of a disk. These characters may make up a program, a document, a spreadsheet, a picture or chart, or almost anything that can be stored. Virtually everything that is stored on a diskette is stored in a file.

File name: Each file that is stored on a disk must have a unique name that will identify that particular file from all other files on the diskette. The file name consists of two parts: the file name and an optional extension. When a file extension is used, the file name must be separated from the extension by a period (.).

Creating a File Name

    File name: A file name may consist of up to eight characters (there can be more characters in more recent versions of the operating system) including letters, numbers, and any of the following special characters: $ % @ - { } ! #. Blank spaces are not allowed in a file name.

    Extension: The use of a file extension is optional, but it is usually a good idea to use one. Typically, the extension is used to identify the kind of information that is stored in the file; in fact, the Works program will automatically assign an extension to your file depending on the contents. For example, an extension of "WKS" shows that spreadsheet information is stored in the file, while an extension of "WPS" indicates that the file contains word processing information. When an extension is used, it becomes part of the file name and must normally be used when referencing the file. File extensions cannot be more than three characters long and can use the same characters that are valid for the file name.

	LAB1.WPS
Valid File Names	EXER#1.SSF
	PROPOSAL.BAT
	TEST1.BAK
	EXER1

	EXERCISE1.BAT	(name too long)
	LAB 1.WPS	(blank space in name)
Invalid File Names	LAB1.DOCUMENT	(extension too long)
	EXER=1.BAK	(invalid character in name)
	WORD.P R	(blank space in extension)

DOS Disk Commands

The MS-DOS operating system provides a number of powerful and useful **commands** that will make life quite a bit easier for you. Some of these include commands for copying files from one disk to another, erasing old files, checking the contents of a disk, etc. These commands all make use of certain rules or conventions that are consistent from one command to the next and make the DOS commands much easier to learn. In this text, the drive prompt will always be shown before the actual command that will be typed. For example, if the command C>DIR is described, you would type only the DIR, not the C> prompt.

An additional convention that you will see frequently is the use of brackets [ ] to indicate an option that can be used with the basic command. Often, this will contain a lowercase *d* that looks like **[d:]**. This option allows you to enter a disk drive specification that is different from the active drive shown as the prompt character. Should you want to enter a command that would affect drive A when you are using drive C as the active drive, you would type **DIR A:** when you see C>DIR [d:] printed in the book.

➢ The Directory (DIR) Command

The DIR (Directory) command is useful for displaying a list of all files and subdirectories in the current disk or directory. Additionally, the DIR command will provide information concerning the size of the file, the date it was created, and how much room remains on the disk.

The general format for the DIR command is :

C>DIR (d:)

Remember that the [d:] refers to the letter of the disk drive you want to examine. If no letter is given the default drive is used. For example, when you want to view the contents of a disk in drive A, use the directory command:

C>DIR A:

When you use the DIR command to view the contents of the diskette in drive A:, the screen will display information about the disk, including the file name, extension, file size, and the date and time that the file was created. These information categories are shown in Figure 2.2. The summary line at the bottom of the listing shows how many files were listed and the amount of free space that remains on the disk.

Figure 2.2

The information that will appear after you issue the DIR command.

```
A>DIR

Directory of A:FILES
Filename   Extension   File Size   Date     Time
TEST1      BAT              4025   9-22-90   6:10p
LETTER     WPS              5113   9-22-90   6:11p
ENG_101    WPS              1756   9-22-90   6:10p
ACCT200    WKS                50   7-02-90  10:23a
           6 File(s)   5789 bytes free
```

Finally, you should notice that the period (.) that normally goes between the file name and the extension does not appear in the directory listing; however, the period is still part of the file name, and you will need to type it when you refer to the file.

➤ *Using DIR with the Wide (/W) or Page (/P) Options*

The DIR command offers two options that make using the command much easier. The /W (wide) option, when used with the DIR command, will display the file names and extensions across the screen. The size, date, and time columns are not displayed, so this option is most useful for finding the name of a given file. When used with the /W option, the DIR command will display many more file names at one time on the screen. This result of of the /W is shown in Figure 2.3.

Figure 2.3

Display more filenames on the screen with the /W option.

```
C>DIR A:/W

Directory of A:\
COMMAND COM    SHOW EXE    SHIP    EXE    PROCOM COM    ENGL  WKS
MODE    COM    FIND BAS    MSKEY COM     SPRINT EXE     SYST  BAT
FDISK   BAT    PROG GX1    CONFIG OLD     FORMAT BAT    MOUSE COM
TRANS   WPS    MENU
            17 Files    40578 bytes free
```

The /P (page) option will provide the standard DIR listing that was shown in Figure 2.2, except that the listing will pause when the screen is full. If you press the ENTER key after the screen has paused, another screen full of file names will be listed. This will continue until all files in the directory have been listed.

This option is handy when you want to see all the information on your files but have too many files to fit on one screen.

Here are some commonly used examples of the DIR command:

C>DIR	Lists all files on drive C: (the C: drive is the default drive as shown by the C> prompt).
C>DIR A:	Lists all files on the disk in Drive A:.
C>DIR A:/W	Lists all files on Drive A:. The listing is in the wide format with five columns of file names across the screen.
C>DIR/P	Lists all file names on the default drive (C:). Because you included the /P option, the listing will pause when the screen is full.

➤ *MS-DOS "Wild Cards" for File Use*

Frequently, you will find that you need to work with a particular group of files when using DOS commands. For example, if you are looking for a research paper with the DIR command, you would like to see only the word processing files. This search can quickly be done with the DOS "wild card" options. A wild card is a special symbol that is used to represent all possible characters or combination of characters. MS-DOS uses two different symbols for wild cards.

The "*" Wild Card

The first symbol is the asterisk (*), which is used to represent any series of characters. To use the asterisk as a wild card, insert it in the file name where you want the substitution to take place. For example, you could put asterisks in both the file name and extension positions and see all files regardless of name or extension. This DIR command would appear as:

C:DIR *.*

Another example is seen when you want to display all the word processing documents created by your Microsoft Works program. (these files use the WPS extension):

C:DIR *.WPS

This command lists all files on the C: drive that begin with EX, have any remaining characters, and have an extension of .SSF. Files could include EXERCISE.SSF; EXER1.SSF; EX12.SSF; and the like.

C:DIR EX*.SSF

This DIR command lists all files that begin with EXER, have any remaining four characters, and have any file extension. Notice that this DIR command would not list the EX12.SSF file listed by the previous DIR command, since all the letters EXER do not appear.

C:DIR EXER*.*

The "?" Wild Card

The second type of wild card is the question mark (?). The concept governing the use of the ? wild card also applies to the asterisk; however, only one character is substituted instead of a series of letters that were substituted for the asterisk.

C:DIR EX?.*

This DIR command displays all files with a three letter file name that starts with EX and has any character in the third position.

➤ *The DOS FORMAT Command*

Diskettes are manufactured in an unformatted fashion, since the diskettes might be used in various types of computers. This means that when you purchase the diskettes, they are not ready to store data and programs. They need to be formatted for your computer by the MSDOS system. This formatting process establishes areas on the disk that are made up of tracks and sectors. The format routine also creates an area for a diskette directory, which is used to store a disk *table of contents* that tells MSDOS what is on the diskette. Data is stored in the areas defined by the tracks and sectors, while the directory area is used by MSDOS to identify which tracks hold what data.

To format a new diskette, use the DOS FORMAT command:

C>FORMAT [d:]

Recall that the [d:] in the format command is the letter of the drive that contains the diskette to be formatted. When the disk is formatted, your screen will display information as illustrated in Figure 2.4.

Figure 2.4

*Formatting a 5^1/4" disk
to prepare it for use.*

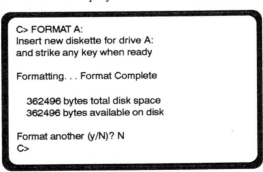

```
C> FORMAT A:
Insert new diskette for drive A:
and strike any key when ready

Formatting. . . Format Complete

   362496 bytes total disk space
   362496 bytes available on disk

Format another (y/N)? N
C>
```

For example, to format the diskette in drive A: you would enter:

C>FORMAT A:

You will then be prompted to insert your diskette in drive A: and instructed to "Press any key when ready." Once you are sure the diskette is properly in drive A: and press the Enter key, the formatting process will begin. When the format is complete, you will be asked if you would like to format another disk. If you enter an "N" (for no), you are returned to the default drive prompt. If you enter a "Y" (for yes), the process is repeated. You can also reformat an existing disk, but **all data will be lost during the format,** so be sure you are formatting the correct disk.

Format Command Volume (/V) and System (/S) Options

The Format command provides for two different options that allow you to assign a name to a diskette or to make a diskette a startup disk. If you use the **/V** or Volume option, you will be prompted to provide a VOLUME label or name for the diskette. This allows you to give the disk a name of up to 11 characters and can be useful in identifying a disk. This label is displayed when you use the DIR command to examine a disk. To format a diskette with a label called DATA, use this command:

C>FORMAT A:/V

Then, when prompted by the system, type DATA as the volume or disk label.

The **/S** or system option instructs MS-DOS to make the diskette being formatted into a bootable diskette. This means that MS-DOS will copy a special system file to the diskette as it is formatted. This format command would be:

C>FORMAT A:/S

The presence of this file will allow you to use the diskette as the startup diskette to boot your computer and is handy when you are working with dual floppy drive computers.

SPECIAL NOTE: Be careful NOT to format the hard disk, drive C:, since this can cause all data stored on the disk to be lost.

➢ *The DISKCOPY Command*

When you have saved work to your disk, you may want to make a copy of the entire disk to use as a backup. The DISKCOPY command is an easy way to do this by making a duplicate copy of an entire diskette. The general format of the DISKCOPY command is:

C>DISKCOPY (d1:) (d2:)

The [d1:] specification refers to the letter of the drive that contains the **source** diskette or the diskette that you want to copy. [d2:] is the drive that contains the new, blank diskette which is called the **destination** diskette. For example, if you wanted to make a copy of a diskette, you would place the original in drive A: and a blank diskette in drive B: and then enter:

C> DISKCOPY A: B:

After you press the Return or Enter key, you will be prompted to insert the diskettes in the drives and then press the Enter key.

The DISKCOPY command will also format the destination disk as it makes the copy, so be sure you do not have something on the destination disk you want to keep! The DISKCOPY command even lets you make copies of diskettes when you have only one diskette drive. In this case, enter:

C> DISKCOPY A: A:

During this DISKCOPY procedure, the system would first ask you to insert your source diskette into the drive. This would be the original diskette that you want to copy. The system would then read some of the source diskette, copy the data into the computer memory, and then ask you to insert the destination diskette which is your new, blank diskette. This diskette would be formatted and the data held in the computer's memory would be copied to it. Then the system would ask you to insert the source diskette again. This disk switching would continue until the entire source diskette was copied to the new destination diskette.

➤ *The CHKDSK (check disk) Command*

The DOS Check Disk (CHKDSK) command will provide you with a status report for the disk and memory specifications of the computer you are using. This command is handy when you want to find out if the disk you are using might be damaged or when you want to determine how much memory is installed on the computer and is currently available for use.

The general format of the CHKDSK command is:

C>CHKDSK (d:)

When this command is typed, the diskette in the specified drive is checked and a report similar to the one in Figure 2.5 is displayed.

Figure 2.5

The CHKDSK command will show you the status of your computer and disk.

```
C> CHKDSK A:

    362496 bytes total disk space
     22528 bytes in 3 hidden files
     52224 bytes in 23 user files
    309172 bytes available on disk

    655360 bytes total memory
    616512 bytes free

C>
```

File Processing Commands

The MS-DOS operating system provides a number of commands that allow you to manipulate individual files or groups of related files. While there are a number of MS-DOS commands available, many are used in specialized situations. Others are helpful to most personal computer users and are included here.

➤ The MS-DOS COPY Command

The COPY command allows you to make a duplicate copy of an individual (or group of) file(s). The general format of the COPY command is:

C>COPY (d1:)Filename1   (d2:)Filename2

In this example, "Filename1" is the name of the existing file you want to copy, while "Filename2" is the name you want to give to the new duplicate file. If you do not specify the drive designation (d1: or d2:), MS-DOS will assume that both files are on the default drive (drive C: in this case). You can also omit the file name for "Filename2," in which case MS-DOS will name the new file with the same name as the old file. You should be aware that the original file and the new copy with the same name cannot both be on the same drive (if you try this, you will receive an error message). To avoid this and make a duplicate of the file on the same drive, rename the file as you copy it by assigning some new name for "Filename 2."

➤ Examples of the Use of the COPY Command

To copy a file from one disk to another keeping the same file name:

C>COPY LAB1.WPS   A:

This command will cause the file "LAB1.WPS" on drive C: to be saved using the same name on drive A:.

Copying a file to a different file name on the same disk:

C>COPY LAB1.WPS   LAB1.BAK

Here, the file on drive C:, LAB1.WPS, will be copied with a new name called LAB1.BAK and will be stored on the same drive, C:.

Using wild cards in the COPY command:

Wild cards can be used with the copy command (see previous section on how to use wild cards) to allow you to copy selected groups of files. For example, to copy all files with the WPS (word processing files) extension from drive C: to drive A:, you would type:

C>COPY *.WPS   A:

If you wanted to copy all files from drive A: to drive C:, type:

C>COPY A:*.*

➤ *Using the TYPE Command*

The TYPE command allows you to "type" or list the contents of a file to the screen. The TYPE command is entered as:

C>TYPE [d:]Filename

This command will cause the contents of the file that you specify with the file name to be displayed on the screen. You should, however, be aware that many files will not "type" correctly on the screen with this command. This is because many programs use special characters when the files are saved and, as a result, only the program that created the file can read the file properly. This means that if a file you type appears as "garbage" on the screen, it is probably stored by a program in a special way; it does not mean that the file is damaged!

➤ *Using the PRINT Command*

The PRINT command does the same thing as the TYPE command, except that it prints the file on the printer rather than using the screen.

C>PRINT [d:]Filename

Use this command in the same way you use the TYPE command, and remember that some characters may not be printable. To be sure you will not have this problem, it is a good idea to always *Type* a file to the screen before you try to print it to make sure that it is stored in a format that is readable.

➤ *Using the ERASE Command*

The ERASE command erases or deletes files from the disk. The command can also be used with DOS wild cards to erase groups of files.

C>ERASE [d:]Filename

If the drive designation [d:] is not specified, the file to be removed must be on the default drive. Otherwise, you must provide the letter of the drive on which the file is located. You can also use wild cards in the file name to remove groups of files, much like the COPY command.

Using the ERASE command to remove the file "EXER1.WPS" on drive A:

C>ERASE A:EXER1.WPS

Using ERASE to remove all files with the "SSF" extension on drive A:

C>ERASE A:*.SSF

CAUTION: You can use the erase command to erase an entire disk by entering C> ERASE *.*. This will erase all files on the disk. In this case, since no drive designation is specified, this would be drive C:, the default drive. When you use this command, you are asked to verify that this is what you want to do. Make **sure** you specify the correct drive and you have the correct diskette in the drive. Once the files are erased, they cannot easily be recovered.

➤ *Using the RENAME Command*

Occasionally, you might want to assign a different name or extension to an existing file. This can be done with the RENAME command:

C>RENAME [d:]Filename1 Filename2

Like the Copy command, Filename1 refers to the existing file, while Filename2 is the new name you want to assign the file. This command differs from the COPY command in that no new file is created; rather it simply assigns a new name to the original file.

To rename a file called EXER1.WPS that is stored on drive A: to EXER1.BAK:

C>RENAME A:EXER1.WPS EXER1.BAK

➤ *Miscellaneous DOS Commands*

CLS (Clear Screen)

This command will clear the display screen. To execute it, type:

C> CLS

Setting DATE and TIME

These commands will allow you to change the system DATE or the system TIME. Type in the command and respond to the prompts:

C>DATE   or   C>TIME

The MSDOS File Directory System

Once you begin to work with the computer, you will probably find that you are saving quite a few files of information and that you are having a hard time recalling just what was in each one. One way to relieve this problem is to use subdirectories, which allow you to subdivide a disk (either floppy or fixed) into many different areas. This technique allows you to save related files in the same place so that even if you forget what the file name is, you still have a good idea of where to look for it. For example, you might elect to set up a subdirectory for each subject area that you are interested in. Such a file organization might look like the one in Figure 2.6.

Figure 2.6

Files are stored in directories on the disk so that you can group similar files.

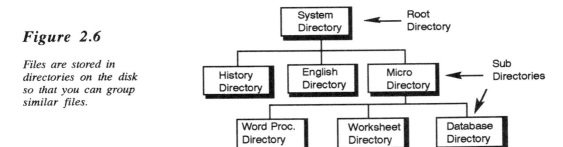

While this type of directory structure is helpful when using the large storage capacities of a hard disk, it can also be helpful when using standard floppy diskettes. This directory structure has a "root" or "system" directory as its highest level and is the directory or portion of the disk that you will usually be in when the system first boots up.

You should also remember that if you try to use a command that is not in the active subdirectory, an error may result. This is particularly common when trying to use DOS commands from a directory other than the one in which the command is stored. One final point: Name your subdirectories in the same manner and use the same rules that you use to name files (not over eight characters, no blanks, etc.).

Managing Directories

➢ The Change Directory (CD) Command

The CD or Change Directory command allows you to move to a new directory or subdirectory. For example, to move from the System Directory to the English subdirectory, you would enter CD\English from the C prompt (C>). Notice that a backslash is used to separate the Change Directory command from the directory name. This convention is expected when using DOS and helps eliminate confusion. The general format for the Change Directory command is:

C>CD\[path]

Remember that the [d:] allows you to specify which disk drive you want to execute the command on. The [path] option allows you to state which directory you would like to use. Finally, when the directory you are changing to is on the default drive, you may omit the drive designation [d:].

To illustrate how this command might work, assume that you want to change the active directory from the System Directory to the History Directory. The command for this would be **CD\History**. To return to the System directory issue the command **CD** which will move to the next higher directory level. Next, assume that you would like to change the active directory from the System directory to the English Directory. The correct command to do this is **C>CD\English**. Figure 2.7 illustrates how this might work.

Figure 2.7

Change to a different directory with the Change Directory command.

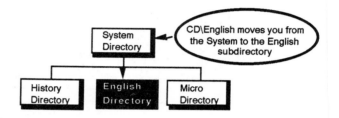

➤ The Make Directory (MD) Command

The MD or Make Directory command allows you to create a new, empty directory or subdirectory on a disk. This is very much like creating a new file folder by writing the name on the folder and preparing it to hold documents and information in the future. The general command format is:

C> MD [d:] [path]

If you wanted to add a new subdirectory for a science research project on the default drive C:, you would type **MD\SCIENCE** from the root or top directory. Figure 2.8 illustrates how this directory would be added to the existing file structure.

Figure 2.8

Adding a directory using the Make Directory command.

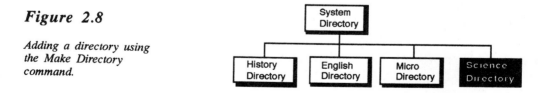

Now assume you were in the System Directory and wanted to create a subdirectory for Accounting beneath the Micro Directory. You would enter:

C> MD\MICRO\ACCOUNT

The addition of this new subdirectory is seen in Figure 2.9. Note that **you must abbreviate Accounting** to keep the directory name to eight characters or less.

Figure 2.9

You can also add subdirectories under other directories.

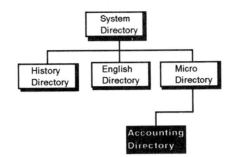

➤ *The Remove Directory (RD) Command*

The Remove Directory command is used to delete an existing directory from a disk. The general format of the RD command is:

RD [d:][path]

MSDOS will not allow you to remove a directory that contains files or has active subdirectories under it. This will prevent you from accidentally erasing files in the directory. To remove a directory, you must first erase all the files in the directory. You also will need to remove any active subdirectories below the directory you are trying to delete. If you try to remove a directory that contains active files, DOS will give you an error message. See the "Erasing Files" section for information on erasing files.

To remove the Accounting subdirectory shown in Figure 2.9, you would issue this command:

C:>RD\MICRO\ACCOUNT

➤ *Some General Comments About Directories*

To move back to the system-level directory (or the top-level directory) from a lower-level directory, enter the CD command with the backslash (\) but do not enter a directory name:

C>CD

If you simply enter the CD command without a backslash, the name of the current subdirectory you are using will be listed to the screen:

C>CD

MSDOS Control Keys

There are several special keys or key sequences that perform a number of useful operations on your microcomputer. When a key is shown as CTRL/*key*, this means that you must hold down the CTRL key while you press the key shown to the right of the slash.

➤ F3...Repeat the Last Command

The F3 Function key will display the last DOS command entered. If you press the ENTER key after the F3 key, the command will be executed again.

➤ Shift/PrtSc...Print the Current Screen

This combination of keys will print the current contents of the screen to the printer. This command will not print the graphics characters that appear on the screen.

➤ Rebooting the System

CTRL/ALT/DEL

You will probably find that you will want to restart the system to change programs or to ensure a clean start. To perform this "warm boot," hold the CTRL/ALT/DEL keys down together. You must have a bootable diskette in the default drive when you perform the warm boot. You should use these key strokes with caution, as anything that is stored in the random access memory (including data you have entered but not yet saved) of the computer when you reboot will be lost.

➤ CTRL/S...Pause Screen Display

The use of this key combination control sequence will temporarily stop the screen display from scrolling. This is normally used when you type a long document to the screen or perform the DIR command. The CTRL/S stops the screen display. Press any other key to continue the display.

➤ CTRL/C...Terminate the Current DOS Command

This key combination will terminate the DOS command being executed.

➤ CTRL/P..Turn Printer On/Off

This key combination is used to toggle output to your printer. Press the CTRL/P once and anything that is subsequently displayed on the screen is also sent to your printer. Press the key combination a second time and output to the printer is canceled.

Chapter 2 Self Test

1. Determine whether the following file names are valid or invalid.

    PAPER.TXT
    RESEARCH#1.WPS
    LAB 1
    LAB#12.SSF
    BUDGET.SSF
    MEMBERS.DB

2. Write the directory command to list the names of all files that begin with the word LAB. The files may have any kind of file extension.

3. Write the FORMAT command to format a diskette in drive B:. Format this diskette so that you can use it to boot your computer system.

4. Write the command to copy a file called MASTER.WPS that is currently on drive C:. Copy this file onto the diskette in drive A: and name the new file TEST1.WRK.

5. Write the command to copy all the files from drive C: to drive A:.

6. The command to delete a file called LAB1.WPS from the diskette in drive A: is:

7. Write the command to create a directory called SAMPLES. Create this directory on the diskette in drive B:.

8. Write the command to change to a subdirectory called TESTS. This subdirectory is below the directory called MGT180. Assume that you are currently in the system level directory and the directories are on the default drive.

9. What set of keystrokes will reboot your computer system?

10. How can you print information currently displayed on the screen?

Hands on Practice

To complete this session, you will need one $3^1/_2$ or $5^1/_4$ inch DS/DD diskette, depending on the type of computer you will use.

1.   Boot your system by turning on the computer and the monitor (insert your startup disk in drive A: if you are using a dual floppy system). After entering the Date and Time, if prompted, the DOS prompt will appear on the screen (A> or C>). Insert your diskette in floppy disk drive A: and enter Format A:. The system will ask you to be sure the disk is in the drive; you should press Enter when ready. The formatting process should take approximately two minutes. After the format is complete, you will be asked if you want to format another diskette. Respond by typing NO, and the DOS prompt will appear again. Finally, set the default drive so that it is the same as the startup disk.

2.   Enter the DIR command and then revise it using wild cards to list the name and size of any file that has an extension of .BAT.

3.   Now use the DIR command with the page option to list only names of the files that have a file extension of .RFT.

4.   List the names of all files that begin with the letter F and have any file extension. List the files using the wide option of the DIR command.

5.   Copy a file called TIME.COM from drive C: or your startup diskette in drive A:, to your new diskette. Name the new file EXERCISE.BAT.

6.   Use the CHKDSK command to check your new diskette.

7.   Use the RENAME command to rename the file on your new diskette from EXERCISE.BAT to LAB1.TXT. Now execute the DIR command to list all files on the diskette in drive A:.

8.   Erase all the files that you have on your new diskette. Execute the DIR command to make sure there are no files left on this diskette.

9.   Remove your diskette and turn your machine and monitor off.

3

Introduction to Microsoft Works

Application Programs

Most office and professional environments require at least four types of computer application programs. These four types of application programs are:

 Word Processor: With a word processing program, you can create and revise letters, papers, and documents of almost any type. Once you have created the document, you can move paragraphs and sentences from one place to another. You can also highlight text by underlining, making the text bold, printing the text in italics, and even making the text smaller or larger. The word processor will automatically number your pages and justify your margins when you print the document. In most word processing programs, you can copy segments of one document into another document. You can even have the word processor check the spelling of the words in the document.

 Spreadsheet: A spreadsheet program will allow you to create electronic worksheets. You can have the spreadsheet automatically produce totals and averages, find the largest or smallest number in a series of numbers, calculate payments, and perform many other functions. If the spreadsheet is designed correctly, you can change a single number in the spreadsheet and have all totals, averages, and formulas automatically recalculated. The spreadsheet normally has a charting or graphing module that will allow you to create bar, pie, line, and other types of charts from the spreadsheet data. These charts can be used as visual aids in presentations.

 Database: Database management programs will allow you to create electronic filing cabinets. You could create a file of names and addresses, inventories, recipes, employees, clients, or any type of information you want. Once you have entered the data into your files, you can create reports, produce mailing labels, create form letters, and make inquiries about the information that you have stored in the database. The data from several different files can be combined to create an almost endless combination of files.

Telecommunications: The telecommunications program allows you to access other computer systems. You could use the telecommunications program to transfer data from your system to another system or transfer data from the other system to yours. You can also use your computer system to browse through the information on other computer systems. You can use the telecommunications program to access many of the computer service companies such as *CompuServe* or *Dow Jones*. This can provide you with easy access to an endless wealth of information.

All of these application programs can be used to improve the productivity of a professional office or an individual. These programs can be purchased individually or as an integrated package. When the programs are purchased individually, each program is usually more powerful and provides more capabilities than those that are purchased as an integrated package. However, there are several drawbacks to purchasing individual programs.

First, the total of all costs for four different programs will usually be higher than the price of an integrated package. Second, each program will probably use a different set of commands or *user interface*. This means that you will need to learn how to use four programs rather than one.

Third and most important is integration. The term *integration* means that you should be able to create information in one program and combine that information with information created by a different program. This indicates that you should be able to create a spreadsheet, create a chart from the data in the spreadsheet, and then copy both the spreadsheet data and the chart into a word processing document. In fact, you should be able to combine information from any of the four programs with information from any of the other programs. When you use different programs, this ability to integrate information is usually very difficult. It sometimes requires the running of several programs, some of which you may not have, and multiple export and import operations. In many cases the integration cannot be accomplished at all. In other cases it cannot be accomplished without losing much of the information from one of the programs.

With an integrated package, these four programs come as a single application. Each of the four programs are usually referred to as a *module,* with each module performing one of the four basic tasks mentioned earlier. In a truly integrated package, the task of combining information from the different modules is greatly simplified. The ability to integrate is the strength of an integrated package. An additional advantage of an integrated package is that you only need to learn one program rather than four. The commands or *user interface* are the same for each module.

Using Microsoft Works

Microsoft Works is an integrated software package vended by *Microsoft Corporation.* The Microsoft Corporation is well established and has an excellent reputation in the industry. The Works package contains all four of the aforementioned modules. It is a powerful package that contains a wealth of features in each module and is probably one of the best, and easiest, packages to integrate. The user interface is extremely friendly and is consistent between each of its modules. In most cases, Works provides three different methods of entering commands. First, you can select commands from a set of menus. Each menu contains a different set of commands and is tailored for a specific type of operation. Second, you can use a control key or alternate key sequence to select a command. This approach is usually faster but is not recommended when you first begin to use Works. You should first learn Works by using the menus.

When you get comfortable with its menus, you can begin to learn the control and alternate keys used for commands. The third method is by using a mouse. If you have a mouse installed on your system, you can use it to select options from the menus. This is probably the easiest approach; however, it does require the additional mouse hardware and software to control the mouse.

Starting Microsoft Works

Starting the Works program may be different on different systems. The way it is started depends on whether you are using a floppy disk system, a hard disk system, or a network. It may also depend on how your particular system is configured and any special command files that have been set up on your system. In general, you should be able to start Microsoft Works using one of the following methods.

➤ Floppy Disk System

You must first boot your system using a *System Startup Disk*. Once your system is booted you insert your *Works Program Disk* in the A: drive. Make sure your default drive is set to A: and enter **WORKS**.

       1. Boot your system using a Startup Disk.
       2. Insert your Works Program Disk in drive A:.
       3. Insert a formatted disk in drive B:. This will be for your data.
       4. Type *WORKS* at your DOS prompt.

➤ Hard Disk System

Boot your system from the hard disk. Next, use the *CD* command to change to the directory named Works. This should place you in the directory that contains the Microsoft Works program. Finally, type **WORKS**.

       1. Boot your system from the hard disk.
       2. At the DOS prompt enter *CD WORKS*.
       3. At your next DOS prompt enter *WORKS*.

➤ Networked Systems

Networked systems may be dramatically different depending on the network being used and the configuration of the system. You should consult your network manual for booting from any network system you may be using.

The Works Startup Screen

When you first start Microsoft Works, you will be provided with a startup screen similar to the one shown in Figure 3.1. This screen uses the typical format for all Microsoft Works screens. Across the top of the screen is a menu bar. This particular menu bar has three menus available. They are the **File** menu, the **Options** menu, and the **Help** menu.

The longer, vertical box along the left side of the screen is referred to as a *pull down* menu. The idea of a menu is similar to a menu in a restaurant. The menu contains all the items that the restaurant has to offer. You select the items that you want from the menu. In most cases, the item on the menu is prepared only one

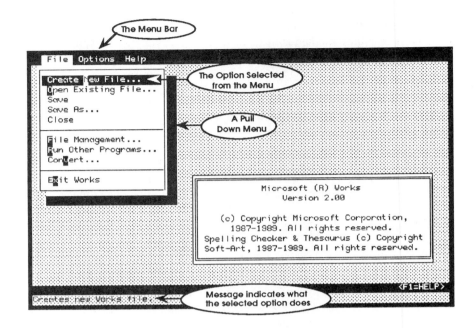

Figure 3.1

When you first start Microsoft Works you will be provided with an initial start up screen. This screen will have the File menu pulled down.

way, so you do not need to provide any other information. In other cases, such as ordering a steak, you need to provide other information, like the type of steak, how it is to be cooked, and its size.

Microsoft Works menus are similar to these restaurant menus. The startup screen in Figure 3.1 shows the **File** pull down menu. *Pull down* menus provide you with a list of options or choices that are available. To use Microsoft Works, you normally pull down one of its available menus and then choose an option from the menu. Note the *ellipsis* points (...) that follow the **Save As...** option in the *File* menu. These *ellipsis points* mean that the Save As option has a *dialog box* that goes with the option. A *dialog box* allows you to specify more information needed by the option. Any option on a menu that has ellipsis points following it will have an accompanying dialog box.

➤ *Using Pull Down Menus*

Generally, there are two ways to choose an option from a pull down menu. The first way is to use your *up* or *down* arrow keys to move the highlight bar to the option you want to select then press the *Enter* key. The second way is to enter the appropriate letter for the option. This letter is normally the first letter in the name of the option but not always. In cases where more than one option on a menu starts with the same first letter, some other letter in the option name will be used to select the option. The letter you need to use will be highlighted.*

If you have a mouse installed on your system, there is a third way to select an option from a menu. To use your mouse, hold down the left button of the mouse and *drag* the mouse's cursor down the menu until you have your option highlighted. Once you have your desired option highlighted, release the mouse's button and the option will be selected.

---

*   Microsoft Works has several types of screens available. The way the letter required to select an option is displayed depends upon the screen type you have set in the Screen Colors option of the Works Settings. For more information on Works Settings, see Chapter 6 of this text.

Normally, these pull down menus are hidden. You will only see the menu bar at the top of the screen. If the menus are hidden, here are two ways to get the pull down menus. First, you can press the **Alt** key. When you press this key, one of the letters in each of the options on the top menu bar will be highlighted. Next, you can press the letter that is highlighted in the menu bar that corresponds to the pull down menu you want, such as **Alt** and **F** for the *File* menu. You can also use your mouse. If you use the mouse, place the mouse's cursor on any letter of the option you want and press the mouse's left button. This will pull the selected menu down so you can choose an option from the menu.

➢ Using Dialog Boxes

If an option in a pull down menu has *ellipsis* points following it, this means that more information is needed in order to execute the option. In those cases, you will be presented with a dialog box. The dialog box is used to provide the additional information needed. A dialog box may have several types of boxes within it. Examine Figure 3.2. This dialog box has three different types of elements in it: *text boxes, check boxes, and buttons.*

    Text Boxes: Text boxes are used when you must provide detailed information. You must type in the text that is required for each text box entry. To move your cursor from one text box to another, you must press the **Tab** key. If you are using a mouse, you may position the mouse's cursor anywhere within the text box and press the left mouse button. This will place your cursor in that text box.

    Check Boxes: Check boxes are used to indicate whether you want an option used with the command. Check boxes contain options that are set either **ON** or **OFF**. These boxes use brackets [ ]. These boxes will contain either an X for ON or a space for OFF. You can *toggle* the check box ON and OFF by pressing the space bar. In some cases, the check box may contain a hyphen (-). This will be discussed later.

    Buttons: Buttons are used to indicate how a command is to be carried out. Buttons are always enclosed in the < > symbols. You can select only one of the buttons in the dialog box. The selected button is the one that has the symbols highlighted. To change the selected button, you tab to the button you want to choose or select it using the mouse.

Some menus may also contain list boxes or option boxes. Examine the dialog box in Figure 3.3.

    List Boxes: Sometimes you will be presented with a box that contains a list of items. These list boxes also have scroll bars. A scroll bar is the small shaded bar on the right side of the box. This scroll bar indicates what relative portion of the list of items is visible

Figure 3.2

Some Works dialog boxes have **Text** *boxes to enter data,* **Check** *boxes to select options, and* **Buttons** *to specify how a menu selection is to be carried out.*

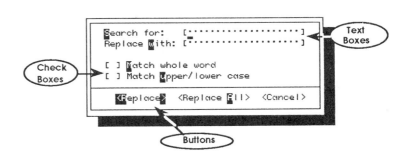

Figure 3.3

*Some Works dialog boxes
have Option boxes, to set
options on and off, and List
boxes to choose a selection
that is listed in the box.*

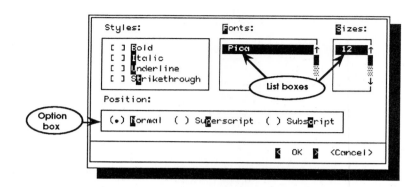

in the list box. You can only select one item from a list box. When the item is
selected, it is highlighted and used when the command is executed. To get into the
list box, you use the Tab key. Once you are in the list box, you use the arrow key to
select your choice from the list. There may be choices that are not visible in the list
box. This is because there may not be enough room in the text box to display all of
the available items. If you use your up or down arrow keys the hidden items will
scroll into view so they can be selected. The position of the scroll bar will indicate
whether there are hidden elements in the list box.

Option Boxes: Option boxes are used to list options that may be used with the command being
executed. To select an option from the list, you first use your Tab key to get into
the option box. Next, use your arrow keys to move the diamond to the option that
you want to use. You can only select one option from an option box.

If all of these different types of boxes seem a bit confusing, don't worry about them now. As you work
with Microsoft Works in the remainder of this text, you will become comfortable with the different types of
boxes.

Works' File Management Utilities

Along with the four general modules - Word Processing, Spreadsheet and Graphics, Database, and
Telecommunications - Microsoft Works also includes a series of *File Management* utilities. These utilities
perform functions similar to the MS-DOS commands covered in Chapter 2 of this text. They can be used
in place of most of the MS-DOS commands that perform the same function, but it is still extremely
important for you to understand the use of MS-DOS.

To access the *File Management* utilities, you must first pull down the *File* menu. Then you can use your
down arrow key to move the highlight bar to the File Management option of the *File* menu *or* you can press
the **F** key (for File Management). When you choose this option from the menu, you will be provided with
an additional submenu similar to the one shown in Figure 3.4.

To select an option from this menu, you can use either your *Up* arrow key or *Down* arrow key to move the
highlight bar to the option you want to choose and then press the Enter key, or you can use your highlighted
letter or your mouse.

Figure 3.4

*Microsoft Works has a set of file
and disk management utilities that
can be selected from a menu. This
menu is pulled down using the File
Management option from the File
menu.*

➢ *Copy File*

This option allows you to make a copy of an existing file. When this option is selected, you will be
provided with a dialog box similar to the one shown in Figure 3.5. This dialog box lists the files available
on the current subdirectory or disk. The first step is to identify the file that you want to copy. This can be
done in one of two ways.

The first way is to specify the file name in the *File to copy:* text box. If you use this approach, you must
specify the entire file name, including its file extension. You can also specify the entire path if the file is
not on the current disk or default directory. The current disk and default directory are listed in the
Directory of: entry below this text box.

The second way to specify the file to be copied is to tab into the **Files** list box and use your down arrow key
to highlight the file. If the file you want to copy is not on the current default directory or disk, you can
change the default by tabbing into the *Directories:* check box and using your arrow keys to select a new
disk drive or directory. If you do this, you must press the Enter key to get a listing of the files on the new
disk or directory.

Once you specify the file to be copied, by either entering its name in the *File to copy* text entry or choosing
it in the *Files* list box, you must press the Enter key to choose the *OK* button. You will then be provided

Figure 3.5

*The Copy File option will
allow you to make copies of
files. You can select the file
to be copied from the list box
or you can enter the file name
in the text box entry. If the
file you want to copy is not
listed, you can use the
Directories list box to change
drives or directories.*

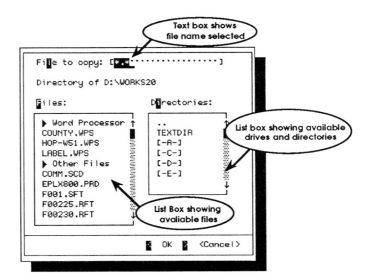

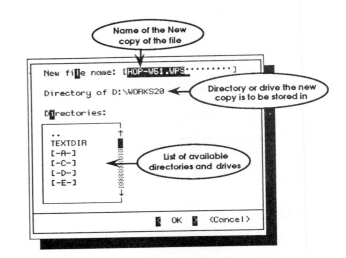

Figure 3.6

*After you specify the file to be
copied, you must specify the new
copy's file name and where you
want the copy placed. You enter the
new file's name in the text box and
select the directory and disk from the
list box.*

with the dialog box shown in Figure 3.6. To complete this portion of the *Copy* option, you must enter the
name of the new copy of the file. You can specify the entire path name if you do not want the copy placed
on the default drive and directory, or you can change the default drive and directory using the Directories
list box. To complete the copy, you must press the Enter key to choose the *OK* button.

When the copy is completed, the original File Management submenu shown in Figure 3.4 will be
displayed. You must choose the *Cancel* button to cancel this submenu or press the *Esc* key.

➤ Delete File

This option from the File Management submenu can be used to delete a file. When this option is selected,
you will be provided with a dialog box similar to the one shown in Figure 3.7. The only difference
between this dialog box and the one shown in Figure 3.5 is that you specify the file you want to delete in
the *File to delete:* text entry. You can use the same method to specify the file to delete as those discussed
earlier in the *Copy File* option. Once you have specified the file to delete, you must press the Enter key to
choose the *OK* button.

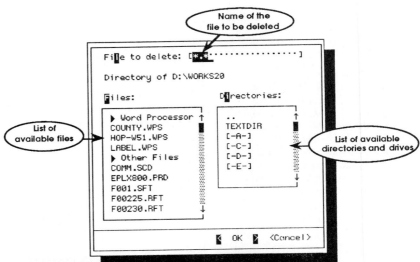

Figure 3.7

*You can use the **Delete File**
utility to remove a file from
a directory or disk. You
can specify the file's name
in the text box, or you can
select it from the list box.*

Figure 3.8

*When you use the **Delete File** utility you will be asked to verify the deletion. If you choose the **OK** button, the file will be deleted. If you choose the **Cancel** button, the file will not be deleted.*

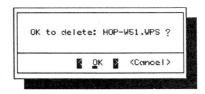

Microsoft Works will then provide you with the button box shown in Figure 3.8. This box asks you to verify the deletion of the file. If you want the file deleted, you can press the Enter key to choose the *OK* button. If you want to cancel the deletion, you must press the Tab key to select the *Cancel* button and then press the Enter key.

➢ Rename File

The *Rename File* option of the File Management submenu allows you to change the name of an existing file. This option works like the Copy File option. You are initially provided with a dialog box like the one shown in Figure 3.5. You specify the file you want to rename by entering its name in a *File to rename:* text entry area or selecting it from the *Files:* list box and pressing the Enter key.

Once you have specified the file you want to rename, you are provided with a dialog box similar to the one in Figure 3.6. You must enter the new name for the file in the text area of this dialog box and press the Enter key. This will complete the renaming of the file and return you to the File Management submenu.

➢ Create Directory

The *Create Directory* command will create a new directory or subdirectory. When you choose this command, you will be provided with a dialog box like the one in Figure 3.9. You must then enter the name for the directory in the *Create Directory:* text entry area. Next press the Enter key to choose the *OK* button. The directory will be created on the default disk drive and under the current default directory.

If you want to change the default disk drive or the default directory, you can use the *Directories:* list box to change them. To change the defaults, tab to the *Directories* list box and use your arrow keys to highlight the drive or directory you want to choose as the default and then tab to the *OK* button and press your Enter key.

Figure 3.9

*The **Create Directory** utility will allow you to create a new directory or subdirectory. You must specify the new directory's name in the text box. You can also change the drive or directory that the new directory will be created in by choosing it from the list box.*

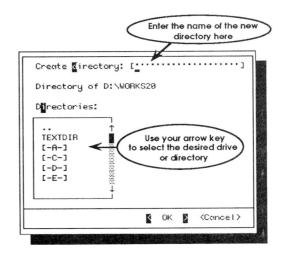

➤ Remove Directory

The *Remove Directory* option is used to delete a directory or subdirectory. When you choose this option, you will be provided with a dialog box similar to the one shown in Figure 3.9 except it will be a *Remove Directory* dialog box. You can choose the directory or subdirectory you want to remove by entering its name or selecting it from the *Directories* list box. To remove the directory, you must tab to the *Remove* button and press the Enter key or press the letter **R** to choose the R*emove* button.

You may get an error message when you try to remove a directory. This normally happens if you try to remove a directory that currently contains files. To remove the directory, you must first delete all the files in the directory. You can use the *Delete File* option discussed earlier to do this. If you want to delete all the files in the directory so that you can remove it, you should use the *.* wild card in the file name of the *Delete File* dialog box. Make sure you select the correct default directory before you use this wild card. Once you have deleted the files in the directory, you can use the *Remove Directory* option to remove the directory.

➤ Copy Disk

The *Copy Disk* option is used to make a copy of an entire disk. This option exits to MS-DOS and executes the DISKCOPY command so it works as if you had entered the command at the DOS prompt.

If you have only one diskette drive, Works will go directly to the disk copy operation on drive A:. If you have two floppy disk drives, you will get dialog boxes like the ones shown in Figure 3.10. In the first dialog box, you choose the drive that contains the original diskette, the one you want copied. In the second dialog box, choose the drive that contains the new diskette, the drive that you want your original diskette copied to.

Figure 3.10

When you use the Copy Disk utility you must first specify the drive that contains the original disk you want copied. Next you must specify the drive that will contain the new copy of the disk. If you only have one disk drive, you will not be asked to specify drives.

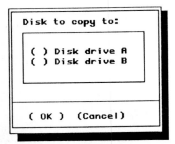

➤ Format Disk

The *Format Disk* option works like the MS-DOS *Format* command. If you have only one diskette drive, Works will go directly to the formatting operation. If you have multiple disk drives, you are provided with a dialog box similar to one of those shown in Figure 3.10. You must choose the disk drive that contains the disk you want formatted and then choose the *OK* button. The disk in the selected drive will then be formatted using the standard DOS format options.

Figure 3.11

You can use the Set Date/Time option to modify the system date or time. When you enter the new value, you must include the colons or slashes.

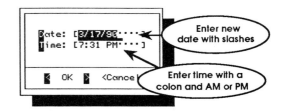

Enter new date with slashes

Enter time with a colon and AM or PM

➤ Set Date & Time

The *Set Date & Time* option can be used to change the date and time used by Microsoft Works when you specify any command that requires a date or time. When you choose this option, a dialog box similar to the one shown in Figure 3.11 will be displayed. To change either the date or time, use your Tab key and tab to the entry you want to change. Type in your new date or time and choose the *OK* button.

This completes the options under the **File Management** utilities. The remainder of the options under the **File** menu will be covered at a more appropriate time.

The Options Menu

There are several options in the **Options** menu that will be covered at this point. This menu, as with some other menus, will contain different options at different times. The options available depend upon what application module you happen to be using at the time you choose the **Options** menu. We will assume that you have just started Microsoft Works when we show the **Options** menu now. This menu is shown in Figure 3.12.

The first option on the Options menu is *Works Settings*. This option will be covered in Chapter 6.

Figure 3.12

The Options menu has several choices. Primary use for this menu (for now) will be to access the calculator, alarm clock, or phone dialing.

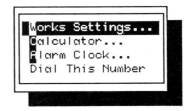

➤ Calculator

Microsoft Works includes a calculator feature that is similar to a normal handheld calculator. To access the calculator feature, you choose *Calculator* from the **Options** menu. When you do this, a small calculator like the one in Figure 3.13 will be displayed. You use the calculator in much the same way that you use a normal calculator. You can use either the number keys at the top of the keyboard or the numeric keypad on the right side of the keyboard. If you use the numeric keypad, you should make sure the *Num Lock* key has been pressed and *Num Lock* is turned on.

To cancel use of the calculator, you can tab to the *Cancel* button and press the Enter key or you can press the *ESC* key. When you cancel the calculator, you will get your menu bar back so that you can choose other menus and options.

Figure 3.13

To use the calculator, you use the numeric keypad. You must make sure you have the Num Lock set on. If you choose the Insert button, the contents of the calculator display will be inserted in the document you are working with at the time.

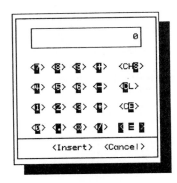

➤ Alarm Clock

The *Alarm Clock* option allows you to define messages that will be displayed on a certain date and time. You would use this if you were working in Works and wanted to be reminded of an appointment or other important meeting. To set an alarm, you choose *Alarm Clock* from the **Option** menu. This will display the dialog box shown in Figure 3.14.

Figure 3.14

The Alarm dialog box allows you to specify a message to be displayed at a certain date and time. You can also use the Frequency to specify how often the alarm is to be displayed. This dialog box is also used to change or delete existing alarms.

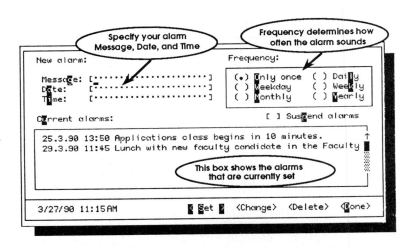

To enter an alarm you would type, in the *Message* text area, the message you want displayed at a specified date and time. Next, tab to the *Date* text area and enter the date you want the alarm to be displayed. Then, tab to the *Time* text area and enter the time. In both the Date and Time areas make sure you use the same format as those displayed at the bottom of the dialog box.

When you complete the *Time* entry for the alarm, you must next tab to the *Frequency* box on the upper righthand side of the screen. You would use your arrow keys to choose one of the options for the frequency that you want the alarm sounded. Next, tab to the *Set* button to set the alarm.

You could now define another alarm using the same approach described above, or you could tab to the *Done* button to complete setting alarms.

To Modify an existing alarm, tab into the *Current Alarms* box and use your arrow keys to highlight the alarm you want to change. You could then edit any of that alarm's settings and choose the *Change* button.

To delete an alarm, tab into the *Current Alarm*s box and use your arrow keys to highlight the alarm you want to delete. Next, tab to the *Delete* button and press the Enter key.

When the appropriate date and time arrive a message box similar to the one shown in Figure 3.15 will be displayed and the bell on your computer will be sounded. If you press the *Esc* key or choose the *OK* button, the box will disappear and the alarm will remain unchanged. If you choose the *Snooze* button, the box will disappear and the alarm will be sounded again in ten minutes. If you choose the *Reset* button, the Alarm dialog box will be displayed and you can change the alarm settings.

Figure 3.15

When it is time for an alarm to go off, the alarm's message, date, and time will be displayed. If you choose Snooze, the alarm will go off again in 10 minutes.

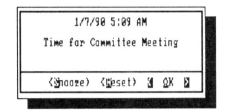

➢ Dial This Number

This option can be used to have Microsoft Works dial a telephone number for you. You can dial any number that is in a word processing, spreadsheet, or database document. For example, if you had a list of names and phone numbers in a database, you could query the database for the person you wanted to call, select the phone number field in the database, and then have Works dial the number for you.

To use this option, you must have a modem that will operate at a transmission rate of 1200 baud.* Next, you should check your Works settings to make sure you have the correct *Modem Port* and *Dial Type* set. To set these Works settings, choose *Works Settings* from the **Options** menu. The dialog box for this option is shown in Figure 3.16.

The two settings you are interested in are the *Modem Port* and *Dial Type*. To set these, tab to the appropriate option box and use your arrow keys to move the small diamond to the appropriate settings. For the *Modem Port*, you must first determine which port your modem is using. For the *Dial Type*, determine

Figure 3.16

*Use the **Settings** dialog box to set the **Modem Port**, and **Dial Type** before you try to use the **Dial** option. These settings determine how Works' will try to use your phone.*

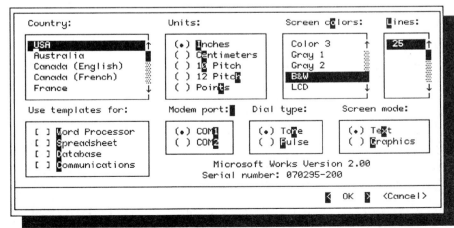

---

* See the Appendix, "Telecommunications Concepts", for a discussion of baud rates, modem ports, and dial types.

whether your phone line is set up for touch tone (tone) or a rotary dial (pulse). Once you have the correct settings, press the *Esc* key to cancel this dialog box.

To dial a number, select the number from a document, spreadsheet, or database by holding down the shift key and using your right or left arrow keys. Next, pull down the **Options** menu and choose *Dial This Number*. Works will be busy for several seconds and you will get a check box. When this check box appears, pick up your telephone receiver and choose the **OK** button by pressing the Enter key. If the call was not completed and you want to cancel automatic dialing, choose the *Cancel* button or press the *Esc* key.

Getting Help While Using Works

Microsoft Works has an online help facility. The help facility works in two modes. First, you can use a help menu to access the facility. When this approach is used, you can choose the category of help you want from an option box and then you can choose help on a particular type of operation you want to perform.

The second type of help is called a context sensitive help. This type of help looks at the type of operation you are trying to perform and provides help on that particular operation.

➢ Using the Help Menu

To get help using the help menu you would pull down the **Help** menu from the top menu bar or press the **F1** function key. A menu like the one shown in Figure 3.17 would be displayed. If you use your arrow keys to highlight the *Using Help* option, you will be provided with a screen that explains how to use the help menu. If you highlight the *Help Index* option you will be provided with a screen similar to the one in Figure 3.18.

Figure 3.17

*To use the online help system of Microsoft Works you choose **Help** from the top menu bar. You can then choose what type of help you want.*

Figure 3.18

*The **Help Index** option will allow you to get help in any part of Works. You would choose the **Topic** from the list box; then Works displays detailed help on that topic.*

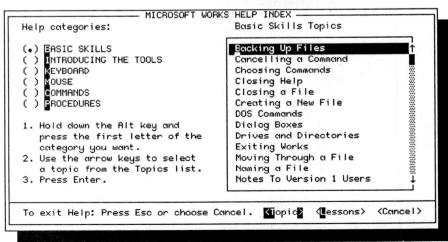

On the left side of the screen is a set of *Help Categories*. You can use your *Up* and *Down* arrow keys to move the small diamond to the category of help you need. When you move the diamond to a new category, the list of *Topics* in the list box on the right of the screen will change. To select a topic, you would tab into the list box and use your *Up* and *Down* arrow keys to highlight the topic that most closely fits what you need help with. When you have the topic highlighted, press your Enter key to get detailed help on the topic. An example of a detailed help screen on the topic *Backing Up Files* is shown in Figure 3.19.

Figure 3.19

Works will provide a detailed help description when you choose a topic from the Topics list box.

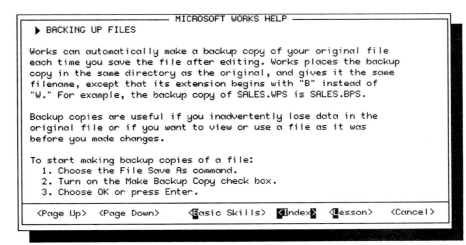

There are several buttons on the detailed help screen that should be explained. The *Page Up* and *Page Down* buttons at the bottom of the screen can be used to move backwards or forwards on the help screen. The *Basic Skills* and *Index* buttons will return you to the *Help Index* screen shown in Figure 3.19. The *Lesson* button will execute a Tutorial lesson on how to use the selected topic. In order to use this button, you must have the Microsoft Works Tutorial Files installed on your system. The *Cancel* button will cancel the help session. Choosing the *Cancel* button would be the same as pressing the *Esc* key.

➣ *Context Sensitive Help*

When you use *context sensitive help* in Microsoft Works, you need to pull down a menu first and highlight an option on the menu. Once you have the option highlighted, you need to press the **F1** function key. This will provide you with help on the option you had highlighted at the time you pressed the **F1** function key. The help screen will be a detailed help screen like the one shown in Figure 3.19.

➣ *Getting Started*

This option from the **Help** menu will provide you with a screen that explains the basics of creating documents, spreadsheets, and databases using Microsoft Works. You can use your Page Up and Page Down keys to browse through a series of screens that provide information on using the different Works modules.

➣ *Keyboard*

The *Keyboard* option will provide you with a listing of the **F1** through **F10** function keys and other key combinations that can be used as short cuts to menu options in Microsoft Works. An example of one of the Keyboard Help screens is shown in Figure 3.20.

Figure 3.20

*The **Keyboard** help
screen explains the
keys or key combina-
tions used to perform
certain types of short
cut operations.*

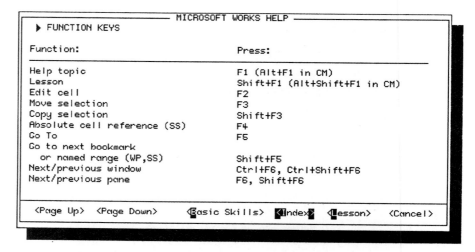

The help screen in Figure 3.20 indicates that you can use the **F1** key to get Help or use the **F3** key to move a selection to a new location. It also indicates that you can use a **Shift/F3** to copy a selection to a new location. You can use the buttons at the bottom of the screen to page up or down the listing of functions, return to the *Basic Skills* or *Topics* screens, or *Cancel* the help session.

➤ Mouse

If you choose the *Mouse* option from the Help menu, a series of screens that explain how to use the mouse in Microsoft Works will be displayed. You have the same buttons on this screen that you have on the other Microsoft Works help screens.

➤ Works Tutorial

This is the last option on the Help menu. If you choose this option, you will be guided through a series of tutorials that will teach you how to use Microsoft Works. In order to use these tutorials, you must have the tutorials files available on your disk.

Conclusion

This chapter has been a brief introduction to using Microsoft Work's *File Management* utilities, some of the menu options, and the *Help* facility. Its intent was also to cover some basic material necessary for using Microsoft Works. You should review the material and answer the questions in the *self-test* before moving on to the tutorial for this chapter.

Chapter 3 Self Test

1. List three advantages of purchasing an integrated package over purchasing separate packages for the four common application programs.

2. List the steps necessary to start Microsoft Works using your computer system.

3. List the three menus available from the Microsoft Works start up screen.

4. What do ellipsis points (...) mean if they follow an option on a Works menu?

5. What is the purpose of a dialog box?

6. List two ways you can select an option from a Microsoft Works menu using your keyboard.

7. How would you select an option from a Works menu using a mouse?

8. Determine whether each of the following is a list box, a check box, a text box, a button, or an option box.
    a. [X] Match Whole Word
    b. (♦) Justified
    c. File Name: [..........]
    d. <OK>
    e. Directory of: [...............]

9. Which option do you choose from the File menu to get the menu for the File Management utilities?

10. What two dialog boxes are provided when you use the Copy File for the File management utility?

11. What is probably the problem when you try to remove a directory and you get an error message? How would you correct the problem so you could remove the directory?

12. Which option would you choose to access the Works calculator?

13. Before you can use your keyboard's numeric keypad to operate the Works calculator, you must set your keypad. What key is used to set the keypad to be used with the calculator?

14. How do you delete an alarm?

15. When an alarm goes off, how do you set it to go off again in 10 minutes?

16. Before you can use the Dial This Number option from the Options menu, you must have a _____ and it must be set to _____ BAUD.

17. Explain what is meant by Context Sensitive help.

18. What function key can be used to get the Help dialog box?

Chapter 3 Tutorial

The purpose of this tutorial is to help you become familiar with Microsoft Works, using its File Management utilities, some of its options, and the Help system. As you work through this tutorial, you should concentrate on the approach of selecting menus and menu options and using dialog boxes. Before you begin this tutorial, you should:

1. Know how to start Microsoft Works on your computer system.
2. Be familiar with the keys on your keyboard.
3. Have a blank, unformatted diskette for your machine.

You will be guided through the tutorial step by step. Throughout the tutorial, you will be instructed to perform certain operations. When you are asked to perform an operation, the print style will change and look similar to the following:

❑   **When you see type in this style, you should perform the requested operation.**

Starting Microsoft Works

As noted earlier in this chapter, there are several ways to start Microsoft Works depending on what type of system you are using. Determine which type of system you have and then boot your system and start Works.

❑   **Boot your computer system.**

❑   **Change to the Works directory if necessary.**

❑   **Start Microsoft Works.**

Once you have started Microsoft Works, you should have an opening screen menu similar to Figure 3.21.

Figure 3.21

You should now have this screen displayed. The letters in the pull down menu may not be highlighted exactly like the ones shown here, but they should be highlighted. The way they are highlighted will depend upon what kind of monitor and graphics capabilities you have on your machine.

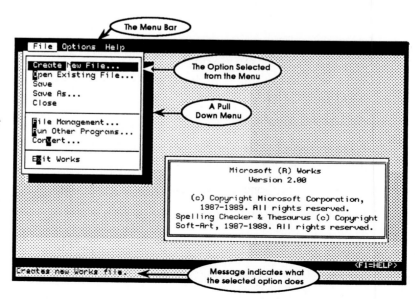

You should note several things about your screen. First, note the top *menu bar*. The **File** menu option should be highlighted. This means that the menu you have pulled down is the **File** menu. Next, notice the entry in the pull down menu that is highlighted. This entry should be the *Create New File* entry. This indicates that if you choose an option now, by pressing the Enter key, you will be choosing the highlighted entry. Also notice that one letter in each of the other menu options is also highlighted. If you enter one of these letters, you will be choosing that option. Finally notice the message line at the bottom of your screen. This line explains what the selected menu option will do. These items are noted in Figure 3.22.

Figure 3.22

*The startup screen will have the **File** menu pulled down and the **Create New File** option selected. The Message line explains what the selected option will do.*

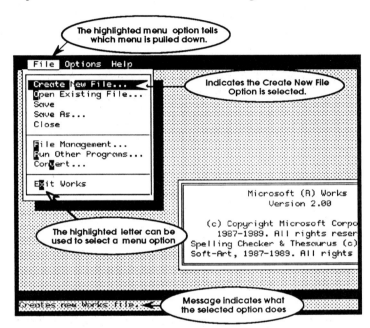

➢ Setting an Alarm

Before you begin using the file management utilities, you will set an alarm to go off 10 minutes from now. To set the alarm, you will need to move to the **Options** menu. Since it is the menu to your right, you can use your right arrow key to move to this menu. Move to the **Options** menu now.

❑ **Press your right arrow key once.**

You should now have the *Options* menu displayed. Press your down arrow key twice to highlight the *Set Alarm* option.

❑ **Press your down arrow key twice.**

Your options menu should now look like Figure 3.23.

Now press your Enter key to choose the option selected. This should provide you with the *Set Alarm* dialog box.

❑ **Press the Enter key.**

There are four steps to setting an alarm. The first step is specifying the alarm message. Assume that you wanted to set an alarm that would tell you that it was time to go to lunch with your computer user's group.

Figure 3.23

*To set an alarm you must choose
the Set Alarm option from the
Options menu.*

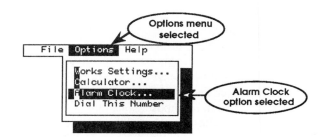

You would enter this in the *Message* dialog box. The message that you will enter is too long to be displayed in the message text box, so as you enter it, the message will *scroll* to the left. Do this now.

❑ **Enter the following in the *Message* dialog box.**

Lunch with the Computer User's Group in 10 minutes.

The next two steps will be to specify the date and time the alarm is to go off. Assume you want it to go off 10 minutes from now. Look at the current date and time at the bottom left side of your screen. Set your date to that date and the time 10 minutes after the time displayed. Remember, the date is entered as MM/DD/YY and the time is entered as HH:MM AM (or PM).

❑ **Tab into the *Date* text entry.**

❑ **Set the date to the current date.**

❑ **Tab to the *Time* text entry.**

❑ **Set the time 10 minutes later than the current time.**

The last step is to set the **Frequency**. You only want the alarm to go off once, so you should place the diamond in the *Only Once* option.

❑ **Tab to the *Frequency* option box.**

❑ **Use your arrow key to place the diamond in the *Only Once* option.**

Now you must set the the alarm. Since the letter **S** is the highlighted letter for the *Set* button, you can simply press the S key to choose this button.

❑ **Press the letter S key.**

Your dialog box should now look similar to the one shown in Figure 3.24.

Figure 3.24

*After you set an alarm, the alarm is
displayed in the Current Alarms
box and you are able to set another
alarm. To exit the Set Alarms
dialog box you must tab to the
Done button and press the Enter
key. If you want to change or
remove the alarm, tab into the
Current Alarms box, highlight the
alarm with your arrow keys, then
tab to the appropriate button and
press the Enter key.*

To exit the Set Alarms option, you must tab to the **Done** button and press the Enter key.

    ❑   **Tab to the *Done* button and press Enter.**

In 10 minutes your alarm will go off and the alarm box will be displayed. When this happens, the **OK** button should be highlighted as the default button. Press the Enter key and the alarm will be canceled.

Using the File Management Utilities

To get used to the file management utilities and some of the different dialog boxes, you will use some of the utilities. To start this part of the tutorial, you will need one unformatted diskette.

The first step is to pull down the **File** menu. You do this by pressing the *ALT* key and then the *F* key for the *File* menu.

    ❑   **Press the ALT key to access the menu bar.**

    ❑   **Press the F key to choose the File menu.**

You should now have the menu shown in Figure 3.25.

Figure 3.25

To pull down a menu, you must first press the ALT key. This selects the top line menu bar. Next you must press the highlighted letter in the menu you want. To get the File menu you would press ALT F. This menu will allow you to use the File Management utilities. The Esc key will cancel a menu.

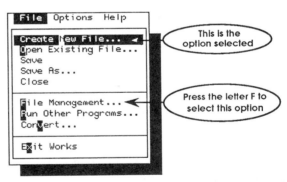

If you have the wrong menu pulled down you can press the *ESC* key to cancel the menu and try the ALT and F keys again. Notice that several of the letters in the menu are highlighted. The highlighted letters are the letters you would use to select an option from the menus. The option that should currently be highlighted is the *Create New File* option. To select the *File Management* menu, you would press the F key again. You should do this now.

    ❑   **Press the F key to select the File Management option.**

You should now have the menu shown in Figure 3.26.

➢ *The Format Disk Option*

This option will allow you to format a diskette. What will happen will depend upon the number of disk drives you have on your machine. If you only have one disk drive, the *Format Disk* option will immediately execute and ask you to insert your diskette in the drive. If you have a machine with multiple disk drives, you will be provided with an option box. You would use your arrow keys to move the diamond to the drive designation that contains the diskette you want formatted, then press the Enter key to choose the *OK* button. You will then be prompted to insert your diskette and press the Enter key. Do this and the formatting process will begin.

Figure 3.26

The File Management menu allows you to work with files and disks. Since there are no letters highlighted, you can select an option using your arrow keys. You can also press the first letter in an option. When two or more options begin with the same first letter, the first option in the menu that begins with that letter will be selected. Press the letter again, and the next option will be selected.

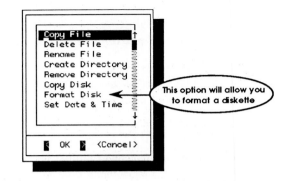

❏ Use your down arrow keys to move the highlight to the *Format Disk* option and press the Enter key.

❏ If you get an option box, use your arrow keys to place the diamond beside the drive designation that contains your diskette and press the Enter key.

❏ Insert your unformatted diskette.

❏ Press the Enter key.

When the formatting process is completed, you will be asked if you want to format another diskette. Enter N for *no* and you will be returned to the File Management menu.

❏ Enter *N* when you are asked if you want to format another diskette, and press the Enter key.

➢ *Creating a Directory*

You can also use the File Management utilities to create a directory. To do this, you must first select the *Create Directory* option from the File Management menu. Next you must specify the name of the directory and the drive or directory you want the directory created on. You will start this process now.

❏ Use your arrow keys to highlight the *Create Directory* option.

❏ Press the Enter key.

You should now have a dialog box similar to the one shown in Figure 3.27. Notice the line that reads *Directory of:*. This entry specifies where the default directory and drive are. Your new directory will be created here. You may need to change this so it shows the drive that contains the diskette you just formatted. To change the directory and drive, you should tab into this list box, use your arrow keys to select the appropriate drive, and press the Enter key. This will change the default drive.

❏ Press the Tab key once. This will place your cursor in the *Directories* list box.

❏ Use your down arrow key to highlight the drive that contains your formatted diskette.

❏ Press the Enter key.

The new default drive should be displayed by the *Directory of:* entry and your cursor should be back in the *Create directory:* text box.

The next step is to name your new directory. Assume you will keep your assignments in this directory, so you will name the directory **Assnment**. Remember, the directory name can be no longer than eight characters. To do this, you would enter the directory name and press the Enter key.

Figure 3.27

*To create a directory, you must first change your default drive by tabbing to the **Directories** list box and highlighting the drive. Next you enter the name of the new directory in the **Create directory** text box. When you press the Enter key, the directory will be created on the default drive. If you want to create a subdirectory, select the drive and then select the directory you want the subdirectory created under.*

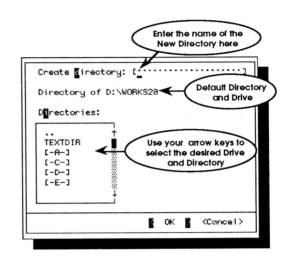

❏ Enter *ASSNMENT* in the *Create Directory* text box.

❏ Press the Enter key.

When the directory is created, you are returned to the File Management menu.

➤ Removing a Directory

You have created a directory, but you are not sure that it was created. You will use the *Remove Directory* option to see that the directory was actually created. To remove a directory, you choose *Remove Directory* from the File Management menu, highlight the directory you want removed, and press the Enter key. This time you don't really want to remove the directory, you only want to see that it has been created, so simply choose *Remove Directory*, check to see if the directory exists, then press the Esc key to cancel the menu.

❏ Highlight the *Remove Directory* option.

❏ Check the *Directories* list box to see that your directory exists.

❏ Press the ESC key.

You should now be back at the File Management menu.

➤ Using the Calculator

You have already used one of the options under the **Options** menu. This was the *Set Alarm* option. Your alarm should have gone off by now. Now you will use the *calculator*. The calculator is located in the **Options** menu, so you will need to pull this menu down. You should currently have the File Management menu on your screen, so you will need to cancel this menu and then pull down the **Options** menu and choose the *Calculator* option.

❏ Press the *ESC* key to cancel the File Management menu.

❏ Press the *ALT* key to highlight the top menu bar.

❏ Press the *O* (letter O) key for the Options menu.

❏ Press the letter *C* for the Calculator option.

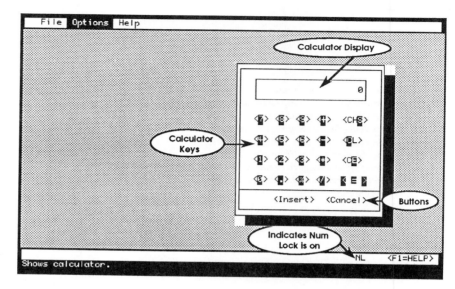

Figure 3.28

*To get the calculator you choose the **Options** menu. Next you choose the **Calculator** option. To use the numeric key pad you must have the **Num Lock** set on.*

You should now have a calculator displayed like the one shown in Figure 3.28.

When you first select the calculator, you may not have the *Num Lock* set on. This is indicated on the status line near the bottom of the screen. If you don't have the *Num Lock* set on, you should do this now. See Figure 3.28.

❏ **Set the Num Lock on by pressing the Num Lock key. Check your status line to make sure you have it on.**

You use the calculator as you would use any calculator. You use the numeric keypad and some of the other keys to calculate formulas. For example, suppose you wanted to find the average of the numbers 58, 99, and 73.7. You would sum the three numbers and divide by 3. Do this now.

❏ **Enter 58 and press the + key.**

❏ **Enter 99 and press the + key.**

❏ **Enter 73.7 and press the / key.**

❏ **Enter 3 and press the = key.**

Your calculator should now display 76.9. To use the *CHS*, *CL*, and *CE* keys, you can use the S, C, and E keys respectively. You can also use your Tab key to tab to any calculator key and choose the key by pressing the Enter key. If you were in an application module of Microsoft Works, you could use the Insert button on the calculator to insert your answer into the Works document. For now, choose the *Cancel* button to cancel the calculator or press the *ESC* key.

❏ **Press the ESC key to cancel the calculator.**

Using the Help Menu

The Help system in Microsoft Works is an excellent source for getting help on any function that Works has. You can access the Help system in one of two ways. The first approach is from the **Help** menu. The second approach is by using the **F1** function key. If you use the function key, you will get *context sensitive* help.

Figure 3.29

*The **Help** menu is pulled down from the top line menu bar. You press ALT to activate the menu bar and then press H for Help. To get more detailed help on a subject, you choose the subject from the **Help** menu.*

Pull down the Help menu now. The help menu is shown in Figure 3.29.

❑ **Press the ALT key and then the H key to get the Help menu.**

Now suppose you wanted to use some *DOS* commands that were not available from the File Management utilities, but you did not know how to do this. Your best approach is to start with the *Help Index*. You can do this by either pressing the letter H for Help Index or selecting the option using your arrow keys and the Enter key.

❑ **Press the letter H for Help Index.**

You should now have the dialog box shown in Figure 3.30.

On the left side of the keyboard is a list of help categories. To choose a category, you hold down the *ALT* key and press the first letter of the category you want help with. For example, *ALT/C* would provide you help with Microsoft *commands*. To *browse* through the topics of a category, you would use your *page up*, *page down*, or *arrow keys*. To try the help system, you will get help with *Opening a File*. Do the following:

❑ **Enter ALT/P. This chooses the Procedures topic.**

❑ **Press your Page Down key until you get to the topics that begin with the letter O. If you go too far, use your Page Up key to move backwards through the list.**

❑ **Use your arrow keys to highlight the *Opening a File* topic.**

❑ **Press the Enter key.**

Figure 3.30

*The **Help Index** allows you to select a category of help or an index topic. If you select a category, a list of topics for that category is displayed. If you select a topic, a detailed description of the topic is displayed.*

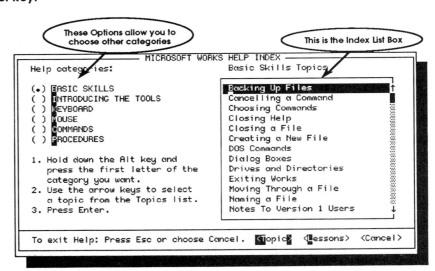

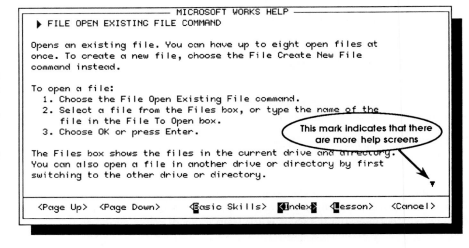

Figure 3.31

The help topics provide detailed help on how to use a command or option. Normally there are several screens for a topic. You get to the additional screens with the Page Down key.

You should now have a help screen like the one in Figure 3.32. There are more screens for this topic. To see the other screens you can press the *Page Down* or *Page Up* keys. View the next two screens now.

❑ **Press the Page Down key to view the next screen.**

❑ **Press the Page Down key to view the third screen.**

To cancel the help session, you can press the *ESC* key.

❑ **Press the ESC key to cancel the help session.**

Exiting Microsoft Works

This will complete your introduction to Microsoft Works. To exit Works you should pull down the **File** menu and choose *Exit* from this menu.

❑ **Press Alt/F to pull down the File menu.**

❑ **Press X to choose the Exit option.**

Conclusion

This completes your first chapter with Microsoft Works. While working through this chapter and the tutorial, you should have become familiar with using the menus and the dialog boxes. Your familiarity with these will be necessary for the next chapter. If you had any problems with the tutorial, you should work through it again before moving to the next chapter.

4

Introduction to Word Processing

Most people use a microcomputer for word processing more than they do for any other single purpose. Word processors are used to create and edit documents, letters, papers, or almost anything that would be considered reading text. Once the document is created, you can modify it by correcting mistakes, replacing one word or phrase with another word or phrase, moving and copying text, formatting text, and adjusting margins and page breaks, as well as copying text from other documents. Microsoft Works' word processor will also check the spelling of your document and offer suggestions for any misspelled words.

When you first start using a word processor, you should simply think of your microcomputer as an electronic typewriter. Most of the principles used in typing are also used in word processing. As you get comfortable with the word processor, you will find yourself using more and more of its capabilities.

Before you begin, we will review some of the items on the word processor's screen and explain some additional items. The word processor's screen is shown in Figure 4.1.

Works' Word Processing Screen

Top Line Menu: The idea of the menu bar was discussed in Chapter 3. Each option on the menu bar has a pull down menu. You can access these menus by pressing the **Alt** key or by pointing to the menu option and pressing your mouse's left button.

The Ruler: The ruler provides information about the length of the line for the text or document you are working with. The ruler is normally specified in inches. The left bracket ([) indicates the left-hand margin of the line, and the righthand bracket (]) indicates the right-hand margin. Although there are none shown, the ruler may also show any tab settings that have been set. The numbers on the ruler mark inches across your page, and each dot on the ruler marks one-tenth of an inch.

Figure 4.1

The top portion of a word processing screen. The menu bar is across the top of the screen. The screen has a ruler across the screen to show your position on the page. If you have a mouse, you will have a mouse cursor, either a square or an arrow depending upon the type of monitor you have.

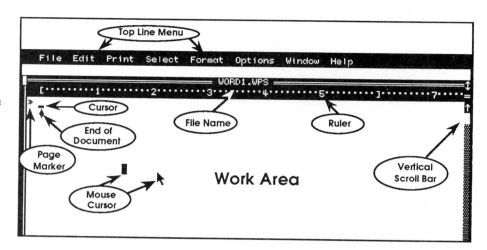

The Cursor	The word processor's cursor is the small underline in the upper left of the work area. It is used to indicate where the characters that you enter will be placed in the document.
End of Document Marker	The diamond (◆) indicates the last line of your document.
End of Page Marker	This marker(») indicates the end of a page. You will have one of these each time an end of page is detected.
The Mouse Cursor	These symbols indicate the position of the *mouse's* pointer. If you have a mouse installed, you will have one of these symbols. The rectangle is used on most screens. The arrow is used in graphics screen mode.
The File Name	This area contains the current name of the document you are working with.
Vertical Scroll Bar	This bar is used to show your current location in the document relative to the beginning or end of the document. As you enter a large amount of text, the rectangle in the scroll bar will move down the bar. If the bar is halfway down the screen, you are at the middle of your document. If you are using a mouse, you can also pull this bar to move to a different location in the document.
The Work Area	The majority of the screen is your work area. It is in this area that you will enter the text for your document.
	There are also several items at the bottom of the Word Processor's screen. These items are shown in Figure 4.2.
Horizontal Scroll Bar	This is similar to the vertical scroll bar except that it indicates your horizontal position on the line rather than your vertical position in the document. Since your line may be too long to fit on the screen, this will help you know your relative position to the beginning or end of the line.

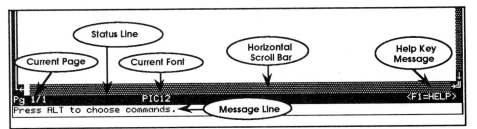

Figure 4.2

The bottom of your screen contains the Status line, the Horizontal scroll bar, and the Message line.

The Status Line	The status line is the second line from the bottom of the screen. This line will contain different items at different times. It is normally used to indicate that certain options are set on.
Current Page	This tells you which page the cursor is currently on out of the total number of pages in the document.
Current Font	This indicates the *Font* that is currently being used. The font specifies the shape and size of the character printed.
Help Key Message	This indicates that you can get help by pressing the **F1** function key.
Message Line	This is the bottom line. Microsoft Works will normally display a message to you on this line. The message will tell you what you need to do next, or it will indicate what the selected option on a menu will do.

Word Processing Terminology and Concepts

As you work through this chapter, you will need to understand some common terms that apply to word processing and Microsoft Works. These terms are defined in the following paragraphs.

Wordwrap: The term *wordwrap* refers to the ability of the word processor to automatically sense the end of a line and wrap to the next line. This means that you do not need to press the Enter key at the end of each line. In fact, you should not press Enter.

Text Attributes: For our purposes, text attributes are underlines, bold, italics, superscripts, subscripts, or any other special characteristics to make the text appear different. These attributes are applied to the text to make it stand out from the other text.

Formatting: For now, formatting will refer to the text alignment. Text alignment refers to the position in which the text appears on a line. The text can be on the *left* side, *right* side, *centered*, or spread across the entire line (*justified*).

Selecting Text: Selecting text refers to specifying a group of characters that you want some special function performed on. Selecting a block of text allows you to perform a function on an entire block of text rather than performing the function on the text one character at a time. This selected block may be as small as one character, or it may be as large as the entire document.

Toggle: The idea of a toggle is like a push button switch. If a function is on and you press the switch, the function is turned off. If the function is off and you press the switch, the function is turned on. Many of the options available in Microsoft Works function like a toggle switch to set the options on and off.

Default: Defaults are options or selections that are used when no specific option or selection is specified.

Paragraphs: In Microsoft Works, a paragraph is all text that appears between two *Enter* keys. A paragraph may be as large as an entire document, or it may be as small as nothing. The word *nothing* is used here to help be precise in the definition of a paragraph. For example, if you pressed the Enter key two times in a row, you would have created two paragraphs. The first Enter key would terminate one paragraph, and the second Enter key would create a new paragraph. The second paragraph would appear as a blank line, but Microsoft Works would treat it as an entire paragraph.

Creating a New File

Microsoft Works stores all of its documents in a file. When you want to create a new document, you choose the *Create New File* option from the **File** menu. This option will provide you with an option box that lets you specify the type of file (Word Processing, Spreadsheet, Database, or Telecommunications) you want to create. This process is shown in Figure 4.3.

Once you have specified the file type you want to create you are provided with a screen for that type of file. The screen will be empty at this point.

➤ *Inserting and Deleting Text*

When you use the Microsoft Works' word processor, your cursor is in what is referred to as the *insert mode*. This means that if you enter text anywhere in a document, the new text is added to the document. If you enter the new text between existing text, the text that follows the new text is pushed forward. During this pushing process, the *wordwrap* feature of the word processor will push words onto new lines.

There are several ways to delete text in Microsoft Works. The simplest way is to delete the text one character at a time. Two of your keyboard keys can be used to delete a single character. The first key, the *Backspace* key, deletes the character that appears to the left of the cursor. The second key, the *Delete* key, deletes the character that the cursor is sitting on.

Another way to delete text is to select the text as a block and then use either the *Delete* option from the **Edit** menu or the *Delete* key. You would normally want to use this blocking approach if you wanted to delete a large block of text. If you only want to delete a few characters, use your *Backspace* or *Delete* keys.

Figure 4.3

*To create a new word processing document you select the **Create New File** option from the file menu. Next you would choose the **New Word Processor** option from the application dialog box.*

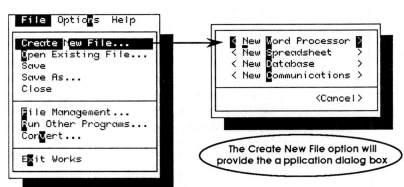

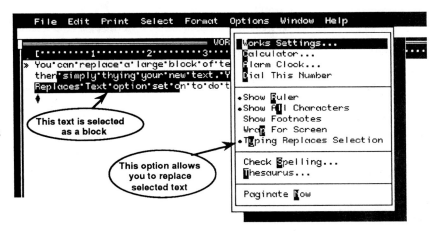

Figure 4.4

You can replace a block of text by selecting it and then typing new text. You must have the **Typing Replaces Selection** *option turned on for this to work. The diamond in front of an option indicates that the option is set on.*

Because the word processor is always in *insert mode*, if you want to replace a word you need to first delete the old word and then insert the new word. For example, if you want to change the word *is* in a sentence to the word *are*, you would delete the word *is* and then enter the word *are*.

You can also *replace* a block of text with new text. To do this you would select the old text as a block and then simply begin entering your new text. You must have the *Typing Replaces Selection* option on for this to work. This approach is shown in Figure 4.4.

Using the Undo Option

There is an *Undo* option on the **Edit** menu. This *Undo* option will remove the last change you have made. This is especially important if you delete a large block of text by mistake. If you happen to do this, you can pull down the Edit menu, choose the *Undo* option, and the text will be placed back where it was originally.

It is important to remember that you can only undo your last operation. For example, if you delete a paragraph and immediately choose the *Undo* option, you can get the paragraph back. If you delete a paragraph and enter a new word, or perform any operation, you cannot get the deleted paragraph back. Also, you cannot undo any operation performed on a disk. For example, if you delete a paragraph and then save your file, you cannot undo your save.

Applying Text Attributes

Microsoft Works has three basic types of *attributes* that can be applied to text. These attributes are Underline, Bold, and Italic. You can also use any combination of these three attributes. For instance, you can apply both bold and underline attributes to text, and the text will be printed as **bold and underlined.** Or you could use all three and have the text printed as ***bold underlined italics.***

These attributes can be applied to the text as it is entered, or you can apply the attributes to existing text. In either case, you can use the **Format** menu shown in Figure 4.5 to select the attribute you want applied to the text.

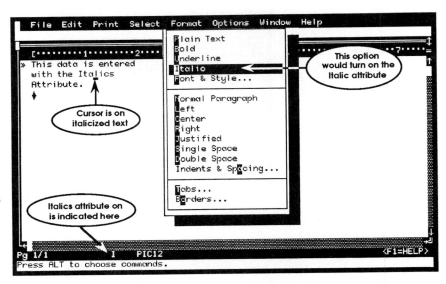

Figure 4.5

*You can use the **Format** menu to assign attributes to text. If your screen is in text mode, the text is displayed in bold or color. If you are in graphics mode, the text will be displayed with the assigned attribute. The attribute that is on is shown on the status line.*

If you want to apply the attributes to text as you enter it, you need to understand how Microsoft Works marks the text that has attributes. When an attribute is first chosen from the format menu, Microsoft Works will insert a special control character in the document to indicate that the attribute is on at this point. This control character is not visible to you; however, you should remember that it is there. When you have completed entering your text and you want to switch back to your normal type style, you must choose the *Plain* option from the Format menu. This operation inserts another control code that sets all the special attributes off. Again, you cannot see the control code, but it is there. This provides a beginning and ending point for the attribute or attributes that are to be applied during printing. By storing a control code at the beginning and the ending of text, Works allows you to insert new text in the middle of existing text and have the new text use the same attributes as the existing text.

If your screen is in *text mode* when you enter text that has an attribute applied to it, the text is displayed in *bold* on the screen. It does not matter which attribute or combinations of attributes you have set on, all the text is displayed in bold even if the attribute is underlined or italics. When the document is printed, the correct codes will be sent to the printer to turn on the printer's underline or italics characteristics so that the text will print with the correct attribute.

Short Cuts

You can also use the following CTL key combinations to set attributes on and off.

Keys	Action
CTL/Spacebar	Plain
CTL/B	Bold
CTL/U	Underline
CTL/I	Italic

Works will show you which attribute is being applied by displaying a character on the *Status Line*. This character is displayed near the middle of the *Status Line*. This is shown in Figure 4.5. The status line will indicate the attribute being applied as you enter the text. Also, any time you place the cursor on text that has an attribute, the characters that represent the attributes that are set on will be displayed on the status line.

You would normally keep your screen in the *text mode* because the characters are displayed more clearly. Microsoft Works will also support a *graphics mode*. This mode will display text as it would be printed, that is, underlined text would be displayed underlined and italicized test would be in italics. To set the screen in *graphics mode,* you would choose the *Graphics* option from the *Works Settings* dialog box. You can access the dialog box from the **Options** menu. The *Works Settings* dialog box is shown in Figure 4.6.

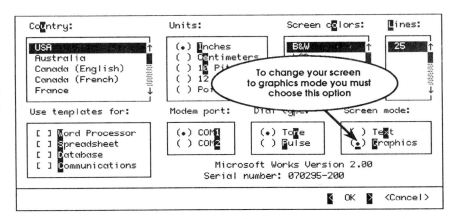

Figure 4.6

You can use the Works Settings options from the Options menu to change to a graphics screen. When your screen is in graphics mode, italics, bold, and underline will display with their attributes.

Aligning Text

You can also use the **Format** menu to specify how text will be aligned. There are four types of alignment that can be used. These are centered, left, right, and justified. Centered alignment will center the lines in the middle of the document. The middle of the document is determined by dividing the distance between the left margin and the right margin by two. Left alignment will start the first character of a line in the first printable position to the right of the left margin. This provides a smooth left margin but a ragged right margin. Right alignment will align the text against the right margin, and the text will flow to the left. This provides a smooth right margin and a ragged left margin. Justified alignment will spread the text all the way across the line, inserting spaces to guarantee smooth margins on both the left and right sides of the document. Most of the text in this book is printed using justified alignment. All four of the alignments are shown in Figure 4.7.

Short Cuts	
Control key combinations can be used to set alignments on and off.	
Keys	**Action**
CTRL/X	Normal Paragraph
CTL/L	Left Alignment
CTL/C	Center Alignment
CTL/R	Right Alignment
CTL/J	Justified Alignment
CTL/1	Single Space
CTL/2	Double Space
CTL/5	1-1/2 Space

Text alignment always works with entire paragraphs. This means if you set the alignment for any part of a paragraph, the entire paragraph will use the alignment. Remember that a paragraph is any text between two Enter keys, and a paragraph can be a single line or even a single character.

Figure 4.7

You can align text one of four ways. Left alignment is the normal alignment. You would use center alignment for titles. Right alignment is sometimes used for tables. The justified alignment can be used to make a document more professional looking.

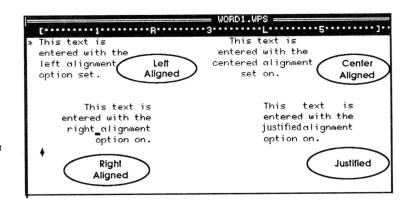

Using the Show All Characters Option

When you are normally entering text into a document or modifying a document, you only want to see the text or characters that will be printed. You should realize that there are many characters in the text that do not print. These characters mark your spaces, paragraphs, page breaks, and several other items. The display of these special characters can be turned on by choosing the *Show All Characters* option from the **Options** menu.

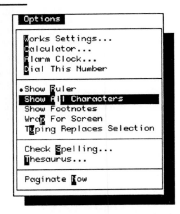

This *Show All Characters* option is used as a toggle. The first time you choose it, the characters are displayed. The next time you choose it, the option is turned off. The diamond indicates that the option has been turned on. Figure 4.8 shows each of the special characters used by Microsoft Works.

Copying Text

Many times, when you create a document, you find that you need the same text in several places. You could retype the text, but if it is long or complex you may make a mistake that would need to be corrected. When you are using a word processor, you have a second option for duplicating this text. This option is to copy the text. You can copy any amount of text: a page, paragraph, phrase, word, or even a character.. When you copy text, you not only copy the text but you also copy any attributes and alignment that might be applied to the text.

To copy text, you must first select the text as a block. After you have selected the text you want copied, you will need to choose the *Copy* option from the **Edit** menu. Once you have selected the *Copy* option, you will be asked to select the new location by moving your cursor and pressing the Enter key. When you do this, you will have a duplicate copy of your selected text at your new location. The *Copy* option is on the **Edit** menu shown in Figure 4.9.

Character	Meaning
»	End of a page.
Date	Place holder for special types of data such as times and dates.
◆	End of document.
→	Indicates TAB key was entered.
•	Indicates space bar was entered.
¶	End of a paragraph.
↓	End of a line but not end of a paragraph.

Figure 4.8

*The **Show All Characters** option will display hidden characters on your screen. Each character has a special purpose to Microsoft Works. The first three characters in this table are always displayed. The last four characters are only displayed when the **Show All Characters** option is turned on.*

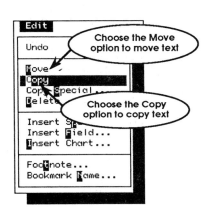

Figure 4.9

The Edit menu has options that allow you to copy and to move text. In each case you must select your text as a block, choose the correct option from the Edit menu, move your cursor to the new location, and press the Enter key.

Moving Text

There will also be times when you want to move text from one location to another. Moving text is similar to copying text, except that the moved text is deleted from its current location and inserted in a new location.

You use the same processes to move text as you use to copy it. You must first select the text as a block and then choose the *Move* option from the **Edit** menu. You will then be asked to select the new location and press the Enter key. After you move your cursor, using any cursor movement keys or commands, and press the Enter key, your text will be moved.

With either the *Copy* or *Move* options, you can cancel the operation before you complete it by pressing the *ESC* key. Also remember that you have the *Undo* option. If you accidentally move or copy the text to the wrong location, you can use the *Undo* option of the **Edit** menu to undo the copy or move. You will want to move text when it is in the wrong location and needs to be placed in a new location. You will want to copy text when you want to leave the original text where it is but want the same text in other locations.

Selecting a Block of Text

When you want to perform operations such as copying, moving, deleting, and assigning attributes to a large area of text, the text must be selected as a block. There are several ways to do this. The first approach is to press the **F8** function key. You then use your arrow keys, or other cursor movement keys, to highlight the text you want in the block. The second way is to hold down your *shift* key while you use your arrow keys, or other cursor movement keys, to define the block. There is also a third way if you have a mouse. To use the mouse, you place your cursor on the first letter of the block you want to select. Next, while holding down the mouse's left button, *drag* the mouse until you have your text highlighted. Once you have the text selected, you can choose many of the options discussed in this text and the option will be applied to all of the text you have selected.

If you need to cancel a block of text, you can simply move your cursor and the block will be canceled. When text has been selected as a block, it will be shown in *reversed video*. Figure 4.10 shows a group of text that has been selected as a block.

Short Cuts	
You can press F8 multiple times to select fixed areas of text	
Keys	**Action**
F8 Two Times	Select Word
F8 Three Times	Select Sentence
F8 Four Times	Select Paragraph
F8 Five Times	Select Document

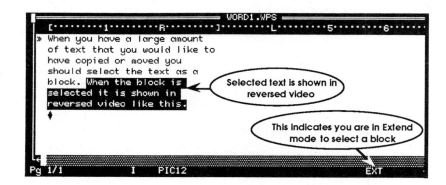

Figure 4.10

You can select a block of text by pressing the F8 function key and then using your arrow keys to define the block. When you use this method, an EXTEND message is indicated on the Status Line.

Moving Your Cursor

There are many ways to move your cursor while you are working in a document. The arrow keys are the simplest way; however, they are also usually the slowest way. Figure 4.11 shows each of the keys that can be used and how they move the cursor.

Printing a Document

There are two steps necessary to print a document. First, you must set up your printer. After you have set up the printer, you can print your document.

➤ Setting Up the Printer

To print a file, you must have the file opened and in a Works window. The first step in printing a file is to set up the printer. To do this, you pull down the **Print** menu. Next, you will need to select the *Printer Setup* option from the Print menu. This option will provide you with the dialog box shown in Figure 4.12.

Figure 4.11

The arrow keys can be used to move through a document; however, they are slow if you want to move large distances. Some of the other keys on the keyboard will move your cursor large distances. You should get familiar with these other keys to save yourself time

Key	Movement
←	Left one character
→	Right one character
↑	Up one line
↓	Down one line
Ctrl/←	Left one word
Ctrl/→	Right one word
Ctrl/↑	Up one paragraph
Ctrl/↓	Down one paragraph
Home	To beginning of line
End	To end of line
Ctrl/Home	To beginning of file
Ctrl/End	To end of file
Page Up	To beginning of screen
Page Down	To end of screen

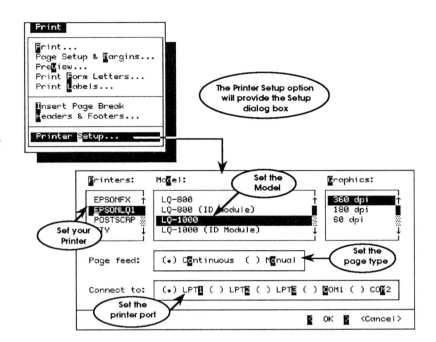

Figure 4.12

*The **Print** menu contains the **Printer Setup** option. The Printer Set option allows you to specify the printer type and model you will be using. You must also specify the way the paper will be fed into the printer and the port the printer is connected to. If you have any incorrect setting, the document will probably not print correctly.*

At this point, you will need to know four things about your printer and your system. First, you will need to know what type of printer you are using and select the appropriate printer in the *Printers* list box. The printers that are available to you in this box are the ones that you installed when you installed Microsoft Works. You will also need to know the particular printer model. For more information about the printers, you should consult your Microsoft Works documentation.

Next you will need to know how the paper will feed the paper. In most cases, this will be continuous forms. Finally, you will need to know whether your printer is connected to a parallel port or a serial port and which port it is connected to. Normally, this will be a parallel port and will be called *LPT1*. Once these list and check boxes have been set correctly, you can select the *OK* button. This will return you to your document so you can print it.

➢ *Printing the Document*

After you have set up the printer, you will need to pull down the **Print** menu again and select the *Print* option from this menu. This will provide you with the dialog box shown in Figure 4.13.

To print the file, you need to specify the number of copies you want in the *Number of Copies* text box and select the *Print* button. You can also use the text boxes in the dialog box to print specific pages of the document, print the document to a file, and specify that the file is to be printed in draft quality. Draft quality prints a little faster than the standard letter quality, but the print is not as clear.

➢ *Using Print Preview*

Before you actually print a document, you should preview the document. The preview option will show you what the document will look like when it is printed. To preview a document, you choose *Preview* from the **Print** menu.

Figure 4.13

From the **Print** *dialog box ,you can specify the number of copies you want. You can also use this dialog box to print selected pages or print to a disk file rather than the printer. Your document will print in letter quality form unless you specify draft quality on this dialog box.*

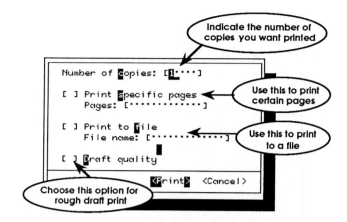

Since the printed output would be much larger than the screen can clearly show, the Preview *'crops'* the document. When the document is cropped, it appears too small to read, but you can get a general feel for what the finished product would look like. To cancel the print *Preview,* you can press the *ESC* key. An example of a Preview screen is shown in Figure 4.14.

Saving a File

If you have just created a file or made changes to a file and you want to keep the new file or changes that you have made, you must save the file before you exit Microsoft Works. Saving a file will copy the contents of the computer's memory to a file stored on a disk. To save a file, you should pull down the **File** menu and then select one of the save options from this menu. There are two save options on this menu as

Figure 4.14

The print **Preview** *will allow you to see how the document will print. The document is reduced to fit on the screen, one page at a time. You can also print while in* **Preview** *by pressing the* **P** *key.*

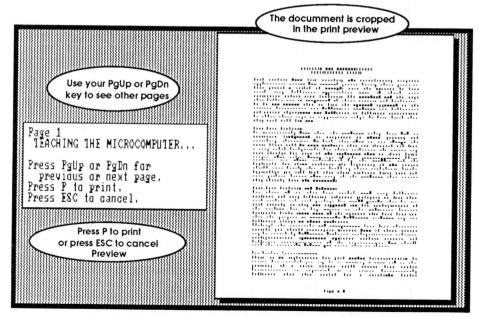

Figure 4.15

*The **File** menu is used to save a file. It has two save options. You would use the Save option to save changes to a file that already exists on a disk. You would used the Save As option to save a new file.*

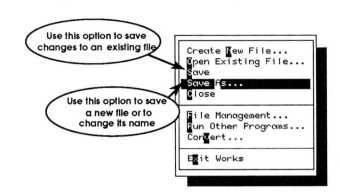

shown in Figure 4.15. Thes are shown in Figure 4.15. The first option is the *Save* option. If you select this option, the file will be saved under the same name and in the same directory or on the same disk drive that it originally resided on. If it is a new file with a name such as WORD1.WPS, Microsoft Works will present the *Save As* dialog box.

If you select the *Save As:* option from the **File** menu, you will be provided with the *Save As:* dialog box shown in Figure 4.16. Notice that the text box contains the file name *WORD1.WPS*. This is the default file name for all new word processor files. If you want to change the file name, you can use your arrow and delete keys to change the name. You would normally use this *Save As* option the first time you save a file or if you want to change the name of the file or disk drive the file is to be saved on.

The *Format* box allows you to specify the format for the saved file. There are three options here. Each option will specify that the file is to be saved under a different format. The *Works* format will save the file with all the formatting necessary for Microsoft Works to remember where the paragraphs, underlines, indents, etc., should be placed. This would be the way you would normally want to save the file. The *Text* format will save the file, but no formatting is saved. This option will place a carriage return (CR) at the end of each paragraph only. The *Printed Text* option will save the document with all the special characters needed for printing. You would use this format if you were going to use a different computer system to print the document.

Figure 4.16

The Save As dialog box allows you to specify the name of the file and the format for the file. You should use this option the first time you save the file or if you want to change the name or location of the file. You can also use this option to make a copy of the file. To make a copy, simply save the file with a different name.

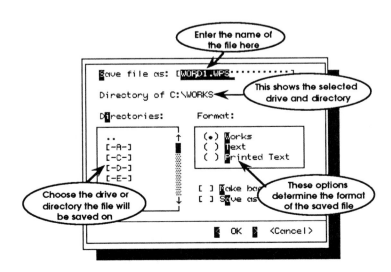

Also notice that this dialog box has one list box. This box lists all the available disk drives and any subdirectories under the current directory. If you want to change the drive or directory where the file is stored, you can either enter the entire path in the *File Name:* text box or select the correct disk drive or directory from the *Directories* list box.

Conclusion

This chapter has introduced some new word processing concepts and terminology. These concepts concern themselves with the basics of word processing. These concepts, along with the following tutorial, should provide you with enough skills to be productive with the word processing module of Microsoft Works. The remaining chapters will add some additional skills necessary to use all the power of Microsoft Works' word processor.

Chapter 4 Self Test

1. What symbols are used on the word processor's ruler to indicate the left and right margins of the page?

2. Explain what is meant by *wordwrap*.

3. How is an option that toggles turned on and off?

4. What does Microsoft Works consider a paragraph?

5. Which menu and menu option are used to create a new word processing document?

6. What is the difference between using the Backspace and the Delete keys to delete text?

7. How would you delete an entire paragraph from a document?

8. What is the function of the Undo option?

9. How does Microsoft Works show which attribute is being applied to the text being entered?

10. How can you get Microsoft Works to show the actual text attributes on your screen?

11. Explain the difference between left alignment, right alignment, centered alignment, and justified alignment.

12. List the steps necessary to copy a large portion of text from one area to another.

13. Explain the difference between moving and copying text.

14. Explain two ways to select a block of text.

15. List the four things you must know about your printer before you can use the Printer Setup.

16. Which menu and menu option would allow you to print multiple copies of a document?

17. Explain the purpose of the Print Preview option.

18. What Save option would you use to save a file for the first time?

Chapter 4 Tutorial

In this tutorial, you will create a new word processing document. During the creation of the document, you will enter text, delete text, format text as you enter it, format text that has already been entered, move and copy text, and use the *Print Preview*. When you have completed the document, you will print and then save your document.

To start the tutorial you should boot your machine using the appropriate steps for your machine, and then start Microsoft Works.

   ❏ **Boot your machine and start Microsoft Works.**

After Works has loaded, you should have the screen shown in Figure 4.17.

Figure 4.17

*This is the initial Works screen. You should get this screen each time you start Works. The File menu is pulled down and the **Create New File** option is selected.*

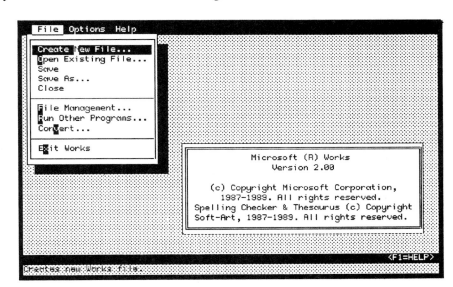

Opening the Document

To create a new word processing document, you should choose the *Create New File* option. Since this is the default option, you can simply press your Enter key to choose the option.

   ❏ **Press your Enter key to choose the *Create New File* option.**

You should now have the applications option box displayed. It is on this option box that you specify the type of file you want to create. Since the word processor is the default file type when you start Works, the *New Word Processor* option should be highlighted. Remember that the highlight indicates the option that will be chossen. To choose the *New Word Processor* option, press the Enter key.

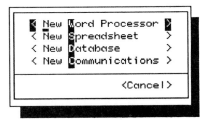

   ❏ **Press your Enter key to choose the *New Word Processor* option.**

This should take you into the word processing module of Microsoft Works, and you should have a screen similar to Figure 4.18. This screen is an empty word processing screen. To make sure that you will see

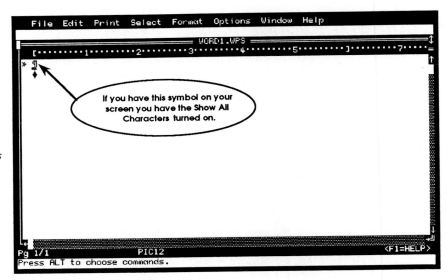

Figure 4.18

*An empty word processor
screen. If you have the
paragraph symbol on your
screen, then you have the*
Show   All   Characters
*option turned on. If you do
not have this symbol, you
should turn the* **Show All
Character** *option on.*

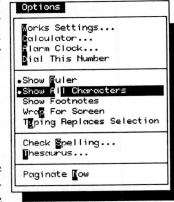

everything as it is discussed in this tutorial, turn your *Show All
Characters* option on. This option may already be set on for your
machine. If you see a paragraph symbol (¶) above your cursor, the option
is set on. If you do not see this symbol, turn on the *Show All Characters*
by doing the following:

❑   **Press the Alt key.**

❑   **Press the O key to get the** *Options* **menu.**

❑   **Press the letter L key to select the** *Show All Characters*
    option.

Look in the top lefthand corner of the screen. You should have three
characters like those in Figure 4.18. Remember that the » symbol represents a *page break*. After you have entered enough text to fill an entire
page, you will see a second one of these symbols. This will indicate the beginning of the second page.
Each additional symbol will indicate the beginning of a new page.

Remember that the blinking underscore is your cursor. This will indicate where text is entered or deleted.
A paragraph symbol should be above the cursor. This indicates that you have one empty paragraph at this
point. The last symbol on the screen is the diamond. This indicates the end of the file or the bottom of
your document.

To make sure that you see the correct items as you work through this tutorial, you will need to set one more
option. This option will set your screen in *text* mode. To do this, do the following:

❑   **Press the ALT key to activate the menu bar.**

❑   **Press the letter O key to pull down the** *Options* **menu.**

❑   **Press the letter W key to choose** *Works Settings.*

This should provide you with the dialog box shown in Figure 4.19. You now need to set your screen to
Text mode.

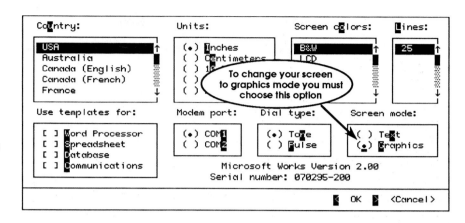

Figure 4.19

You will need to set your screen so it is in text mode to work the tutorial. To do this, set the Text option in the Works Settings dialog box.

❑ Tab to the *Screen mode* option box.

❑ Press the letter X key to choose *Text*.

❑ Press the Enter key to choose the *OK* button.

This should have your machine set with the correct options for the tutorial.

Entering Text

You should now have your blank word processor screen. To begin the tutorial, enter the following three lines. Since you will want each line to be treated as a paragraph, press the Enter key at the end of each line. On the last line, enter your full name.

❑ **Enter:** Microcomputer Applications. **Press Enter.**

❑ **Enter:** Tutorial #1. **Press Enter.**

❑ **Enter:** your full name. **Press Enter.**

Notice that each time you press the space bar, a small dot appears. This is so you can see the number of spaces you have entered. Also notice that the paragraph symbol appears at the end of each line. This is because you pressed the Enter key at the end of each line.

Now enter the following paragraph. **Do not press the Enter key at the end of each line;** let the word processor's *wordwrap* feature force you to the next line. Before you begin the paragraph, press the Enter key once to get a blank line between your name and the new paragraph you are about to enter.

❑ Press the Enter key.

❑ **Enter:** Microcomputers are the basic tool of most business people. They are as common as typewriters in most professional offices. Unlike other machines, such as automobiles which get more expensive each year, microcomputers are getting cheaper and more powerful each year. As a professional, you will need to know how to use the microcomputer.

When you have completed entering these lines, your document should look like Figure 4.20.

Figure 4.20

Your screen should look like this after you have completed entering your paragraph. You should have noticed the lines automatically wrap when you reached the end of a line. You can see your right margin on the ruler.

Inserting and Deleting Text

You can insert characters in the text anywhere you need to. To see this, use your arrow keys to move your cursor to the *t* in the word *the* in the first line of the paragraph you just entered and then enter the words *beginning to be*.

❑ **Move your cursor to the** *t* **in the word** *the* **of the first line of your paragraph.**

❑ **Enter:** beginning to be **so that the line reads:**
   Microcomputers are beginning to be the basic tool of most

Notice that words were pushed down to new lines as you entered the new text. This again is because of the word processor's wordwrap feature. You can insert characters anywhere in the document simply by moving your cursor to the new position and entering the text.

Now suppose you want to delete the words *such as automobiles*. To do this, move your cursor to the comma in the third line. Press the delete key until you have deleted the comma and the words *such as automobiles*.

❑ **Move your cursor to the comma in the third line.**

❑ **Press the Delete key until the words** such as automobiles **have been deleted.**

This is one way to remove characters from the text. You can also remove characters by using the *Backspace* key. Unlike the *Delete* key, which deletes the character directly above the cursor, the *Backspace* key will delete the character to the left of the cursor.

To replace words or characters, you need to take two steps. First, delete the characters by using the Backspace or Delete keys. Next, insert the new characters by typing them in.

You can also replace text by blocking the text you want to replace and then typing in the new text. In order for this to work, you must have the *Typing Replaces Selection* option set on in the **Options** menu.

Formatting Paragraphs

Notice that the right hand margin of the paragraph you entered is ragged. It is not aligned evenly. When text is aligned with a smooth righthand edge, it is referred to as being *justified*. Most of the paragraphs in this manual are justified. To justify a paragraph, you must use the ***Format*** menu. Your cursor should be within the paragraph you just entered. Now pull down the **Format** menu.

    ❑ **Press the *Alt* key.**

    ❑ **Press the *T* key to get the *Format* menu.**

You should now have the *Format* menu pulled down. It should look like Figure 4.21.

Figure 4.21

*The **Format** menu allows you to specify the alignment for paragraphs. You can use your arrow keys or press the highlighted letter to select an option. If you need to cancel the menu without selecting an option, you can use the ESC key.*

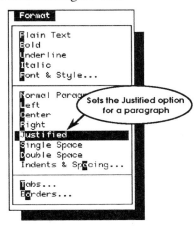

If you do not have this menu, press the *Esc* key and try again.

Notice the Justified option in the second block of options on the menu. To justify the paragraph, you need to select this option. Select this option now.

    ❑ **Press the J key to select the *Justified* option.**

This is the one way to specify the alignment for a paragraph. Simply place your cursor anywhere in the paragraph and use the format menu to select the alignment.

Now assume that you wanted the paragraph double spaced. This was one of the options in the Format menu. Try this on your own.

    ❑ **Double space the paragraph.**

Entering Underlined, Bold, and Italic Text

The **Format** menu also lets you specify Plain, Underlined, Bold, and Italic text. You can set these options before you enter the text. Then, as you enter the text, it will apply the selected attribute to the text being entered. Before you try this, you need to be aware that the attribute you specify will not be displayed on the screen. You will only see the actual attribute when you print the document.

Press the *Cntl/End* keys to move to the end of your document. Press the Enter key twice so that you get a blank line between your first paragraph and your new paragraph. Now access the **Format** menu and set the *Bold* attribute on.

❑ Enter *Cntl/End* to move to the bottom of your document.

❑ Press the Enter key twice.

❑ Press the *Alt* and *T* keys to get the *Format* menu.

❑ Press *B* for the *Bold* option.

Your screen may appear to have lost all the text you have entered. If this has happened, look at the vertical scroll bar on the right side of your screen. Notice that the scroll bar is near the bottom of the screen. This indicates that your cursor is near the bottom of your document, so there must be text above the cursor. You can use your *Up* arrow or *Page Up* keys to see the text above the cursor. If you do move your cursor, remember to move it back to the bottom of your document before you continue.

Now enter the following sentence:

❑ **Enter:** One of the advantages of a word processor is that you can format text in different ways.

Notice that, in this case, the text you entered is displayed as brighter (bolder) characters than the other text. Most importantly, notice the letter **B** on the left of the status line like the one shown in Figure 4.22. This B indicates that you have the bold format turned on. Remember that attributes must be turned on and then turned off. If you enter more text, the new text will also have the bold attribute. To turn the bold attribute off, you will need to select the *Plain* option from the **Format** menu. Do this now.

Figure 4.22

The attributes that are turned on are indicated on the status line.

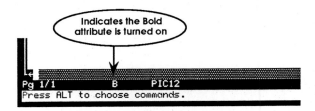

❑ Press the *Alt* and *T* keys.

❑ Press the *P* key.

Now try one yourself. Use the Format menu to set Italics on, enter the following sentence, and set the format back to Plain. Remember that when you print the document the line will print in italics, but it will be displayed as bold on your screen.

❑ Set the Italics format on.

❑ Enter: *Italics is an example of a different text format.*

There are quicker ways to set character formats. This quicker approach uses *Cntl* keys. These control keys avoid the need to access the menu and choose a format. The *Cntl* keys to set the formats are:

Cntl/B	Sets on the Bold attribute.
Cntl/I	Sets on the Italics attribute.
Cntl/U	Sets on the Underline attribute.
Cntl/Spacebar	Sets on the Plain attribute.

You can also combine formats by having more than one format turned on. To try this, enter the following control keys:

❏ **Enter Cntl/B**

❏ **Enter Cntl/I**

❏ **Enter Cntl/U**

Notice that you now have all three letters on your status line indicating that all three formats are turned on. Now enter the following line. Remember that your line will not be displayed as italics and underlined, but it will print that way.

❏ **Enter:** You can also combine different types of formats.

❏ **Press the Enter key.**

Now enter *Cntl/Spacebar* to set the formatting back to Plain.

❏ **Enter Cntl/Spacebar.**

➤ *Applying Formats to Blocks of Text*

You can also apply formats to text that you have already entered. To do this, you must select the text as a block. There are three steps in selecting a block. These steps are:

1. Position your cursor at the beginning of the block.
2. Press the F8 function key.
3. Use your arrow keys to highlight the text.

To try this, use your page up and arrow keys to move your cursor to the first word in the first paragraph. This is the word *Microcomputers*. Now suppose that you wanted to underline this word. You will need to select the word as a block and then set the attribute on. You should underline this word now using the following steps:

❏ **Place the cursor on the *M* in** Microcomputers.

❏ **Press the F8 function key.**

❏ **Use your right arrow key to highlight the word** Microcomputers.

❏ **Enter Cntl/U to set underline on.**

Now cancel the block by moving your cursor.

❏ **Press the Down Arrow key.**

You can also use the same process to remove attributes from text, except that you must choose the *Plain* option from the **Format** menu or use the *Cntl/Spacebar* keys.

Using the Graphics Screen

You can see your text with all of its attributes displayed if you switch to the graphics screen. In order to do this your machine must have some type of graphics capabilities. To switch to a graphics screen, you need to set the option from the *Works Setting* menu. Remember, you set the *Text* screen on at the beginning of this tutorial. Set the graphics screen on now.

❏   Press the ALT key to activate the menu bar.

❏   Press the letter O for the *Options* menu.

❏   Press the letter W for the *Works Setting* option.

❏   Press the Tab key until your cursor is in the *Screen Mode* option box.

❏   Press the letter G for *Graphics*.

❏   Press the Enter key for OK.

Your screen should have changed and the word *Microcomputers* should now be underlined. Press your *Page Down* key to see the other text you assigned attributes to.

❏   Press your Page Down key once.

Your screen should now look like the one shown in Figure 4.23.

You changed the screen mode so you could check your text and ensure that you had the correct attributes assigned. This screen is more difficult to read and causes more strain on the eyes than the text screen, so you should shift back to the text screen now.

❏   Press *ALT, O, W*.

❏   Tab to the *Screen Mode* option box, press *X*, and press your Enter key.

Aligning Text

Remember that formatting refers to the alignment of text on the page. You can format text as you enter it or you can format blocks of text that have already been entered.

Assume that you want the first three lines of your document centered. To center this text, you would select the three lines and assign the *Center* format from the **Format** menu. Do this now by using the following steps:

Figure 4.23

The word processor with its screen in graphics mode will display under-lines, italics, and bold characters. This helps you see exactly what the text will look like, but the characters are not as clear.

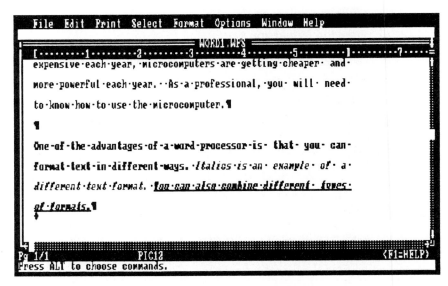

❑ Press *Cntl/Home* to move to the beginning of your document.

❑ Press the *F8* function key to start the block.

❑ Press the Down arrow key three times to define the block.

❑ Press the *Alt* and *T* keys to get the Format menu.

❑ Press the *C* key to choose the Center option.

❑ Press the Down arrow key to cancel the block.

You could have centered the lines without selecting them as a block. Since each line is considered a paragraph, you could have positioned your cursor on each line and selected the *Center* option from the **Format** menu. If you had used this approach, you would need to do it three times, once for each line.

Now try one on your own. Assign the *Single Space* format to the last paragraph of your document. Remember, to do this you should:

❑ Define the last paragraph of the text as a block.

❑ Choose the *Single Space* option from the *Format* menu.

❑ Cancel your block.

Using the Undo Option

There are times when you are working with Microsoft Works that you may make a mistake and perform an operation that you did not mean to perform. For example, you may format a paragraph and accidentally press the delete key rather than choosing a format option. This mistake would delete your paragraph. Microsoft Works is *somewhat* forgiving of this type of mistake.

Works keeps track of the **last** operation you perform. If the operation was a mistake, you can use the *undo* option in the **Edit** menu to correct the mistake.

To see this, we will delete the first three lines of the document and then have them recovered. Follow the next few steps carefully or you may lose the lines permanently.

The first step will be to select the first three lines as a block and delete them.

❑ Enter *Cntl/Home* to move to the top of your document.

❑ Press the *F8* function key to start the block.

❑ Press the Down arrow key three times to select the first three lines.

❑ Press the *Delete* key to delete the block.

Your lines should now be deleted. Now, before you perform any other operation, you must pull down the **Edit** menu and select the *Undo* option.

❑ Press the *Alt* and *E* keys to get the Edit menu.

You should now have the menu shown in Figure 4.24.

The *Undo* option should be highlighted, so you can choose this option by pressing your Enter key.

❑ Press the Enter key to choose the Undo option.

Figure 4.24

*The **Undo** option in the **Edit** menu will allow you to undo your last change. You must remember that Works will only keep track of your last change, so you cannot undo changes that were made prior to your last change*

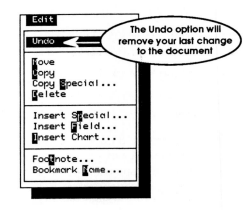

You should now have the lines back in your document.

You can undo almost any operation, but remember that you can only undo your last operation. As you learn Microsoft Works, you should keep this option in mind. When you make a mistake, try the *Undo* to correct the mistake.

Copying Text

Now assume you wanted to make a copy of your first three lines and place the copy at the bottom of your document. You could retype the lines but you may make errors as your retype them. An easier way is to copy the lines. Remember, to copy lines you first select the lines as a block, choose *Copy* from the **Edit** menu, move your cursor to the new location, and press the Enter key. These steps are shown in Figure 4.25.

- ❏ **Press CNTL/Home to move to the beginning of your document.**
- ❏ **Press F8 to begin the selection of the block.**
- ❏ **Press the Down arrow 3 times to select the block.**

Figure 4.25

*To copy a block of text you must first block the text, then choose the **Copy** option from the **Edit** menu, move your cursor to the place you want the copy, and press the Enter key.*

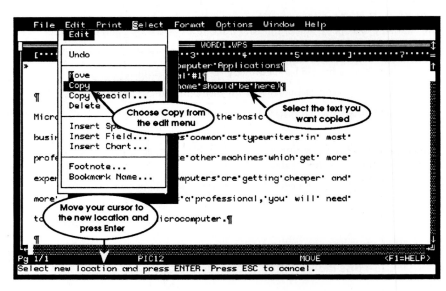

❑   Press *ALT* and *E* to get the *Edit* menu.

❑   Press *C* for *Copy*.

❑   Press *CNTL/END* to move to the end of your document.

❑   Press your Enter key to complete the *Copy*.

Your text should now be copied to its new location. Remember, you move text using the same approach except that you choose the *Move* option from the **Edit** menu.

Printing the Document

➢ Setting Up the Printer

You will now print your document. You should do two things to print the document. Make sure you have the correct *Printer Setup* and then print the document. The first thing is to set up the printer. Remember that to do this, you use the *Printer Setup* from the **Print** menu. Pull this menu down now.

❑   Press the Alt and P keys.

❑   Press the S key to choose the *Printer Setup* option.

You should now have the *Printer Setup* dialog box shown in Figure 4.26.

You will need to determine the correct options to set for your printer. Since almost all printers and computer configurations are different, we cannot provide specific examples for you here. If you cannot determine any of your printer settings, try the ones shown in Figure 4.26. They will probably let you print the document, but some things may not print correctly. Make sure the options in this dialog box are set for your printer and then press the Enter key. Make sure your printer is turned on and *online*.

❑   Set the options for your printer.

❑   Press the Enter key.

If you get an error message when you try to print a document or the document simply does not print, it may be because of these settings. If this happens, you will need to refer to your system and printer manuals for help. If your document prints but does not print your underline, italics, or bold characters correctly, it is usually because you have the wrong model set in this dialog box.

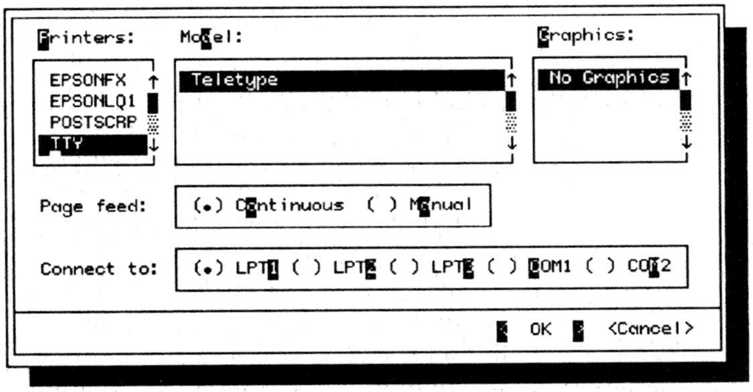

Figure 4.26

*The **Printer Setup** dialog box specifies the information for your printer. The TTY printer is a standard teletype printer. It will not print the underlines, italics, and bold letters, but it will normally allow you to print.*

➤ *Previewing the Document*

Before you print the document you would want to preview it to ensure that it looks correct. To do this, pull down the **Print** menu and choose the *Preview* option.

❑   Press the *Alt* and *P* keys to get the Print menu.

❑   Press the *V* key to get the Preview dialog box.

You should now have the *Print Preview* box shown in Figure 4.27.

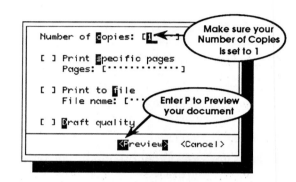

Figure 4.27

*Use the **Preview** option to set your **Number of Copies** before you preview your document. After you set your Number of Copies, press the **P** key to preview.*

Make sure the *Number of Copies* text box contains 1 for one copy and press the Enter key. This should preview your document, and you should get a screen like the one in Figure 4.28.

❑   Press the Enter key to preview your document.

You can now print your document. Before you print the document, make sure your printer is turned on and set *online*. Next press the letter **P** to print your document.

❑   Make sure your printer is online.

❑   Enter *P* to print your document.

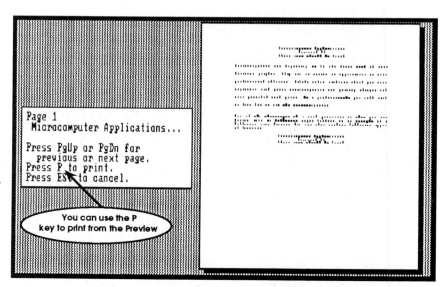

Figure 4.28

*The **Print Preview** option will allow you to view your file the way it would be printed. Use this to check your page breaks, indentations, and other formatting before you print the document. If you press the letter P while you are in Preview, the document will be printed. Press ESC to cancel Preview.*

Saving the Document

You now need to save your document to your diskette. Before you start the save operation, notice the name of your document. This is displayed at the top of your screen. The current name of the document should be **WORD1.WPS.** This is the default name Microsoft Works assigns documents when you originally create them. Since you would want to save your document under a better name, you would need to use the *Save As* option from the **File** menu. Select this option now.

❑ **Press the** *Alt* **and** *F* **keys to get the File menu.**

❑ **Press the** *A* **key to choose the Save As option.**

You should now have a dialog box like the one shown in Figure 4.29.

Figure 4.29

The Save As dialog box allows you to specify the disk and the directory your file will be saved to. Tab into the Directories list box and highlight the drive or directory you want. You must enter the file's name in the Save file as: text box.

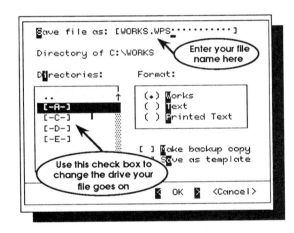

To save the file as a word processing document, make sure you have the Works format indicated in the *Format* box. Next, enter the name you want your document saved under. If you want it saved on any disk or in any directory other than the one indicated by the *Directory of:* setting, you will need to enter the drive designator and path with the file name. For example, if you wanted the file saved on drive B: under the name TUT-WP1, you would enter B:TUT-WP1 and then press the Enter key. You do not need to enter the file extension. Microsoft Works will add a file extension of WPS to your file name. This extension is used by Works to note the file as a word processor file. Save your file now.

❑ **Enter the name and path to save your file under.**

❑ **Press the Enter key.**

Your file should now be saved.

If you need to make corrections to the file at a later time, you can open the file and edit it. To open the file, choose *Open Existing File* from the **File** menu. You will be presented with a dialog box similar to the *Save As* dialog box. Enter your file name, including the drive designator and the file extension *WPS* in the *File Name* text box, and the file will be opened.

Exiting Microsoft Works

Your last step to complete this exercise is to *Exit* Works. To do this, select the *Exit* option from the **File** menu.

❑ **Press the *Alt* and *F* keys to get the File menu.**

❑ **Press the *X* key to Exit Microsoft Works.**

Depending upon the type of system you are using, you may get a message that says:

```
Insert COMMAND.COM Disk
```

If you get this message, you will need to insert your *System Startup* disk to return to DOS.

Conclusion

You have just completed your first word processing tutorial. The purpose of the tutorial was to get you familiar with some of the elementary functions in the word processing module of Microsoft Works. As you work through this text, you will gain more expertise with the word processor.

If you had trouble with the tutorial, you should work through it again. The information provided in the tutorial is necessary for the remainder of the text. The only way to be efficient with a software package is to be so comfortable with it that the operation of the package becomes second nature to you.

You should now remove any of your diskettes from the drives and turn your machine and monitor off. If you printed your document, you should remove it from your printer.

Hands on Practice

Exercise 4.1

Using Microsoft Works' Word Processing module, create and print the following document. Make sure you format the text the way it is shown here. Enter your full name and the current date on the second and third lines. Your document will not look exactly like the one shown here because your lines will not be as wide as these.

Exercise 4.1
(your name)
(today's date)

Buying a Computer System

Buying a computer system is much the same as buying an automobile. There are dozens of dealers and dozens of models to choose from. You can get a basic computer system, or you can buy special packages that provide an *unlimited* number of options. Like automobile dealers, most computer dealers will haggle over the price and many have begun to take trade-ins.

One of the primary concerns when selecting a dealer is service. Computers, like other machines, occasionally break down and require maintenance. Most dealers will **service what they sell;** however, they hesitate to service systems that were bought from mail order and discount houses.

Another item that you should consider is **technical support**. There will be times when you need help with a technical problem. These problems range from connecting a printer or modem to installing software. Training should also be a consideration. Many dealers will provide a free class that will help you with the basics of using the system.

You should remember that buying the hardware is only part of the cost of a computer system. <u>After you buy the hardware, you still need software and programs to make your system productive</u>. Although you will want to buy some of your software, there are many large libraries of public domain and **shareware** software. Public domain software is free and there is no licensing agreement. With Shareware software, you are encouraged to try the software. If you find it useful, you are asked to pay a *nominal* fee.

Hands on Practice

Exercise 4.2

Using Microsoft Works' Word Processing module, create and print the following document. Make sure you format the text the way it is shown here. Enter your full name and the current date on the second and third lines. Your document will not look exactly like the one shown here because your lines will not be as wide as these.

Exercise 4.2
(your name)
(today's date)

Today's computer systems are cheaper and more powerful than they were only one year ago. Each year the prices go down, while the speed and the power of the systems increase. You can buy a computer system for under 1,000 dollars. Five years ago the same system would have cost 3,000 dollars.

If the automobile industry had kept pace with the computer industry, a **Rolls-Royce** would sell for under 1,000 dollars and it would get over 1,000 miles to a gallon of gas.

Most microcomputers today can hold at least 640,000 characters of data in memory. Many have moved over the 3 million character limit. They work at speeds measured in *nanoseconds*. A nanosecond is 1/1,000,000,000 of a second. The types of work performed by computers have moved past pure number crunching and into the areas of graphics, music, art, and science. Some computer systems even display an amount of **artificial intelligence**.

In the future, computers will continue to go down in price while they go up in performance. It is estimated that by the year 2000 over 90 percent of American households will own a microcomputer.

Once you have created and printed the foregoing document, make the following changes and print your document again.:

a.   Format the first three lines (exercise, name, and date) so that they are Bold.

b.   Add the following line as a document title. Place the line above the first paragraph. Format the line in   Bold Italics and center the line.

Today's Computer Systems

c.   Change the format for the second paragraph so that the entire paragraph is formatted in italics.

d.   Change the formatting for the word *nanosecon*ds from italics to underlined in the third paragraph.

e.   In the last paragraph, change the number 2000 to the words *two thousand*.

f.   Move the last paragraph so that it is the first paragraph.

g.   Copy your name and date to the end of your document. Change the alignment to *left for your name and date*.

h.   Double-space the entire document.

i.   Print two copies of your document.

Working with Documents

In this chapter, you will be introduced to some additional word processing concepts. These concepts will deal primarily with the formatting of the text and layout of the printed document. Before we cover the formatting concepts, a few additional editing concepts will be discussed.

Additional Editing Features

➢ Searching for Text

There are times, especially in long documents, when you want to locate a word, phrase, or term. You may want to do this to add to the phrase or to correct the phrase. Rather than reading the entire document to find the phrase, you can have Microsoft Works search for the word, phrase, or term. This is much faster and much more accurate.

There are two things that must be remembered when you search for text. The first is that the search is always conducted in a forward fashion. This means that Works starts at the current location of the cursor and searches all the text from that point to the end of the document. If your cursor is below the text before you start the search, Microsoft Works will not find it.

The second thing to remember deals with how characters are matched. Assume that you wanted to search for the word *is*. Realize that the two characters in the word, *i* and *s*, are embedded in the words th*is*, de*cis*ion, di*s*cussion, parenthe*sis*, and many other words. If you were to perform a straight character search, you would find these words along with the word *is*.

To perform a search, you use the **Select** menu and choose the *Search* option. This will provide you with a dialog box like the one shown in Figure 5.1.

In this example, we are searching for the word *soft*. This is entered in the *Search for:* entry. Since we do not want to find the words softy, software, Microsoft, etc., we have marked the *Match Whole Word* option. This option forces a match on entire

Figure 5.1

*The **Search** option from the **Select** menu
will allow you to find a word or phrase.
If you are looking for part of a word, do
not set the **Match Whole Word** option
on.*

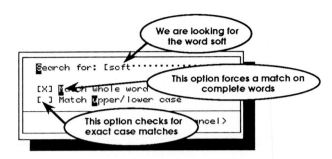

words. A *word* is defined as any number of characters between spaces or any number of characters
beginning with a space and ending with a punctuation mark. The last option is *Match Upper/Lower Case*.
This forces the search to check upper and lowercase characters for an exact match. We did not select this
option because we want to find the word *Soft* if it begins a sentence. When you press the Enter key, the
first occurrence of the word *soft* will be located and highlighted. To search for the next occurrence of the
same word, you would press the **F7** function key.

Searching for Special Characters

You can also search for special characters such as tab marks, paragraph marks, and page breaks. To search
for these special characters, you must enter *special character codes* to represent them. These special
character codes are listed in Figure 5.2.

Searching Using Wild Cards

You can also use wild cards in the *Search for:* text. Wild cards are used here in the same way they are used
in MS-DOS file names. The asterisk (*) is substituted for any number of characters. For example, the
search text **Lab*** would find *LAB1, Laboratory, Label,* etc. When the question mark is used as a wild card,
it will only be substituted for one character. For example, **Lab?** would only find *Lab1, LabA, laba,* etc.,
and would not find *Label* or *Laboratory*.

➤ Searching for and Replacing Text

There may be times when you would like to replace one word or phrase with a different word or phrase.
For example, suppose that your company changes its name from *First Federal Bank* to *Second National
Bank*. Also assume that the original name occurred in a document several times. You could use the *Search*
option to find each occurrence of the name and manually delete the old name and enter the new name.
Works has a better approach. It can search for the old name and automatically replace it with the new
name. This approach is much faster and less prone to error.

Figure 5.2

*Works will search for
special codes. To search
for special characters, you
must enter the code to
represent the character.*

Character	Code	Character	Code
Tab mark	^t	Paragraph mark	^p
End-of-line mark	^n	Manual page break mark	^d
Non-breaking space	^s	Optional hyphen	^-
Non-breaking hyphen	^~	Caret (^)	^^
Question mark	^?	White space	^W
Any character	?	Any ASCII character	^#
		Where # is the ASCII code	

Figure 5.3

*The **Replace** option will allow you to change each occurrence of a word or phrase. The buttons at the bottom of the dialog box are used to determine how the replacement is performed.*

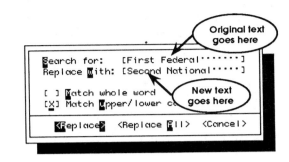

Searching for and replacing text is similar to searching for text. In fact, it actually performs a search prior to performing the replace. The primary difference is that you must enter replacement text. When the text you are trying to replace is found, you have an option to replace the text or ignore the replacement. An example of the *Replace* dialog box is shown in Figure 5.3.

You enter the text you are searching for in the *Search for:* text box. You then enter the new text in the *Replace with:* dialog box. In our example, you would enter *First Federal* in the *Search for:* text box and *Second National* in the *Replace with:* text box.

The *Match Whole Word* and *Match Upper/Lower Case* applies to the *Search for* text and works the same as it does for the *Search* option.

The three buttons at the bottom of the dialog box are used to execute the option. If you choose the *Replace* button, the text is searched from the cursor forward. Each time the *Search for* text is found, you are presented with the *Replace* dialog box. If you choose **Yes** from this dialog box, the text is replaced. If you choose **No**, the text is not replaced. In either case, the search continues to the next occurrence where the *Replace* dialog box is presented again. This continues to the end of the document or until you select the *Cancel* button from this box. The *Replace All* button will replace all occurrences of the text without asking you to verify each replacement.

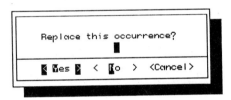

When the text is found and replaced, the following two rules apply:

1. If the original text has attributes (underline, bold, or italics) applied to it, the new replacement text will also have these attributes.

2. Capitalization of the replacement text is matched with the original text. For example, if you search for the word *some* and replace it with the word *most* and Works finds the word *Some*, it will replace *Some* with the word *Most*.

You should also remember that if you make an error entering either the *Search for* text or the *Replace with* text, you can use the *Undo* option to undo your changes.

Setting TABS

Tabs are specially marked positions placed on the ruler of the document. Each time you press the **Tab** key, the cursor moves to the next tab marker. Microsoft Works has several types of tabs.

Left: When you specify a left tab, you are specifying that the text aligned on the tab is to be aligned with the leftmost characters beneath each other. As the text is entered, it will flow to the right of the tab mark. This provides a smooth, even, left edge but may make a ragged right edge.

Center: A centered tab will force the text placed on the tab mark to flow both to the left and to the right of the tab mark. This will align the text in the middle of the tab mark but will probably cause uneven edges on both the right and the left of a column.

Right: The right tab mark will align the text with the rightmost characters beneath each other. The text will flow to the left as it is entered. This type of tab mark will provide a smooth right edge, but it will probably provide an uneven left edge for a column of data.

Decimal: A decimal tab is used when you want to enter a column of numbers. Since text will always be aligned left, right, or centered, these types of tabs are not appropriate for numbers. For numbers, you want the digits aligned on the decimal point. The decimal tab will force this. As the numbers are entered, they will flow to the left until you enter a decimal point. Once the decimal point is entered, the numbers will flow to the right.

An example of each type of tab is shown in Figure 5.4.

Figure 5.4

When tabs are set, you must specify the alignment for the tab. Text is aligned when you press the Tab key.

Left Tab	Centered Tab	Right Tab	Decimal Tab
Computers	Computers	Computers	1945.53
Disks	Disks	Disks	100.00
Cables	Cables	Cables	33.75
Discounts	Discounts	Discounts	.053

A tab leader can also be assigned to each tab. A *tab leader* is a set of characters that will be printed in all blank spaces that precede the tab. Leaders are normally used for things like *Tables of Contents*. They are used to help guide your eye to the data at the other end of the tab. Figure 5.5 shows tabs with leaders.

Figure 5.5

Tab leaders are used to guide the reader's eye to the data that is at the other end of the tab.

Chapter 1 1
Chapter 2 12
Chapter 3 24

Tabs can be placed on the ruler anywhere in a document. Once a tab is placed on a ruler, any new text that is entered below the tab can use the tab. Text that has already been entered cannot use the new tab. To allow existing text to use the new tabs, you must select the text as a block before you set the tabs. The tab will remain on the ruler until it is replaced by another tab or is deleted.

To insert the Tab markers, you choose the *Tabs* option from the **Format** menu. This will present you with the dialog box shown in Figure 5.6.

When you create a document in Microsoft Works, a default tab is placed every 0.5 inches. These are not noted on the ruler. There are two ways to define the location of a new tab. First, you can enter the *position* of the tab. For example, if you wanted a tab 2 1/2 inches from the left margin, you would enter 2.5.

Figure 5.6

*The **Tabs** dialog box allows you to specify tab marks at locations on your ruler. When you specify the tab, you must also specify the alignment for the tab and the tab leader, if you want one. To complete the tab, you must select the Insert button.*

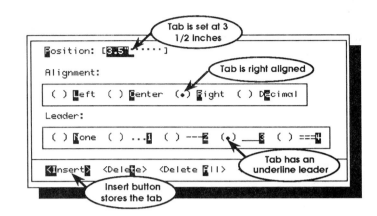

The second way to define the tab location is to hold down the *control* key and use your arrow key to move your cursor to the location where you want the tab. As you move the cursor, its position is displayed in the *Position* text box.

Once you have the position indicated, you must specify the tab alignment. You can do this by tabbing to the alignment box and using your arrow keys to move the diamond to the desired alignment. You can also use your *ALT* and highlighted letter keys to do this. Next, you must specify the leader. Either tab into the leader area and use your arrow keys or use your *ALT* and highlighted letter keys. The last step is to tab to the *Insert* button and press enter, or use *ALT/I*.

To *change* or *remove* a single tab mark, you must enter the tab location or use your *control* and arrow keys to position your cursor on the tab mark of the ruler. You can then tab into the other boxes to modify the tab. You must finally choose the *Insert* button to change the tab. To delete a tab, highlight the tab and choose the *Delete* button. To clear all tabs, choose the *Delete All* button.

Once you have set tabs, the tab marks will be displayed on your ruler. Each tab mark will be displayed differently depending on the alignment you have selected for the tab. If the tab has been assigned a leader, the leader character will be displayed to the left of the tab marker. The left and righthand margins are also displayed on the ruler. An example of a ruler with tab marks is shown in Figure 5.7.

Figure 5.7

Tab marks are displayed on the document ruler with an indication of the alignment and leaders.

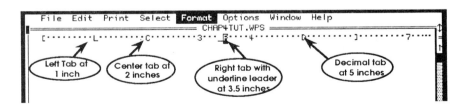

Setting the Print Margins

To have total control of the way your document is printed, you must set up the layout of the page. Page layout refers to the size of the page and the amount of the page that is to be used for margins. Standard typing paper is 11 inches long and 8 1/2 inches wide. Wide computer paper is 11 inches long and 17 inches wide. Once you specify the size of the page and the size of the margins, Microsoft Works determines how

Figure 5.8

A document may have up to 6 margins specified. The top and bottom margins specify the distance from the top and bottom edges of the paper to the first or last line of text on the page. The left and right margins specify the distance from the left and right edges of the paper to the first or last characters on a line. The header and footer margins specify the distance from the header or footer lines to the edge of the paper.

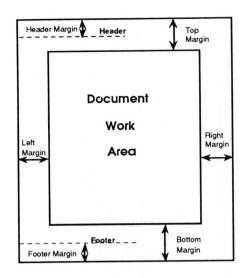

to set the right and lefthand margins for the document work area. The work area is set based on the size of paper you have defined and the size of your margins. There are actually six margins that Works uses. Before we explain these margins, examine the diagram of a page layout in Figure 5.8.

Top and Bottom Margins: These margins refer to the amount of space from the top edge of the paper to the top edge of the first line of text printed and from the bottom edge of the paper to the bottom of the last line printed. The standard for term papers and documents is 1 inch for both top and bottom margins.

Left and Right Margins: These margins refer to the amount of white space between the leftmost edge of the paper and the beginning of the leftmost character and between the end of the rightmost character and the right edge of the paper. For standard typing purposes, these should also be 1 inch. One exception to this would be the left margin. If the document is to be bound on the lefthand side, you should use a left margin of 1.5 inches.

Header and Footer Margins: Headers are text that appears across the top of each page of a document. This text uses the chapter title and page number as a header. Footers are text that appears at the bottom of each page. An example of a footer might be a page number. Header and footer margins refer to the amount of white space between the top of the header and the top edge of the page and the bottom of the footer and the bottom edge of the page, respectively. Onehalf inch header and footer margins are recommended for most documents.

To set the page size and the margins, you choose the *Page Setup & Margins* option from the **Print** menu. This option will give you the dialog box shown in Figure 5.9.

To set the *Page Length, Page Width,* or any of the *margins,* you must tab to the appropriate text box and enter your measurement for these margins. All measurements for these margins should be specified in inches.

Figure 5.9

The Page Layout & Margins dialog box is used to specify the location of all margins for the document. You can also use this dialog box to specify the page size and starting page number.

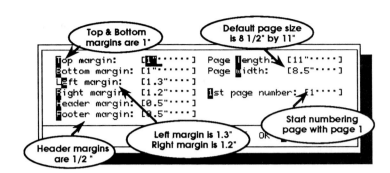

Another text box of importance in this dialog box is the *1st Page Number* text box. If you are printing page numbers on your document, you can use this text box to indicate the first page number. Suppose you were using Microsoft Works to write this book. You would not want the entire book to be in a single document. You would probably store each chapter as a different document, but when you printed the book you would want consecutive page numbers. To get these consecutive numbers, you would print the first chapter beginning with page 1. Then, when you print the second chapter, you would change the *1st Page Number* so that Chapter 2 begins with the page number after the last page of Chapter 1. You would continue this by setting the *1st Page Number* for Chapter 3 as the first page number after the end of Chapter 2, and so on.

Using Headers and Footers

As mentioned earlier, headers are lines of text that appear at the top of each page of a document, while footers are lines of text that appear at the bottom of each page. Microsoft Works uses two different approaches to defining headers and footers. The first approach uses the *Headers & Footers* dialog box from the **Print** menu. This dialog box is shown in Figure 5.10.

To define header or footer information using the dialog box, you enter the header or footer information into the *Header* and *Footer* text entries. There are special codes that can be used to align and print header and footer information, such as date and time, in the headers and footers. These codes are shown in Figure 5.11.

To use these special characters in the *Headers* or *Footers* text box of the dialog box, the code must precede any text that you want printed in the header or footer. For example, if you wanted to print a header with your name on the left side and the date on the right side, you would enter the header as:

&lJames R. Jones&r&d

It is important to realize that you can enter as much information as you want in the *Headers* and *Footers* text boxes; however, since this header or footer can only be one line, Work$ will only print as much as will

Figure 5.10

The Headers & Footers dialog box is used to specify one-line headers and footers. Special codes are used to set the alignment for the headers and footers.

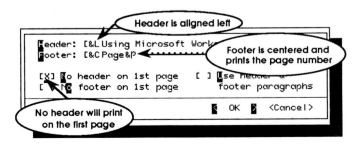

Figure 5.11

*To align headers and footers and
to print certain data such as
dates and times, special codes
must be placed in the header and
footer lines. These codes are
preceded by ampersands.*

Code	
&l	Align the characters that follow on the left margin.
&c	Center the characters that follow between the margins.
&r	Align the characters that follow on the right margin.
&p	Print the page number.
&f	Print the file name.
&d	Print the date.
&t	Print the time.
&&	Print a single ampersand.

fit between the left and right margins of the page. When your headers & footers consist of a single line and are fairly simple, you should define them in the *Headers & Footers* dialog box.

The second approach to defining headers and footers allows you to define multiple line headers and footers. This approach also allows you to assign attributes to the text and set your own tab marks for the header or footer. Use this approach, when you want more control over how the headers or footers are to be printed. To use this approach you enter the header directly on the screen as if it were part of the text. To tell Microsoft Works which header to use (the one in the dialog box or the one entered on the screen), you need to set the *Use header & footer paragraphs* option ON from the *Headers & Footers* dialog box. This is the dialog box shown in Figure 5.10.

Once you set this option ON, you will get two new lines on your screen. An example is shown in Figure 5.12. The **H** indicates the *Header* paragraph, and the **F** indicates the *Footer* paragraph. To define your new header, move your cursor to the line and type whatever you want to use as the header. You can use the *Tabs* option of the *Format* menu to set tabs, assign *attributes* to text using the *Format* menu or *Cntl* keys, or do anything to the header or footer that you can do to normal text.

You can also create multiple-line footers; however, you can have only one paragraph as a header or footer. This is an important concept. Since the Enter key marks the end of a paragraph, you cannot press the Enter key to start a new header line. You must use the **Shift and Enter** keys. This places an end-of-line mark in the header but does not create a new paragraph.

When you print the document, Microsoft Works will either use the header and footer defined in the *Headers & Footers* dialog box or the one defined in the *Header* and *Footer* Paragraphs, depending on the option set in the dialog box. If the option is OFF, the dialog box headers are used. If the option is turned ON, the paragraphs are used.

Before we finish our discussion of headers and footers, we need to note two other options in the Layout dialog box in Figure 5.10. It is common not to have headers or page numbers on the first page of a document. The *No Header on 1st Page* and *No Footer on 1st Page* are used to control this. When the option is set on, headers or footers will not print on the first page of the document.

Figure 5.12

*The Use headers & footers para-
graphs option allows you to enter
your headers and footers into the
text as normal lines. You must set
the option on in the Headers &
Footers dialog box.*

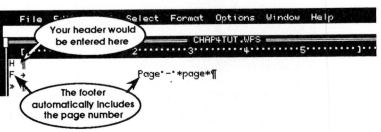

Using Footnotes

Works will allow you to place *footnotes* in your document. When a footnote is inserted into a document, Works inserts a footnote *mark*. This mark is normally a footnote number; however, you can specify your own footnote mark. You are then provided with a footnote *pane*. You enter the text for your footnote in this pane. When the document is printed, the footnote marks are printed in the text where you inserted the footnote, but the footnote text is printed at the end of the document.

To insert a footnote, you choose the *Footnote* option from the **Edit** menu. This will provide you with an option box. This box is used to define the footnote mark. Choose the *Numbered* option if you want numbered footnotes, choose the *character* option if you want to specify your own footnote mark. If you choose the *Character* option, you will need to tab to the *Mark* box and enter your footnote mark. Next, choose the *OK* button.

After you choose the OK button, you will be presented with a *Footnote pane*. An example of a *Footnote pane* is shown in Figure 5.13. Your cursor will be in the pane, and you would enter the text for the footnote. When you have completed entering the footnote, press the **F6** function key to move your cursor out of the footnote pane and into your document.

If the *Footnote pane* is not on your screen, when you insert a footnote it will be displayed. To remove the pane from your screen, you can close the pane. To close the pane, turn the *Show Footnotes* option from the **Options** menu off.

You can edit a footnote if the pane is displayed. If it is not displayed, turn the *Show Footnotes* option on from the **Options** menu. To edit the footnotes, use your **F6** function key to move into the pane. Now edit the footnote as if it were normal text and use the **F6** key to move back to your document. To move a footnote, select the footnote marker, choose *Move* from the **Edit** menu, move your cursor to the new location, and press the Enter key. You can *Copy* a footnote by using the same approach as a move, but choose *Copy* from the **Edit** menu. To delete a footnote, select the footnote mark and choose *Delete* from the **Edit** menu.

Figure 5.13

*When footnotes are entered in the document, a footnote mark is placed in the document. A **Footnote pane** is presented and you enter the footnote text in this pane. To move between the pane and the document, you use the F6 function key.*

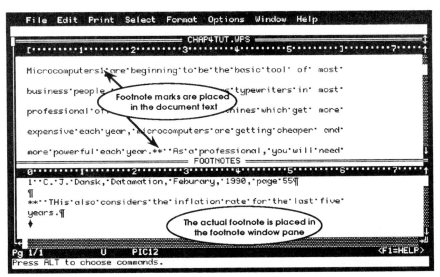

Using the Spell Checker

Microsoft Works includes a builtin dictionary that contains over 50,000 words. This dictionary is used with Works' spell checking feature. Works will not only check the spelling of words but it will also check for irregular capitalization and double words. A double word error occurs any time the same word occurs two or more times consecutively.

To spell check a document, you choose the *Spelling* option from the **Edit** menu. When the spell checker finds a word that is not in its dictionary, Works will show you the word and allow you to correct the spelling. If you do not know the correct spelling, Works will provide you with suggestions for the correct spelling of the word. This is shown in Figure 5.14.

Figure 5.14

The spelling checker will check for any word that is not in its dictionary. When it finds a misspelled word, the word is highlighted. If you choose the Suggest button, several suggested spellings of the word are given.

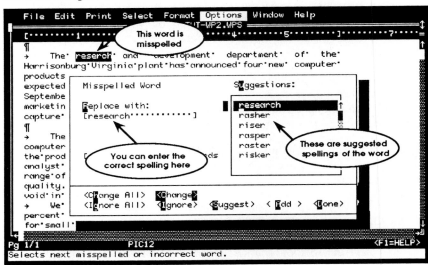

This dialog box has several areas. In the upper-left corner is an indication of the error found. The *Replace with:* text box will contain the misspelled word when it is initially found. You could correct the spelling of the word here or choose the *Suggest* button. If you choose *Suggest*, a list of possible spellings will be provided. You can use your arrow keys to choose one of the suggested spellings.

The functions of the buttons on the dialog box are:

Change All:	Will correct the spelling of this word in the remainder of the document.
Ignore All:	Works will ignore this word or treat it as a correctly spelled word for the remainder of the document.
Change:	Will substitute the word with the word in the *Replace with:* text box.
Ignore:	Will ignore the spelling of the word in this case but will continue to catch the spelling in the remainder of the document.
Suggest:	Provides a list of suggested spellings.
Add:	Adds the word to your personal dictionary. You should only do this for commonly used words.
Done:	Terminates the spell checker.

Although spell checkers appear to be the ultimate saving grace for poor typists and poor spellers, you cannot rely on them as a proofreading tool. The spell checker checks spelling, but it does not check grammar and punctuation. You can have a perfectly spelled paragraph, but the paragraph may not make sense. Read the following paragraph:

> Win you use a spell checking, your should be very carefully. Spell checking is a very god tool however they cannot displace spoof reading. There design is for correct spelling only. Since your can spell wording correct but use they wrong words, you con right documents that makes absolutely know cents at all.

The preceding paragraph would pass through your spell checker with no errors. This should prove to you that there is no replacement for good proofreading skills.

Conclusion

This completes the coverage of concepts for this chapter. You should complete the following self-test before you move to the hands-on tutorial.

Chapter 5 Self Test

1. When you perform a Search, where does the search start and in which direction is the search performed?

2. Which Search option will keep Microsoft Works from finding a character match in the middle of a word?

3. Write the Search criterion to find any word that contains the letters *able*. These letters may be at the beginning, end, or middle of a word.

4. If you were to perform a search for the letters *The* and you did not specify Match Whole Word but you did specify Match Upper/Lower Case, which of the following words would be found?

    the   The   Theater   therefore   another   GATHER   weaTher

5. Complete the following Replace dialog box. Assume you want to replace the word Table with the word Chair.

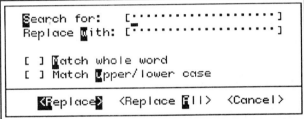

6. Determine whether each of the following columns is left, right, center, or decimal aligned:

Steps	95.	1000.	Tires
Pillows	3.50	22.	Crank shafts
Windows	1,598.88	395.88	Handle
Chair	3.898	0.00	Door

7. What is a tab leader?

8. List the six margins that can be set in the Layout dialog box.

9. What is the difference between a header and a footer?

10. Microsoft Works has two kinds of headers. What determines which header to print?

11. Write the Header that would be used in the Headers & Footers dialog box to print the date on the left, your name in the center, and the time on the right of the header.

12. How do you keep headers and footers from printing on the first page of a document?

13. What function key is used to move into and out of the Footnote window pane?

14. How would you move a footnote from one location to another?

15. List three types of errors that the spelling checker can find.

16. Why should you not rely on the spelling checker to proofread your document?

Chapter 5 Tutorial

In this tutorial, you will be making changes to a document that has already been created. In the last tutorial, you were led through the tutorial with precise steps. In this tutorial, we will assume that you know how to choose options from the menus, and therefore we will simply tell you to choose an option rather than indicating the exact keys to press.

Opening a Document

The document you will be using is stored on your tutorial's files disk. You should have this disk available before you start the tutorial. You should now start Microsoft Works and choose *Open existing file* from your **File** menu.

❏ **Boot your system and start Microsoft Works.**

❏ **Choose *Open existing file* from the *File* menu.**

This should give you an *Open* dialog box similar to the one in Figure 5.15.

If you do not have most of the files shown in this dialog box, you may need to change drives or directories. You can do this by choosing the drive or directory from the *Directories* list box or by specifying the drive or directory path in the *File to open:* text box (i.e., A:*.W*). In either case, you must press the Enter key to load the file names from the new drive.

The file you want to modify is called **TUT-WP2.WPS**. Move into the *Files* box by using your tab key. Now use your arrow keys and highlight the file named TUT-WP2.WPS. Next select the *OK* button and press the Enter key. This should load the TUT-WP2.WPS file.

❏ **Select TUT-WP2.WPS.**

❏ **Select OK.**

After the file has been loaded, you should have a screen similar to Figure 5.16. You may need to turn the *Show all characters* on to get your screen exactly like this.

Figure 5.15

The Open existing file dialog box is used to load a file into memory. You can enter the name of the file in the text box or you can select the file from the Files list box. Use the Directories list box to change drives or directories.

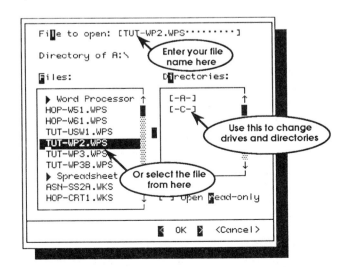

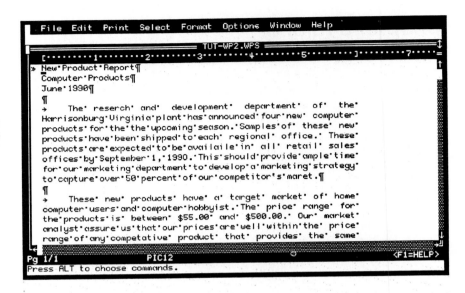

Figure 5.16

*This is a copy of your
tutorial file. Notice that
the file has the Show All
Characters set on. You
will be using this file to
edit for this tutorial.*

Searching for Text

The word *ample* is in the sixth line of the text. Suppose you did not know where the word was, but you
wanted to find it. We will use the *Search* option of the **Select** menu to find this word. To do this, pull
down the **Select** menu and choose the *Search* option.

- ❑ Pull down the *SELECT* menu.
- ❑ Choose *SEARCH* from this menu.

You should now have the dialog box shown in Figure 5.17.

To perform the search, you need to enter the string of characters you want to find in the *Search for:* text
box and then select the *OK* button. To demonstrate the search process, leave the *Match whole word* option
off.

- ❑ Enter ample in the *Search for:* text box.
- ❑ Select the *OK* button.

You should now have the letters *ample* in the word **samples** highlighted. This is because the word *samples*
contains the characters in the word *ample*. Since you did not check the *Match whole word* option, **samples**
was found. To repeat the search and find the next occurrence of the word, press the **F7** key.

- ❑ Press the F7 function key to find the next occurrence.

Figure 5.17

*To search for a string of text, you enter the text
in the **Search for:** text box of the Search dialog.
To find the text the cursor must be at the beginning of your document.*

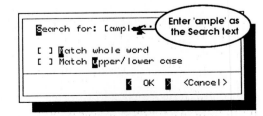

You should now have the word **ample** highlighted. When Microsoft Works finds a segment of text using the *Search* option, it selects the text as a block. You could now use any of the other options that works on blocks, and the option would be applied to the text that is found by the search. If you have the *Typing Replaces Selection* option turned on, you could replace this text with whatever you entered. You should now use your arrow keys to cancel the block. Do not press the Enter key or you will delete the block.

❑ **Use your arrow keys to cancel the block now.**

Replacing Text

The word *computer* appears in the text several times. Assume that you wanted to use the word *microcomputer* instead. You can have Microsoft Works search for the word *computer* and replace it with the word *microcomputer*. To do this, you use the *Replace* option from the **Select** menu. The *Replace* menu is shown in Figure 5.18.

Figure 5.18

*The **Replace** option in the **Select** menu will allow you to search the entire document for a word or phrase and replace it with a different word or phrase. You can also check each occurrence before it is replaced if you choose the **Replace** button rather than the **Replace All** button.*

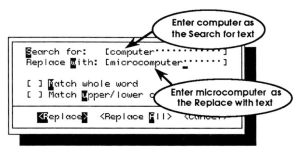

In the *Replace* dialog box, you enter the original word (*computer*) in the *Search for:* option and the new word (*microcomputer*) in the *Replace with:* option. Since you also want to replace the word *computer*, we will not select the *Match Whole Word* option. Also, do not select the *Match Upper/Lower case* option, since you want to replace the word *Computer* when it begins a sentence. Before you start the replace, you will need to move your cursor to the top of the document. Perform the search by doing the following:

❑ **Enter** *Ctrl/Home* **to move to the top of the document.**

❑ **Choose the** *Replace* **option from the** *Select* **menu.**

❑ **Enter** computer **in the** *Search for:* **text entry.**

❑ **Tab to the** *Replace with:* **entry and enter** microcomputer.

❑ **Select the** *Replace* **button.**

Your search should stop on the first word *computer* and display the dialog box shown in Figure 5.19. You want to change this occurrence, so select the **YES** button. The second occurrence of the word *computer* should then be found. Continue replacing all occurrences of the word.

❑ **Replace all occurrences of computer.**

Figure 5.19

*The **Replace** option box appears each time the Search text is found. Choose YES to replace the word. Choose NO if you do not want the occurrence replaced.*

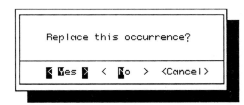

Setting Tabs

As discussed earlier, there are four kinds of tabs that can be set in Microsoft Works. Tabs are used to guarantee column alignment. These tabs are set using the *Tabs* option from the **Format** menu. When you set tabs, the tab marks are placed on the ruler. This ruler and the tabs take effect for all new text that is entered below the point that the tabs were set and before any new ruler takes effect that does not have the tabs. We will begin by setting tabs for columns beneath the line that reads:

```
Product    Plant      Price     Date
```
❑ **Move your cursor to the blank line directly below this line.**

You need to enter the tabs here so that the tabs will take effect for this blank line and the new lines that you will enter below it. We want to enter a *Center* tab for the Product, a *Left* tab for the Plant, a *Decimal* tab for the Price, and a *Right* tab for the Date. To set a tab it takes three steps. You must specify the position of the tab, specify the type of tab, and insert the tab. All of these steps are done from the *Tabs* option of the **Format** menu.

❑ **Pull down the *Tabs* dialog box from the *Format* menu.**

Your dialog box should look like the one in Figure 5.20.

To set the first tab, hold down your *Cntl* key and use your right arrow key to move the ruler's cursor to 1 inch. This will also be shown in the *Position* text entry. Now tab to the *Alignment* box. Use your arrow keys to move the diamond to the *Center* option. Now tab to the *Insert* option and press Enter. This should set your first tab.

❑ **Hold down the *CNTL* key and use your right arrow key to position the tab at 1 inch.**

❑ **Tab to the *Alignment* box and use your arrow key to choose *Center*.**

❑ **Tab to the *Insert* button and press Enter.**

Using the same approach, enter the following three tab settings:

❑   **2.5"   Left**

❑   **4.5"   Decimal**

❑   **6"   Right**

Figure 5.20

*The **Tabs** dialog box allows you to specify the position of the tab. You can enter your position in the text entry, or you can use your CNTL key and arrow keys to position the tab. You can also set the alignment and the tab leader in this dialog box.*

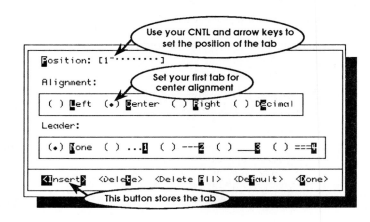

Figure 5.21

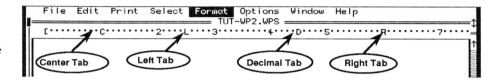

After you set your tabs, they should be displayed on your ruler.

All four of your new tab settings should be displayed on your ruler. These are shown in Figure 5.21. If any of your tabs are incorrect, use your *Ctrl* keys and arrow keys to move to the *tab mark* and correct the error. Now choose the *Done* button to move back to your document.

❑ **Select the *Done* button.**

Next, you need to enter the data for your columns. Enter the following four columns. Remember to press the Tab key each time you want to move to your next tab setting.

❑ **Enter the following lines. Use your tab key between line items.**

```
    Laser Disk      Harrisonburg      495.50      September
 Bubble Memory      Elkton            125.00         August
         Drams      Richmond          345.75      September
Optical Reader      Harrisonburg      475.00        October
```

If your columns do not align properly, you have made a mistake entering your tabs. To correct your mistake, you must first select all the lines you have entered. This is so that any changes will affect each line. Once you have selected the lines, you can use the *Tabs* option to correct your tabs. To remove a tab, move the ruler's cursor to the *tab mark* and select *Delete*. To change a tab, highlight the tab and make your changes. To clear all tabs and start over, select the *Delete All* button.

Another option that is available for tabs is the *Leader*. A leader, as its name implies, is used to guide, or *lead*, the reader's eye to the data that is at the other end of the tab. Microsoft Works has four different styles for leaders. They are shown in Figure 5.20, in the *Leader* dialog area. A leader is assigned to a tab. To see how leaders work, we will use leaders to complete a table for product managers in our document.

❑ **Move your cursor to the blank line below the line that reads:**

```
Manager                Product
```

Now pull down the *Tabs* dialog from the **Format** menu. This time, you will set a tab leader for your tab. After you specify the location of the tab, you will need to tab into the *Alignment* box and select the *Right* alignment. This will align your text to the right of the tab mark and give you a smooth right-hand margin. Next, you will need to tab into the *Leader* box and use your arrow keys to move the diamond to the periods (. . . .) leader before you *Insert* the tab. Set your tab now by doing the following:

❑ **Choose *Tabs* from the *Format* menu.**

❑ **Enter 5 for 5 inches in the *Position* entry.**

❑ **Tab to the Alignment entry and use your right arrow key to move the diamond to *Right*.**

❑ **Tab to the Leader box and use your right arrow key to move the diamond to the second entry (♦) . . . .).**

❑ **Tab to the *Insert* button and press Enter.**

❑ **Enter *ALT/D* to choose the *Done* button.**

Now enter the following four lines. Don't forget to use the Tab key to move to your tab positions.

```
T. J. Jones ................... Laser Disks
C. B. Dix .................... Bubble Memory
K. P. Miller ....................... Drams
C. J. Thomas .............. Optical Reader
```

Defining the Headers and Footers

We will now enter a multipleline header. Remember, to enter a multipleline header you must set this from the *Headers & Footers* option of the **Print** menu. Pull down the **Print** menu and choose the *Headers & Footers* option. This dialog box is shown in Figure 5.22. Next, set the *Use header & footer paragraphs* option.

Figure 5.22

The Use headers & footers option deter-mines which header type will be used when the document is printed.

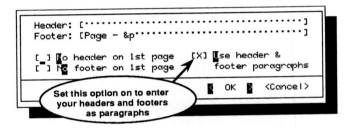

- ❏ Pull down the *Print* menu.
- ❏ Choose the *Headers & Footers* option.
- ❏ Enter the *Alt/U* to set the Use header and footer paragraphs option on.
- ❏   Choose the *OK* button to remove the dialog box.
- ❏ Enter *Cntl/Home* to move to the top of your document.

You should have two new lines in your document. The first line is your header line. To enter a header, you simply type what you want as the header. In your case, you will enter your name on the first line. You will underline your name. On the second line, you will enter your city and state. Before you start, you must remember that this header must be a single paragraph. Rather than pressing the Enter key to start a new line in the header, you must press the *Shift/Enter* keys. Enter your header by doing the following:

- ❏ Set the underline attribute on.
- ❏ Enter your full name.
- ❏ Turn off the underline attribute.
- ❏ Enter Shift/Enter to insert a line feed.
- ❏ Enter your city and state.
- ❏ Press the Down arrow key.

You should now be on the *Footer* line. This line has a default footer that will print the page number. This is indicated by the **page** place holder. The place holder prints in the center of the page, because both the header and the footer have tabs for the center of the page. You can see this on your ruler.

Assume that you want the *date* printed on the left side of the Footer and the *page number* on the right side. To get this footer, you will need to enter a special control key for the date and then delete the word *Page* - and insert a tab to push the page number to the right. Do this now.

❑ **Make sure you are on the Footer line with your cursor at the left margin.**

❑ **Enter *Cntl/D* to get a date place holder.**

❑ **Use your Delete key to delete the spaces and the letters *Page* -. Leave the characters *page* in the line.**

❑ **Press the Tab key once to push the *page* to the right side of the page.**

This should complete your headers and footers. The top three lines of your document should now look like the ones shown in Figure 5.23.

Figure 5.23

The header and footer paragraphs contain the header and footer text.

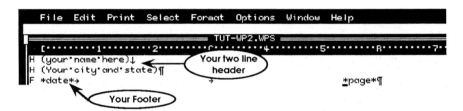

Inserting Footnotes

Footnotes are used to add additional information or to cite references and sources of information. A footnote consists of a footnote mark, usually a number, and the footnote text. To insert a footnote, you position your cursor at the point where you want the footnote mark placed and then choose *Footnote* from the **Edit** menu. Next you specify whether you want the footnote mark to be a *Number* or a *Mark* in the *Footnote* dialog box. Then you are provided with the footnote window. To try this, you will insert a footnote at the end of the second sentence of the second paragraph. This mark should come right after the $550.00 in that sentence.

❑ **Move your cursor to the end of the second sentence in the second paragraph.**

❑ **Choose the *Footnote* option from the *Edit* menu.**

❑ **Choose *Numbered* from the footnote mark dialog box.**

❑ **Choose OK.**

You should now have a footnote window like the one shown in Figure 5.24.

Your cursor should now be in the footnote pane. Now type your footnote text.

❑ **Enter: These prices were prepared by the marketing department based on projected demand.**

This will complete the footnote. Now use your **F6** function key to move out of your footnote pane and into your document.

❑ **Press the *F6* function key.**

Figure 5.24

Each footnote has a marker and a text entry. The marker is in the document and the text is in the Footnote pane. If you have more than one footnote, they will all be stored in one pane. You can scroll your pane just like you scroll a document. Use your F6 function key to move in and out of the footnote pane.

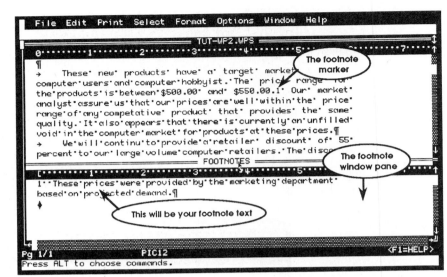

Spell Checking the Document

The next thing you will do to this document is check the spelling. Before you begin spell checking the document, you should understand a few basics about the spell checker's dictionary.

First of all, you must realize that the spell checker uses a dictionary to check the spelling of words. Not all English words are stored in this dictionary. Many words that are seldom used or very specific to a discipline will probably not be found in the dictionary, and Works will think they are misspelled. If the spell checker cannot find a word, this does not necessarily mean that the word is misspelled. It simply means that the word is not in the dictionary.

Second, words that have prefixes or suffixes may not be found, since these prefixes and suffixes change the spelling of the word. Possessive forms can also be missed. In general, formal names will not be found. There are just too many formal names to be placed in the dictionary.

When you ask Microsoft Works to suggest the spelling of a word, it uses a combination of the spelling and the phonetic sound of the misspelled word to find its suggestion list. Just because it cannot suggest the correct spelling does not mean that the word you are trying to use does not exist.

The spell checker checks from the current position of the cursor forward, to the end of the document. Therefore, you should move to the top of your document before you begin checking the document. Once you are at the top of the document, start the spell checker by selecting *Check Spelling* from the **Options** menu.

❑ **Move your cursor to the top of the document by entering** *Ctrl/Home.*

❑ **Select** *Check Spelling* **from the** *Options* **menu.**

The first few misspelled words you will probably find will be in your name and address. If these are correct, enter *ALT/I* to ignore the misspelled words.

❑ **Enter** *ALT/I* **to ignore your name and address if they are found as misspelled. Stop when you find the word** research.

Figure 5.25

Use the Suggest button to get a list of possible spellings for the misspelled word. If the correct spelling of the word is not listed in the suggestions, you can enter the correct spelling in the Replace with: dialog box.

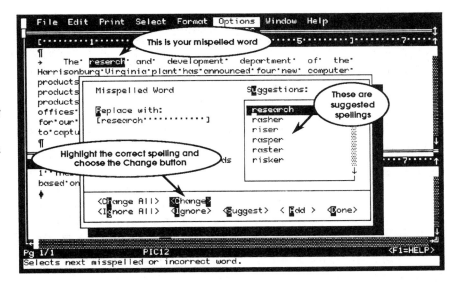

The first misspelled word, *reserch,* is highlighted directly above the *Check Spelling* dialog box as shown in Figure 5.25. The misspelled word is also shown in the *Replace with* entry of the dialog box. If you know the correct spelling of the word, you could enter it now or use your arrow keys to correct the spelling in the *Replace with* text box.

Assume that you do not know the correct spelling of the word and want Works to provide you with some possible spellings. To do this, you would choose the *Suggest* button. Do this now.

❏ **Choose the Suggest button.**

You should have six words in the *Suggestions* dialog box. The correct spelling of the word, *research*, is highlighted. To select this spelling, press the Enter key. The misspelled word at the top of your screen should now be replaced, and the next error should now be found.

The next error should be a repeated word. This is indicated in the upper-left side of the dialog box. Works should have *the* in the R*eplace with* text entry. Choose the *Change* button to replace the double word with the single word and then continue checking your entire document. Remember, you should first read the line that contains the word to get the context of the word. If you cannot correct the spelling of a misspelled word, choose the *Suggestions* button.

❏ **Choose Change to remove the double word.**

❏ **Continue checking the entire document. Use the *Ignore* button when the spell checker catches a proper name as a misspelled word.**

Microsoft Works does not automatically check the spelling of your footnotes as it checks the rest of the document. This is because the footnotes are kept in a separate *pane*. To check the spelling of the footnotes, you must use the **F6** function key to move your cursor into the footnote pane and then start the spelling checker. To complete this part of the tutorial check the spelling of the text in your footnotes.

❏ **Press the *F6* function key to move to the Footnote pane.**

❏ **Check the spelling of the text in your footnotes.**

Using the Page Setup Options

The *Page Setup & Margins* option of the **Print** menu is used to specify the page size, its margins, and starting page number. This setup has predefined default settings which will normally be appropriate. There may be times when you want to change these default settings. In your case, you will want to change the *Left* and *Right* margins to 1 inch and the *Top* margin to 1.2 inches. You should change the top margin because your header is two lines long. This will provide more space between the header and the first line of the document. The *Page Length*, *Page Width*, and *Bottom* margins are probably appropriate for the paper you are using.

Most of the entries in the *Page Setup & Margins* dialog box are text entries. To change an entry, simply tab into the entry box and make your changes. You should now pull down the setup dialog box and make the following settings. When you complete your changes, your *Page Setup* dialog box should be like the one in Figure 5.26.

- ❏ Choose the *Page Setup & Margins* option from the *Print* menu.
- ❏ Set the Top Margin to 1.2".
- ❏ Set the Left Margin to 1".
- ❏ Set the Right Margin to 1".
- ❏ Press the Enter key to complete the Setup dialog.

Figure 5.26

Use the Page Setup & Margins dialog box to change your margins. You need to make the top margin larger because you will have a two line header.

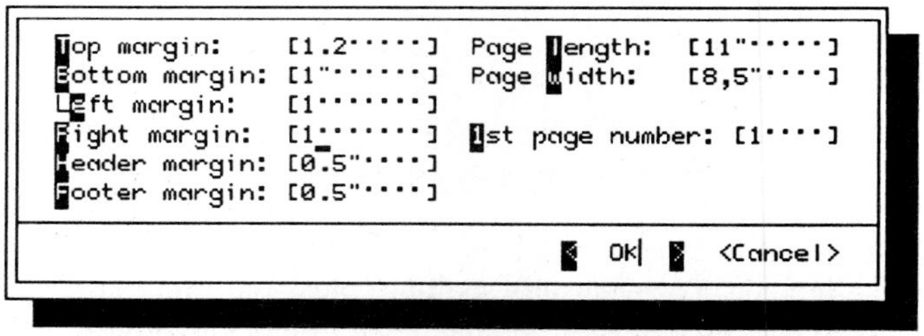

```
Top margin:      [1.2"·····]   Page Length:   [11"······]
Bottom margin:   [1"·······]   Page Width:    [8,5"·····]
Left margin:     [1"·······]
Right margin:    [1_"······]   1st page number: [1····]
Header margin:   [0.5"·····]
Footer margin:   [0.5"·····]

                                        ▌ OK▐ ▌   <Cancel>
```

Saving the Document

You should now save your document. Use the *Save As:* option and save the file under a different name. This will allow you to save your completed document and still have the original to use again.

- ❏ Use the *Save As:* option from the *File* menu and save your file under a different name.

When you save a file, the page setup options are saved with the file. Therefore, you would not need to reset the options each time you load and print the file.

Printing the Document

You should now print your document. Check your *Printer Setup* option to make sure it is set for the correct printer first. Then use the *Print Preview* option to view your document and print one copy.

- ❏ Use the *Printer Setup* from the Print menu and make sure your printer settings are correct.
- ❏ Make sure your printer is turned on and online.

❑ Use the *Preview* option from the Print menu to preview your document

❑ Print one copy of your document.

Conclusion

This completes your second word processing tutorial. You should now use the *Exit* option of the **File** menu to exit Microsoft Works and turn your computer off. Remove your printout from the printer.

If you need to make any corrections, you can edit your document again. Just remember to open the file with the name under which you saved your corrections.

Hands on Practice

For this assignnment, which contains spelling many errors, you will use the file named HOP-W51.WPS. A copy of the file is shown in Figure 5.27. The file, before your changes, should be like this except for the margins.

1. Insert the following table as Table 1. When you enter the table, use Tabs with Leaders.

```
                    Table Number 1
      Geographic Area                    Population
      Northeast  --------------------- 55,573,890
      Southeast  --------------------- 35,720,000
      Northwest  --------------------- 22,100,000
      Southwest  ---------------------- 7,567,889
      Midwest    ---------------------- 9,213,500
```

2. Insert a footnote at the end of the paragraph that introduces Table 1. Place the marker after the word census. Use the text below.

   [1] US Bureau of the Census, 1910 Census Summary, March, 1913.

3. Insert the following table as Table 2. Set appropriate tabs for each column.

```
                    Table Number 2
         State           Percent            Class
      New York            4.850         North East
      Georgia             2.000         South East
      Illinois            1.300            Central
      California         11.050           Mid West
      Washington          3.671         North West
```

4. Replace every occurrence of US with United States.

5. Change the footnote at the end of the paragraph that introduces Table 2. Change the title of the article to Population Changes in America.

6. Change the print margins. Set the Top and bottom Margins to 1.5". Set the Left Margin to 1.5" and the Right Margin to 1".

7. Create a header. Place your name on the left side of the header and place the Print Date on the right side of the header. Set the header so that it will not print on the first page. Use the Headers & Footers dialog to create this header.

8.   Create a footer. Place the Print Time on the left side of the footer. Place the Page Number on the right side of the footer. Use the Headers & Footers dialog box to create this footer.

9.   Spell check the entire document.

10.   Change the spacing of the entire document to double spaced.

11.   Print your document. Start your page numbers with page number 5.

Figure 5.27

Practice WP2-A
Author:

Population Growth
in the
United States

This paper is dedicated to an examination of the population growth of the continental US. Alaska and Hawaii have intentionally been omited. The paper covers the years between 1900 and 1988.

n the early 1900s, the large concentrated populations were located in the Northeastern portion of the US. This was primarily because this time peroid saw a huge influx of immigrants. Since most of of the immigrants were from the European countries adn imigrated through Ellis Island in New York, it was natural that tehy would remain in this region. A second reason for the population being concentrated in this area was industry. During this time period the North East was about teh only industialized area in the US. These industries provided a huge job market for unskilled labor.

The table below shows the percent of US population for five geographc areas. These figures are based on the 1910 census.

Place Table 1 Here

Improved relations with other countries, especialy the Latin American countries, also helped stimulate the growth of the south west. This growth occurred during the 1930 through 1948 period.

The table below lists five states, their percent of change, and whether this change was an increase or decrease. The table's base year is 1920 and the percent change is based on the year 1955.

Place Table 2 Here

For most of us today, the West Coast, brings to mind the large overcrowded cities like Seattle, Los Angles, and San Francisco. We also think of the high cost of living in that area. We should remembr that the west cost was not always like that. In the early 1900s the West Coast offered opportunities to the aggresive American. It it has been the intro-duction of heavy industry, especially the computer industry, that has changed this area.

In conclusion, there are several major reasons for the heavy sheft in population from the North East to the West Coast.

Begining around 1930 with improved transportation methods, population growth began to increase in the western portion of the US. This was primarily because of the over crowding in the east and the increased competetion for jobs. Other reasons for this shift in the population include an increased opportunity to own land. Much of the west coast was sparsely settled to this time and land was cheap. Opportunities were good for because there were few established businesses and the area was experiencing a high growth rate.

6

Advanced Word Processing Features

This will be your final chapter on the Microsoft Works Word Processor. In this chapter, we will cover some of the more advanced features of the word processor. Some of these features include changing margins within a document, creating hanging indents or bullets, outlining paragraphs, changing print styles, using subscripts and superscripts, inserting special characters, using the thesaurus, using multiple windows, and using a split window.

Formatting Paragraphs

➤ *Changing the Left and Right Margins*

There are times when you will want to change margins for only a part of the document. You would normally do this to separate special comments, notes, or quotes from the standard text.

Microsoft Works will not allow you to change margins directly. Margins are set for the entire document

and are used to specify the amount of white space at the top, bottom, left, and right of the printed text. In order to change margins for only a part of the document, you must indent the paragraphs. Remember, to Microsoft Works, a paragraph is all text that lies between two paragraph markers. A paragraph marker is inserted each time you press the Enter key.

To set the format for paragraphs, you access the **Format** menu and select the *Indents & Spacing* option. This would provide you with the dialog box shown in Figure 6.1.

Notice the *Left Indent* and the *Right Indent* items in the dialog box. These allow you to specify an indentation for paragraphs. This indentation is normally specified in inches and refers to the number of inches from the left or right margins that are set in the *Page Setup & Margins* option. If you

Figure 6.1

*The **Indents & Spacing**
option is used to change
the margins for specific
paragraphs. You can
also set the paragraph
alignment, spacing, and
determine how the text is
treated with other text
near it with this option.*

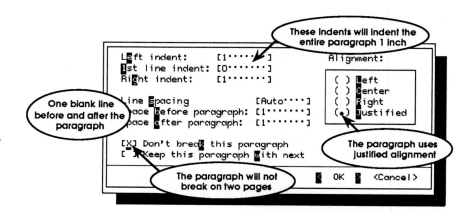

wanted to offset a paragraph by 1 inch on the left and 1 inch on the right, you would specify 1 in the *Left indent,* and *Right indent* text areas.

There are several other important options in this dialog box. The *1st Line Indent* is used to define the indentation for the first line of a paragraph. If you wanted all paragraphs to automatically be indented 1/2 inch, you could specify this in the *1st Line Indent* text box. If you do this, you will not need to press the Tab key for each paragraph.

The *Line Spacing* option will allow you to change the spacing to single, double, triple spacing, etc. You can also specify fractional spacing. You enter a number in this entry to change spacing. For example, you would enter 1.5 for line and a half. *Auto* in this entry tells Microsoft Works to use the standard line spacing for the *font* you are using. These settings give you more flexibility in determining the line spacing than the options on the **Format** menu. The **Format** menu only has single, double, and 1 1/2 spacing options.

Space Before and *Space After* specify the number of blank lines in front of the paragraph and the number of blank lines after the paragraph. This book is printed with one blank line before each paragraph.

The *Alignment* option allows you to align all lines in the paragraph. These work just like the **Format** options. If the *Don't break this paragraph* option is marked, Microsoft Works will keep the entire paragraph on one page. You may want to use this option on short two or three-line paragraphs.

If the *Keep this paragraph with next* option is marked, this paragraph and the next paragraph will be kept on the same page. You could use this to guarantee that all lines in a table were kept on the same page, since each line in a table is normally treated as a paragraph.

To change the format of a paragraph, you need to position your cursor anywhere within the paragraph and then choose the *Indents & Spacing* option from the **Format** menu. When you get the dialog box, the options in the box will indicate which options are set for the paragraph. If you want to format more than one paragraph, you must select all the paragraphs as a block. When you pull down the *Indents & Spacing* dialog box with multiple paragraphs selected, the text boxes are blank, option boxes have nothing selected, and the check boxes have a dash (-). If you change any of these boxes, all paragraphs will use the new options. If you leave them as they are, the options will not change for the individual paragraphs. This will leave any special formats for individual paragraphs unchanged.

Figure 6.2

*The **Borders** option will create borders around paragraphs. When the border is created, it will run from the left margin to the right margin. If you want to restrict the size of the border, you will need to use the **Indents & Margins** option to change your margins.*

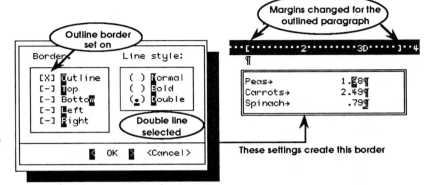

> ## Using Borders

Works will also allow you to place *borders* around paragraphs. There are three different types of borders. These are single, double, and bold line borders. Borders can be placed *above, below, to the left,* or *to the right* of a paragraph. You can also *outline* a paragraph. To apply borders to a paragraph, you must first select the paragraph as a block. Next, you would select *Borders* from the **Format** menu. This would present the dialog box shown in Figure 6.2. Finally, set the border and the line style from the dialog box and choose the *OK* button.

When you define a border, the border will be drawn from the left margin of the paragraph to the right margin. If you want a narrower border, you will need to change the margins by indenting the paragraph. You can do this with the *Indents & Margins* option of the **Format** menu.

> ## Creating Hanging Indents or Bullets

A *hanging indent*, often referred to as a *bullet*, occurs when the first line of the paragraph extends past the left margin of the paragraph. This approach is commonly used when you have a list of items that you want numbered or lettered, like questions on a test. To help make this idea clear, examine the following paragraph.

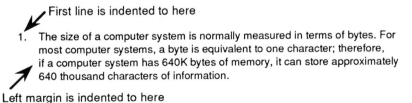

In the preceding example; the bullet is the number '**1.**'. Notice that the margin for the text in the paragraph is aligned on the left, but the number for the paragraph extends to the left of the paragraph's margin. To create a hanging indent, you can indent the paragraph using the aforementioned *Indents & Spacing* option. Then, in the 1st Line Indent, you would indent the paragraph a negative number (this is sometimes called outdenting), such as -0.5". The paragraph shown earlier has a *Left indent* of 0.75 inches and a *1st Line indent* of -0.5 inches.

```
Left indent:      [0.5"····]
1st line indent:  [-0.5"····]
Right indent:     [0"······]
```

You can also create hanging indents using a control key. To use this approach, you enter whatever you want for your bullet and then press the *Tab* key. Next, mark the *hanging* indent by entering *CTRL/H and* then enter your text. The text will use a one half inch indent from the left margin. You can enter the *CTRL/H* anywhere within the paragraph.

➢ *Copying Paragraph Formats*

If you have a paragraph format defined for one paragraph and want to copy that format to other paragraphs, you can use the *Copy Special* option from the **Edit** menu. This would allow you to set up one paragraph the way you want it and then copy that format to the other paragraphs. To copy the format, you must first place your cursor in the paragraph that has the format you want to copy. Next choose the *Copy Special* option from the **Edit** menu. Then you would select the paragraphs you want to copy the format to and press the Enter key. You will be provided with the option box shown on the right in Figure 6.3. Choose the *Paragraph Format* and *OK* button and the formats will be copied.

Figure 6.3

One way to format several paragraphs is to set the format for one paragraph and then use the Copy Special option to copy the format into other paragraphs.

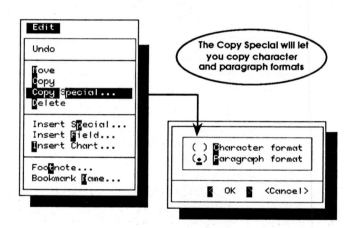

Formatting Characters

➢ *Changing Print Styles*

There are two characteristics of print styles. The first of these is referred to as the *font*. A character font determines the shape of the character. You may have noticed that this text uses several different shapes for the characters that are printed. For example, the section titles have one shape while the reading text has another shape. This is because they are printed in different *fonts*.

The second characteristic of a character is its *size*. A *font's* size is normally measured in points. This manual also uses different font sizes. The greater the number of points for a character, the larger the character. A point is 1/72 of an inch. Several different *fonts* and *point sizes* are shown in the following lines:

This is 8 point elite.

This is 12 point elite.

This is 14 point chansery.

This is 18 point helvetica.

Figure 6.4

*The **Font & Style** option will allow you to select different fonts and font sizes. The fonts available depend upon the type of printer you have specified in the **Printer Setup** option.*

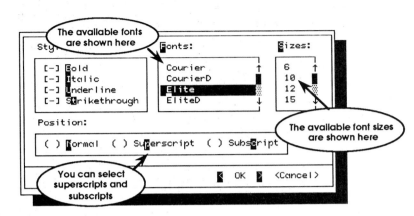

To change the font and font size, you use the *Font & Style* option from the **Format** menu. The dialog box for this option is shown in Figure 6.4.

The fonts and the font sizes that are available are dependent on the type of printer you are using. Not all printers can print all fonts or all sizes. The *Font & Style* dialog box will list the fonts and sizes available based on the type of printer you have selected in the *Printer Setup* option of the **Print** menu. The printers available are based on the printers selected when you install Microsoft Works. The fonts available are shown in the *Fonts* list box, and the sizes available are shown in the *Sizes* list box.

Although Microsoft Works cannot display characters of different sizes on your monitor, most printers can print them. When you select the different fonts and sizes, you will see very little difference on your screen. The characters will be displayed as standard characters, but the word-wrap will take their size into consideration. This means that your line may not wrap when it reaches the right margin on the ruler if you are using a font that is smaller than the standard font for Microsoft Works. The line may wrap before the right margin if you are using a larger font. The *status line* will also show the font and the font size you are using.

➢ *Subscripts and Superscripts*

Subscripts are characters that are printed than the normal characters lower on the line. In this sentence, the word *Subscript* is lowered and printed as a subscript. *Superscripts* are raised higher than the normal characters. In this sentence, the word *Superscript* is printed as a superscript. Subscripts and superscripts are normally used when you write formulas like the following:

$$X_i = (Y_1...Y_n) \, Z^y...Z^n$$

Although formulas are a common use for subscripts and superscripts, they are also used in standard text. The number for a footnote or an end note is an example of a superscript used in standard text. Subscript and superscript printing can also be controlled by the *Font & Style* dialog box.

Short Cuts	
Key	**Action**
Ctrl/+	Superscript
Ctrl/=	Subscript
Ctrl/s	Strikethrough

➢ *The Strikethrough Attribute*

The other options in the *Font & Style* dialog box are used to specify the character attributes. These are the same as they are on the **Format** menu, except for the *Strikethrough* option. If you choose this option, the selected text will be printed with a dashed line through each character, ~~like this~~.

➤ *Inserting Special Characters*

There are times when you want special types of characters inserted into the text of a document. For example, you may want to force a page break to keep certain text on the same page or to separate text onto two pages. Other cases might be for a non-breaking hyphen. If you were to enter a date as 8-19-90, Works would interpret this as a hyphenated word and it might break the date onto two lines. Even simple text, such as a person's name like *James R. Jones*, should not be broken onto two lines. Special characters like nonbreaking hyphens and nonbreaking spaces can be used to prevent this.

The first way to insert special characters is to use the *Insert Special* option from the **Edit** menu. This option's selection box is shown in Figure 6.5.

Figure 6.5

*The **Insert Special** option of the Edit menu can be used to insert special types of characters. Some of these options are actual characters, like hyphens. Others are place holders, like a date. You can also insert these characters with short cut keys.*

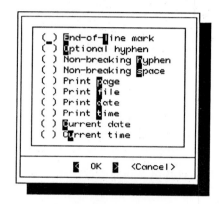

To insert the special characters using the *Insert Special* option, position your cursor where you want the special character and then choose the *Insert Special* option and make your selection. Since you are inserting a character, you can choose only one of these special characters at a time. If you wanted two special characters together, you would need to access this option twice and make two different choices.

Microsoft Works will also allow you to insert these special characters using combinations of keys. A list of the key combinations along with a description of the character's function is shown in Figure 6.6.

Using Bookmarks

Bookmarks are markers that are placed in a document that allow you to quickly move to a specific area of a document. Think of this as folding down the corner of a page. When you want to reference the page, you simply look for the folded corner. In Works, *Bookmarks* are placed in the text of the document and given names. To create a bookmark you choose the *Bookmark,* option from the **Edit** menu. This provides you with the dialog box shown in Figure 6.7.

Once you have created a bookmark, you can use the *Goto* option from the **Select** menu to move directly to the bookmark. When the *Goto* dialog box is displayed, you can use your arrow keys to select the bookmark you want to go to. This is shown in Figure 6.8. You can also use the *Goto* dialog box to move to a specific page within a document. If you want to go to a specific page, enter the page number in the text entry.

End-of-Line Mark [Shift/Enter]	This character is inserted when you want to terminate a line but you do not want to press the Enter key because the Enter key would indicate the end of a paragraph.
Manual Page Break [Cntl/Enter]	This character forces a new page wherever it is entered.
Optional Hyphen [Cntl/-]	This hyphen is used to indicate where a word should be broken if it needs to be placed on two lines.
Non-Breaking Hyphen [Cntl/Shift/-]	This will guarantee that the hyphen is treated as part of the word and the word will not be broken onto two lines.
Non-Breaking Space [Cntl/Shift/Spacebar]	The space will be treated as part of the word and will not allow two words to be broken onto two lines.
Print Page [Cntl/p]	Will print the current page number wherever it is entered.
Print File [Cntl/f]	Will print the file name wherever it is entered.
Print Date [Cntl/d]	Inserts the current date into the document as text.
Print Time [Cntl/t]	Insert the current time into the document as text.
Current Date [Cntl/;]	Will print the current date whenever the file is printed. This differs from Print Date in that this date will change each time the file is printed.
Current Time [Cntl/Shift/;]	Will print the current time whenever the file is printed.

Figure 6.6

*Each of the special characters in the **Insert Special** option box can be inserted using short cut keys. The table on the right lists the short cut keys and their function.*

Figure 6.7

*To create a bookmark, you choose the **Bookmark Name** option from the Edit menu and name the bookmark. All existing bookmarks are displayed in the Bookmark dialog box. You cannot have two bookmarks with the same name.*

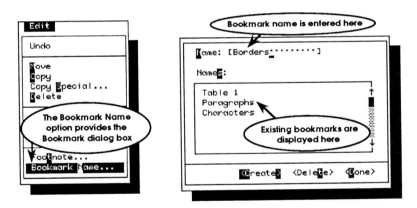

Figure 6.8

*To move to a bookmark, choose **Goto** from the Select menu. In the dialog box, use your arrow keys to select the bookmark to go to. If you enter a number in the Go to: text entry, you will be moved to the page corresponding to the number entered.*

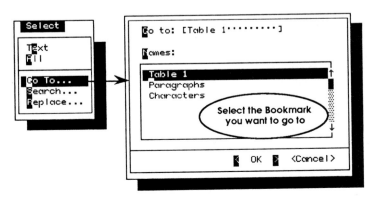

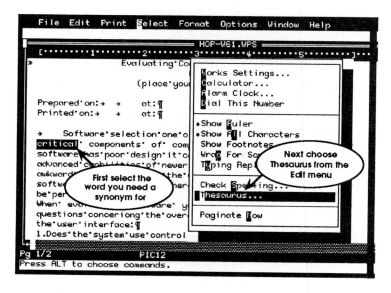

Figure 6.9

To use the Thesaurus to find a synonym, you must first select the word you need the synonym for. Next choose the Thesaurus option from the Options menu.

Using the Thesaurus

The thesaurus in Microsoft Works can be used to find alternate words that have the same meaning as your word. This alternate word would be a synonym. This can improve your writing style by eliminating words or phases that are overused or by simply finding the right word to express a thought. To use the thesaurus, you must select your word as a block first. Next, you would choose the *Thesaurus* option from the **Options** menu. These steps are shown in Figure 6.9.

When the *Thesaurus* option is chosen, a dialog box like the one in Figure 6.10 is displayed. On the left side of the dialog box, the meaning of the word is displayed. Each meaning is marked with a character to indicate the use of the word, (a) adjective, (n) noun, (v) verb, etc. On the right side of the dialog box is a list of synonyms. You use your arrow keys to select the *Meaning* of the word. This will provide you with a new list of synonyms. Next use your Tab key to move into the *Synonyms* list box. Use your arrow keys to select a synonym and choose the *Change* button. This will substitute your selected word with the chosen synonym. You can get a list of *synonyms* for a *synonym* if you highlight a synonym and choose the *Suggest* button.

Figure 6.10

The Thesaurus dialog box provides meanings of a selected word and synonyms for the word. You need to choose your meaning first, then choose your synonym. To substitute the synonym, choose the Change button.

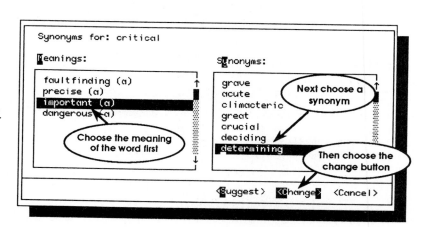

Working with Windows

Works keeps all opened documents in a *Window*. You may think of a window as being a *porthole* that you look through to see a portion of memory. The window can be as large as the screen, or it can be as small as one inch. So far, you have used only one window. This section discusses how to split a single window and how to use multiple windows.

➤ Using a Split Window

Microsoft Works will allow you to split your window into two *panes*. You can then move one part of your document in one pane while another part of the document is in the other pane. This allows you to view nonadjacent parts of your document. An example of a split window is shown in Figure 6.11.

Figure 6.11

To split a window, choose the Split option from the Window menu. Next, use your arrow keys to move the double bar to the point you want the window split and press the Enter key. To return to one pane, choose Split again and move the double bar back to the top of the screen.

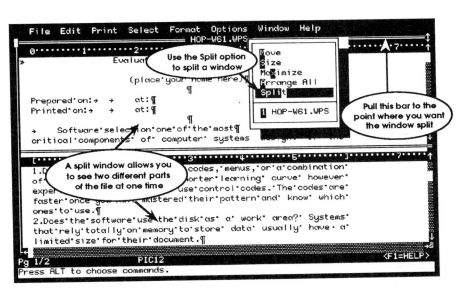

To split the window, you choose the *Split* option from the **Window** menu. This displays a double line at the top of the screen. You can use your arrow keys to move the line where you want to split the window. To accept the window, press the Enter key. Once the window is split, one copy of the document appears in each of the window *panes*. You can then scroll each *pane* independently to view a different part of the file in each pane.

To scroll or edit in a pane, you must have your cursor in that pane. To move your cursor from one window pane to another, you press the **F6** function key. To close the split window and return to a single pane, choose the *Split* option from the **Window** menu and use your arrow keys to move your double line to the top or bottom of the screen. Press the Enter key to accept the window.

➤ Using Multiple Windows

To Microsoft Works, a window is an open file. You can have up to eight windows open at one time, assuming that you have enough memory to hold the file in the window. Each file will reside in its own window. Whenever you use the *Create new file* or *Open existing file* options from the **File** menu, a new window is created. If you open a file, the file is loaded into the new window and becomes the active file.

Figure 6.12

*You can have multiple
windows open at one time.
If you size the windows,
more than one window can
be displayed on the screen.
You can use the Move
option on the Window
menu to arrange windows.*

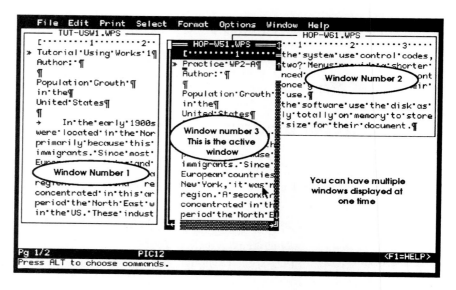

Once you have windows open, you can *Size* the window and *Move* windows around on the screen. This will allow you to see parts of different files. A screen with three different windows is shown in Figure 6.12.

To size a window, choose the *Size* option from the **Window** menu. Next, use your arrow keys to move the borders of the window until you have it the size you want. To complete the sizing of the window, press the Enter key. The window will be redrawn to fit within its new borders. Once you have a window sized, you can use the *Move* option to *drag* the window to position it where you want it. The *Maximize* option can be used to *explode* the window to the full screen. If you set *Maximize* off it will reduce the window to is previous size. The *Arrange All* option will arrange all your windows so that they are all displayed on the screen.

To move between windows, you can use the **Window** menu. This menu has all the open windows listed at the bottom. To move into a window, pull down the **Window** menu and enter the number of the window you want to move into. You can also use your keyboard to move between windows. **Ctrl/F6** will move you to the *next* window. **Ctrl/Shift/F6** will move you to the previous window.

➤ *Copying Between Windows*

To copy from one word processing document to another, both documents must be open and in windows. You must first make the window that contains the text you want copied the active window. Do this by choosing that file from the **Window** menu or using your *CTRL/F6* keys. Next, select the block of text you want copied and choose the *Copy* option from the **Edit** menu. You will then get the following message:

```
Select new location and press Enter or press Esc to cancel.
```

Next, pull down the **Window** menu or use your *CTRL/F6* key to choose the file that you want to copy to. When that file becomes active, move your cursor to the location where you want the text copied and press the Enter key. The text will then be copied into your new document.

Figure 6.13

*The **Works Settings** option determines default settings for most Works' operations. These settings can be changed to change the defaults.*

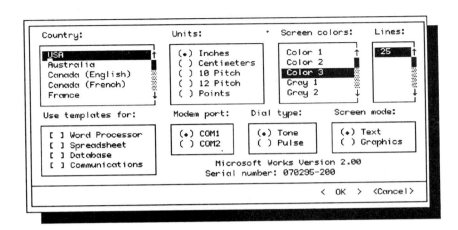

The SETTINGS Option

The *Settings* option of the **Options** menu will allow you to change some of the default settings in Microsoft Works. The settings control how Works performs certain operations. The *Settings* dialog box is shown in Figure 6.13.

Country   This option will change the default page length, page width, currency symbol, date order, and month name (abbreviated or full) for dates to the format used by specific countries.

Units   This setting selects the default unit of measure. Works normally uses inches, but if you choose one of these options, the menus that require you to enter measurements will allow you to enter your measurement in this new form. Works will internally convert them to inches when it uses the measurements.

Color   When you install Microsoft Works, you specify the type of monitor and video card you will be using. Works then selects the appropriate setting for this dialog box. You can try different settings to get different colors on your screen. If you do not have a color monitor, you should set this option to B&W.

Lines   This option determines the number of lines Works will display on the screen. If you have a VGA video card, you can specify more than 25 lines.

Modem Port   This specifies which internal serial port your modem is connected to. If you have a modem but cannot connect to another machine, try changing the modem port.

Dial Type   This option specifies the type of telephone line used for the modem. Tone is for a *touch tone* line and Pulse is for a *rotary* line.

Screen mode   This option determines how the screen will be written to. *Text* should be the normal mode. It gives the clearest text. *Graphics* mode is used when you want to display italics, underlines, and bold characters.

Options Not Covered

Several of the word processing commands and options have not been covered in these three word processing chapters. The *Insert Field* and *Insert Chart* commands of the **Edit** menu require knowledge of the *Spreadsheet* and *Database* modules. These commands are covered in Chapter 14.

The *Print Merge* and *Print Labels* commands of the **Print** menu are also not covered because they require knowledge of the Database Module. These are also covered in Chapter 14.

Chapter 6 Self Test

1. How do you change the right and left margins for a single paragraph within a document?

2. How would you set an automatic indent for each paragraph in a document?

3. Explain how you could force Microsoft Works to place three consecutive paragraphs on the same page.

4. How do you limit the *width of a border?*

5. Give two ways you can create a hanging indent.

6. Explain how you copy a paragraph format.

7. Explain what a *font* is.

8. How does Microsoft Works determine what *fonts* are available to you?

9. Which is larger, a 10 point font or a 15 point font?

10. What is the difference between a *subscript* and a *superscript*?

11. How would you print a word with a strikethrough?

12. How do you insert a subscript or superscript?

13. Give two ways to insert a special character.

14. What is a non-breaking space?

15. What is a *Bookmark*?

16. Why would you use a *Thesaurus*?

17. What key is used to move between window *panes*?

18. What is a window to Microsoft Works?

19. How do you move between windows in Microsoft Works?

20. What is the function of the GO TO option in the Word Processor?

21. What options can you set using the Settings option?

Chapter 6 Tutorial

In this tutorial, you will be using two documents that have already been created. During the tutorial, you will be making changes to these documents.

Opening the First Document

The first document you will be working with is stored on your tutorials files disk. You should now start Microsoft Works, select *Open existing file* from the Works **File** menu, and load the document named TUT-WP3.WPS.

   ❏ **Boot your system and start Microsoft Works.**

   ❏ **Select *Open existing file* from the *File* menu.**

   ❏ **Select *TUT-WP3.WPS* from the list of files.**

   ❏ **Press ENTER.**

Using Multiple Windows

➢ Opening a New Window

Before we begin editing the file you just opened, we will need to open another window and copy some text from that window. Remember that a window is simply another file. To open the new window, you use the **File** menu and select *Open existing file*. Once you have done this, Microsoft Works presents you with the same *Open* dialog you used to open your original file. Open the file named *TUT-WP3B.WPS* now.

   ❏ **Choose *Open existing file* from the *File* menu.**

   ❏ **Select the file named *TUT-WP3B.WPS*.**

   ❏ **Press Enter.**

After Microsoft Works loads the file, it should be displayed on your screen. Your original file, *TUT-WP3.WPS*, will be gone from the screen, but it is still in memory. To see the other file and practice changing windows, you need to select the other window from the **Window** menu.

   ❏ **Pull down the *Window* menu.**

You should now have the menu shown in Figure 6.14.

Figure 6.14

*The **Window** menu lists all available files. To make a file active, use your arrow keys to highlight the file name and press the Enter key or enter the window number.*

Notice the lower portion of the **Window** menu. This area lists each file that has been opened and is in a window. To make a window the active window, you need to choose the file name. You can do this by using your arrow keys, pressing the file's number, or using your mouse. Move to your first file now by pressing the number 1.

> ❑ **Press the number 1.**

You should now have the first file on your screen.

So you can better see what you are doing, use the *Arrange All* option from the **Window** menu to get both windows on your screen.

> ❑ **Choose** *Arrange All* **from the** *Window* **menu.**

Your screen should now look like Figure 6.15.

Figure 6.15

This screen has two windows open. The window in the left is the active window. You can tell your active window because of the scroll bars at the bottom and on the right. To move between windows, use your Window menu or your control and F6 key.

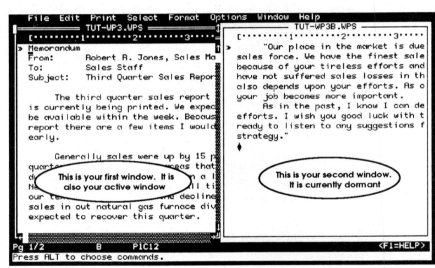

➤ *Copying Text Between Windows*

Assume that you wanted the contents of the second file included in the first file. You can do this by using the *Copy* option of the **Edit** menu. Remember, to copy text you must select the text to be copied, choose *Copy* from the **Edit** menu, place your cursor where you want the copy inserted, and press the Enter key. You use exactly the same approach to copy between windows.

First move to your second window and select the text. This time you will use your control keys.

> ❑ **Enter** *Ctrl/F6* **to change windows.**
> ❑ **Select both paragraphs as a text block.**

Your next step is to choose the *Copy* option and move your cursor to the point where you want the copied text inserted. This will be in your first window, so you will need to change windows before you complete the copy.

> ❑ **Choose** *Copy* **from the** *Edit* **menu.**
> ❑ **Enter** *Ctrl/F6* **to change windows again.**

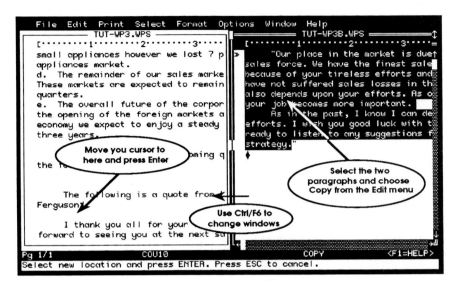

Figure 6.16

To copy between windows, select the text you want copied. Next use Ctrl/F6 to activate the window you want to copy to. Then position your cursor and press Enter.

You should now be back to your original document. Now, move your cursor to the place where you want the text inserted. This will be toward the bottom of your document. Then press the Enter key.

❏ **Move your cursor to the blank line following the sentence that reads:** The following is a quote from the president, Richard R. Ferguson.

❏ **Press the Enter key.**

Your text should now be copied. This process is shown in Figure 6.16. If you have made a mistake and have the text in the wrong place, you can use the *Undo* option to undo your copy. You can then try the copy again.

Before you go to the next step, choose the *Maximize* option from the **Window** menu to enlarge your work area.

❏ **Choose** *Maximize* **from the** *Window* **menu.**

Indenting Paragraphs

You indent paragraphs that you want set off from the rest of the text, such as quotes. You have such a quote in your document. This is the quote you just copied from your second file. Before you can format the paragraphs, you must select both paragraphs. Next, you need to choose the *Indents & Spacing* option from the **Format** menu.

❏ **Select the two paragraphs that you just copied.**

❏ **Select the** *Indents & Spacing* **option from the Format menu**

You should get the dialog box shown in Figure 6.17.

The left and right indent options are used to offset the paragraph. The measure that you enter in these areas is the amount of offset from the current left and right margins. In your case, you want 1 inch offsets from both the left and right margins. Assume that you want a blank line above the paragraph. This blank line can be set using the *Space before paragraph* option. Also assume that you want the margins justified. You

Figure 6.17

To indent paragraphs within a document, you use the Indents & Spacing option from the Format menu. Set the left and right indents to the number of inches you want the paragraphs indented.

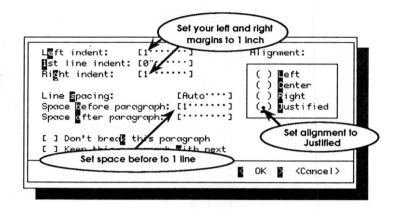

can do this with the *Alignment* option. Use your Tab key to move to the appropriate areas and make the following settings:

❑ **Set the following options in the *Indents & Spacing* dialog box:**

           Left Indent   1"

           1st Line Indent   0"

           Right Indent   1"

           Line Spacing   Auto

           Space Before   1

           Alignment   Justified

❑ **Choose the *OK* button.**

The paragraph should now be offset and justified. You needed to select both paragraphs because you wanted to format more than one paragraph. If you had wanted to format only one paragraph, you could have just placed your cursor in the paragraph rather than selecting it.

Changing Print Styles

Remember that the types of print styles available are controlled by the printer you are using. Also remember that the two items that can be set are the *font* and *size*. To demonstrate the use of fonts and font sizes, we will change the font and the font size for the two paragraphs you just copied.

To change the font and size, you must use the *Font & Style* option from the **Format** menu. Since this option applies formats to characters and not paragraphs, you must make sure you have all your characters selected before you set the format. Both paragraphs should still be selected. If they are not selected, select them again and choose the *Font & Style* option from the **Format** menu.

❑ **Make sure both paragraphs are selected.**

❑ **Choose the *Font & Style* option from the *Format* menu.**

You should now have the dialog box shown in Figure 6.18. The number of available fonts and sizes may differ depending on the printer you have selected in the *Printer Setup* option.

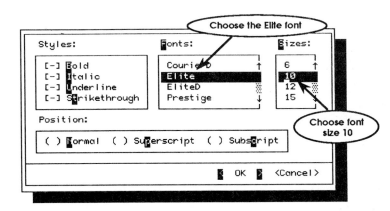

Figure 6.18

Use the Font & Style option from the Format menu to change print styles. The fonts that are available are determined by the printer selected in the Printer Setup option of the Print menu.

Before going further, we need to discuss the upper-left options (Bold, Italic, Underline, and Overstrike). These options can have one of three settings, On (X), OFF (blank), and No Change (-). When you have a block of text selected and pull down this dialog box, the settings are No Change (-). This means that if any text in the selected block has this format assigned to it, the format will not be changed. If you set the format ON, you are setting the format on for all text in the block. If you set the format OFF, it is set off for all the text in the block. You can set the format on and off by pressing the space bar.

The next option box specifies the *Position* of the text on the line. This will be discussed in the section under *Superscripts and Subscripts*.

The first dialog list box chooses the *font*. The fonts that are available depend on the printer you have set in the *Printer Setup* option. You can use your Up and Down arrow keys to look at the available fonts and their sizes. When you have a block of text selected and you pull down this dialog box, no font is selected. To select a font, you must move into the list box. Use your Tab key to move into the *Fonts* list box and highlight the *Elite* font.

❑ Tab to the *Fonts* selection box.

❑ Use your arrow keys to select the *Elite* font.

Once you have a font selected, the available sizes for that font appear in the *Sizes* box. You want to print the selected paragraphs in a smaller font size. To do this, tab to the *Sizes* box and select size **10** and then choose the *OK* button.

❑ Tab to the Sizes box.

❑ Use your arrow keys to select size 10.

❑ Choose the *OK* button.

This should have set the appropriate font and style for the paragraphs. You should not have noticed much change on your screen. If you look at your ruler, you will see that some of the characters appear to be past the right hand margin. This is because Works has adjusted the line for printing. The characters themselves have not changed. This is because the screen cannot display the text style. When you print the document, the correct print style will be used. You can tell what font and size are being used if you place your cursor on any character and look at the status line. See Figure 6.19.

If you pull down the *Font & Style* menu but do not have any text selected, the dialog box will highlight the settings for the character the cursor is currently sitting under. This is one way to find the setting for a

Figure 6.19

Works will indicate the font and font size of the character at the cursor's position on the status line.

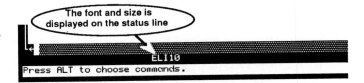

particular area of text. Also, any formats that were set using the *Font & Style* dialog cannot be turned off using standard format options. They must be turned ON or OFF, using the *Font & Style* dialog box.

Using Bookmarks

To complete the next section on *hanging indents,* you must move your cursor to the list of items that are lettered *a,b,c,d,e*. To help you find this text, a bookmark has been inserted at the first item in the list. You will use the *Goto* option from the **Select** menu to go to the bookmark. Choose this option now.

❏ **Choose the *Goto* option from the *Select* menu.**

You should now have a dialog box like the one in Figure 6.20.

Figure 6.20

*You can use the **Goto** option to move directly to a bookmark. Before the bookmark can be used, it must be inserted in the document at the correct location.*

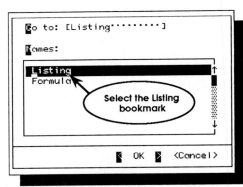

To move to the bookmark location, use your arrow keys to select the bookmark name and choose the *OK* button. This should place your cursor on item *a.* of the five items in the document.

❏ **Choose the *Listing* bookmark.**

❏ **Choose the *OK* button.**

Creating Hanging Indents

Remember that a hanging indent allows the first line of a paragraph to extend past the left margin. To create the hanging indent, you indent the *left margin,* then set the *1st Line Indent* so that it is to the left of the left margin. We will begin by creating a paragraph format for the first item, item a., listed under the sentence that reads *"The following points are also from this quarter's sales report."* Your cursor should be at this point. Choose the *Indents & Spacing* option from the **Format** menu.

❏ **Choose the *Indents & Spacing* option from *Format* menu.**

To create the hanging indent, you will need to set the *Left indent* to .4 inches and set the *1st Line indent* to -.4. Since you will be printing the document at 10 characters per inch, this should provide a bullet that is four characters to the left of the left margin. You also want a blank line between this paragraph and the paragraph above it. Therefore, you should set the *Space before paragraph* option to 1 line. Make the following settings in the dialog box and press Enter to accept the format.

❏ **Set the following options in the Character dialog box:**

Left indent:	**.4"**
1st line indent:	**-.4"**
Space Before Paragraph:	**1**

❏ **Press the Enter key.**

If you examine the paragraph now, you will see that the first line is moved to the left of the paragraph margin and the remaining lines are aligned on the left margin. This is shown in Figure 6.21.

Figure 6.21

The bullet for the hanging indent will be set out from the left margin of the text. The remainder of the paragraph will be aligned on the left margin, 1 inch in from the other text.

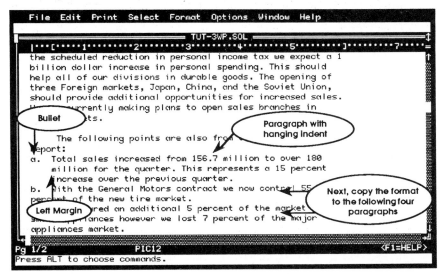

Copying Paragraph Formats

Once you have a paragraph formatted, you can copy that format to other paragraphs. This allows you to work with one paragraph and get it correct and then quickly apply the same format to other paragraphs. We will do this with the remaining items under the paragraph you just formatted. These are items b.,c.,d., and e.

To copy a format, you place your cursor in the paragraph that has the format you want copied and then choose *Copy Special* from the **Edit** menu. Next, select the paragraphs you want to copy the format to and press the Enter key. Do this now.

❏ **Make sure your cursor is in the paragraph you just formatted.**

❏ **Choose *Copy Special* from the *Edit* menu.**

❏ **Select items b. through e. (the next four paragraphs) as a block.**

❏ **Press the Enter key.**

You should now have the *Copy Special* check box.

Since you want to copy the paragraph format and not the character format, use your arrow keys to choose *Paragraph*, and press the Enter key.

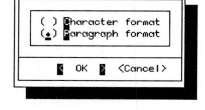

- ❏ Choose *Paragraph Format.*
- ❏ Press the Enter key.

All five paragraphs should now be formatted.

You can also copy character formats. You perform the copy the same way as you do for paragraphs, except you choose the *Character format* option from the *Copy Special* check box rather than the *Paragraph format*.

Subscripts and Superscripts

If you noticed in Figure 6.18, there is a *Position:* selection box in the *Font & Style* dialog. You can use this option to create *subscripts* or *superscripts*. You could do this using the same procedure used to change fonts and font sizes. An easier way is to use *Ctrl keys*.

Ctrl keys can be used for most things that we have been using the menus to do. When you begin using a software package, you should stick with the menus. As you get comfortable with the package, you will find that control keys are often easier and quicker. The inside cover of this text contains a list of all the control keys for the word processing module.

The control keys you use to insert a subscript are **Ctrl/=**.

The control keys you use to insert a superscript are **Ctrl/Shift/=**.

The control keys you use to shift back to plain text are **Ctrl/Spacebar**.

To see how these work, we will enter a formula into the document. Remember that the screen cannot display the subscripts or superscripts, but the printer can print them. The formula needs to be entered after the sentence that reads: *Sales quotas for the upcoming quarter will be based upon the following formula.* This sentence should be directly below your cursor.

The formula you want to enter will be:

$$\text{Quota} = (\text{Year}_1 \ldots \text{Year}_5)^{\text{Annual}/3}$$

- ❏ **Move your cursor to the blank line that follows the sentence:** Sales quotas for the upcoming quarter will be based upon the following formula.

As you enter your formula, watch the status line. The = on the status line indicates that you are in subscript mode, and the + indicates that you are in superscript mode. Now enter your formula by doing the following:

- ❏ **Type:** Quota = (Year
- ❏ **Enter** Ctrl/= **to set subscript mode.**
- ❏ **Type:** 1

❑ **Enter** Ctrl/Space Bar **to shift back to plain text.**

❑ **Type:** . . . Year

❑ **Enter** Ctrl/= **to shift to subscript mode.**

❑ **Type:**5

❑ **Enter** Ctrl/Space Bar **to shift back to plain text.**

❑ **Type:**)

❑ **Enter** Ctrl/Shift/= **to shift to superscript mode.**

❑ **Type:** Annual/3

❑ **Enter** Ctrl/Spacebar **to shift back to plain text.**

You will notice that your subscripts and superscripts are displayed as bold characters. If you move your cursor to one of the subscripted characters, you will see an equals sign (=) on the status line to indicate that the text is a subscript. For a superscript, the status line shows a plus sign (+).

Inserting Special Characters

Special characters are characters that are not treated as standard text. They are used to insert special types of data into a document. We will use several of these special characters to illustrate how they work.

First, you will insert the current date on the first line of your document. You will do this using the *Insert Special* dialog box of the **Edit** menu. This *Special Character* dialog box is shown in Figure 6.22. Before you insert the date, you should have your cursor where you want the date placed. Since this is at the end of your first line, you can use the *Ctrl/Home* and *End* keys to move your cursor there.

❑ **Enter** *Cntl/Home.*

❑ **Press the** *End* **key.**

Now insert the *Current Date* character by using the following steps:

❑ **Pull down the** *Insert Special* **dialog box from the Edit menu.**

❑ **Move the diamond to** *Current Date* **option.**

❑ **Press Enter.**

This should have the current date after the word *Date:*.

Figure 6.22

*The **Insert Special** option will allow you to place special character codes in your document. These special codes allow you to insert dates, nonbreaking spaces and hyphens, end of line marks, etc. These can also be entered with control codes.*

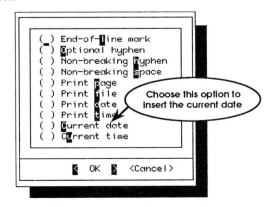

Sometimes when you insert special characters this way, you may not get the actual text. You may get two question marks (*??*) or a place holder such as **date**. These are referred to as *place holders*. This happens when the special character cannot determine exactly what text to insert. For example, if you choose *Print Date*, Works cannot determine the date until the document is printed.

The last special character you will enter is the *manual page break.* You will enter this so that the quote you copied from your second window will begin on a new page. You can choose Manual Page Break from the **Print** menu or you can use the *Ctrl* and *Enter* keys. We will use the *Ctrl/Enter* method for this example. Move your cursor to the beginning of the line that reads; *The following is a quote from the president, Richard R. Ferguson.*

❑   **Move your cursor to the beginning of the line that reads:** The following is a quote from the president, Richard R. Ferguson.

❑   **Enter Ctrl/Enter.**

Notice the line of periods across the screen and the new page marker below the line. The periods indicate a manual page break.

Using the Thesaurus

The *Thesaurus* will provide you with a list of synonyms for words that you have selected. To see this work, assume you did not like the use of the word *Generally.* You could use the thesaurus to find a *synonym* for the word. To find a synonym, you must first select the original word and then choose *Thesaurus* from the **Options** menu.

❑   **Select the word** Generally. **This is the first word in the second paragraph.**

❑   **Choose** *Thesaurus* **from the** *Options* **menu.**

You should now have a *Thesaurus* dialog box like the one in Figure 6.23.

The *Meanings* dialog box indicates that the only meaning for this word is *In all.* Often there will be more than one meaning listed. In these cases, you would select the one that is closest to the way you have used the word. On the right side of the dialog box are the synonyms. To choose a synonym, tab into this list box and highlight the synonym. Finally, choose the *Change* button to accept the synonym.

Figure 6.23

*The **Thesaurus** option of the Options menu will provide a list of synonyms for a word. To use the Thesaurus, select your original word, choose the* **Thesaurus** *from the* **Options** *menu, highlight the synonym you want to use, and choose* **Change**.

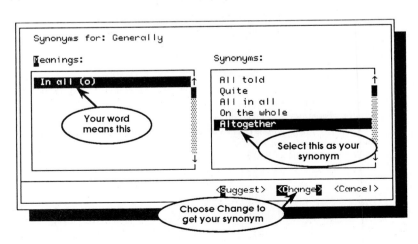

❏ Highlight the *In all* meaning.

❏ Tab to the *Synonym* list box and choose *Altogether.*

❏ Choose the *Change* button.

Altogether should now have replaced the word *Generally.*

Using a Split Window

There are times when you would like to be able to view two portions of your document that are not adjacent to each other. For instance, you may need to reference a table while you are writing about the table. You can do this in Microsoft Works if you use a *split window.*

To create a split window, you choose the *Split* option from the **Window** menu. Next, you use your Up and Down arrow keys to move a horizontal double line to where you want the screen split and press the Enter key. Try this now.

❏ Enter *Ctrl/Home* to move to the top of your document.

❏ Choose the *Split* option from the *Window* menu.

❏ Use your arrow keys to move the horizontal bar to the middle of the screen.

❏ Press the Enter key.

Your screen should now look like Figure 6.24.

You can now use your cursor movement keys to scroll one part of the screen. Try this now.

❏ Use your arrow or page down keys to scroll the window your cursor is in.

Notice that only one part of the screen scrolls. You can jump to the top half of the screen by pressing the **F6** function key. Try this now.

Figure 6.24

You can use the Split option from the Window menu to create a split screen. Use this when you want to view two non-adjacent parts of a file.

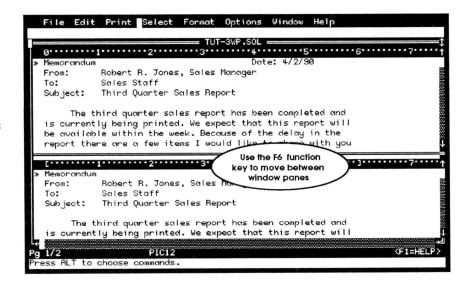

❑ Press the *F6* function key.

❑ Use your arrow keys to scroll this part of the window.

You can use the **F6** function key and your *cursor movement keys* to move any part of the file into either part of the screen.

It is important to remember that you only have one copy of the file; you are merely looking at that copy using a split window.

To close the split screen and move back to the single screen, you must choose the *Split* option again and then move the horizontal bar to the top or bottom of the screen and press the Enter key. Do this now.

❑ Choose *Split* from the *Window* menu.

❑ Use your arrow keys to move your bar to the top of the screen.

❑ Press the Enter key.

Completing the Tutorial

This completes the tutorial for this chapter. You should save your document. Use the *Save As:* option and save the file under a different name. You should also print your document. Use the *Preview* option from the **Print** menu to print the file. Finally, you should exit Works.

❑ Use the *Save As* option to save your file.

❑ Use the *Preview* option to print your file.

❑ Exit Works.

Conclusion

This is your final chapter on the Works Word Processor. By now you should be fairly proficient with its use. You should remember that a word processor is a tool to help you improve your written communications. You should make frequent use of this tool.

Hands on Practice

Exercise 6.1

For this practice problem, you will be using the file named HOP-W61.WPS and the file named HOP-W61B.WPS. These files should be on your tutorials disk. Complete the following changes. Use the copy of the file on the next page to determine where to make the changes.

1. Use the Font & Style dialog to format these lines so they will print with a font of pica and a size of 14.

2. Place your name here.

3. Use Insert Special and insert the Current Date for *Prepared on:* and Current Time for *At:*.

4. Use control keys and insert the Print Date for *Printed on:* and insert the Print Time for *At:*.

5. Use the *Indents & Spacing* dialog and create hanging indents for these paragraphs. Use a left and right indent of 1 inch and move the bullet 1/2 inch to the left of this indent. Also, space one line before the paragraphs.

6. Open the files named HOP-W61B.WPS. Copy all the data in this file to this location. Once you have the data copied, create a **Bold** border around the four numbered questions in the data.

7. Enter the following formula here: $ST_n = P_2 \ (W^{PR3}-W)^{PW2}$

8. Use Insert Special and insert a non-breaking space to keep the name Steven S. Jobs on one line.

9. Use the *Indents & Spacing* dialog box to indent this quote 1 inch on both margins. Use the *Font & Style* dialog to print this in italics, font elite, and size 10 points.

10. There are three bookmarks placed in this text. Each bookmark in in front of a word. Use the *Goto* option to find each bookmark. After you find the bookmark, use the *Theasurus* to find a synonym for the word that follows the bookmark.

11. Spell check the document.

12. Print your document.

1 →
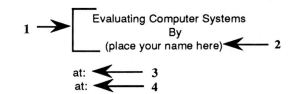

Evaluating Computer Systems
By
(place your name here) ← 2

Prepared on: at: ← 3
Printed on: at: ← 4

     Software selection is one of the most critical components of computer systems design. If the software has poor design, it cannot take full advantage of the advanced capabilities of newer machines. If the software is awkward to use, it costs the user in time and errors. If the software is too limited, there are too many things that must be performed by hand.

     When evaluating software, you should ask the following questions concerning the overall operation of the system and the user interface:

5 →
1.   Does the system use control codes, menus, or a combination of the two? Menus provide a shorter learning curve; however, experienced users prefer to use control codes. The codes are faster once you have mastered their pattern and know which ones to use.
2.   Does the software use the disk as a work area? Systems that rely totally on memory to store data usually have a limited size for their documents.
3.   Does the vendor have a 24-hour Help Line to answer questions? This is especially important for beginners.
4.   How well is the documentation written? Too much documentation is written assuming that you already know the software.

6 →

     Speed of the text searching is also a consideration for word processors. When evaluating the speed of the total system, you should use the following formula:

7 →

     When the founder of Apple Computer Systems, Steven S. ← 8
Jobs, made the following comment, most people laughed:

9 →
     "When you first purchase a computer system it appears to be much faster than anything you would ever need. As you use the system, it appears that it is slowing down, like it is getting tired of working. The machine is not getting tired, you are performing more work with it and you are growing accustomed to it. Because of this you should try to obtain the fastest machine you can when you purchase your first machine. No matter how fast your machine is, you will eventually outgrow it."

     Typically users look at price when they evaluate software. Although price must be a consideration, it should not be an overriding one. You could buy a 10 cent pencil and a dollars' worth of paper rather than buy a word processor if you are concerned with price. Money spent on software that will not fulfil your needs is wasted money, no matter how much you save.

7

Introduction to Spreadsheets

The electronic spreadsheet has rapidly become one of the most popular applications used on personal computers. These spreadsheets, which allow the PC user to quickly calculate and compare all sorts of data, are based on the manual accounting ledger sheet, or "worksheet." The original concept of the paper worksheet provided the user with a neat and accurate method to record columns of information. The computerized spreadsheet dramatically extends the power of the paper worksheet yet at the same time makes the ledger concept much easier to use. Since the spreadsheet program uses the computer, numbers and values can be changed with the results instantly updating the screen. Further, it is now possible to use the power of the computer to transform numbers into powerful charts that convey information at a glance. Finally, the electronic spreadsheet provides you with a number of easy to use formulas to find answers to sophisticated problems such as the calculation of loan payments, finding the average of a group of numbers, and other common problems.

Manual Worksheet Basics

Since the Microsoft Works computer based spreadsheet, like all spreadsheets, has its origins in the paper worksheet, it is a good idea to develop the basic concepts there. The manual spreadsheet utilized a grid format which is comprised of horizontal rows and vertical columns. This format allows the user of the manual system to work with a related column of numbers in order to sum them, to find an average, or to look for errors. Each row usually consisted of information about some given object of interest such as an item or person, while the columns contained related values for each object of interest. An example of this relationship is shown in the spreadsheet displayed in Figure 7.1 where each row contains information about a given product such as diskettes or ribbons. Each column contains information such as unit cost or net cost which has an individual value for each row entry.

Figure 7.1

A sample manual worksheet in which rows of information are entered and calculated by hand.

7/15/90	Purchase Order Worksheet					Page 1
Item Description	Unit Cost	Quant. Purch.	Total Cost	5% Discount	Net Cost	
Diskettes	8.50	25	212.50	10.23	201.87	
Pens	1.25	100	125.00	6.25	118.75	
Paper	12.49	20	249.80	12.49	237.31	
Ribbons	4.75	250	1,187.50	59.38	1,128.12	
Totals			1,774.80	88.75	1,686.05	

When you look at this manual worksheet, you will notice that quite a bit of the data in each row and column can readily be calculated from information contained above or to the side. For example, total cost can be calculated as unit cost x quantity purchased. This table format, which has served well in manual systems for many years, forms the foundation for the automated spreadsheet found in Microsoft Works.

Electronic Spreadsheet Basics

The spreadsheet in Microsoft Works provides you with access to all the power and computing capabilities of the computer's processor in place of the old paper worksheet, pencil, and calculator used in past manual systems.

With the electronic spreadsheet, the keyboard takes the place of the pencil in the manual system. This change allows you to copy repeated data instantly, use auto repeat keys for faster entry, and save the file to disk so that your work can be recalled later without reentry. Even the traditional eraser is still available in the form of the Delete key.

The old calculator is also replaced by the computer, which allows you to easily enter a long string of numbers. With the calculator, if you make an entry mistake, you must reenter all the numbers; the computer allows you to correct just the error. Further, the electronic spreadsheet can store and recall literally millions of entries quickly and accurately. By design, calculators perform simple functions. Spreadsheets, on the other hand, can be as simple or as complex as you need to make them.

➤ Rows, Columns, and Cells

Like the manual worksheet, the Microsoft Works spreadsheet is composed of rows and columns. **Rows** run horizontally across the screen, while columns run vertically. Each row is numbered, and in the Microsoft Works spreadsheet, the row numbers run consecutively from 1 to 4,096. The vertical **columns** in Works are identified through the use of capital letters, which start with A and increase to B, C, D, etc. When the number of columns reaches Z (26 columns), an additional letter is placed in front so the column is labeled AA, AB, AC, and so forth. Works provides for up to 256 columns ending with the label IV.

The intersection of a row and a column is called a **cell**. The cell provides a "box" in which you can enter numbers or other information that you want the spreadsheet to keep track of and manipulate. Works provides an ample number of cells for you to enter data into with a maximum of 4,096 x 256 = 1,048,576 cells available!

➤ *Using Rows and Columns in the Spreadsheet*

Normally, you will store information about a particular object or item of interest in a row. Some examples include information about a person, place, thing, or virtually anything that you want to keep information about. For example, in Figure 7.2, row number 3 contains information about Alice Bowers. This information includes her hours, pay rate, and gross pay. Row number 5 has information about Carol Kurtz and so forth.

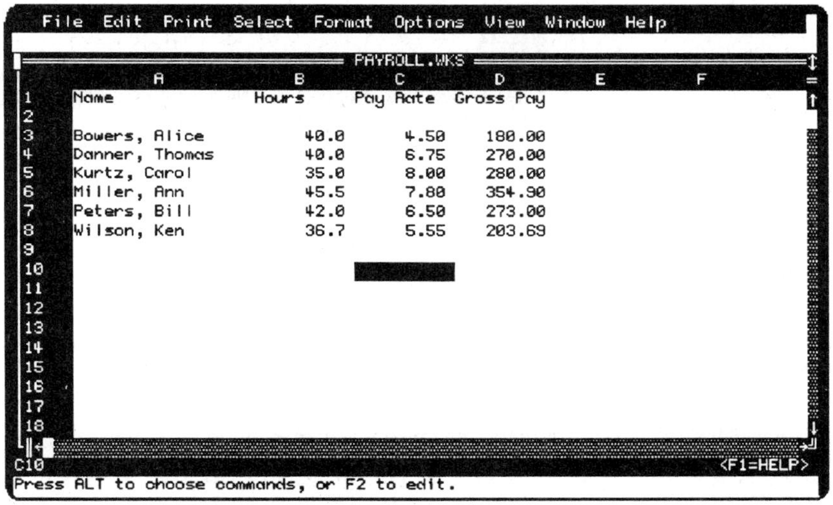

Figure 7.2

A sample Works spreadsheet. Notice the similarity to the manual worksheet seen in Figure 7.1.

Columns run vertically and normally contain information that pertains to the object on the row. In the sample spreadsheet, you can see that column A contains information on the employee's name, while column B holds information on hours, column C for pay rate, and so forth.

➤ *Defining the Active Cell*

Individual cells, formed by the intersection of the rows and columns, represent the fundamental building blocks of the electronic spreadsheet. Think of a cell as a holding area for data, much the same as a mailbox holds letters. Each cell is referenced by both the letter of its column and the number of its intersecting row and is illustrated in Figure 7.3.

This combination of a letter and a number is referred to as the **cell coordinate**. For example, when referencing the cell highlighted in Figure 7.3, you will find that the cursor (the highlighted box) is at the intersection of column D and row 9. Thus, the cell coordinates are **D9**. When specifying a cell coordinate, it is important that you always specify the letter of the column first. Finally, remember that the cell coordinate refers to a location in a spreadsheet, while a given cell is a special area that contains data.

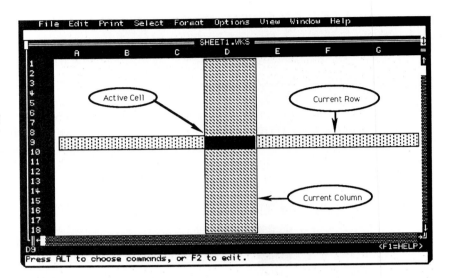

Figure 7.3

The active cell is located at the intersection of the row and column that are currently in use.

Cell Contents

A cell can contain **labels**, **values**, and **formulas** or a combination of all three. Labels are usually names: employee name, title, and the like. A label can be made up of alphabetic, numeric, or alphanumeric (a combination of both alphabetic and numeric characters) data. Labels, by their nature, cannot be used in any kind of arithmetic function or formula.

Values always consist of numbers and special numeric characters such as dollar signs, commas, and decimal points. Since values are numbers, they can be used in any type of arithmetic function and in formulas. Formulas are numeric operations that are performed on values. Formulas may contain cell coordinates, numbers, or a combination of both. For example, you could write a formula such as A2+5 which would take the contents of cell A5 and add 5 to it.

You should be sure that you understand the differences between these three types of data. For example, if you entered 5*100 as a label, the characters 5*100 would be displayed, not 500.

Spreadsheet Formula Concepts

Spreadsheet cells often contain formulas that perform some mathematical operation such as adding two numbers or finding the average of a range of numbers. The formula, although entered into the cell, displays only the answer on the computer screen. Thus, you can think of the formula as being behind the screen with only the answer displayed for your use. This important concept is shown in Figure 7.4.

Figure 7.4

The contents of the cell shown in the upper row will display as shown in the lower row.

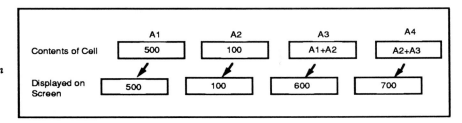

This diagram shows that the formula entered into cell A3 is A1+A2. The formula will take whatever value is stored in cell A1 (500 in this case) and add it to the value in A2 (which is 100) in the spreadsheet shown in Figure 7.4. The result of the formula (600) will be displayed in cell A3. This displayed answer, 600, would now be considered the value of cell A3. This value can now be referenced by other cells, such as cell A4, which uses the cell A3 in its formula.

This ability to reference the contents of a cell is very handy, since a change in referenced cell A2 would automatically update the result displayed in cell A3. Such a change is shown in Figure 7.5. This simple ability to quickly update is the key that provides the electronic spreadsheet with much of its power.

Figure 7.5

When cell A2 is changed, notice how the other cells are updated.

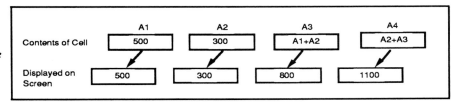

➤ Formula Development

A formula consists of two or more values, cell coordinates, or functions (discussed in the next chapter) which are separated by an arithmetic operator. When you use cell coordinates in a formula, the contents of that cell must be either a numeric value or another formula. If the cell contains a label (even if the label is a number), it will be treated as a value of zero (0).

Formulas are written as algebraic equations and follow the same rules for evaluation as does simple algebra. One difference between standard algebraic operations and spreadsheet operations is that implied operations are not supported in the spreadsheet. Therefore, to multiply 2 by 12, you would have to enter 2 * 12, not 2(12) as you might in standard algebra.

➤ Formula Evaluation Order

Parentheses first, from innermost set to outermost set.

Exponents next, from left to right.

Multiplication and division next, from left to right.

Addition and subtraction next, from left to right.

➤ *Formula Evaluation Symbols*

( )   Parentheses; these must always be used in pairs.

+   Addition

-   Subtraction

*   Multiplication

/   Division

^   Exponents

The Works Spreadsheet Screen

Microsoft Works' spreadsheet screen is very similar to the word processor's screen. A layout of this screen and a description of its parts are found in Figure 7.6.

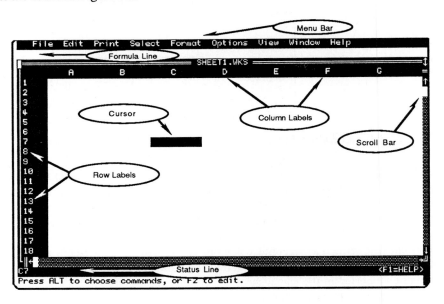

Figure 7.6

The Works Spreadsheet Screen. The screen can provide you with very helpful information that will save you quite a bit of time.

Menu Bar:	Access the menus the same way you did in the word processor, using the ALT key or by dragging the mouse.
Formula Line:	The formula line displays the contents of the current spreadsheet cell, which is now highlighted by the cursor.
Column Labels:	These letters are used to identify the column that is directly below.
Row Labels:	These number the row directly to the right.

<table>
<tr><td>Cursor:</td><td>The cursor is a horizontal bar that is always as wide as the column it is positioned in. The highlighted cursor also indicates the current or active cell.</td></tr>
<tr><td>Scroll Bars:</td><td>There are horizontal and vertical scroll bars, which show the approximate location of the cursor in the spreadsheet. They can also be used by the mouse to scroll through the spreadsheet.</td></tr>
<tr><td>Status Line:</td><td>The status line is similar to the status line in the word processor and displays the cell coordinates of the current cell.</td></tr>
<tr><td>Current Cell:</td><td>These coordinates show where the cursor is located.</td></tr>
</table>

Spreadsheet Navigation

The Works spreadsheet has over a million cells available for use; however, it is quickly apparent that only a few will fit on the computer screen at one time. Therefore, you need to be able to move around the spreadsheet or *navigate* using some of the methods that are provided by Works. Some of these methods may already be familiar to you from the word processing module and include use of the arrow keys, page up and down keys, and perhaps the general use of the mouse. However, you will probably find that there are times where you would greatly benefit from these additional spreadsheet navigation commands.

<table>
<tr><td>Arrow Keys:</td><td>The four arrow keys move the highlighted cursor one cell in the direction of the arrow. You can also hold down an arrow key to move the cursor rapidly in one direction. Works will automatically move the spreadsheet for you to keep the cursor in view: If you move from cell A18 to A19, you will see row 19 appear on the screen and row 1 disappear from the top.</td></tr>
<tr><td>PgUp/PgDn:</td><td>As the name implies, these keys (Page Up and Page Down) will move the spreadsheet up or down a screen or page at a time. These keys are handy to use when you need to move many rows up or down.</td></tr>
<tr><td>Ctrl/PgUp:</td><td>The PgUp and PgDn keys are helpful when you want to move up or down, but what happens when you want to move sideways across columns? To move right a screen at a time, hold the Ctrl (Control) key down and press the PgDn key. This will move you from column A to column H instantly. Similarly, the Ctrl/PgUp combination will move you one screen to the left. Notice that the highlighted cursor will stay in the same relative position on the screen as the spreadsheet moves.</td></tr>
<tr><td>Home:</td><td>The Home key will move the cursor horizontally to the "A" column, staying in the same row. Like the PgUp and PgDn keys, the Home key can be used with the Ctrl key to gain extra results; when the Ctrl/Home key combination is used, the cursor will instantly move to cell A1 in the upper-left corner of the spreadsheet. This is a navigation command that you will probably use quite a bit when you want to get to the top of your spreadsheet quickly.</td></tr>
<tr><td>End:</td><td>The End key works a bit differently than the other navigation keys in that it refers to an "active" area of your spreadsheet. The active area of your spreadsheet is the part of the sheet in which you enter information into cells. For example, if you have entered information into columns A through G and press the End key, you will move into column G, which is the last "active" column. Like the</td></tr>
</table>

Home key, the row being used will not change with the use of the End key. This is very useful when you return to a spreadsheet and want to move directly to the place where you last entered data.

Ctrl/End: The End key can also be enhanced through the use of the Ctrl key in much the same manner as the Home key. The Ctrl/End combination will move you to the bottommost active cell in your spreadsheet.

Ctrl/Arrow: The Ctrl/Arrow key combinations provide you with another very flexible navigation option. This key combination will move the cursor to a "boundary" cell in the direction of the arrow key that was pressed. This boundary cell is the last occupied cell before a blank cell is encountered. For example, if you wanted to move down a long column of numbers to the last number in the list, you would use the Ctrl/Down arrow key combination. This is a very valuable navigation command that will save you quite a bit of time as you become more proficient in the use of the spreadsheet.

GOTO (F5): The GOTO or F5 key gives you the ability to move instantly to a given cell coordinate. To use the F5 key, just press F5 and then enter the cell coordinate (A6 as an example) and press Return. Your cursor will instantly move to the cell desired.

Entering Data into the Spreadsheet

You will find that entering data into the spreadsheet is very easy if a few simple rules are remembered. Works will automatically decide if the data you enter into a cell is a label, value, or formula depending on how you enter the data.

Label Entry: If the first character that you enter into a cell is a letter of the alphabet or the data contains non-numeric characters, the data is assumed to be a label. Remember that labels can contain any type of character, but you cannot perform any arithmetic functions with labels. If you wanted to enter a number as a label, you should precede the number with a double quote. Labels are aligned to the left of the cell by default.

Value Entry: If you enter a number or a numeric symbol, such as a dollar sign or decimal point into a cell, Works will automatically infer that you are dealing with numeric data. Numeric data is aligned to the right of the cell by default.

Formula Entry: If the first character that you enter is an equals sign (=), the data that you enter is treated as a formula. The equals sign alerts Works that the characters after the sign are part of a formula, not text. An example of a problem that could occur when the sign is not used is when you enter a formula like A1+A2. Since the first character is an A, the formula will be treated as a label, not a formula. When you put the equals sign in front to make the entry =A1+A2, Works will correctly recognize the expression as a formula. Formulas are always evaluated at the time they are entered, and the result of the formula is displayed in the cell.

The actual entry of the information is very easy; just position the cursor over the cell desired, type the label, data, or formula, and press Enter. Pressing Enter will finalize the entry into the cell but will not move the cursor from the cell it is on. Frequently, you will find that you wish to enter data into a cell and move directly to another cell to enter additional information. This can be done directly by simply pressing any arrow key after you have completed the data entry in the cell. The arrow key acts like the Enter key and at the same time moves to the next adjacent cell.

➤ *Changing the Contents of a Cell*

Frequently, you will find that you want to alter the contents of a given cell. Perhaps the easiest way to do this is to enter new data into the cell by moving the cursor to the cell in question and typing it in. The new data will take the place of the original data, which is erased.

Cell Editing: To edit the contents without changing all of the cell by retyping, position your cursor on the cell and press the F2 Edit key. When the F2 key is pressed, the contents of the cell, such as a formula, are displayed on the formula line. You can then use the arrow keys, backspace, or delete keys to edit the contents of the cell. This is extremely useful when you want to change a small part of a formula without retyping it from scratch.

Deleting Cells: To delete the contents of a cell, position your cursor on the cell and press the Delete key. This will erase the contents of the cell and place you in the entry mode so that you can enter new data. If you want to leave the cell blank, press the Enter key after you press the Delete key.

➤ *Selecting a Block of Cells*

Occasionally, you want to perform some operation, such as changing the appearance of an entire group of cells. To do this, you must first identify the cells of interest as a **block**. In the Works spreadsheet, a block must be a square or a rectangular group of cells. There are three ways to select a block, any of the which will allow the selection of the block in the spreadsheet.

The Extend Key: Position your cursor on the first cell of the block to be selected and press the **F8** extend key. Next, use your cursor keys to extend the highlighted block into the other cells you want to change. When you have highlighted all the cells you want, then perform the operation. You need to press the Esc key or move your cursor to cancel the block.

Shift/Cursor: Position your cursor on the first cell of the block and then hold down the Shift key and any cursor movement key (arrow, PgDn, etc.) to highlight the block desired. Next, perform the function you want and press the Esc key to cancel the block. This method is fast, easy, and allows you to be sure that the block is as you want it.

Mouse: Use your mouse to move the cursor to the first cell in the block and then hold down the left mouse button and drag the mouse to highlight the block. When all cells are highlighted, release the button and complete the function or press the Esc key to cancel the function. Perhaps the quickest method of all, the mouse works great if you have one on your computer.

Whichever method you use, you will highlight a block of cells similar to the block shown in Figure 7.7.

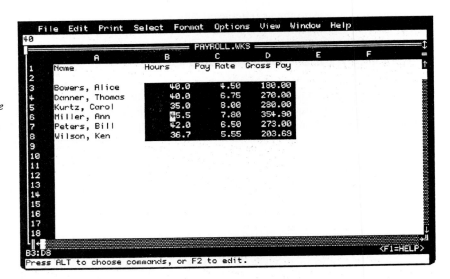

Figure 7.7

You can use the F8 key, the Shift/arrow keys, or the mouse to select a block of cells. Blocks can then be copied, moved, or erased.

➤ Formatting the Cell Contents

The use of the formatting options in the Works spreadsheet allows you to customize the appearance of your spreadsheet in a manner similar to the character formatting process in the word processor, in which you selected bold print, italics, and so forth. You will often find that when you enter data into a cell, you will want to format or display the data so that it includes dollar signs, a specific number of decimal positions, commas, and the like.

You can specify the format for a cell before or after data is entered into it by positioning the cursor on the cell to be formatted and then pulling down the **Format** menu either through the use of the mouse or by using the ALT/T key combination. This menu works exactly like the Format menu in the word processor, except that the format options differ slightly. The spreadsheet Format menu provides you with a list of all the possible formatting options and is shown in Figure 7.8.

Since spreadsheets typically deal with numbers, the majority of the formats on the Format menu are used for formatting numeric information and allow you to determine the way in which numeric data will be displayed in the spreadsheet. All of these options, except the General format, require that you also specify the number of decimal positions that are to be displayed to the right of the decimal point.

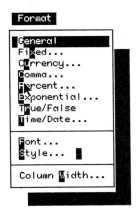

Figure 7.8

*The spreadsheet **Format** menu which can be used to change the format and appearance of one or more cells in the spreadsheet.*

You will be asked for the number of decimal positions to include after selecting the format option from the menu. Figure 7.9 shows you how each format will display the values of formatted cells.

Figure 7.9

Different spreadsheet formats that can be used in Works.

Cell Value	0.889	13.887	2589.98	2345678.89
General	0.889	13.887	2589.98	2345678.89
Fixed	0.89	13.89	2589.98	2345678.89
Currency	$0.89	$13.89	$2,589.98	$2,345,678.89
Comma	0.89	13.89	2,589.98	2,345,678.89
Percent	88.90%	1388.70%	258998.00%	234567889.00
Exponential	8.8E-01	1.39E+01	2.59+E03	2.35E+06

General: The general format serves as the default format. This format will display only those decimal positions to the right of the decimal point that are significant. This format is often sufficient for most numeric information.

Fixed: This format allows you to instruct Works to display a given number of decimal positions. The number that is in the cell being formatted is automatically rounded to the nearest displayed decimal.

Currency: This format is the same as Fixed, except that it also displays the dollar sign adjacent to the leftmost digit and it displays commas. Naturally, you would want to use this format option when dealing with dollar amounts.

Comma: The Comma format is the same as the currency format, except that no dollar sign is displayed. This format is helpful when you want to display a column of currency amounts but only want a dollar sign included with the first number.

Percent: This format is used to display percentages. You should remember that percentages are based on the number 1 as equal to 100%. This means that 10% would be entered as 0.1 and then formatted with the percentage option, which would yield a display of the desired 10%. Similarly, the number 10 is shown as 1,000%. You will be asked to specify the number of decimal places to be displayed.

Exponential: This format is used for scientific notation. It is normally used for very large or very small numbers that would be difficult to use in the spreadsheet. To determine the actual number of an exponential number, you simply move the decimal. If the number that follows the E is negative, move the decimal to the left. For example, 5.056E-03 is actually 0.005056. If the number following the E is positive, move the decimal to the right. For example, 5.67E+5 is 567,000.

Logical: This format is used for a special type of cell that is not normally encountered. For full information, you should refer to the Works documentation.

Time/Date: This format allows you to enter and work with times and dates in the spreadsheet. Numbers are stored in the cell and then analyzed as either a time or date depending on how you specify the format option. The complete use of this format option is covered in the next chapter.

➤ *Setting Cell Styles*

You probably noticed that below the basic format options on the Format menu is the Style option. Styles are similar to the format options found in the word processor module of Works and allow you to further enhance your spreadsheet display and printout. When you select the Styles option, you will see a dialog box like the one displayed in Figure 7.10.

The Alignment box within the Style dialog allows you to specify how you want data to be displayed in a cell. The General, or default alignment, automatically right aligns values and left aligns labels. If you do not specify any Style option, you will automatically get the General style.

Figure 7.10

*The **Style** dialog box allows you to align or change the appearance the contents of a cell.*

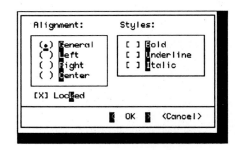

The Left align option positions all kinds of data starting at the left border of the cell, while the Right align option positions all data starting at the right side of the cell. The Center option will center the data in the cell. These simple commands can be used to give your spreadsheet a neat appearance that allows you to read it easily.

The Bold, Underline, and Italic commands are used the same way as they are in the word processor and can be used to alter the appearance of any data in any cell. You will find these commands helpful for setting off titles, column headings, and the like.

➤ *Setting Column Width*

The Width option is used to change the column width from the default value of 10 characters. It is important to realize that when you alter the width of a column, you affect the width of **all** cells in the column. Therefore, the minimum width of the column must be at least as wide as the largest cell entry. To set the width of a column, position the cursor on any cell in the column and select the Width option from the Format menu.

When the Width dialog box is displayed, the current column width will appear in the box. If you have not changed the width of the column before, the default width of 10 will be in the box, as shown in Figure 7.11.

Figure 7.11

*The **Width** dialog box allows you to change the width of the cell by typing in the number of spaces you desire.*

Cells actually have two widths: the width of their contents and their displayed width. While this may seem a bit confusing at first, remember that what is displayed in a cell and what is actually entered in the cell (like a formula) may well be different. When you alter the column width, you are actually changing the width of the *display*, not the width of the cell contents. The content width is system set and can accommodate up to 256 characters, which is usually more than enough. You might want to think of the cursor as being a window into the cell with the width of the cursor being the width of this window, as shown in Figure 7.12.

Figure 7.12

Comparing the contents of a cell with the display of the cell.

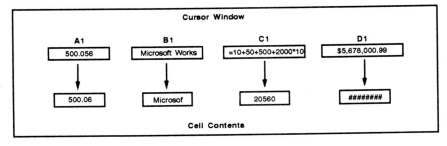

The top blocks show the actual contents of the cells, while the lower blocks show what is displayed in the cell position. In the first cell, cell A1, the decimal places have been set to two, so the rightmost decimal is truncated. Cell B1 shows what happens when a label display width is smaller than the cell's contents. The rightmost characters are not displayed; however, the data is still in the cell. You could make the column wider to see the entire contents of the cell. Cell C1 illustrates the display when a cell contains a formula. The formula is larger than the display window; however, the result of the formula, the cell's value, is not, so the entire number is displayed. Cell D1 displays number signs (#) instead of the number which indicates the cell's width is too narrow to display the entire number. Widen the column width to correct this.

Conclusion

You are now familiar with many of the basic spreadsheet concepts required to use the Microsoft Works spreadsheet and have learned the basic concepts of data entry, displayed contents of cells, formula use, and general formatting. You should complete the chapter review to be sure of your understanding, as these concepts form a foundation for later spreadsheet use.

Chapter 7 Self Test

1. In a spreadsheet, Rows run _____ and use _____for their labels. Columns run _____ and use _____ for their labels.

2. What is a coordinate in a spreadsheet?

3. What would be the coordinate of the fourth cell in the fifth row?

4. What is the difference between a <u>label</u> and a <u>value</u>?

5. What is the difference between the <u>contents</u> and the <u>value</u> of a cell?

6. Write formulas to carry out the following operations:

   a. Subtract cell A3 from cell B4 and multiply the result by 5.

   b. Add the contents of columns C, D, and E in row 5.

   c. Add cells A1, A2, and A3, and subtract the contents of cell A4.

7. How would you enter the formula A3*A4+A2 into a cell?

8. Explain what is meant by referencing a formula from another cell.

9. How can you change the formula in a cell without retyping it?

10. Explain three ways to select a block of cells.

11.   If cell C7 contained the value 3456.783, how would it be displayed for each of the following formats? (Assume the format is set for two decimals.)

        General   _____

        Fixed   _____

        Currency   _____

        Comma   _____

        Percent   _____

        Exponential   _____

12.   Using one step, how would you make all cells from A2 through G12 Bold by using the Style option?

13.   What happens when the width of a column's display is smaller than the contents of the cell and the cell contains a label? What happens when the cell contains a number?

Chapter 7 Tutorial

In this tutorial, you will create a spreadsheet that will calculate total cost, as shown in Figure 7.13:

*Figure
7.13*

*Total Cost
Spreadsheet*

		TUT-SS7.WKS					
A	B	C	D	E	F	G	H

		Quantity	Unit	Total	Selling	Total	Discount	Total
Description	On Hand	Cost	Cost	Price	Retail	Percent	Profit
Printer Cables	10	$12.90	129.00	23.59	235.90	10.00%	$83.31
Diskette Cases	500	$1.75	875.00	2.98	1,490.00	13.00%	$421.30
Printer Paper	3,000	$25.90	77,700.00	37.10	111,300.00	20.30%	$11,006.10
Mouse Pads	92	$4.80	441.60	8.90	818.80	15.70%	$248.65
3 1/2" Diskette	15,000	$1.33	19,950.00	2.35	35,250.00	25.00%	$6,487.50

Creating the Empty Spreadsheet

To create a Microsoft Works spreadsheet, start Works as usual. When the initial screen is displayed, use the arrow keys or mouse to move the selection diamond to Spreadsheet, or simply enter an *S*. Next, select the New option, since you are creating a new Spreadsheet. This process is shown in Figure 7.14.

Figure 7.14

*Create the new spreadsheet by
moving the highlight to
"New Spreadsheet" and
pressing Enter.*

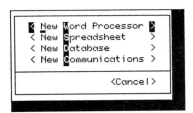

To create the new spreadsheet, follow these steps:

❑ **Start Microsoft Works.**

❑ **Select "Create New File" from the File Menu.**

❑ **Select "New Spreadsheet" and press Enter.**

Once these steps are completed, you will see an empty spreadsheet screen like that shown in Figure 7.15.

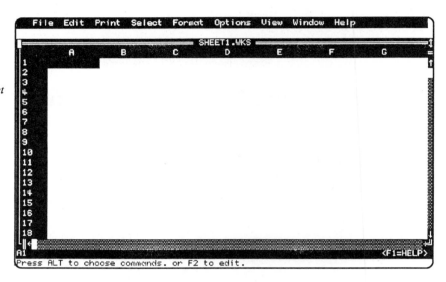

Figure 7.15

The new Works spreadsheet screen. The cursor is automatically located in cell A1. The spreadsheet will be called SHEET1.WKS until you save it later on.

Some Quick Practice on Navigation

Before entering any data into the spreadsheet, you should take a moment to try some of the navigation commands mentioned earlier. As you move through the spreadsheet, notice that the current position of the cursor is always shown at the bottom left corner of the screen. Also, take special note of the position of the scroll bars on the right side and bottom of your screen as you move the cursor around the spreadsheet. These bars can give you an idea of where you are in the spreadsheet. First, try these steps:

❏ Use the Arrow keys to move the cursor to cell G14.

❏ Press the Home key to move back to cell A14.

❏ Now try the PgDn and PgUp keys to move up and down one screen at a time. You should also try the Ctrl/PgDn key to move one screen to the right and Ctrl/PgUp to move one screen to the left.

❏ Hold the Ctrl key down and press the Down arrow key to move to row 4096, the very bottom of the spreadsheet. Next, use the Ctrl/right arrow to move the cursor to cell IV4096, which is the bottom right corner of the spreadsheet.

❏ At this time, use the Ctrl/Home key combination to instantly return to cell A1, the home cell.

❏ Finally, use the F5, Goto key to move instantly to cell GZ2088 by pressing the F5 key and entering the cell coordinates GZ2088. Next, use the Ctrl/Home option to return to cell A1.

Entering Title and Column Headings

The cursor should now be positioned on cell coordinates A1 (use Ctrl/Home if it is anywhere other than cell A1). In this cell (A1) and the next cell down (A2), you will enter a title for your spreadsheet and your name.

Remember that after you enter the data in a cell and you want to move to another cell, you do not need to press the Enter key. You can simply use the arrow keys to move the cursor and enter the data.

Enter the following in cells A1 and A2:

❑ **Enter "SPREADSHEET TUTORIAL 1" in cell A1 (Do not type the parentheses).**

❑ **Enter your name in cell A2.**

The spreadsheet should now look like Figure 7.16.

Figure 7.16

The initial spreadsheet entries. Remember to press Enter or the Down arrow key after you type the cell contents. This enters the information into the cell.

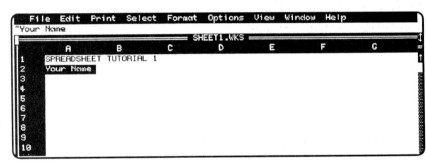

You will now want to begin entering column headings in the spreadsheet to show the type of information contained in each column. Start entering the headings by moving the cursor to cell A6 and enter the following in cells A6 and B6:

❑ **Type "Description" in A6 and press the Right arrow key.**

❑ **Type "On Hand" in cell B6 and press Enter.**

When you have completed the entry of these cells, the spreadsheet should look like Figure 7.17.

Figure 7.17

When you enter the first titles, don't be alarmed that they run together. This indicates that the column is not wide enough to hold the data.

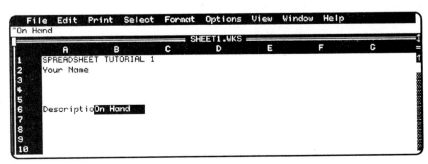

Take a special look at cells A6 and B6 where it appears as though you have lost the last character in the word <u>Description</u>. Don't worry, everything is fine, and remember that the cell's contents can be larger than the cursor. When you entered the words <u>On Hand</u> in cell B6, the <u>O</u> in the word <u>On</u> was displayed over the <u>n</u> in the word <u>description</u>. This is because column A is not wide enough to display the entire word, a problem we will correct shortly. For now, complete the entry of the column headings in row 5 by entering them as shown in Figure 7.18, but do not worry about any special formats or column widths at this time.

Figure 7.18

Entering the row 5 titles. Press the Right arrow key after typing each title.

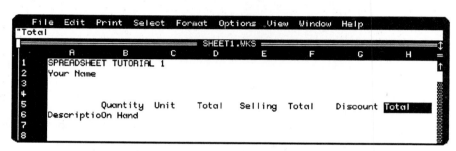

The exact steps for entering the row 5 titles are:

❑   **Move the cursor to cell B5 and type "Quantity" and press the right arrow key.**

❑   **Next, type "Unit" in cell C5 and press the Right arrow key.**

❑   **Continue to type the titles in row 5, and use the Right arrow key to enter the title and move to the next cell until all row 5 titles are entered.**

When all of the row 5 titles are entered, enter the row 6 titles shown in Figure 7.19.

Figure 7.19:

Finishing the row 6 titles.

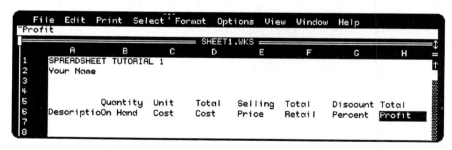

❑   **Move the cursor to cell C6 with the arrow keys and type "Cost"; then use the Right arrow key to move to cell D6 as you did earlier.**

❑   **Finish entering all other row 6 titles until your spreadsheet looks like Figure 7.19.**

➤ *Setting the Column Width*

You now need to adjust the width of column A so that it will be wide enough to display all the item descriptions and titles. This is done with the Width option from the Format menu, which is shown in Figure 7.20.

Figure 7.20

Setting the column width using the Format Width option.

In the Width dialog box, specify the width as the maximum number of characters that will be in the column. Set the width of column A to 20 characters now by using the following steps:

❑ Move the cursor to cell A6.

❑ Pull down the Format menu with the ALT/T key combination or mouse.

❑ Select the Width option.

❑ Enter 20 as the Width.

❑ Press Enter.

The cursor in column A should now be wider, and the entire word <u>Description</u> should be displayed.

Entering Spreadsheet Data

The next step is to enter the data for columns A, B, and C in rows 8, 9, 10, 11, and 12 using the information in Figure 7.21. DO NOT include any commas when you enter numbers such as <u>3000</u>. The spreadsheet program will do this for you automatically later on when you format the entries.

❑ Move the cursor to cell A8, type "Printer Cables"; then press the Right arrow.

❑ Enter the Quantity of the cables (10) into cell B8 and press the Right arrow.

❑ Enter the Unit Cost (12.90) into cell C8 and press Enter.

❑ Enter the rest of the products, quantities, and costs shown in Figure 7.21 in the same manner.

Figure 7.21

*Enter the spreadsheet data
in columns A through C
by pressing the Right
arrow or the Enter key
after typing the entry.*

```
   File  Edit  Print  Select  Format  Options  View
 1.33
 ╞═══════════════════════════════ SHEET1.WKS ═══════
 ▐                    A               B        C        D
 1 │SPREADSHEET TUTORIAL 1
 2 │Your Name
 3 │
 4 │
 5 │                             Quantity  Unit    Total
 6 │Description                  On Hand   Cost    Cost
 7 │
 8 │Printer Cables                    10   12.9
 9 │Diskette Cases                   500   1.75
10 │Printer Paper                   3000   25.9
11 │Mouse Pads                        92    4.8
12 │3 1/2" Diskettes               15000   1.33
13 │
```

➤ *Formatting the Cells in a Column*

Now that some of the data is entered into the spreadsheet, you will need to format it. When you look at the data in column B, you will see that some of the entries need to have commas inserted. Further, data in column C also needs to be reformatted, because we need to display dollar amounts that require two decimals to appear at the right of the decimal point.

Recall that to apply a special format to a group of cells in one step, you must first select the cells as a block. Once the cells are selected, the format can be set by selecting the appropriate format from the Format menu; in this case, you will use the Comma format option. Works will ask you to specify the number of decimal positions you want to the right of the decimal point through the use of a dialog box like the one shown in Figure 7.22.

Figure 7.22

*Select the number of
decimal positions you
want to display in the
Decimals dialog box.*

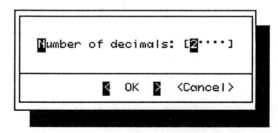

Format the cells in column B now by following these steps:

❑ **Move the cursor to cell B8.**

❑ **Press the F8 (Extend) key and then press the Down arrow key to highlight cells B8 through B12.**

❑ **Select Comma from the Format menu.**

❑ **Enter 0 for the number of decimals.**

❑ **Press Enter.**

Next, format the entries in column C as follows:

❑ **Move the cursor to cell C8.**

❑ **Select a block consisting of cells C8 through C12 again using the F8 and Down arrow keys.**

❑ **Select Currency from the Format Menu.**

❑ **Enter 2 for the number of decimals.**

❑ **Press Enter.**

The spreadsheet should now look like the one shown in Figure 7.23.

Figure 7.23

Formatted spreadsheet contents

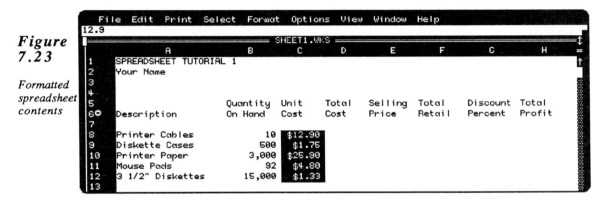

➢ *Entering the Total Cost*

Now that you have completed the entry of most of the labels and data, you can use the power of the spreadsheet to compute some of the values, such as the total cost for each product. The total cost value can easily be calculated by multiplying the item's unit cost by the quantity on hand. This calculation can best be done by using a formula in the spreadsheet; for example, in cell D8, the formula would be B8 * C8. Remember that when entering a formula, you must start the formula with the equals sign (=).

Now, enter the formula into cell D8.

❑ **Move to cell D8.**

❑ **Enter =B8*C8.**

❑ **Press Enter.**

➢ *Using the Fill Down Option*

Cell D8 should now display the value 129. To compute the value for the other total costs, you could go ahead and type in the same basic formula in cells D9 through D12; however, Microsoft Works has a unique feature that will perform this process for you. Called the Fill Down feature (found in the Edit menu), it will copy the contents of the first cell in a block to all the cells below it that are also in the same block. Further, when formulas that contain cell coordinates are copied, each cell row coordinate in the formula is increased by one as the copy takes place, so you can perform what is called a **relative copy,** or fill. This very powerful feature will copy the formula you specify and make changes relative to the rows you copy it to. To see firsthand how this feature is used, follow these steps:

❑   **Be sure the cursor is still in Cell D8.**

❑   **Select cells D8 through D12 as a block.**

❑   **Pull down the Edit menu and select the Fill Down option.**

With the block of cells still highlighted, change the format of the values for cells D8 through D12 to the comma format with two decimals, as you did earlier.

❑   **Format the Total Cost cells to Comma with two decimal places.**

❑   **Press ESC to cancel the block.**

➢ *Entering the Selling Price*

The next step in the construction of the spreadsheet is to enter the selling price for each product. This value should be entered starting in cell E8, as shown in Figure 7.24. After you have entered all the values for the cells, format the cells using the Comma format with two decimal places.

Figure 7.24

*Enter the Selling Price
information the same way
that you entered the
Quantity on Hand data.*

❑   **Enter the price figures for cells E8 through E12.**

❑   **Format these cells using the Comma format with two decimal places.**

When you have completed the data entry and the format on the selling price data, your spreadsheet should look like Figure 7.25.

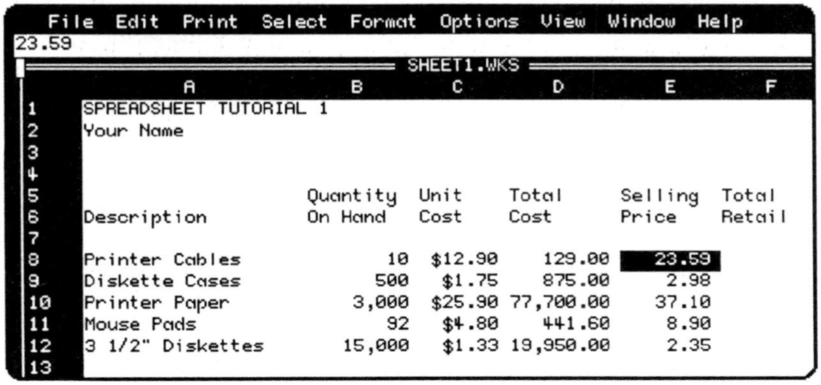

Figure 7.25

The intermediate spreadsheet.

```
    File   Edit   Print   Select   Format   Options   View   Window   Help
23.59
═══════════════════════════════ SHEET1.WKS ═══════════════════════════════
▌            A              B        C         D          E         F
1   SPREADSHEET TUTORIAL 1
2   Your Name
3
4
5                       Quantity  Unit      Total    Selling   Total
6   Description         On Hand   Cost      Cost     Price     Retail
7
8   Printer Cables          10    $12.90    129.00    23.59
9   Diskette Cases         500    $1.75     875.00     2.98
10  Printer Paper        3,000    $25.90 77,700.00    37.10
11  Mouse Pads              92    $4.80     441.60     8.90
12  3 1/2" Diskettes    15,000    $1.33  19,950.00     2.35
13
```

➢ Entering the Total Retail Column

You now need to develop and enter the formula that will calculate the Total Retail values. This value is found by multiplying the cells in the Quantity on Hand column by the Selling Price column. For row 8, this would be B8 * E8. Follow these steps to enter this formula in cell F8, and use the Fill Down function to copy the formula into rows 9 through 12.

❑ Enter =B8*E8 in cell F8.

❑ Select cells F8 through F12 as a block.

❑ Use Fill Down from the Edit menu to copy the formula.

❑ Now format this column using the Comma format with two decimal places.

When you are done with the entry of the formulas, you will notice that cell F10 now contains number signs (##########) rather than the actual value of the total retail. Remember that this happens when the width of the cell is too small for the value that needs to be displayed, so use the Column Width option from the Format menu and change the column's width to 12.

❑ Select the Column Width option from the Format menu.

❑ Enter 12 for the column width.

❑ Press Enter.

➢ Entering the Percent Discount Column

Now, enter the percent discount column information found in Figure 7.26 in the same manner that you entered the Quantity on Hand data and then adjust the format with the following steps:

❑ Enter the percent discount information.

❑ Format as percentages with two decimal positions using the Format menu.

Figure 7.26

*Enter the Percent discounts
in the same way as the
earlier information.*

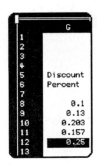

	G
1	
2	
3	
4	
5	Discount
6	Percent
7	
8	0.1
9	0.13
10	0.203
11	0.157
12	0.25
13	

➤ Computing the Total Profit

To compute total profit, take the total retail price and then subtract the sum of the total cost and discount amount. To arrive at the discount amount, just multiply the discount percent times the total retail price. To develop the formula to do all this, it is a good idea to develop first the formula in English using the parentheses to identify the procedure that should be done first. This formula would look like this:

Total Retail - (Total Cost + (Total Retail * Discount Percent))

The next step would be to convert this formula to a spreadsheet formula that uses the appropriate cell coordinates in place of the English descriptions. This formula will be entered into cell H8, and then the Fill Down option from the Edit menu will be used to copy the formula into the other cells. Finally, the cells should be formatted using the Currency format, and the column will need to be widened to 14 spaces.

❑ Develop and enter the spreadsheet formula in cell H8.

❑ Use Fill Down to copy the formula into cells H9 through H12.

❑ Format the cells as Currency format with two decimal places.

❑ Set the column width to 14 characters.

When you have completed the preceding steps, your spreadsheet should look like Figure 7.27.

```
 File  Edit  Print  Select  Format  Options  View  Window  Help
═══════════════════════════════ SHEET1.WKS ═══════════════════════════════
        A            B       C        D       E        F         G        H
1  SPREADSHEET TUTORIAL 1
2  Your Name
3
4
5                  Quantity Unit    Total   Selling  Total    Discount Total
6  Description     On Hand  Cost    Cost     Price   Retail    Percent  Profit
7
8  Printer Cables       10  $12.90   129.00  23.59     235.90  10.00%      $83.31
9  Diskette Cases      500   $1.75   875.00   2.98   1,490.00  13.00%     $421.30
10 Printer Paper     3,000  $25.90 77,700.00 37.10 111,300.00  20.30%  $11,006.10
11 Mouse Pads           92   $4.80   441.60   8.90     818.80  15.70%     $248.65
12 3 1/2" Diskettes 15,000   $1.33 19,950.00  2.35  35,250.00  25.00%   $8,487.50
13
```

Figure 7.27 *The Completed Spreadsheet.*

Aligning the Column Headings

You are almost done with the spreadsheet, but you have probably noticed that the column headings really do not line up very well with the data in the columns. This is because Works aligns labels (like your column headings) on the left side of the cell, while data and formulas are aligned to the right side. To align the headings with the numeric data, you will need to use the Align option box, which is located in the Style dialog box of the Format menu. The Align option in the Style dialog box is shown in Figure 7.28.

Figure 7.28

Use the options in the
Style dialog box to align
the titles of the
spreadsheet.

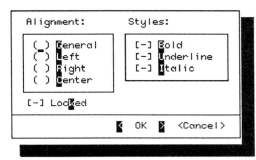

To properly align all the labels with their column of numbers, you first need to select all the labels in cells B5 though H6 as a block. Next, you will adjust the style of the labels by using the following steps:

❏   **Select cells B5 through H6 as a block.**

❏   **Select Style from the Format menu.**

❏   **Select Right from the Style dialog.**

❏   **Press Enter.**

Printing the Spreadsheet

The spreadsheet is now complete, and you are ready to print it. However, since the finished spreadsheet is too wide to fit on your screen, it also will not fit on a standard page of paper. One way to be sure that the printout will fit on a page is to print with smaller characters by changing the print **font**. Fonts are used in the spreadsheet in the same way they are used in the word processing section of Works. To change fonts, select the Font option from the Format menu. Pull down the Format menu now and select the Font option. You should get the Font dialog box shown in Figure 7.29.

The actual print fonts and sizes that are available to you will depend on the type of printer that you have available, but the following process is the same regardless of printer type. First, select the type of font you want, such as pica, and then tab to the Sizes box and select the size (such as 8). Finally, press the Enter key to accept the font selection. Print the spreadsheet by pulling down the Print menu, selecting Print, and pressing Enter. Works will next present a Dialog box that allows you to choose from several special Print options; for now accept these as they are by pressing Enter.

Figure 7.29

*Change print fonts with the **Fo**nt dialog box.*

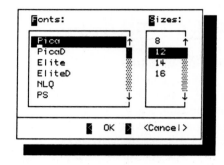

❑ **Select Font from the Format menu.**

❑ **Set the font to Pica size 8.**

❑ **Press Enter.**

❑ **Select Print from the Print menu.**

❑ **Accept Print options.**

Saving the Spreadsheet

You should now save the completed spreadsheet to your disk. Be sure that your diskette is in drive A: or another appropriate drive. To save, use these procedures.

❑ **Pull down the File menu and select the Save option.**

❑ **Use the TAB key to move to the box called Other Drives and Directories.**

❑ **Now, use the arrow key to move the highlight over the drive you want to use, and then press Enter.**

❑ **Finally, type in the name TUT-SS7 (this stands for Tutorial lesson, spreadsheet chapter 7) and press Enter. NOTE: While you could enter any name for the file, here you should use the one given, since you may need to use the file again. Also, notice that Works will automatically add the .WKS extension to indicate that the file is a spreadsheet.**

Works should now save the file to your disk. You can be sure that the file was saved by watching the disk drive indicator light, which should light up when you save the file. When you are sure that the file has been saved, exit Works.

Hands on Practice

Exercise 1: Introduction to Data Entry and Formatting

Using the Spreadsheet module of Microsoft Works, create the spreadsheet illustrated in Figure 7.30 by entering the information from the figure into the cells shown. You will have the opportunity to format the data later on, so just enter it as shown for now.

Note: When you enter the names of the month, Works will automatically assume that you want to use a special date function and only record the abbreviation of the month (such as jan for January). To avoid this, enter a quotation mark (") before you type each month name: This will specify to Works that the entry following must be treated as a label (or word) and not some special function.

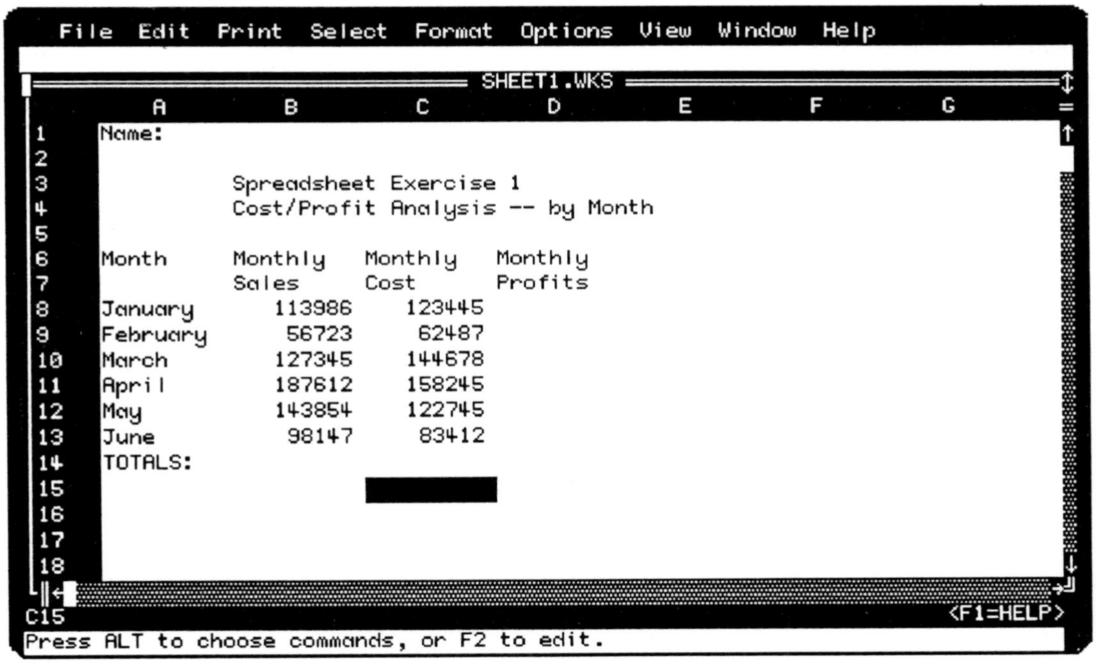

```
  File  Edit  Print  Select  Format  Options  View  Window  Help
═══════════════════════════════ SHEET1.WKS ═══════════════════════════
        A          B          C          D          E       F        G       =
1  Name:                                                                      ↑
2
3             Spreadsheet Exercise 1
4             Cost/Profit Analysis -- by Month
5
6  Month        Monthly     Monthly     Monthly
7               Sales       Cost        Profits
8  January       113986      123445
9  February       56723       62487
10 March         127345      144678
11 April         187612      158245
12 May           143854      122745
13 June           98147       83412
14 TOTALS:
15                          ███████████
16
17
18
C15                                                             <F1=HELP>
Press ALT to choose commands, or F2 to edit.
```

Figure 7.30 *Exercise 1 Spreadsheet.*

When you have completed the basic data entry, adjust the spreadsheet as follows:

1. Change the style of your name so that it is in bold type. Also, change the style of the titles (Spreadsheet assignment 1 and Cost/Profit Analysis--by Month) so that it is styled with both bold and underlined type. Finally, change the style for the word TOTALS: so that it appears in bold type.

2. Alter the style for the names of the months so that the names align with the right side of the cell instead of the left.

3. Underline the column headings of Month, Sales, Costs, and Profits. Also, underline the last Sales, Costs, and Profit entry just above the Totals row.

4. Use a formula with cell references to calculate profits for January (Sales minus Costs) and then Fill Down to copy the formulas for the other months.

5. Develop a formula in cell B14 to add up all the Sales, and then use the Fill Right command to copy the formula to the Total cells for Costs and Profits.

6. Change the format for all the numeric cells to Dollar Format with two decimal positions. After you make this change, you will have to adjust the column width to 13 positions.

7. Save the file under the name **HOP-SS71** (hands on practice, spreadsheets chapter 7, exercise 1) and then print the completed spreadsheet.

Exercise 2: Formula Development and Data Revisions

Enter the information shown in Figure 7.31 into a new Works spreadsheet and then make the changes as instructed. The data shown in the figure is not formatted, so just enter it as it is and format it later. Also, you will need to expand the width of column A to 18 spaces to be sure the titles fit.

Be sure to enter the data in the first three columns as values, and then use formulas to compute all the data in the last four columns. The numbers in the last four columns of row 8 are for you to use to check your formulas with. Do not enter these numbers as values; use formulas.

```
 File  Edit  Print  Select  Format  Options  View  Window  Help
========================= SHEET1.WKS =========================
         A          B        C        D        E        F        G        H
 1  NAME:
 2
 3  Spreadsheet Exercise 2
 4
 5  Customer        Previous  New               Current  Carrying  Total    Minimum
 6  Name            Balance   Purchases Returns Balance  Charge    Owed     Payment
 7
 8  Reynolds Tires   1000      575      100       1475   55.3125  1530.3125 202.8125
 9  IMB Corp.        2590      500        0
10  X Mart            430        0        0
11  Arctic Airlines  2500     3000     1500
12  Accidental Petro. 500      500      500
13  Gallery Art      1200      300      199
14
15
16
17
18
A15
Press ALT to choose commands, or F2 to edit.
```

Figure 7.31 *Initial Spreadsheet Data for Exercise 2.*

1. Compute the current balance for each customer as the Previous Balance plus New Purchases minus Returns.

2. Compute the Carrying Charge as 3 3/4 percent of the Current Balance.

3. Compute the Total Owed as the Current Balance plus the Carrying Charge.

4. Compute the Minimum Payment as 10 percent of the Current Balance plus the entire Carrying Charge.

5. Add up all of the cells in the Current Balance, Carrying Charge, and Total Owed columns to arrive at a total amount that is owed to our firm in each of these categories. These totals should be placed on row 15.

6. Format the spreadsheet so that the first numeric entry in each column of data is in the Currency format with two decimal positions. The totals should also be formatted as currency with two decimals. All other numeric entries should be formatted with the Comma format and two decimals. A sample, formatted column would look like this:

```
Previous
Balance

$1,000.00
 2,590.00
   430.00
 2,500.00
   500.00
 1,200.00
```

7. Adjust the column width as required to display all the data in each column.

8. Right align all the titles in rows 5 and 6 except for the Customer Name title.

9. Save the spreadsheet as **HOP-SS72**.

10. Adjust the print font as required to print the spreadsheet on one page, and print the spreadsheet.

Exercise 2: Part B

1. Assume that the following returns have just been received:

IMB Corp: $1,250

Gallery Art $486 (enter in place of the original $199.00)

X Mart $235

Update the spreadsheet by entering only these cells of information: if you have used formulas correctly, this is all you will need to do. Change the title of the spreadsheet to Assignment 2: PART B, and print the spreadsheet.

Exercise 3: Formulas and Formatting

Use the spreadsheet module of Works to create a spreadsheet just like the one shown in Figure 7.32.

```
 File  Edit  Print  Select  Format  Options  View  Window  Help
                        ═══ SHEET2.WKS ═══
            A            B           C          D          E          F          G          H
  1  NAME
  2                                       STOCK MARKET PORTFOLIO
  3  Spreadsheet Exercise 3
  4
  5        Stock       Purchase     Number     Broker    Current    Percent    Amount
  6        Name      Price/Share   of Shares    Fee     Price/Share  Change    Profit/Loss
  7
  8  Biotech, Inc.     $115.75        200                 $105.50
  9  BDM Corp.           8.50          50                   8.00
 10  Cress Financial     5.30          25                   7.50
 11  Micro/Systems      30.44          87                  30.44
 12  Wilson Technology  22.10         100                  42.10
 13  Diamond Rental      6.15       3,000                   7.10
 14  Spartan Trucking   10.10      10,000                  21.50
 15                                                                          _____
 16        TOTAL:                                                             $0.00
 17
 18
A17
Press ALT to choose commands, or F2 to edit.                                      <F1=HELP>
```

Figure 7.32   *Exercise 3 Spreadsheet.*

Enter the data provided as values and change the width, style, and format as required. Then complete the spreadsheet as follows:

1. The Broker Fee is computed as 2.73 percent of the Total Cost of the stock (Total Cost = Number of Shares * Purchase Price/Share). Format this as dollar with two decimals for the first entry and comma with two decimals for the rest.

2. Compute the Percent of Change, which is calculated as:

$$\text{Percent Change} = \frac{\text{Current Price/Share - Purchase Price/Share}}{\text{Purchase Price/Share}}$$

Format this column as percentages with two decimal positions.

3. Compute the Amount of Profit or Loss by calculating the total value of the stock minus all costs and the purchase price initially paid. This calculation is shown as:

Profit or Loss = (Current Price * Number of Shares) - ((Purchase Price * Number of Shares) + Broker Fees)

4. Format the Profit/Loss column the same way as the Broker Fee column.

5. Center the labels (column titles) over all of the columns. Underline the second row of labels.

6. Use Bold format for the stock names.

7. Underline and develop a formula to find the total for the Profit/Loss column. This total should be put in place of the zeros in cell G15.

8. Print the spreadsheet out on one page of paper, changing the print font if needed.

9. Save the spreadsheet under the name HOP-SS73 and then turn off the computer.

8

Using Spreadsheet Functions

The Works spreadsheet provides a number of special features that increase its power and ease of use. Special functions allow you to answer complex financial questions with ease while others perform tedious mathematical equations quickly and accurately. Finally, you also have the ability to insert, move, and delete columns or rows of information. You will find that these special capabilities will make using the spreadsheet much easier.

Inserting/Deleting Rows and Columns

Frequently, you will find that you need to add an extra row or column in a spreadsheet that already contains data. Works allows you to do this by using the Insert option found in the Edit menu. When the Insert option is selected, Works will present you with the Insert dialog box, which allows you to specify if you want to insert a row or a column. These menus are shown in Figure 8.1.

Figure 8.1

*Use the **Insert** or **Delete** options to add or remove rows or columns when using an existing spreadsheet.*

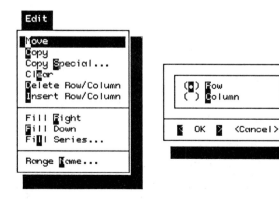

➤ *Inserting Rows*

To insert a new row, position the cursor anywhere on the row immediately **below** the point where you want the new row inserted. The new row will then be inserted directly <u>above</u> the cursor. Therefore, if you want a new row between rows 6 and 7, you must position the cursor on row number 7 before inserting the new row.

You can also insert multiple rows at one time by selecting (as a block) the number of rows to be inserted. For example, if you wanted to insert five new rows between rows 6 and 7, select a block of cells (in one column) in rows 7, 8, 9, 10, and 11. Then choose the Insert option from the Edit menu. Now, select the Row option from the Insert dialog box and press Enter. The new rows would be inserted above row number 7, and all rows would be renumbered. You should also be aware that Works knows that rows have been inserted and will adjust your formulas accordingly, so you will not have to change them.

➤ *Inserting Columns*

The insertion of new columns is accomplished in the same manner as the insertion of rows, except that new columns are inserted. To insert a single new column, position the cursor in the column to the **right** of where you want the new column inserted. Then use the Insert option from the Edit menu and select columns from the Insert dialog box. For example, to insert a new column between columns C and D, position the cursor in column D, select the Insert option from the Edit menu and the column option from the Insert dialog box. A new column would then be inserted between the old columns C and D (and will be labeled as column D).

To insert multiple columns, use the same approach as for inserting multiple rows, but highlight multiple columns instead of rows. Should you wish to insert three new columns between columns C and D, select as a block any three adjacent cells in columns D, E, and F. Then use the Insert option from the Edit menu and specify columns. When the new columns are inserted, all existing columns are relabeled appropriately.

➤ *What Happens to the Formulas When Adding Rows and Columns?*

You should recall that when you entered formulas in the previous chapter, you used cell references to denote which cells to add, multiply, and so forth. When you insert new rows and columns, however, the cell positions change; so you might wonder if you need to alter your formulas each time you make an insertion. Fortunately, the answer to this question is No, since Works takes care of this problem for you.

To illustrate this concept, assume you had the formula =A1 + B1 stored in cell C1. If you inserted a new column between columns A and B, the new column would become column B and the old column B would now become column C. If the formula was not adjusted for this change, the formula =A1 + B1 would now reference the new column, which would be blank. The Works spreadsheet has been programmed to identify this problem, and when you insert new rows or columns, Works reconstructs all the formulas automatically. This reconstruction of the formula references allows the formulas to identify correctly the new location of the cells, as shown in Figure 8.2.

Figure 8.2

Changes in the spreadsheet after a new column is added.

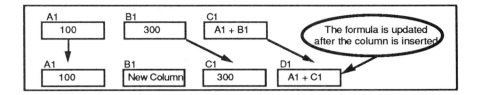

➤ Deleting Rows and Columns

To delete rows and columns, use the same approach that you used to insert rows and columns, except that you should highlight the rows or columns that you want to delete. Once the desired rows or columns are highlighted, use the Delete option from the Edit menu and select the appropriate entry from the Delete dialog box, which is used in the same fashion as the Insert dialog box.

Caution: When you delete rows or columns, be aware that the deletion may affect formulas referencing the deleted cells. Usually, when this situation occurs, you will see the notation "Err" in the affected cell. You should also be aware that the spreadsheet component of Works does not have an Undo like the word processor. Once the rows or columns are deleted, they are gone for good.

Copying and Moving Cells

You have already seen that the ability to copy cells from one area of a spreadsheet to another can save you quite a bit of work through the use of the Fill Down or Fill Right commands. While this method can work very well in many instances, there are some limitations, including the inability to copy a cell to a higher position in the spreadsheet or copy a cell to the left of the spreadsheet. The Fill Down and Fill Right also require the cells you are copying to be adjacent to each other. When you encounter these situations, a better approach is to use the Copy command from the Edit menu.

The Copy command in the spreadsheet is very similar to the copy methodology used in the word processing section. First, highlight a cell or block of cells that you want to copy. Next, select the Copy option from the Edit menu, after which the message line in Works will appear like this:

Now, move the cursor to the target cell where the data will be copied to, and press Enter. If you are copying a block of data, position the cursor in the upper-left cell of the target range (the cells into which the block will be copied) and press Enter. The data will be copied to its new location. When formulas are copied from one location to another, any cell coordinates are automatically adjusted during the copy.

You can also move cells from one location to another by using the same kind of process as the Copy procedure. To Move cells, identify the cells as a block, select Move from the Edit menu, position the cursor on the new location, and press the Enter key.

➤ *Relative and Absolute Cell Addresses*

When inserting, deleteing or copying rows or columns of cells, the formula references in affected cells will be automatically updated. For example, when each row is copied down as the result of a Fill Down operation, the value one (1) is added to the row coordinate. Similarly, each time a cell is copied to the right, the column coordinate is increased by one letter. This same process holds for those times when a cell is moved upward in the spreadsheet; 1 is subtracted from the row coordinate. You can see in Figure 8.3 that when the contents of cell A2 are copied to cell A4, the formula reference is changed. In this case, the formula refers to the cell directly above it (originally A1), and when it is copied, the reference changes to cell A3.

Figure 8.3

How a relative copy will affect the contents of a cell.

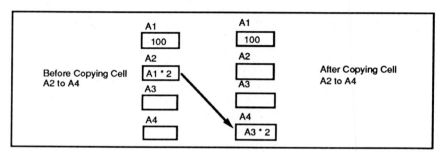

➤ *Using Absolute Cell References*

What happens when you do not want the automatic adjustment of formulas to happen when you copy a cell to a new location? For instance, assume that you had an interest rate value stored in one cell and want to use the rate to compute the payments for several different loans. Since all payments would be computed using the same formula, you enter the formula into one cell and then copy it into all the other cells. However, if the Copy procedure automatically adjusted the cell coordinates in the formula by adding 1 to the current interest rate cell position the copied payment formulas would no longer refer to the correct cell. Figure 8.4 shows how this could happen. To avoid this problem, the formula should always refer to cell B2, the interest rate, even after it has been copied.

Figure 8.4

Notice how the formula changes as it is copied from cell A3 to cells A4 and A5.

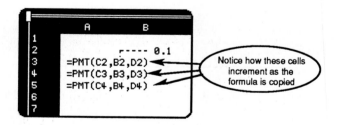

To allow you to control when you want the cell reference to change or not, the Works spreadsheet allows the use of both *relative* and *absolute* coordinates. When you use relative coordinates in a formula and the formula is copied or moved, the coordinates are adjusted. as shown previously. When you use absolute coordinates in a formula and the formula is copied or moved, no adjustment takes place.

Works uses the relative coordinate type as its default; therefore, you must specify if you want a cell coordinate treated as an absolute, or nonmoving, coordinate. This specification is accomplished by placing a dollar sign ($) in front of the coordinate you want to make absolute. Recall at this point that each cell has both a row coordinate and a column coordinate; each of these may be controlled seperately with an absolute notation. This means that you can use up to four combinations of coordinate control, including:

A1: Both the column and row are treated as relative. When the coordinate is copied left or right, the column coordinate is adjusted, and when copied up or down the row coordinate is adjusted. This is the default setting for Microsoft Works.

$A1: Here, the dollar sign causes the column to be treated in an absolute manner while the row remains relative. When the coordinate is copied to different columns (left or right), the coordinate will not change; however, when copied between rows (up and down), it is adjusted as usual.

A$1: This case illustrates relative column and absolute row coordinates. When the cell is copied between columns, the coordinate is adjusted; but when the cell is copied between rows, it will not change.

$A$1: The final case involves absolute references for both the column and row. Here, the cell coordinates will not change regardless of the copy direction. This specification is very often used and would work in the payment situation presented earlier. It is illustrated in Figure 8.5.

Figure 8.5

Use the dollar sign ($) to reference a cell absolutely, which means it will not change when the formula is copied.

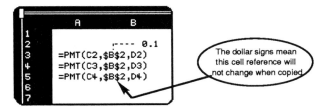

Spreadsheet Functions

Functions are special mathematical routines that have been defined in the spreadsheet software and allow you to perform many different operations without writing complex formulas. Works provides you with quite a few of these functions, and you will find many that will be quite useful to you. Functions used by the Works spreadsheet typically have the following general format:

=Function Name (argument1, argument2, . . . argumentn)

This general format indicates that the first thing to appear in any function is the equals (=) sign, which informs Works that the characters following are a function and not part of a label. A special function name that tells Works what you want follows the equals sign. Finally, several arguments are given which are enclosed in parentheses. These arguments provide the working data for the function in the form of literal values, formulas, cell coordinates, or even other functions. While the number and order of the arguments will vary from one function to another, all required arguments must be specified, and the order of the arguments is important. Perhaps the easiest way to learn the more common functions is simply to use them.

➢ *The Concept of Cell Ranges*

Many functions are designed to determine answers based on a selected block of cells in the spreadsheet. These groups of cells are referred to as *cell ranges* and provide you with complete control over the data that is referenced in a spreadsheet function.

Ranges can be specified as cell coordinates by typing the starting cell and the ending cell separated by a colon (:). For example, if you wished to select a range of cells from cell J4 to J18, the proper range would be J4:J18.

➢ *Describing a Range by Cursor Pointing*

You can also identify a range through the use of the mouse or the shift/arrow keys in the same manner that you did in the selection of a block of cells. To use this technique, enter the function name and the left parenthesis as usual. Next, press any one of the arrow keys and you will see the cell coordinate for the cursor position presented in the function area. Continue to press the arrow key until the cursor is on the first cell you want included in the function range. Now, press the colon (:) key to inform Works that you want to start the range at that point. Again, use the arrow keys to extend the highlight until the entire desired range is covered. Type the right parenthesis, press Enter, and the function is complete.

Once you try this method of range selection, you will find that it is very fast and accurate, since you can visually confirm that the range you select is correct.

➢ *Functions Used in Microsoft Works*

=SUM(range)   This powerful function computes the sum of all cells in a given range of cells. If you wanted to find the sum of all the cells from A5 to A20, the correct Sum function would be =SUM(A5:A20). Works will insert a value of zero for any blank cell or label in the range of cells being summed. Further, if you insert or delete any rows in a range, Works will automatically adjust the range to reflect the new composition of cells.

=AVG(range)   This function computes the arithmetic mean or average of the cells specified in the range. The same rules apply to inserting and deleting rows that apply to the SUM function. The average function excludes cells from the average computation if they are blank; however, a problem arises when a cell within the range contains a label. Labels in the averaged range are interpreted as zero and are included in the calculation of the average. Certainly, you will want to be aware of this, as it can cause your average calculation to be inaccurate. This situation can be seen in Figure 8.6.

Figure 8.6

Using the Average function. Blank cells are ignored, but cells with labels are treated as zeros (0).

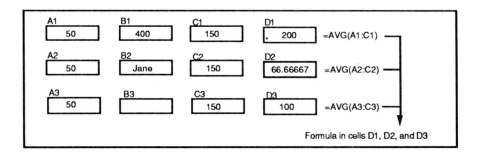

=**MAX(range)**   This function identifies the largest value contained in a range of cells. Again, blank cells in the range are ignored and cells containing labels are considered to be zero. For an example of the Max function, suppose that you wanted to find the highest test score for a group of students, and the test scores were stored in cells D5 through D40. You would then use the function =MAX(D5:D40).

=**MIN(range)**   The MIN function works just like the Max function, except that the minimum value in a specified range is found and displayed. The rules for the use of the Min function are the same as for the Max function.

=**FV(payment, rate, term)**

The Future Value function computes the future value of a given series of payments. This function differs from the functions you have already studied, since three *arguments* rather than a range are required. A typical use of the Future Value function might involve a situation in which you were going to save 50 dollars a month at an annual interest rate of 7 percent for the next 10 years. The question you are interested in is, "How much would you have at the end of the 10 years?" To develop the function to answer this question, you first need to know that the rate argument in the Future Value function is measured on a per period basis. This means that if you have an annual rate, you must convert it to a monthly rate, since you are making deposits on a monthly basis. The term *argument* specifies the number of periods over which the deposit will be made. Again, if you make the deposit monthly, the term must be converted to months. A simple way to remember how to state the rate and term is to be sure that all arguments (payment, rate, and term) deal with the same time increments.

This example would be written as:

=*FV(50,.07/12,10*12)*.

The answer to this problem, as provided by the function, is $8,654.24. While this example uses literal values (given numbers) for the amount, rate, and term, a better approach would be to store these three values in cells and use the cell coordinates in the formula. Then, to try a new amount at the same rate and term, you would only need to change the value in the cell that stores the amount.

The IF Function

The IF statement or function is considered a logical function that is used to test a given condition and then perform certain operations depending on whether the result of the test is true or false. The general format of the IF function is:

$$=IF(condition, True, False).$$

This function consists of four separate components starting with the IF function name. The second part of the function is the condition which is a test of a relationship between two cells or values. For example, the IF function would let you test a condition that cell A5 > 100 (if the contents of cell coordinates A5 are greater than 100). Each condition must be made up of two coordinates or values separated by a "relational" operator such as those listed here:

Operator	Meaning	Example
=	is equal to	A1=100
>	is greater than	A1>100
<	is less than	A1<100
< >	is not equal to	A1<>100
> =	is greater than or equal to	A1>=100
< =	is less than or equal to	A1<=100

The condition being evaluated can be very simple, with a single coordinate or value on each side (A2>10), or could be quite complex, with other functions being evaluated as part of the IF condition. Some examples of allowed IF functions and their descriptions include:

IF Condition	Meaning
=IF(A5+A6 > B5+B6)	If the sum of cell A5 and cell A6 is greater than the sum of cells B5 and B6
=IF (AVG(A1:A25) > 50)	If the average of all cells from cell A1 through and including cell A25 is greater than 50

The preceding conditions are now evaluated to be either true or false. When the condition is evaluated as true, the first operation following the condition is performed and the results of the operation are displayed in the cell that contains the IF function. If the outcome of the condition is false, the second operation is performed instead and the results are displayed in the cell containing the IF function.

For example, suppose you wanted to test the contents of cell A5 to see if it is greater than 100. If it is greater than 100, the condition is true and you want to multiply cell A6 by 2 and display the answer in cell A7. If the test is false (cell A5 is less than 100), you want to multiply cell A6 by 4 and display the answer in cell A7. To do this, you would place the following formula in cell A7: IF(A5>100,A6*2,A6*4).

➤ *The & (AND) Operator*

This option to the IF function allows you to test two conditions at the same time. For example, assume you want to test for conditions in which cell A5 > 82, and at the same time, A12 < 0. If the condition is true, the answer of 30 will be displayed; if false you want to display zero (0). The following function would be used:

$$=IF(A5 > 82 \& A12 < 0,30,0)$$

Interpretation: If A5 > 82 and A12 < 0, then put the value 30 in the cell; otherwise put the value 0 in the cell.

Notice that for this condition to be true, both conditions must be evaluated as true simultaneously.

The IF condition also supports several other logical operators, including OR (|) and NOT (~), as well as functions. These advanced options allow you to incorporate very sophisticated logic into your spreadsheets but are beyond the scope of this text. Those interested in learning more about them should consult the Microsoft Works program documentation.

Using Working Figures

One of the most powerful feature of any electronic spreadsheet is the ability to make a change in one cell and have that change update a large block of cells. This ability to use "working figures" allows you to use the spreadsheet to quickly find answers to "what if" questions that are based on various changes in the spreadsheet data.

To understand how this powerful feature can assist you, assume that you had created a spreadsheet that used the FV (Future Value) function =FV(50,.07/12,10*12) as described earlier. This function would work fine as long as you always deposited 50 dollars at 7 percent for 10 years. However, suppose that you wanted to change your deposit to 75 dollars. You would need to rewrite the complete formula. If the interest rate changed to 7.5 percent, you would need to rewrite the formula again.

The concept of working figures is based on the creation of four cells to be used by the FV function. The first cell would store the Amount, the second the Interest Rate, and the third cell would hold the Term. The last cell would contain the FV function, but in that function you use the coordinates of the first three cells rather than the actual values, as shown in Figure 8.7.

Figure 8.7

Using working figures in a future value function.

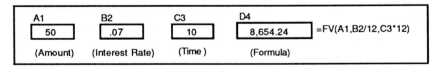

Now, to test the result for a deposit of 75 dollars, all you have to do is to change the value of cell A1, not the entire formula. The formula will automatically recalculate based on the new information and display the new answer. Similarly, to adjust the rate to 7.5 percent, you would change only the value in cell B1. These changes are shown in Figure 8.8.

Figure 8.8

When working figures are changed, the function is automatically updated.

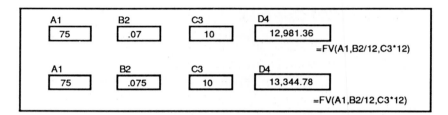

Certainly, this concept saves some time even in this small example, but what if you were dealing with values in many cells? If the formulas in 10 cells had the interest rate entered as a value, and the rate changed, you would need to change 10 formulas. If these same 10 cells used the coordinate of a working figure, only one change would be needed.

Conclusion

The Microsoft Works spreadsheet allows you to develop very powerful yet easy to use spreadsheet analyses. You can even incorporate logical conditions through the use of IF functions and other powerful options. To add even more flexibility, Works offers a number of other functions; some of the commonly used Functions are listed before the self test.

The Works Spreadsheet Functions

The following functions will prove very useful to you as you work with spreadsheets. Each function is first listed as to its purpose with the general format for the function following. Finally, a short description describes what you might expect from the function's use.

Average   =AVG(Range) Computes the average of a range of cells. To find the average of the range of cells C10 through C20, use the average function =AVG(C10:C20).

Choose Cell   =CHOOSE(Choice,List) Choose selects an option from a list depending on the value of Choice. For example, consider the function =CHOOSE(A1-2,2*5,5*10,3*100). If cell A1 contains the value 3, CHOOSE will select the first option and display 10, since 3 - 2 equals 1.

Count Cells   =COUNT(Range) This function displays the number of nonblank cells in the range. To count the cells for the range A15 through A60, enter =COUNT(A15:A60).

Term Invest   =CTERM(Rate,Future Value, Present Value) CTERM gives the number of periods during which you must leave the Present Value invested at the given interest rate for it to grow into the Future Value. For example, the function =CTERM(.07,500,100) computes how many years you must leave 100 dollars invested for the investment to reach 500 dollars at an interest rate of 7 percent compounded annually. The answer in this case is 23.78 years.

Julian Date =DATE(Year,Month,Day) This function returns the Julian date for the specified arguments. The Julian date is the number of days since Jan. 1, 1900. For example, to find the Julian date for November 1, 1990, use =DATE(90,11,01), with the answer being 33178.

Depreciation =DDB(Cost, Salvage, Life, Period) This function uses the Double Declining Balance method to compute the amount of depreciation for a given period. To find the amount of depreciation for the fourth year of an item that costs $10,000, has a salvage value of $1,000, and a life of 10 years, you would use =DDB(10000, 1000, 10,4). The answer is $1,024.00.

Future Value =FV(Payment, Rate, Term) Computes the Future Value of an annuity. If you wanted to find the future value of investing $100 per year at 9 percent for 10 years, enter =FV(100,.09,10), with the answer equaling $1,519.29.

IF Statement =IF(condition,True,False) This function will check to see if a cell meets some condition either true or false. Different actions can then be taken if the condition is true or false.

Maximum =MAX(Range) Determines the largest value in the range. To find the largest value in the range D12 through D46, enter =MAX(D12:D46).

Minimum =MIN(Range) This works just like the maximum function but returns the smallest value in a range.

PI. Function =PI( ) Gives the number 3.14159, the approximate value of the mathematical constant PI (π).

Payment =PMT(Principal,Rate,Term) Computes the amount of a payment given the principal of a loan, interest rate per period, and number of periods. To compute the monthly payment for a loan of $10,000 at 9.5 percent annually for four years, you would use =PMT(10000,.095/12,4*12). The answer is $251.23.

Random # =Rand( ) Returns a random number in the range 0.000001 through 0.999999.

Sum Cells =SUM(Range) Produces the Sum of all numbers in a specified cell range. To find the sum of all numbers in the range B5 through B73, enter =SUM(B5:B73).

Invest Pmt =TERM(Payment,Rate,Future Value) Gives the number of payments necessary to produce a future value given the payment and the interest rate. If you wanted to have $10,000 and you could save $100 dollars per month at an interest rate of 7 percent, how many months would it take? Use the function =TERM(100,.07/12,10000) to find the answer of 79 months.

While these are probably the most commonly used functions, Microsoft Works supports many more. Consult the Microsoft Works documentation for a complete list of all possible functions.

Chapter 8 Self Test

1.   How would you insert three new rows between row 8 and row 9?

2.   Explain how you would delete columns C, D, and F.

3.   If you copied the formula =A1+B1 from cell B3 to cell C5, how would the formula be changed?

4.   Explain the difference between relative and absolute coordinates.

5.   Write the coordinates for the following:

        a.   Column D absolute, row 2 relative.

        b.   Column F absolute, row 7 relative.

        c.   Column G relative, row 8 relative.

6.   Write the function to find the average of all cells from A3 through C10.

7.   Write the function to find the largest number in the range of cells from A1 through G99.

8.   Write the IF function to test cell A7. If the value in cell A7 is less than 10, display cell A7's value multiplied by 2. If the value in cell A7 is equal to or greater than 10, display cell A7's value divided by 2.

9.   Write the IF function to display the average of cells A2 through A20 if the value in cell B3 is less than zero. If the value in cell B3 is equal to or greater than zero, display the sum of cells A2 through A20.

10.   Explain why you would use working figures.

Chapter 8 Tutorial

In this tutorial, you will implement the concepts that have been discussed earlier by loading a partial spreadsheet from your disk and completing most of the column entries.

➤ Problem Description

You are in charge of the credit department of an industrial supplier. When customers place orders with your company, the order is filled and shipped, and an invoice is created. This invoice contains an invoice number, invoice amount, invoice date, and an area that indicates whether this purchase will be charged on a time payment plan. If the invoiced items are to be charged, an area is completed that indicates the number of monthly payments the customer wants to make.

For items that are not charged, your company gives a discount if the invoice is paid within 10 days. If the invoice is not paid within 10 days, the net value of the invoice is due within 30 days. In accounting terminology, your company uses a 2/10 , N/30 (2 percent discount in 10 days, net due in 30 days) payment schedule.

It is your job to keep track of the accounts receivables for your company. Some of the items you need to know include when the first payment is due for charged invoices and the amount of the payment, when the discount period is over and what is owed if the invoice is paid within the discount period, and when the net invoice amount is due. You also need to keep some totals about what amounts are due. You decide that this is a good spreadsheet application, and you develop a spreadsheet similar to Figure 8.9.

File	Edit	Print	Select	Format	Options	View	Window	Help		

"Spreadsheet Tutorial #2
TUT-SS8.WKS

	A	B	C	D	E	F	G	H	I	J
1	Spreadsheet Tutorial #2									
2	Author 1:									
3										
4										
5	Invoice	Invoice	Invoice	Number of	First	Payment	Discount	Discount	Net	Net
6	Number	Date	Amount	Payments	Payment	Due	Date	Amount	Date	Amount
7										
8	1234	8/1/90	10,000.00	24	8/31/90	459.14	Aug 11, 1990	9,800.00	Aug 31, 1990	0.00
9	1235	8/3/90	568.89		9/2/90	0.00	Aug 13, 1990	0.00	Sep 2, 1990	568.89
10	1236	8/3/90	600.00		9/2/90	0.00	Aug 13, 1990	0.00	Sep 2, 1990	600.00
11	1237	8/5/90	7,500.00	24	9/4/90	344.36	Aug 15, 1990	7,350.00	Sep 4, 1990	0.00
12	1238	8/11/90	8,509.90	48	9/10/90	213.80	Aug 21, 1990	8,339.70	Sep 10, 1990	0.00
13	1240	8/13/90	10,000.00	48	9/12/90	251.23	Aug 23, 1990	9,800.00	Sep 12, 1990	0.00
14	1241	8/14/90	7,845.40	42	9/13/90	220.30	Aug 24, 1990	7,688.49	Sep 13, 1990	0.00
15	1242	8/21/90	345.60		9/20/90	0.00	Aug 31, 1990	0.00	Sep 20, 1990	345.60
16	1243	8/21/90	8,901.00	60	9/20/90	186.94	Aug 31, 1990	8,722.98	Sep 20, 1990	0.00
17	1244	8/22/90	4,534.87	24	9/21/90	208.22	Sep 1, 1990	4,444.17	Sep 21, 1990	0.00
18	1245	8/22/90	3,451.00	36	9/21/90	110.55	Sep 1, 1990	3,381.98	Sep 21, 1990	0.00
40	Interest Rate:		9.5%		Total of Invoices:		130,743.66			
41	Days to Due Date:		30		Average Invoice:		4,217.54			
42	Discount Days:		10		Total Due Payments:		3,753.09			
43	Discount Rate:		2.0%		Total Due Discount:		123,363.34			
44	Days to Net:		30		Total Due Net:		4,862.70			
45										
46										

Press ALT to choose commands, or F2 to edit.

Figure 8.9 *Completed Spreadsheet for Tutorial 2.*

➣ Starting the Tutorial

To begin the tutorial, follow these steps to start Microsoft Works and open the file named TUT-SS8.WKS.

❏ **Start Microsoft Works.**

❏ **Select Open Existing File.**

❏ **Open the file named TUT-SS8.WKS**

When the file is loaded, you should have a spreadsheet that has been partially completed. It should look like Figure 8.10, except that it will have 44 rows.

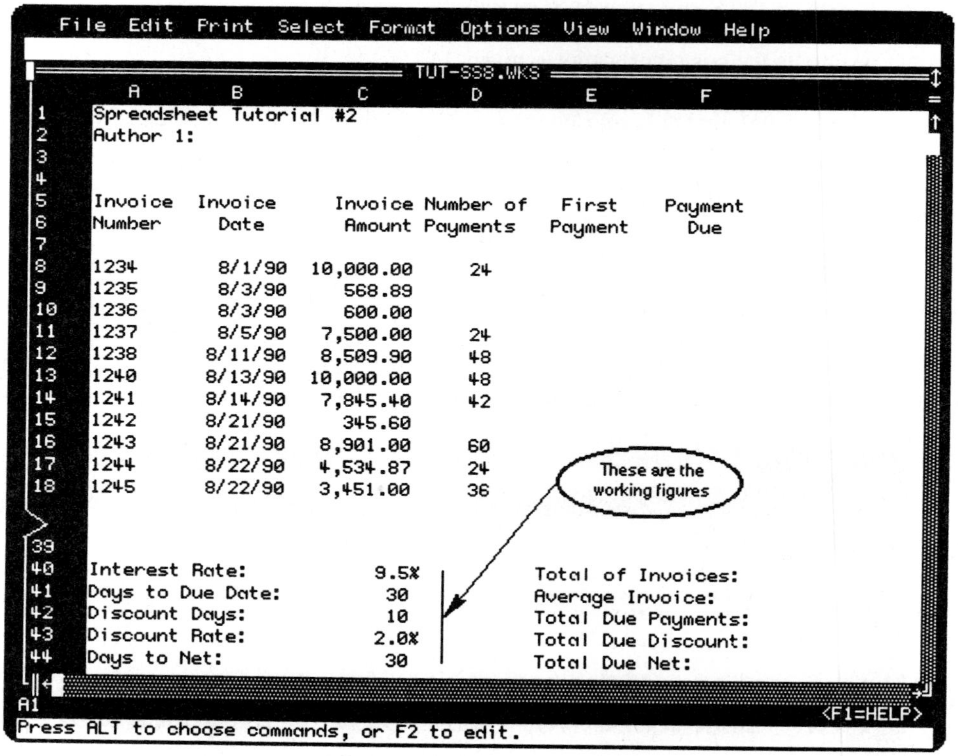

Figure 8.10

This is how the spreadsheet will look right after you load it into Works.

```
   File   Edit   Print   Select   Format   Options   View   Window   Help

   ==================== TUT-SS8.WKS ====================
          A          B          C          D          E          F
   1   Spreadsheet Tutorial #2
   2   Author 1:
   3
   4
   5   Invoice    Invoice             Invoice Number of    First      Payment
   6   Number     Date                 Amount Payments     Payment       Due
   7
   8   1234        8/1/90    10,000.00      24
   9   1235        8/3/90       568.89
   10  1236        8/3/90       600.00
   11  1237        8/5/90     7,500.00      24
   12  1238        8/11/90    8,509.90      48
   13  1240        8/13/90   10,000.00      48
   14  1241        8/14/90    7,845.40      42
   15  1242        8/21/90      345.60
   16  1243        8/21/90    8,901.00      60
   17  1244        8/22/90    4,534.87      24        These are the
   18  1245        8/22/90    3,451.00      36        working figures

   39
   40  Interest Rate:           9.5%        Total of Invoices:
   41  Days to Due Date:         30         Average Invoice:
   42  Discount Days:            10         Total Due Payments:
   43  Discount Rate:           2.0%        Total Due Discount:
   44  Days to Net:              30         Total Due Net:

   A1                                                        <F1=HELP>
   Press ALT to choose commands, or F2 to edit.
```

Before you continue with the tutorial, you will need to enter your name in cell C2.

❏ **Enter your name in cell C2.**

Next, take a moment to look at the working figures you will use in the spreadsheet. Move down to these with the F5 key.

❏ **Press the F5 (GoTo key), type the cell address A44 and press Enter to move down to view cells A40 through C44.**

These will be working figures for this spreadsheet. Notice that you have a working figure for the Interest Rate, which is the rate you charge for invoices that are placed on the time payment plan. Also notice that you have a working figure (equal to 30 days) for the number of days until the due date of the first payment. You should know that this figure may need to be changed, since we occasionally offer a "No Payment for 90 Days" special. Because of this requirement, when you need to calculate Payment Due Dates in the spreadsheet, you will want to use the number of days as the absolute coordinates of cell C41. This is why the Days to Due Date value has been stored separately.

Move back up to the top of the spreadsheet by using the Ctrl/Home key combination.

❑   **Use the Ctrl/Home key combination to move to cell A1.**

➢ *Completing the First Payment Column*

The Invoice Date (stored in cell B8) has already been entered in the correct date format, so you can simply add to it when calculating the First Payment date. To compute the First Payment date in cell E8, you will need to develop a formula as follows:

First Payment = Invoice Date + Days to Due Date

Notice that the first Invoice Date is stored in cell B8 and that the Days to Due Date value is located in cell C41; therefore, the spreadsheet formula should be B8+$C$41. You should also take special note that cell C41 has been specified as an absolute reference through the use of the dollar signs. You will need this absolute coordinate so that when the formula is copied into the other rows, this coordinate will not change. This formula will be entered into cell E8 as follows:

❑   **Enter: =B8+$C$41 into cell E8.**

The value in the cell should now be 33116, but this certainly does not appear to be a date! It is, however, the Julian date, which is the number of days since Jan. 1, 1900. The date figure is now displayed as a number because the cell is using a General format. To convert the date to a Date format, select the Time/Date option from the Format menu as shown in Figure 8.11.

Figure 8.11

Format the Julian date number into the Month, Year, and Day format with the Time/Date dialog box.

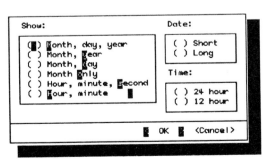

Since you will want the date displayed as MM/DD/YY, select the Month, Day, Year format and the Short format by using the arrow and tab keys to move the diamond to these options. Next, press Enter to accept the format.

❑   **Pull Down the Time/Date dialog from the Format menu.**

❑   **Select Month, Day, Year from the Show box.**

❑   **Select Short (the default setting) from the Date box.**

❑   **Press Enter.**

You should now have 8/31/90 in the First Payment column for cell E8. Now use the Fill Down option from the Edit menu and copy the formula to all the cells in the other rows.

❑   **Select cells E8 through E38 as a block.**

❑   **Select Fill Down from the Edit menu.**

❑   **Press Esc to cancel the block.**

➤ *Completing the Payment Due Column*

This column should display the amount of the monthly payment. When computing the monthly payment, you need to take into consideration that interest is computed monthly based on a declining balance. Because of this, computing the monthly payment is much more complex than simply computing the simple interest, adding it to the invoice amount, and dividing by the number of payments. Fortunately, Microsoft Works has a function that computes this payment, called PMT. Its general format is as follows:

=PMT(principal, rate, term)

In the PMT function, the **principal** is the amount of the loan, which in our case is the amount of the invoice. The **rate** is the periodic rate or the interest rate for each period a payment is made. While the annual rate is known and stored as a working figure in cell C40, customers make monthly payments. Therefore, you will need to convert the annual interest rate into a monthly interest rate by dividing the annual rate by 12. Be sure to reference the rate as an absolute value when using the rate working figure. The final component in the payment function is the **term,** which is simply the number of payments that will be used. This value is stored in column D in the spreadsheet.

To develop the spreadsheet formula for this exercise, follow these steps:

❑   **Enter =PMT(C8,$C$40/12,D8) in cell F8.** Note that you are replacing the PMT function variables with working figures from the spreadsheet.

❑   **Format the cell using the Comma format with two decimals.**

❑   **Cell F8 should now contain the value 459.14.**

❑   **Select cells F8 through F38 as a block.**

❑   **Select the Fill Down option from the Edit menu.**

❑   **Press ESC to cancel the block.**

I Get an Error (ERR) in Some Cells!

Notice that some of the cells contain the word ERR. This error occurs whenever the formula cannot be computed. Move the cursor to the first ERR, cell F9, and then look at the formula in the formula line. The term of the payment refers to cell D9; however, this cell is empty; it does not have a value. This blank cell occurred because this customer did not want to charge the invoice and hence has no "Number of Payments" entry. This same situation is also true of all the other rows that contain the ERR.

To avoid the ERR condition, each cell in the Number of Payments column should be tested to determine if there is an entry or if it is blank. If a cell in the column is blank, then the payment should be zero. However, if there is an entry in the cell, the payment should be computed normally. This relationship can be described in English as:

If the Number of Payments is blank, the payment is zero; otherwise, compute the payment.

This relationship can be converted to a spreadsheet IF function:

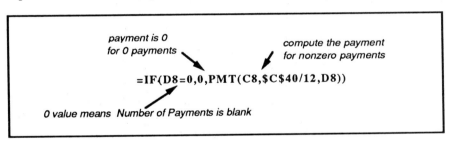

To adjust the PMT function that was entered in cell F8 so that it will perform correctly, use the F2 key to edit the formula in cell F8, and then use the Fill Down to copy the formula, as shown in these steps:

❑ **Press F2 and edit the formula in cell F8 to read as**
   =IF(D8=0,0,PMT(C8,$C$40/12,D8))
   Note: You must delete the = in front of PMT.

❑ **Select cells F8 through F38 as a block.**

❑ **Use Select Fill Down from the Edit menu.**

❑ **Press Esc to cancel the block.**

The first few lines should now look like Figure 8.12. Check the First Payment and Payment Due columns of the first few rows to make sure they are right. If they are not correct, correct your errors before moving to the next column.

Figure 8.12

The Interim Spreadsheet. Be sure to check your figures with these to be sure that everything is correct before moving on.

```
 File  Edit  Print  Select  Format  Options  View  Window  Help
=IF(D8=0,0,PMT(C8,$C$40/12,D8))
================================ TUT-SS8.WKS ================================
        A           B           C          D          E          F
 1  Spreadsheet Tutorial #2
 2  Author 1:
 3                                            Be sure your figures
 4                                               match these
 5  Invoice     Invoice          Invoice  Number of    First     Payment
 6  Number      Date             Amount   Payments    Payment    Due
 7
 8  1234         8/1/90       10,000.00     24        8/31/90    459.14
 9  1235         8/3/90          568.89               9/2/90       0.00
10  1236         8/3/90          600.00               9/2/90       0.00
11  1237         8/5/90        7,500.00     24        9/4/90     344.36
12  1238         8/11/90       8,509.90     48        9/10/90    213.80
13  1240         8/13/90      10,000.00     48        9/12/90    251.23
14  1241         8/14/90       7,845.40     42        9/13/90    220.30
15  1242         8/21/90         345.60               9/20/90      0.00
16  1243         8/21/90       8,901.00     60        9/20/90    186.94
17  1244         8/22/90       4,534.87     24        9/21/90    208.22
18  1245         8/22/90       3,451.00     36        9/21/90    110.55
```

➤ The Discount Date Column

The next column is the Discount Date column. This is a simple column to compute and shows a specified number of days after the Invoice Date and is stored as a working figure at cell C42. Currently this number is 10, but we want the ability to change the number without rewriting the spreadsheet, so a formula using absolute coordinates should be used to set the date.

Once the date formula is developed, the cell must be formatted as a date in the form of: MMM DD, YYYY (Aug 11, 1990). This is the long format of the Month, Day, Year format. To save some time, format the cell before using the Fill Down option, so that as the formula is copied into the other cells, the format for the column will also be copied. Once the cell is formatted, you can use the Fill Down option to copy the formulas. Complete column G now.

❑   Enter = B8+$C$42 in cell G8.

❑   Format cell G8 using the Time/Date format, Month, Day, Year, and Long date option.

❑   Use Fill Down to copy the formula and format to the remaining rows.

Comment: Ideally, if the customer charged the invoice on the time payment plan, there would be no Discount Date. Therefore, for some rows, this cell should be left blank. To do this, we would need to use an IF function and test the number of payments column. If the column were blank, we would leave the date cell blank; otherwise, we would compute the date. Microsoft Works will not allow you to write an IF statement like this. You must always supply some numeric operation on both the true and false conditions of the IF.

➤ **The Discount Amount Column**

The Discount Amount column is the amount that should be received if the invoice is paid prior to the Discount Date. This is calculated using the percentage that is stored at cell C43. The English computation of the Discount Amount would be found as:

*Invoice Amount - (Invoice Amount * Discount Rate)*

For example, to compute the discount rate for the first invoice, you would take the $10,000 invoice amount and subtract $200, which is the product of the Invoice Amount * the Discount rate ($10,000 * 2%). Converting this formula to the spreadsheet would give a formula that would look like: =C8-(C8*$C$43). This formula would then be copied into the other rows.

There is still a problem, since if the invoice is paid on the time test column D8 for zero or a no-payment condition. The complete formula should then read:

$$=IF(D8=0,0,C8-(C8*\$C\$43))$$

Now, complete the Discount Amount column using these steps:

❑ Enter =IF(D8=0,0,C8-(C8*$C$43)) in cell H8.

❑ Format the cell using the Comma format with two decimal places.

❑ Select the remaining rows.

❑ Use the Fill Down option to copy the formula to the remaining cells.

Your spreadsheet should now look like Figure 8.13. Be sure to check the Discount Date and Discount Amount of the first few columns. If they are incorrect, correct the formulas before moving to the next step.

```
 File  Edit  Print  Select  Format  Options  View  Window  Help
                                                                      ‡‡
                        TUT-SS8.WKS
        A        B         C        D       E        F          G            H         ↑
 1   Spreadsheet Tutorial #2
 2   Author 1:
 3
 4
 5   Invoice  Invoice    Invoice Number of  First   Payment    Discount     Discount
 6   Number   Date       Amount  Payments   Payment Due        Date         Amount
 7
 8   1234     8/1/90    10,000.00   24      8/31/90  459.14   Aug 11, 1990   9,800.00
 9   1235     8/3/90       568.89           9/2/90     0.00   Aug 13, 1990      0.00
10   1236     8/3/90       600.00           9/2/90     0.00   Aug 13, 1990      0.00
11   1237     8/5/90     7,500.00   24      9/4/90   344.36   Aug 15, 1990   7,350.00
12   1238     8/11/90    8,509.90   48      9/10/90  213.80   Aug 21, 1990   8,339.70
13   1240     8/13/90   10,000.00   48      9/12/90  251.23   Aug 23, 1990   9,800.00
14   1241     8/14/90    7,845.40   42      9/13/90  220.30   Aug 24, 1990   7,688.49
15   1242     8/21/90      345.60           9/20/90    0.00   Aug 31, 1990      0.00
16   1243     8/21/90    8,901.00   60      9/20/90  186.94   Aug 31, 1990   8,722.98
17   1244     8/22/90    4,534.87   24      9/21/90  208.22   Sep 1, 1990    4,444.17
18   1245     8/22/90    3,451.00   36      9/21/90  110.55   Sep 1, 1990    3,381.98
F8
Press ALT to choose commands, or F2 to edit.
```

Figure 8.13 *The Discount Date and Amount Columns.*

➤ *Completing the Net Date and Net Amount Columns*

The last two columns are completed just like columns E through H. To see how familiar you are with these spreadsheet concepts, complete these last two columns yourself. Here are a couple of hints to get you started.

The Net Date consists of a specified number of days after the Invoice Date and is stored in cell C44 as a Working Figure. Don't forget absolute referencing where needed and format this column in the Month, Day, Year format with the Long option.

The Net Amount is simply the Invoice Amount. Remember that you only have a Net Amount if there are no payments (the cell for the number of payments is equal to zero), so an IF statement might be helpful. This column should be formatted in the Comma format with 2 decimal positions.

➤ *Completing Cells G40 through G44*

❑   **Complete columns I and J (check the figures against Figure 8.9).**

❑   **Move the cursor to cell G40 by pressing the F5 key and entering G40.**

This cell should contain the total of all Invoice Amounts. To compute this total,use the SUM function. The format of the SUM function is SUM(range), where range is the block of cells you want to sum. In this case, the range consists of cells C8 through C38, written as C8:C38. To enter this formula, you will use a new technique called *cursor pointing*. Cursor pointing allows you to start a formula and then move your cursor to the cell coordinates you want placed in the formula. To do this, follow these steps:

❑   **Enter =SUM(in cell G40.**

As you perform the next step, watch the formula line:

❑   **Move the cursor up to cell C8 with the arrow keys.**

Notice that the cell the cursor is positioned on appears in the formula line. Once you reach cell C8, the formula line should show =SUM(C8.

❑   **Enter a colon (:) after the cursor is on cell C8.**

The formula line should now read =SUM(C8:C8.   Now when you move your cursor, only the last coordinate should change.

❑   **Move the cursor to cell C38.**

The formula line should now show =SUM(C8:C38, and this cell range should be highlighted. Complete the formula by entering the closing parenthesis and pressing Enter.

❑   **Enter the closing parenthesis.**

❑   **Press the Enter key.**

Cell G40 should now show 130743.66, which is the sum of all cells from C8 through C38. The next cell, cell G41, should contain the Average of the Invoice Amounts. Remember that you have an average function called AVG. The format of this function is the same as the SUM function: AVG(range). Use the same approach used to enter the SUM function in cell G40 to compute this average, which equals 4,217.54.

❑   **Use cursor pointing to enter the AVG function in cell G41.**

The last three cells that need to be completed are Total Due summaries for Payments, Discounts, and Net. The Total Due Payment is the SUM of cells F8 through F38. The Total Due Discount is the sum of cells H8 through H38. Finally, the Total Due Net is the sum of cells J8 through J38. Enter these formulas using the cursor pointing technique, and then format the cells using the Comma format with two decimals.

❑   **Complete cells G42, G43, and G44.**

❑   **Format cells G40 through G44 using Comma format with two decimals.**

Your totals should look like Figure 8.14.

Figure 8.14

The completed working figures and totals.

39				
40	Interest Rate:	9.5%	Total of Invoices:	130,743.66
41	Days to Due Date:	30	Average Invoice:	4,217.54
42	Discount Days:	10	Total Due Payments:	3,753.09
43	Discount Rate:	2.0%	Total Due Discount:	123,363.34
44	Days to Net:	30	Total Due Net:	4,862.70

You have now completed the initial tutorial and should save the spreadsheet and then print it using the following directions:

❑   **Save the spreadsheet as TUT-SS8A.**

❑   **Change the print font as needed to print the spreadsheet out on one page of paper.**

➢ *Testing the Finished Spreadsheet*

You have completed the spreadsheet, but before you quit the Works program you should take a moment to really see the value of what you have created. Assume you had the following question:

1. If the Interest Rate were changed to 12 percent, what would be the Total Due in payments?

Before answering this question, note the payment amount in cell F32, which should be 959.26. To see what happens at the higher interest rate, follow this step:

❑   **Enter .12 in cell C40.**

Not only did the Total Due Payments change to 3,905.29, but all payments have been recalculated. The payment in cell F32 should now be 1,016.02.

2. If the Discount Days value is changed to 20 days, when is the new Discount Date for invoice 1265?

❑   **Enter 20 in cell C42.**

❑   **Examine cell G38. The date is Feb 9, 1990.**

You should now turn off the computer or close the spreadsheet and continue with the hands-on practice.

Hands on Practice

➤ Exercise 1: Developing Formulas

This exercise will allow you to practice the development and use of formulas that are used to make the most of the entries in the spreadsheet. You should first set up the spreadsheet exactly like the one shown, then develop the correct formulas, and finally use the Fill Down command to copy these formulas to their new positions.

➤ Exercise Scenario

Marge and Joe's Steakhouse was started about five years ago as a family business by Marge and Joe Robins. The restaurant is only open on the weekends (Thursday through Saturday), as Marge is still working as an accountant at the local hospital. Joe spends his week ordering food and preparing the restaurant for the weekend rush. Marge and Joe decided from the start to specialize in very few menu items but to prepare and serve the items carefully; a philosophy that has been very successful judging from the number of repeat customers that patronize the restaurant.

Recently, Joe decided to study the orders of each menu item to see if he could do a better job of ordering food for each week. He decided to use Thursday as a "base" day and to compare the other days with it. This seemed to work fairly well, as the demand for meals has been reasonably consistent and related to the "base" as follows:

Thursday	= Base,
Friday	= 58% above the Thursday base,
Saturday	= 112% above the Thursday base.

While he was studying the demand for each item on the menu, Joe noticed that the demand for ribeye steaks on Fridays increased an extra 20 percent over the usual rise of 58 percent. Joe attributes this to the fact that the local mill has payday on Fridays.

All meals include a tossed salad (8 ounces worth), and the customer's choice of a baked potato or french fries. Joe found that 73 percent of the customers ordered the baked potato while the remainder chose the six ounce portion of french fries. Joe also made the salad available on an individual basis, and he has found that about 18 percent of the patrons ordering the Mega-Burger also purchase the salad.

Beverages are purchased on an individual basis, and at this time, the restaurant offers coffee, tea, and soft drinks. Joe has decided to combine the coffee and tea into one group and all soft drinks into another for order purposes, as these items have a long shelf life and can be ordered in bulk.

Joe has determined that beverages follow the following consumption pattern:

43% of the customers choose coffee or tea,

29% of the customers select soft drinks.

The remaining customers drink water or opt for no drink.

Joe has just purchased a personal computer and is using the Works software and has decided that a spreadsheet could easily accommodate this problem. He started to develop a spreadsheet, as shown in Figure 8.15, but had some difficulty with the formulas and so he has asked you to finish the job. The final spreadsheet should use formulas wherever possible so that a change in the sales level of the base day demand (Thursday) is automatically reflected in the rest of the spreadsheet.

Joe wants each column, except column A, to be 8 spaces wide. Column A should be 15 spaces wide. Pay special attention to the formatting by copying the format shown in the sample (labels left, right, etc.) to be sure that your finished sheet will look just like Figure 8.15.

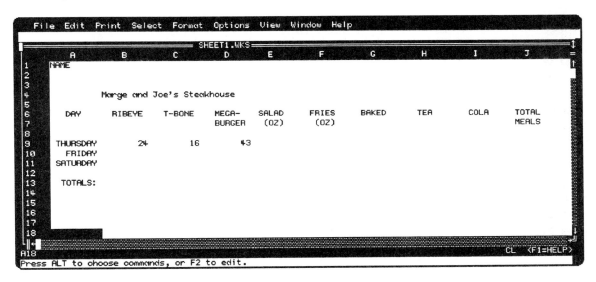

Figure 8.15 *Spreadsheet Illustration.*

When you are done, print out the spreadsheet, changing the font if necessary to be sure it will fit on one page. Be sure to save this spreadsheet as HOP-SS81.

➤ *Exercise 1: Part B*

Joe has just discovered that his estimate for Thursday's ribeye and T-bone steak demand is incorrect. The correct figures should be 33 ribeyes served and 12 T-bones served. Adjust your spreadsheet accordingly to reflect these changes, and after your name, type PART B in bold print. Note: If you have used the correct formulas in the spreadsheet, all you will have to do is to enter the new demand figures in for Thursday. Print this spreadsheet.

➤ *Exercise 2: Developing a Payroll*

The firm that you are working for has decided to use the Works spreadsheet to calculate the payroll. You have been asked to develop a spreadsheet similar to Figure 8.16 to accomplish this task. First, be sure to center all of the titles and set the column width to 8. You should plan to use formulas wherever possible and you will want to use IF statements to calculate the number of overtime hours (over 40 hours) an employee should be paid for. Overtime hours are paid at a rate of 150% of the employee's base pay. Your manager also wants you to compute the average number of hours worked, the average pay rate, regular pay, and overtime pay. Print out the spreadsheet and save it to your diskette as HOP-SS82.

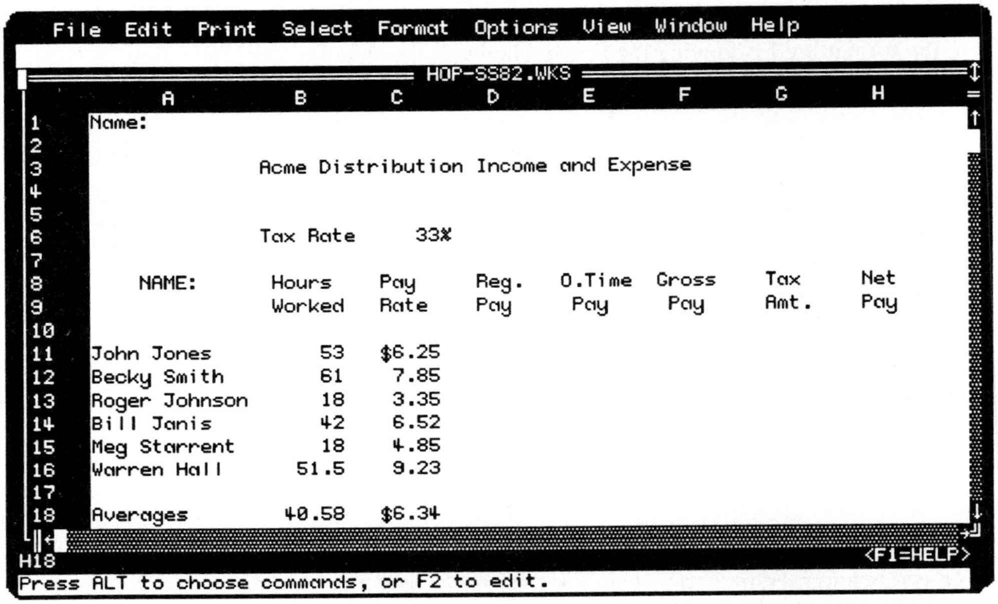

```
 File   Edit   Print   Select   Format   Options   View   Window   Help
══════════════════════════════════ HOP-SS82.WKS ══════════════════════════════
          A          B        C       D        E        F       G        H
 1  Name:
 2
 3             Acme Distribution Income and Expense
 4
 5
 6             Tax Rate     33%
 7
 8             NAME:      Hours    Pay     Reg.    O.Time   Gross   Tax     Net
 9                        Worked   Rate    Pay     Pay      Pay     Amt.    Pay
10
11  John Jones            53     $6.25
12  Becky Smith           61      7.85
13  Roger Johnson         18      3.35
14  Bill Janis            42      6.52
15  Meg Starrent          18      4.85
16  Warren Hall          51.5     9.23
17
18  Averages            40.58    $6.34
H18
Press ALT to choose commands, or F2 to edit.
```

Figure 8.16 *Payroll Calculation Spreadsheet.*

➢ Exercise 2: Part B

You have just found out that the payroll information you received has been adjusted. Use the spreadsheet you developed in Part A and make the following changes:

❑   Change the hours John Jones worked to 37.

❑   Adjust Meg Starrent's hourly rate to $5.35.

❑   Change Roger Johnson's hours to 57.5.

❑   Change the tax rate to 24 percent.

Once you have made these changes, type PART B next to your name and print out the spreadsheet. You do not have to save these changes.

Using Advanced
Spreadsheet Concepts

You have already learned that spreadsheets are extremely powerful tools that can be applied to any number of different situations; however, to reap the maximum reward, you must be able to recognize how various problems best fit into the spreadsheet framework.

The Works spreadsheet provides some powerful special features that allow you to handle many special problems quickly and easily. These features, which are common to most spreadsheet programs, include the use of table-based value lookups, freezing given titles to force them to remain on the screen, and effectively using a split screen. Works also allows you to set spreadsheet recalculation modes to utilize either manual or automatic modes. Each of these features provides you with power and flexibility, but the key to gaining the most from their use is knowing when and how to apply them.

Using Table Lookups

Table value lookup systems are often used in our everyday life. For example, when you go to a store to make a purchase, you often find that you must pay a sales tax based on the amount of the purchase. Typically, the tax is calculated as a percent of your purchase amount; however, you have probably noticed that a straight percentage will often not work correctly due to rounding problems. For example, at a tax rate of 5 percent on a purchase of of 51¢, the tax is 2.5¢ but you are charged 3¢. Therefore, in order to provide consistency, tax tables are used which let the salesclerk look up the exact tax amount.

Figure 9.1

*This is a sample of the kind
of table that is used to
compute sales taxes.*

State Sales Tax Table				
Purchase Amount	Tax		Purchase Amount	Tax
.00 - .10	.00		1.91 - 2.10	.10
.11 - .30	.01		2.11 - 2.30	.11
.31 - .50	.02		2.31 - 2.50	.12
.51 - .70	.03		2.51 - 2.70	.13
.71 - .90	.04		2.71 - 2.90	.14
.91 - 1.10	.05		2.91 - 3.10	.15
1.11 - 1.30	.06		3.11 - 3.30	.16
1.31 - 1.50	.07		3.31 - 3.50	.17
1.51 - 1.70	.08		3.51 - 3.70	.18
1.71 - 1.90	.09		3.71 - 3.90	.19

The table shown in Figure 9.1 illustrates the kind of table used in a manual lookup. The table provides an easy to use and consistent method for computing the required tax. To see how this might work, use the table to find the tax for an item that cost 48¢ by looking down the first column to find the entry between 31¢ and 50¢, noting that 48¢ is less than 50¢, and then refer to the number directly to the right, which equals the tax of 2¢.

This straightforward table method, widely used in many manual systems, forms the logical base for spreadsheet functions which use tables in much the same way. The spreadsheet application requires that you first build a table like the tax rate table in Figure 9.1; however, the spreadsheet differs in that the table can contain both values and/or formulas. To use the table, a Works spreadsheet **LOOKUP** function is available which can match a value in a given cell key with a value in the table. When the values match, the spreadsheet can select a second value from the table in the same fashion that you selected the sales tax amount earlier.

Since the value you wish to find will seldom match a value in the table (in the tax table in Figure 9.1 there is no match for 36¢ or 48¢), you would want the spreadsheet to define a standard logical process to determine when to stop searching for the match. The Works spreadsheet accomplishes this by always specifying data in the table in a specific order, either ascending or descending. Then, when the table is searched, the spreadsheet can determine the appropriate range of values that contains the amount in question.

Microsoft Works contains two LOOKUP functions which work in essentially the same manner but differ in the actual layout of the data table.

➤ *The VLOOKUP Vertical Lookup Function*

One table lookup function available in the Works spreadsheet that is similar to the tax table in Figure 9.1 is the Vertical Lookup function, called **VLOOKUP**. The general format of the VLOOKUP function is similar to functions that you have already used and appears as:

=VLOOKUP(Key Value, Table Range, Offset)

The **Key Value** referred to in the function is the value you are looking for and must be a numeric value or a cell coordinate that contains a numeric value. This value is from the working spreadsheet and is the value that you are trying to match in the table. The key value for the state sales tax table found in Figure 9.1 would be the sales amount.

The **Table Range** describes the area of the spreadsheet that will be searched. The range reference will describe a block of cells in the spreadsheet that contains all the cells that the lookup function will use. The range will always consist of multiple rows and multiple columns. For example, if your table started in cell A20 and had entries to B25, the range would be A20:B25. This is illustrated in Figure 9.2.

Figure 9.2

The VLOOKUP Table Range.

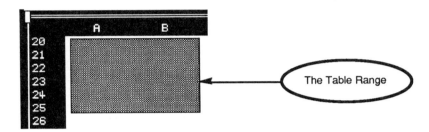

Finally, you will need to specify which column contains the values that you want returned to the spreadsheet from the table. The **Offset** informs the spreadsheet how you will look for a value in the table. This variable represents the number of columns to the right of the lookup value that the spreadsheet will look to find the value you want to retrieve. The offset in the sales tax example would be 1, since you read down the sales amount until you find the amount of the sale and then move one column to the right to find the amount of the tax. This idea can be better understood by referring to Figure 9.3.

Figure 9.3

Using the VLOOKUP function to find the tax for the value .48. The value returned to the spreadsheet is 0.02.

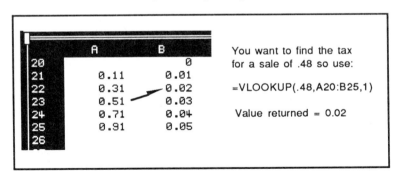

The function in Figure 9.3 specifies the table range as cells A20 through B25. Notice that the table is set up as two columns, with the first column containing the values you wish to compare with the value from the spreadsheet. This column of values (column A) consists of the key values. The second column contains the values that will be returned from the VLOOKUP function.

For example, if you want to find how much tax will be assessed on a given value, look down the first column of Figure 9.3 until you find a number that is equal to or greater than the amount of your purchase. Assume that in this case you are looking for the tax on 48¢. If the number in the key column (the left column) of the table matches the number you are looking for, your tax will be in the column to the right, which would be equivalent to an offset of 1. If your lookup number is less than the number in the table, your tax will be in the row to the right and immediately above where you stopped. In this case, 48¢ is less than 51¢, so you should stop when you get to 51¢ in the first column and move up one row, with the tax being found directly to the right in row 22 and equal to 2¢.

➢ *Using the Key Value in VLOOKUP*

Generally stated, Works uses the key value in the VLOOKUP function to determine which row in the table contains the function result. To do this, Works searches the first column of the table for the first value that matches or exceeds the function's key value. If the spreadsheet finds a match, the result of the function will be found in the row that contains the match. If Works finds a value that exceeds the key value, it uses the row immediately above, which will be the largest value that does not exceed the key value. This selection is automatic and is not something you will have to specify.

➢ *The HLOOKUP Horizontal Lookup Function*

The horizontal lookup function works generally the same as the vertical lookup, except that the data table is constructed in a horizontal fashion. A sample horizontal table is illustrated in Figure 9.4.

Figure 9.4

Using the HLOOKUP function with information located in rows.

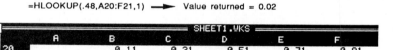

This approach places the key values in a row rather than a column with the keys being found in the first row and the values in the second row. The Works spreadsheet will use this table by first comparing values across the first row (row A in Figure 9.4) until a value is found that is equal to or greater than the key value. If the table value is equal to the key, the function returns the value immediately below the key. If the key value is less than the table's key, the function returns the value to the left of the key, which is the largest value that does not exceed the key value.

The choice to use the vertical VLOOKUP function or the horizontal function is usually determined by the kind of data that you need to include. When you are working with a table of data that is vertical in nature (like the sales tax example), use the VLOOKUP function, and when the data is laid out in a horizontal or row format, the HLOOKUP will be easier to use. Normally, most users find they will use the VLOOKUP function more frequently.

Finally, in both the VLOOKUP and HLOOKUP functions presented, the tables are shown as single dimensional because there is only one row or column used to store results. Both functions can easily be expanded by increasing the offset value to accommodate multiple rows and columns of results.

Freezing Titles in Rows and Columns

You have probably noticed that it can be difficult to keep track of which row or column you are working in when the spreadsheet scrolls down or to the right. While Works will display your current cell location on the status line, you cannot be sure what the column title is after you move down into the spreadsheet and the column headings (titles) scroll off the screen. The same thing happens when the cursor is moved to the right and the row labels and other information to the left are scrolled out of view. This situation occurs because the computer screen acts as a window to the spreadsheet and is much too small to display all the cells at one time. Indeed, you have probably become somewhat frustrated even when working with small spreadsheets; therefore, you can imagine the problems that could result when you work with very large spreadsheets like those encountered in the business world.

Fortunately, Works provides a way for you to stop certain rows or columns from scrolling off the screen by "locking" the selected rows or columns in place. This useful function is activated from the Options menu and is called the Freeze Titles option. The Option menu is shown in Figure 9.5.

Figure 9.5

The Options menu box in which the spreadsheet titles can be frozen or released.

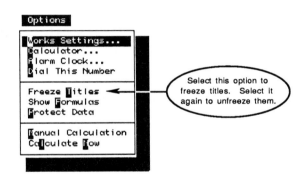

When the Freeze Titles option is selected, rows above and columns to the left of the present cursor position will be frozen or locked in their current position on the screen. When the cursor is moved off the screen with the Freeze Titles option active, titles will stay in their frozen position. This is an excellent way to be sure you are entering data in the correct column or row, since you can always see the titles on the screen.

The Freeze Titles option also provides an easy method to view columns that are located in different positions of the spreadsheet side by side. For example, if you wanted to compare column A with column E, you could freeze column A and then move the cursor to the right until column E scrolls to a position next to column A.

When you want to unfreeze the titles, select the Unfreeze Titles option from the Options menu. The cursor can be at any position in the spreadsheet when the Unfreeze option is selected.

Using a Split Screen

While the Freeze Titles option can be used to hold a given portion of the screen in view at all times, you will find that it can be easier to split the screen into sections and see different parts of the spreadsheet in each window. The Split Screen option can be used to do this and actually allows you to view up to four different portions of the spreadsheet at the same time.

The use of the Split Screen option allows you to divide the screen into multiple windows. Each window can access the entire spreadsheet, so by moving around in different windows, you can have different parts of the same spreadsheet visible in different windows.

➤ *Splitting the Screen with the Arrow Keys*

You can split the screen into multiple windows by selecting the Split option from the Window menu. When this option is activated, Works will display a message as follows:

Use DIRECTION keys to move split and press ENTER.

When this message is displayed, notice the two sets of double lines that appear on the screen: one set at the top and one set on the left side. These double lines serve as boundaries between the windows and also allow you to change the size and number of windows. Use the keyboard arrow keys to move either set or both sets of the double lines to create the windows sizes that are desired. The up and down arrow keys will move the double line at the top of the screen, while the left and right arrow keys move the line located on the left side of the screen. When the windows are the right size for what you want, press the Enter key. Should you decide that you do not want to split the screen after choosing the split option, just press the Escape (ESC) key. To change the size of the windows after they have been created, choose the Split window option again and simply move the bars to the size desired. Figure 9.6 shows a screen split into four windows.

Figure 9.6

Your can split the screen into four components using the Window Split command and then moving the arrows keys to select the sizes of the windows.

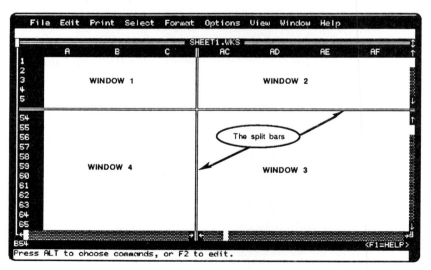

➤ *Splitting the Screen into Windows with the Mouse*

The mouse can also be used to create multiple windows. When no windows are active, Works displays a small double line as shown in Figure 9.7, which looks like an equals sign on the upper-right portion of the screen directly above the mouse scroll line. Move the mouse's cursor to the line and hold down the left mouse button. You can then drag the window bar down to the desired position. This operates like the arrow key, except the mouse replaces the key. Notice that a window bar is also available in the lower-left corner of the screen and is used to split the window vertically.

Figure 9.7

Use the Horizontal Split bars to split the screen with the mouse.

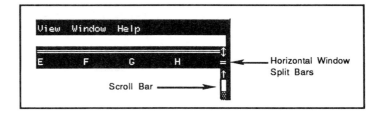

Moving Between Windows

Once the screen is split into windows by either the arrow keys or the mouse, you will want to move from one window to another. This movement is accomplished through the use of the F6 (Next Window) key. Each time the F6 key is pressed, the cursor will move horizontally to the right to the next window. If there are no windows next to the current window, the cursor will move down to the next available window. The cursor will continue to move between windows and will cycle back to the starting window. The SHIFT/F6 (Previous Window) key combination can also be used and will move the cursor in a counterclockwise (reverse) direction. This process is illustrated in Figure 9.8.

➤ Closing Windows

To close the windows and return to the standard screen, choose the Split window option and move the window separator bars back to the top of the screen with either the arrow keys or the mouse. This will close all the windows and leave the screen as it was before windows were opened.

Remember, you only have one copy of the spreadsheet active, even though you may have multiple windows. This means that any change to the spreadsheet from any window is immediately reflected in all windows.

Figure 9.8

Use the F6 key to move from Window 1 to Window 2, 3, 4, and finally back to 1. Each time the F6 key is pressed, you will move to the next window. To use the mouse, just position the cursor in the desired window and click the button.

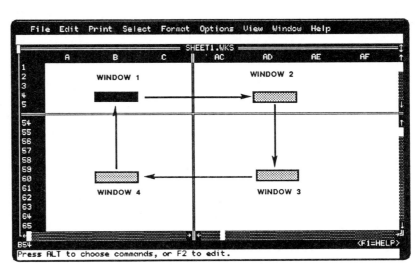

Manual and Automatic Recalculation

Whenever a change is made to any part of the spreadsheet, Works will automatically update all the entries that are affected. This **automatic recalculation** feature of the spreadsheet is very handy and is the default setting for the Works spreadsheet when it is first started. However, when large spreadsheets with many complex formulas are being used, the constant recalculation can be frustrating, since it can be time consuming even on a fast computer. This constant need to stop entering data and wait for the computer can be avoided by instructing Works to turn off the automatic recalculation feature and only recalculate when you tell it to.

➤ Selecting Manual Recalculation Mode

Automatic recalculation can be turned off by selecting the **Manual Recalculation** feature in the Options menu, as shown in Figure 9.9. When the spreadsheet is operating in the Manual Recalculation mode and formulas have been altered but not recalculated, the word CALC will appear on the message line of the spreadsheet to let you know that a recalculation is needed. To instruct Works to recalculate when using the Manual Recalculation option, press the Calc Now (F9) key or select the Calculate Now option from the Option menu. To avoid errors caused by not recalculating after changes when using the manual mode, you should watch for the CALC indicator.

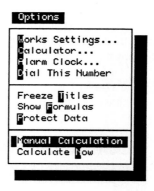

Figure 9.9

*Select the **Manual Recalculation** option to make the spreadsheet update the calculations when you instruct it to.*

To return to the automatic calculation mode, select the Option menu and choose the Manual Recalculation option again. This will turn off the manual recalculation. This type of option, which is selected once for on and then again for off, is an example of a toggled option. To identify which state the recalculation mode is currently set at, pull down the Option menu and look to the left of the word *Manual*. When a black dot is visible next to the option, it means that manual recalculation is active. When you select the option again, the dot will disappear to indicate that the spreadsheet is using automatic recalculation.

Printing and Displaying Formulas

Once data and formulas have been entered into the spreadsheet, only the values are displayed on the screen. While this is usually what you will be interested in, it can lead to a false sense of security, since any possible errors contained in the formulas are "out of sight and out of mind." To avoid this potential problem, experienced spreadsheet users will often display or print the spreadsheet formulas and examine them for typographical errors, logic errors, and the like. Although this examination could be done a cell at a time by moving the cursor to a given cell and looking at the formula line, there is a much easier way that will allow all formulas to be displayed at once.

➤ Displaying Formulas to the Screen

To have all the formulas displayed to the computer screen, select the Show Formulas option from the Options menu, as shown in Figure 9.10. This option also operates as a toggle; select it once and the formulas are displayed; select it a second time and the values are displayed.

Figure 9.10

The Show Formulas option will allow you to see all the formulas in the spreadsheet. When this option is used, the formulas will also print out.

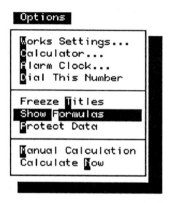

➤ Printing Formulas

Spreadsheet formulas can be printed by selecting the Show Formulas option before printing the spreadsheet. When formulas are printed, the printed columns will become wider to accommodate the longer width of the formulas, and as a result, it is likely that several pages will be needed to print all formulas in the spreadsheet.

Printing Part of a Spreadsheet

Occasionally, only part of a spreadsheet will need to be printed. To do this, first select the area of the spreadsheet to be printed as a block and then choose the Set Print Area option from the Print menu, as shown in Figure 9.11. When the spreadsheet is printed after this selection process, only the highlighted area will print. Should you now want to print the entire spreadsheet, you must reselect the full spreadsheet and use the Set Print Area option again.

Figure 9.11

When you only want to print part of the spreadsheet, use the Set Print Area option located under the Print menu.

Printing Titles on Each Page

The first few rows and the leftmost column usually contain titles or other information that helps identify the contents of the columns and rows and needs to be included on each printed page. However, when a spreadsheet is printed that requires more than one page, these important title rows and columns will only print on the first page. To print these titles on all pages of the spreadsheet, use the Freeze Titles option from the Options menu to freeze the desired information before you print. When the Freeze Titles option is selected, frozen titles will be printed on each page.

➤ Printing Row and Column Labels

The row and column labels are the numbers down the left-hand side of the screen, and the letters across the top of the screen, and are not usually included in a Works spreadsheet printout. Occasionally when you are testing a spreadsheet or checking it for errors, you will want these labels included on the printout. This feature is activated by choosing the Print Row and Column Labels option located in the Print dialog box before printing the spreadsheet. The dialog box shown in Figure 9.12 is displayed when you choose the Print selection from the Print menu.

Figure 9.12

To print the row and column labels, arrow down to this option and press the space bar to select it.

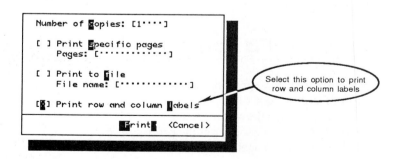

Sorting the Spreadsheet Data

The Works spreadsheet allows you to sort spreadsheet data so that you can quickly arrange it to see various patterns or trends. For example, you might want to sort an expense spreadsheet from the largest expense item to the smallest. This type of sort would be called a **descending** sort. An **ascending** sort would arrange the data from the smallest value to the largest.

To sort data in the spreadsheet, first create a block of cells containing the information you want to sort. Next, pull down the Select menu and choose the Sort option. Finally, choose the sort order (ascending or descending) from the sort options box. When you press Enter to select the options, the data will automatically be sorted. Notice that it is possible to "nest" sorts so that you can sort two or more items at once.

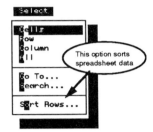

NOTE: When you sort spreadsheet data, **all** the cells in the selected range will be sorted; even the blank cells, which are evaluated as a zero. Since there is not an Undo feature in the spreadsheet, a good practice is to save the spreadsheet *before* you sort it so that you can quickly return to the original sheet if the sort does not perform as you expected.

Making Decisions with Spreadsheets

The real value of an electronic spreadsheet is its ability to manipulate data in ways that can provide information to aid decision makers. It is very important to remember that the spreadsheet cannot reach a decision independently and that the information shown in the spreadsheet is only as good as the data and formulas used in its development. This important concept can easily be forgotten when working with tools as powerful as the Works spreadsheet and probably represents the spreadsheet's biggest weakness.

The types of problems that are very well suited to spreadsheet analysis are often referred to as "what if" questions. Some examples of these kinds of questions include:

> If inflation increased by 2 percent a year for three years, what would happen to my average business expenses?
>
> If the new warehouse was financed for twelve years rather than eight, what would be the additional finance charges?
>
> If production was increased by 20 percent, what would be the additional labor costs?

Assuming that the spreadsheet is formulated correctly, the answers to these and similar questions can be found quickly and easily. Similar questions and techniques are covered in this chapter's tutorial, which will allow you to actually try these techniques yourself.

Conclusion

You have now had the opportunity to try out a number of the more advanced and powerful features that are found in the Works (and most other) spreadsheets. The spreadsheet can also provide an easy and quick way to examine many different what if questions. This flexibility means that managers can better analyze the outcome of many different potential scenarios and thus be better prepared to meet them. This improvement in the decision-making potential is perhaps the key to the usefulness of the spreadsheet concept.

Chapter 9 Self Test

1. Show how you would set up a table to locate a monthly commission rate for the sales representatives of a firm. The sales plan is such that if a salesperson sells over $10,000, a 4 percent sales commission is paid. If sales are over $25,000, a 6 percent commission on sales is earned. Finally, for sales that are over $50,000, 10 percent is paid.

2. In the following table, what are the cell coordinates that will contain the value that is returned if 500 is used as the Key value in an HLOOKUP function?

	A	B	C	D	E	F
1	50	100	350	850	1030	3750
2	1	2	3	4	5	6

3. What is the difference between an HLOOKUP and a VLOOKUP function?

4. If you wanted to freeze the first three rows and the first two columns of a spreadsheet as titles, what cell should the cursor be on when you set the freeze option?

5. Explain two ways to split a spreadsheet screen into multiple windows.

6. What is the difference between automatic and manual recalculation in a spreadsheet? How can these be changed?

7. How can you specify that the cell formulas of a spreadsheet rather than the cell values be printed?

8. You want to print only rows 1 through 5 and columns A through D of a large spreadsheet. What procedure should be followed to do this?

9. How do you get titles printed on each page of a spreadsheet?

10. How can you specify that column and row labels be printed on each page of a spreadsheet?

Chapter 9 Tutorial

This tutorial exercise will allow you to modify an existing spreadsheet stored on disk. The modifications include changing one row of formulas, adding a lookup table, and using other advanced concepts to manipulate the spreadsheet shown in Figure 9.13.

	A	B	C	D	E	F	G	H
	File Edit Print Select Format Options View Window Help							
			TUT-SS9.WKS					
1								
2								
3	Cashflow Projections							
4	Elite Pub and Deli							
5								
6								
7		Income	Income	Income	Income	Income	Income	Total
8		January	Febuary	March	April	May	June	Income
9								
10	Store #1	3,450.00	3,000.00	1,850.00	2,000.00	2,230.00	4,000.00	16,530.00
11	Store #2	7,890.00	7,892.00	12,000.00	8,567.00	5,002.00	6,809.00	48,160.00
12	Store #3	10,000.00	8,500.00	7,540.00	6,570.00	8,050.00	7,500.00	48,160.00
13								
14	Total Income	21,340.00	19,392.00	21,390.00	17,137.00	15,282.00	18,309.00	112,850.00
15								
16	Fixed Expenses							
17	Rent	3,500.00	3,500.00	3,500.00	3,500.00	3,500.00	3,500.00	21,000.00
18	Salaries	5,550.00	5,550.00	5,550.00	5,550.00	5,550.00	5,550.00	33,300.00
19	Telephone	125.00	125.00	125.00	125.00	125.00	125.00	750.00
20	Total Fixed Expenses	9,175.00	9,175.00	9,175.00	9,175.00	9,175.00	9,175.00	55,050.00
21								
22	Variable Expenses							
23	Electric	2,347.40	2,133.12	2,352.90	1,885.07	1,681.02	2,013.99	12,413.50
24	Delivery	1,813.90	1,648.32	1,818.15	1,456.65	1,298.97	1,556.27	9,592.25
25	Misc. Expenses	1,707.20	1,551.36	1,711.20	1,370.96	1,222.56	1,464.72	9,028.00
26	Waste	1,131.02	1,027.78	1,133.67	908.26	809.95	970.38	5,981.05
27	Total Variable Expenses	6,999.52	6,360.58	7,015.92	5,620.94	5,012.50	6,005.35	37,014.80
28								
29	Total Income	21,340.00	19,392.00	21,390.00	17,137.00	15,282.00	18,309.00	112,850.00
30	Minus Total Expenses	16,174.52	15,535.58	16,190.92	14,795.94	14,187.50	15,180.35	92,064.80
31	Profit Before Taxes	5,165.48	3,856.42	5,199.08	2,341.06	1,094.50	3,128.65	20,785.20
32	Taxes	1,627.13	1,214.77	1,637.71	737.44	344.77	985.52	6,547.34
33	Profit After Taxes	3,538.35	2,641.65	3,561.37	1,603.63	749.74	2,143.12	14,237.86
34								
35	Actual Profit Margin	0.17	0.14	0.17	0.09	0.05	0.12	0.13
36	Over/Under Margin	0.05	0.02	0.05	-0.03	-0.07	0.00	0.01
37								
38	===============================Working Expenses===============================							
39	Fixed Expenses							
40	Tax Rate	31.5%		Variable Expenses				
41	Rent	3,500.00		Electric		11.0%		
42	Salaries	5,550.00		Delivery		8.5%		
43	Telephone	125.00		Misc. Expenses		8.0%		
44				Waste		5.3%		
45	Expected Profit Margin:	12.0%						

Figure 9.13 *Initial Tutorial Spreadsheet.*

➤ Starting the Tutorial

The first step is to start the Microsoft Works software and open the spreadsheet file named TUT-SS9.WKS.

❑ **Start Microsoft Works.**

❑ **Open the spreadsheet called TUT-SS9.WKS.**

This spreadsheet is used to project income, expenses, profits and losses, taxes, and other information for the Elite Pub and Deli Company, which currently operates three stores. The spreadsheet contains the income data for each store over a six-month period as well as the total fixed expenses for all three stores over the same six-month period. These fixed expenses are assumed to be the same for each month. Another part of the spreadsheet contains variable expenses, which are calculated as a percent of the store's income.

You will also notice that profits or losses before and after taxes, tax liabilities, and profit margins are also computed in the spreadsheet. Finally, at the very bottom of the spreadsheet are the working figures that are used to make the various calculations. Begin the tutorial by entering your name into cell A11.

❑   **Enter your name in the spreadsheet at cell A1.**

➤ *Using a LOOKUP Table to Calculate Taxes*

The tax figures currently used in the spreadsheet are computed at a fixed rate with the tax rate now stored in cell B40. Since the rate is fixed, no matter how much profit is made before taxes, the taxes are computed at the same rate. You realize that this may change in the future and would like to alter the spreadsheet so that the tax rate depends on the amount of profit that is earned. For instance, if the firm earns $10,000 in profits, it may be taxed at a rate of 18 percent. If $20,000 in profits are returned, the tax rate would be 19 percent, and so forth. The easiest way to accommodate this is to include a tax table, shown in Figure 9.14, in the spreadsheet.

Figure 9.14

This is the manual tax table that needs to be included in the spreadsheet.

Profit More Than	But Less Than	Tax Rate
0	2,001	.00
2,000	3,501	.15
3,500	7,001	.21
7,000	15,001	.31
15,000	40,001	.32
40,000	75,001	.35
75,000	110,001	.36
110,000	150,001	.37

To use the table in a manual fashion, first determine the appropriate profit level range in the leftmost two columns which bracket your firm's figure before taxes. Next, look to the rightmost column to determine the correct tax rate. For example, if the firm's profits before taxes were $22,075, the correct tax rate would be found at the fifth row of the table, which would correspond to a tax rate of 32 percent.

To automate this type of table in a spreadsheet, you must first determine if you want to arrange the table vertically or horizontally. In this case, it would be more convenient to arrange the table vertically, since that form most closely duplicates the table's current format.

HINT:

Recall that a spreadsheet table only uses one column for the key values, while the manual table makes use of two. Fortunately, this presents no real problem, since the spreadsheet lookup function searches for a greater than or equal to condition when it searches a table. Remember that if the condition is equal, it uses the value to the right of the matched key; however, if the condition is less, it uses the lower value above the row where the "matched" key is. This simple relationship will allow you to quickly develop tables that function like the tax table in Figure 9.14.

➢ Entering the Table into the Spreadsheet

Before the tax table can be directly entered, a few small changes need to be made to accommodate the spreadsheet method of table lookups. Remember, when the less than condition is met, the lookup function uses the cell above the matched column. Therefore, if the value 2,001 is used as the less than key, the correct percent rate should be stored in the row above this key. The correct way to enter this table in the spreadsheet is shown in Figure 9.15. Take a few minutes to study this table to be sure you are familiar with its operation.

Figure 9.15

This shows the correct format for the tax rate table as it will appear in the spreadsheet.

	A	B
46		
47		0.00
48	2,001	0.15
49	3,501	0.21
50	7,001	0.31
51	15,001	0.32
52	40,001	0.35
53	75,001	0.36
54	110,001	0.37
55	150,001	0.37

To enter the table, you will need to use an empty area in the spreadsheet. After you inserted two rows for the entry of your name, the spreadsheet ends at row 45, so to keep things separate, start entering the table at row 47, column B, with the value 0.00. Format the entries as shown.

❑ **Move to Cell B47 (use the F5 key to move quickly) Start the tax table by entering 0.00 in B47.**

❑ **Complete the table as shown in Figure 9.15. Remember not to type in the commas; but rather change the format of cells A48:A55 as comma with zero decimal positions. The values in cells B47:B55 should be formatted in the Fixed format with two decimal positions.**

Once the table is entered, all that remains is to enter the lookup function. Since the table has been entered vertically, the vertical lookup must be used. Remember that the format for the vertical lookup is:

LOOKUP(Key value, table range, offset)

➤ *Entering the VLOOKUP Function*

In this case, the key spreadsheet value will be the cells containing the **Profit Before Taxes**. This profit category for January is now stored in cell B31. The lookup table that you just entered is located in cells A47 through B55, so this is entered as the table range. Finally, the offset would be 1, since the table values are located one column to the right of the key value column. If you were to enter it, the function would appear as:

$$VLOOKUP(B31,A47:B55,1)$$

Before you actually enter this function, consider that you will probably want to take advantage of the Fill Down or Fill Right commands to cause the function in cell B31 to be copied into other cells. As this copy is made, you will want the source of the key, the Profit Before Taxes field, to change, but you will not want the table range to change. To avoid this problem, specify the table range with absolute coordinates. This revised function will look like:

$$VLOOKUP(B31,\$A\$47:\$B\$55,1)$$

This function will cause the tax rate from the table to be returned, but you will need more than just the rate to finish the calculation. The complete requirement is to determine the amount of the taxes; therefore, the Profit Before Taxes must be multiplied by the tax rate to arrive at the tax amount. The resulting final formula is:

$$B31*VLOOKUP(B31,\$A\$47:\$B\$55,1)$$

The result of the formula should be stored in cell B32, Taxes, so that's where you should enter the completed formula. Once entered, the formula can quickly be copied to cells C32 through H32 through the use of the Fill Right option from the Edit menu. Now, enter the formula using the following steps:

- ❑ **Move to cell B32.**
- ❑ **Enter =B31*VLOOKUP(B31,$A$47:$B$55,1).**
- ❑ **Select cells B32 through H32.**
- ❑ **Select Fill Right from the Edit menu.**
- ❑ **Use *SAVE AS* option from the File menu to save the spreadsheet as TUT-SS9A.**

When you are done entering these steps, the spreadsheet should have recalculated the tax values. You can check that the values are correct by comparing row 32 with the values shown here:

	A	B	C	D	E	F	G	H
				TUT-SS9.WKS				
32	Taxes	1,084.75	809.85	1,091.81	351.16	0.00	469.30	6,651.26
33	Profit After Taxes	4,080.73	3,046.57	4,107.27	1,989.90	1,094.50	2,659.35	16,978.34

➤ *Freezing Column and Row Titles*

The column headings and row titles have probably scrolled off the screen by this time, making it hard to determine exactly which column you are working with. Choosing the Freeze Titles from the Options menu can prevent this problem. Be sure to recall that when you freeze the titles, you freeze only rows and columns that are above and to the left of the cursor. Since you will want to freeze the column titles located in rows 7 and 8 and the titles in column A, you should move the cursor to cell B9 and select the Freeze Titles option from the Options menu.

❏ **Use the F5 key to move the cursor to cell A7 and then use the arrow keys to position the cursor at cell B9. The titles in rows 7 and 8 should be showing.**

❏ **Select the Freeze Titles from the Options menu.**

Now go ahead and move the cursor around the spreadsheet noticing that the titles do not scroll. You should also notice that with the titles frozen, you have a smaller scrolling area.

➢ *Splitting the Screen into Multiple Windows*

Even with the titles frozen, a spreadsheet of this size can be difficult to edit, since you have to scroll back and forth frequently. An easier way to observe the changes in one part of the spreadsheet while entering new data in another is to split the screen into windows. To split the screen, follow these steps:

❏ **Move the cursor to cell B9.**

❏ **Select Split from the Window menu.**

❏ **Use the Down arrow key to move the bar to row 13.**

❏ **Press Enter.**

➢ *Moving In and Between Windows*

The screen will now be split into two windows, with the cursor in the top window. Now try scrolling in this window by pressing the Down arrow key. Notice that only the top window scrolls while the bottom window remains stationary. To move the cursor from the top to the bottom window, press the **F6** key now. Note that when this window is scrolled, the top window is stationary. You can switch back to the other window by pressing the F6 key again.

To see how much easier working on the spreadsheet can be using windows, scroll the top window until you position row 20 immediately above the window bar. Next, move to the second window by pressing the F6 key and scroll until row 27 is immediately below the window bar. Now the totals for both Fixed and Variable expenses appear together where you can easily view them, as seen in Figure 9.16.

You can also split the screen again and move the vertical window bar to give you a maximum of four windows. The F6 key will allow you to move between these in sequence.

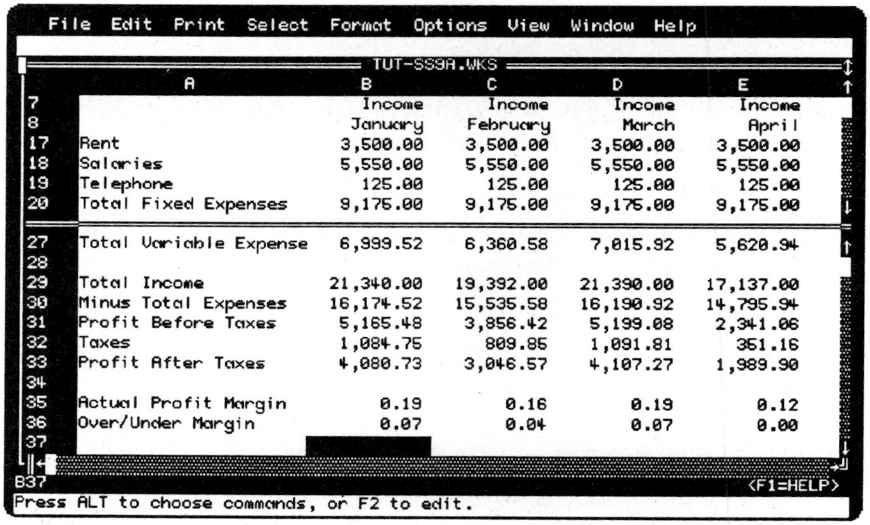

Figure 9.16

Using the split screen to show both fixed and variable costs. Notice that the titles are still in the frozen position in the top window.

```
 File   Edit   Print   Select   Format   Options   View   Window   Help
╔═══════════════════════════ TUT-SS9A.WKS ═══════════════════════════╗
                      A              B          C          D          E
  7                             Income     Income     Income     Income
  8                             January    February   March      April
 17  Rent                       3,500.00   3,500.00   3,500.00   3,500.00
 18  Salaries                   5,550.00   5,550.00   5,550.00   5,550.00
 19  Telephone                    125.00     125.00     125.00     125.00
 20  Total Fixed Expenses       9,175.00   9,175.00   9,175.00   9,175.00
 27  Total Variable Expense     6,999.52   6,360.58   7,015.92   5,620.94
 28
 29  Total Income              21,340.00  19,392.00  21,390.00  17,137.00
 30  Minus Total Expenses      16,174.52  15,535.58  16,190.92  14,795.94
 31  Profit Before Taxes        5,165.48   3,856.42   5,199.08   2,341.06
 32  Taxes                      1,084.75     809.85   1,091.81     351.16
 33  Profit After Taxes         4,080.73   3,046.57   4,107.27   1,989.90
 34
 35  Actual Profit Margin           0.19       0.16       0.19       0.12
 36  Over/Under Margin              0.07       0.04       0.07       0.00
 37
B37                                                            <F1=HELP>
Press ALT to choose commands, or F2 to edit.
```

➤ Displaying Formulas

Before you try displaying the spreadsheet formulas, be sure to turn off the Freeze Titles option by selecting the Unfreeze Titles option from the Options menu. Also, close the windows to move back to a single screen. Finally, select the Show Formulas from the Options menu.

- ❏ Select Unfreeze Title from the Options menu.
- ❏ Select Split from the Window menu and move the window bar back to the top of the screen.
- ❏ Press Enter to complete the Split option.
- ❏ Select Show Formulas from the Options menu.

The formulas should now be displayed on the computer screen. Notice that the columns have been automatically widened to double the width that was set originally so that Works can display all of the formula. This change is only temporary, and the width will change back when the Show Formulas option is turned off.

You will see that some of the cells contain only a number that shows that the cell is occupied with a value. If the cell displays a text entry such as a title, the cell contains a label. All other cells should contain formulas. You can use this option to check formulas and make sure you have entered them correctly.

➤ Printing Formulas with Row and Column Labels

To print formulas, you must first have selected the Show Formulas option so that the formulas are displayed in the spreadsheet. Since the printout showing formulas will also show the double width columns, it is helpful to print titles on each page. This can be done by selecting the Freeze Titles with the cursor in the correct position before you print the spreadsheet. In this case, to make the titles print, move the cursor to cell B9 and select the Freeze Titles option.

❑ **Move to cell A7 and then arrow to cell B9 so that the titles in cells B7 and B8 show on the screen.**

❑ **Select Freeze Titles.**

Since the column width will be quite wide, it is a good idea to select a small print font to be sure that you print as much as possible on each page. The Pica font, size 8 selected from the Font option shown in Figure 9.17, located on the Print menu, is a good one to use.

Figure 9.17

Select print fonts from the
Font *dialog box located*
under the ***Format*** *menu.*

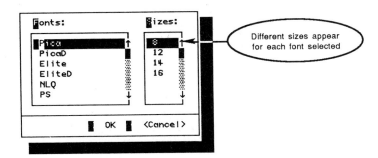

Often, it is helpful to have the row and column labels (A,B,C and 1,2,3, etc.) printed as well. To include the row and column labels on this spreadsheet printout, you must select the Print Row and Column Labels option from the Print dialog box as seen in Figure 9.18. Follow these steps to print:

❑ **Select the Pica font and size 8 from the Font option of the Format menu.**

❑ **Select Print from the Print menu.**

❑ **Select Print Row and Column Labels.**

❑ **Select Print by pressing Enter.**

Figure 9.18

Print the Row (1,2,3) and
Column (A,B,C) headings
with this option.

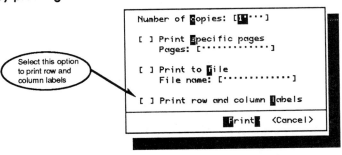

Once the printout is completed, turn off the Show Formulas option.

❑ **Select Show Formulas from the Options menu.**

❑ **Select Unfreeze from the Options menu.**

➤ Sorting the Spreadsheet Data

Assume you have decided to sort the monthly income data for March so that the store incomes are in descending order.

❑   Select D10 through D12 as a block of cells.

❑   Pull down the Select menu and then choose Sort Rows

❑   Press the Tab key then use the right arrow key to select Descending.

❑   Press enter and watch as rows 10, 11, and 12 are sorted.

❑   Now, select cells B10:B12 as a block.

❑   Use the Sort procedure to sort the income figures into ascending order.

The spreadsheet should now look like it did before you started the sort procedures.

➤ Answering WHAT IF Questions

One of the real benefits that result from the use of the spreadsheet is the ease with which what if questions can be asked. Due to the flexible nature of the spreadsheet and the possibility of quick changes, an almost endless number of different questions can be evaluated. A few such questions can be examined based on the tutorial spreadsheet. The answer to each question is based on the answers developed in earlier questions, so it is important that you work with the questions in order.

1.   If rent were raised to $4,500 each month, what effect would it have on total profit after taxes?

Initially, this question appears trivial: If six months are considered and the rent is increased by $1,000.00 each month, profits should decline by $6,000 dollars. However, it is important to remember that tax rates are based on the level of profits, and differing profit amounts will be taxed at different rates. To use the spreadsheet to evaluate this question, first move the cursor to cell H33 and notice that the total profit after taxes is $16,978.34. Next, follow these steps to enter the $4,500.00 rent amount as the new working figure.

❑   Move the cursor to cell A7 and then arrow to B9 (show the labels above B9) and select the Freeze Titles option.

❑   Press the F5 key and then enter H33 to move to cell H33 and observe current profits of $16,978.34.

❑   Use the F5 key to move to cell B41.

❑   Enter 4500 in cell B41.

❑   Move back to cell H33 to see revised profits.

Now return to cell H33, and notice that the total profit after taxes is $12,280.88. This is only $4,697.46 difference, not the $6,000.00 ($1,000 per month) that might have been expected.

2.   If the change to the $4,500 rent per month was made, what effect would this have on the total six month profit margin?

Before we made the change to the rent cost, the profit margin in cell H35 was 0.15 or 15 percent. After the change was made, the profit margin dropped to 11 percent, which represents a 4 percent decline.

3.   If waste was cut by 2 percent, what impact will this change have on our total waste expense?

This is an easy change to make. First, note that the total waste value is stored in cell H26 and is currently $5,981.05. Since waste is a percent of total sales and this percentage is stored in cell F44, all you need to do is change this cell's value by entering 0.033 (which is 3.3 percent and shows a 2 percent decline) in this cell and then note the change in cell H26.

❑   **Enter 0.033 in cell F44.**

The new waste figure is $3,724.05, which is a net decrease of $2,257.00.

4.   If store 1 had increased its sales by $10,000 in January, what effect would this have on the Actual Profit Margin for the six-month period?

The first thing to notice in this instance is that the current 6-month Actual Profit Margin stored in cell H35 is 0.13, or 13 percent. Next, follow these steps to see what happens with this increase in sales. We will use the Split screen option when working with this question to view two parts of the screen at the same time.

❑   **Move the cursor to cell B10.**

❑   **Choose the Split screen option and move the bar on the top of the screen until it is on row 13. Next, move the bar on the left of the screen until it is between columns B and C. Finally, press Enter to split the screen into four windows.**

❑   **Press F6 twice to move to the lower-right window.**

❑   **Move to cell H35 (use the F5 key or the arrow keys) and notice the profit level.**

❑   **Press the F6 key two more times to return to cell B10, and enter 13450 in cell B10 while observing the profit figure in cell H35 reflect the change.**

You will notice that the profit value in cell H35 is instantly recalculated to show the new 15 percent profit level. You should also notice how easy it is to see these changes when using the Split screen option.

This concludes the tutorial exercise, and you should now exit the Works program and turn off your machine.

❑   **Exit Works and reply NO when asked if you want to save your recent changes to TUT-SS9A.WKS.**

❑   **Turn off the computer.**

Hands on Practice

➤ *Exercise 1: Part A*

One of the more common functions that you will want to use in a spreadsheet is the payment function. This function can determine payments for any length of time or amount and can be used to determine an amortization schedule, as shown in this exercise. Since these schedules tend to be rather long, it is very helpful to use the Freeze Titles and/or the Split screen options when you are working on them. Be sure to read the *Hints* for the exercise on the next page.

➤ *Exercise Scenario*

You have decided to purchase a new automobile and have decided on a model that will require you to finance $10,000. Before you go shopping, you want to know what your monthly payment on this loan will be, and you would like to see what the repayment or amortization schedule of the loan will look like. Finally, you want to see the total sum of all the payments you will make. Assume that you can finance the car for 48 months at a rate of 9.00 percent per year.

To develop a solution, first create a spreadsheet like the one shown in Figure 9.19.

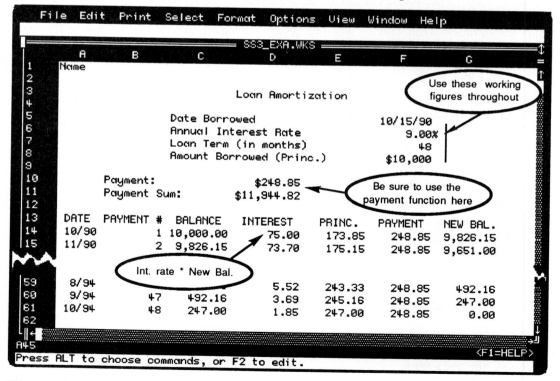

Figure 9.19: Spreadsheet Exercise 1

➢ *Hints for Exercise 1:*

Set up the spreadsheet by first making the DATE column 6 characters wide and all of the other columns equal to 14 characters wide. Right align all the labels in row 13. For simplicity, assume that payments are due every 31 days from the date borrowed and use the Date format option to format dates in the date column.

This spreadsheet makes extensive use of the working figures so DO NOT just type in all the values in row 13 and 14. Rather, you should reference the working figures and use formulas to develop rows 13 and 14. Be sure to use the Payment function in cell D10 (reference the working figures in F6 through F8); if you do not use this function, you will not end up with a zero balance at the end of the spreadsheet. Also, develop your formulas carefully (you will need to use absolute references) and then use the Fill commands to copy them throughout the spreadsheet. Pay special attention to absolute referencing (you will need to use it). Remember that the interest paid each month is charged on the New balance amount, so as the balance is reduced, the interest will decline. Finally, try the **Split screen** option or **Freeze Titles** when examining the spreadsheet to answer questions, as these functions will save time.

All of row 15 in Figure 9.19 was developed with formulas, and once you have this, you are ready to use the Fill command. You should end up with 61 rows in your spreadsheet.

When you are done, save the spreadsheet as **HOP-SS91**. Then change the print font to a size that will let you print on one page, such as Pica, size 8, and print the spreadsheet, including the row and column labels. Next, print the formulas for the spreadsheet, again including the row and column labels.

➢ *Exercise 1: Part B*

You have just decided that you would really like a nicer car, and so you are now planning to borrow $14,000 for 48 months. You have also learned that the interest rate will be 21 percent per year. Change your spreadsheet to accommodate these new figures, type PART B after your name, and then print out the spreadsheet.

NOTE: If you have used the formulas correctly, all you will need to change are the two new figures.

➢ *Exercise 1: Part C*

A friend has asked you to develop an amortization table for her townhouse purchase. She will have to borrow $110,000 at an interest rate that is dependent on the length of the loan and wants you to determine her **monthly** payment if she borrows the money for various periods of time. Each different loan period carries with it a different interest rate with the appropriate rate and loan duration shown below. Develop a vertical table lookup in cells H3:I7 to incorporate this information.

She also wants to find out the total interest charge amount for each of these payment options; do this by subtracting the amount borrowed from the Payment sum. Show this new total in cell G11 and label it "INTEREST PAID". Use the amortization schedule you have developed to answer these questions. Print out the entire spreadsheet for the 10 year option and the first page for the 20 and 30 year options.

INTEREST RATE TABLE:

TIME	RATE (per year)
10 years	9.00%
15 years	9.50%
20 years	10.00%
25 years	10.25%
30 years	10.50%

10

Creating and Using Charts

This chapter will introduce you to the powerful graphing tools offered in Microsoft Works. Graphing or charting tools, as they are called in Works, allow you to represent complex data easily so that it can be quickly understood. Further, charts allow you to make very professional and powerful presentations that allow your audience to focus quickly on the items you are stressing. The old saying "a picture is worth a thousand words" certainly holds true when data is presented in a chart.

➢ Creating Charts

The Works software package refers to spreadsheet graphs as **charts**, a name that differs from some other spreadsheet programs. However, you will find that the method that Works uses to create and display charts is virtually the same as with other software. Works also offers the powerful advantage of supporting nine different types of charts and allows you to specify many more minor variations within each of these graph types. Because there are so many different options available, one of the most important tasks when working with charts is to recognize which chart to use in a given situation. Once you choose the basic type, you can enhance the chart with the addition of special titles, print fonts, and the like.

Chart Concepts

Charts are created from selected data within a spreadsheet. The actual chart exists only when it is displayed on the screen or printed. This technique not only uses less of the computer's memory but also allows you to change the data in the spreadsheet and then redraw it without having to define it from scratch. Finally, you should know that charts are automatically saved when the spreadsheet the charts are based on is saved.

➤ **Chart Terminology**

There are a number of special components that should be defined before a chart can be developed. These components, shown in Figure 10.1, allow you to customize a particular chart to fit your needs.

Figure 10.1

A typical chart showing the titles, scales, and data series. You have many options on how these features are used in the chart.

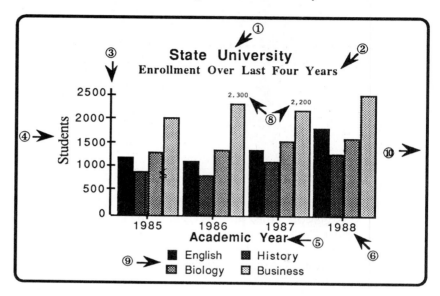

➤ **Chart Component Descriptions**

①　　　**Chart Title:** Appearing on the top line of text on the chart, this serves as the main chart title. Only one main title line per chart is allowed.

②　　　**Chart Subtitle:** The subtitle is printed on the second line of the graph directly below the title. It is normally used to further describe the chart.

③　　　**Scale:** The scale is printed along the left vertical axis of the chart and is used to indicate the assigned value for each position in the chart. The values in the scale will be set automatically by the Works program, but you can assign specific values if you want.

④　　　**Y-Axis Title:** Printing along the Y or vertical axis, this title usually describes the unit of measure for the Y-axis.

⑤　　　**X-Axis Title:** This title is printed below the chart along the horizontal or X-axis and is used to describe the data that is printed along this axis.

⑥　　　**X-Axis Labels:** Labels appear at the bottom of the graph along the X-axis and are used to identify the bars portrayed in the graph. There will be one label for each type of bar.

⑦　　　**1st Data Series:** Each bar in the chart represents one data series, or group of cells, in the spreadsheet. Separate data series are represented by a different shades on the graph; the Works program can support up to six data series in any given chart. Figure 10.1 shows that there are four data series being considered.

⑧   **Data Labels:** Data labels are labels or values that can be printed above the bars in bar graphs and with the data points on line graphs. In Figure 10.1, the data labels are used to specify the actual value of a specific data series.

⑨   **Legend:** The legend is displayed at the bottom of the chart and is used to help identify the data that is represented by each bar. The Legend Box is the same shade as the bar it represents.

⑩   **Chart Border:** The chart border is a box around the chart. This can be set on or off using an option.

Y-axis: This is the vertical axis of the chart and always runs from the top to the bottom of the chart.

X-axis: The horizontal axis of the chart always runs left to right across the chart.

Types of Charts

Works offers a wide variety of chart formats and, as you have seen, allows you to customize these in a variety of ways. Because there are many options, it is important for you to understand that some charts will convey different kinds of data better than others. Therefore, it is a good idea to take a few moments to study the following chart types so that you will be able to choose the appropriate chart to best display your data.

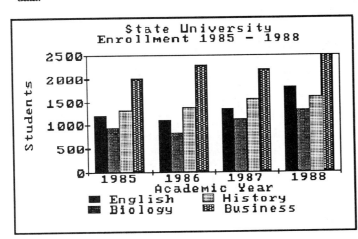

Bar Chart: This example of a bar chart includes four data series, each of which is shown as a bar filled with a different pattern. Data is represented through the use of vertical bars, with each number in the spreadsheet represented by a separate bar. Bar charts are normally used when the data that is being compared is distinct in nature, such as the population in different cities, and the number of majors in a school.

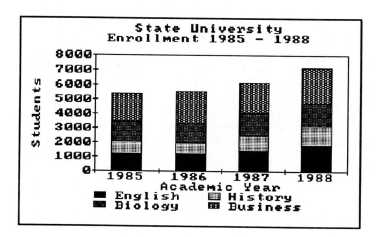

Stacked Bar: *The stacked bar graph stacks bars on top of each other to represent the combined total of a category, which in this case is student enrollment for a given year. Each bar consists of one number from the different series of data. The stacked bar is best used when you are trying to compare entire categories of data.*

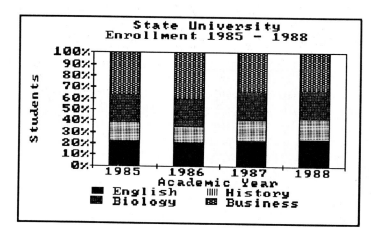

100% Bar: *While this chart looks much like the stacked bar chart, it differs in that the individual data series are charted as a percentage of the whole. Each value in the series is assigned a percent of the bar, and the value is charted as its relative contribution to the total of the bar. Use this chart when you want to compare different categories with all the data.*

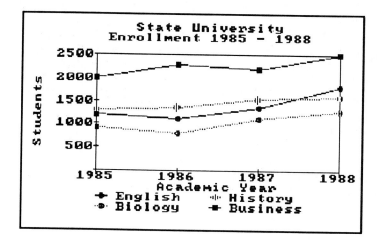

Line Chart: *A line chart displays data in a line format instead of a bar format and is very useful in charting trends in the data. Each line on the chart represents one category, and each point on the chart represents one event or value from a data series. This chart is used to compare changes over time for each set of data.*

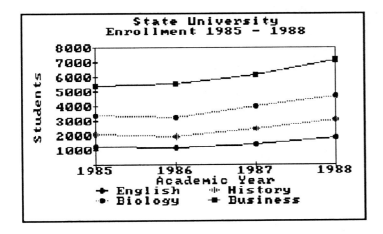

Area Line: *Although the area chart appears to look the same as the line chart, it actually measures and plots each line based on the line below it rather than the X-axis. This is similar to the 100% bar in that it shows the contribution of each category to the sum total. This chart can be used to show the contribution each data set makes to the data as a whole.*

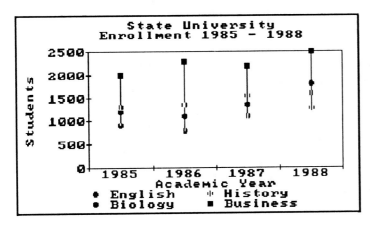

Hi-Lo-Close: *This chart emphasizes the position of a point between two extremes. Designed to display information like that used in the stock markets, it can also be used to represent the High, Low, and current value if items of interest.*

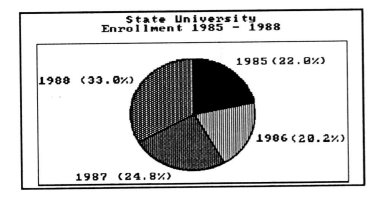

Pie Chart: *A pie chart represents the numbers in a single series as separate slices in a pie. Pie charts are commonly used to show the contribution of each element in a series to the whole and can have one section emphasized or "exploded" for clarity.*

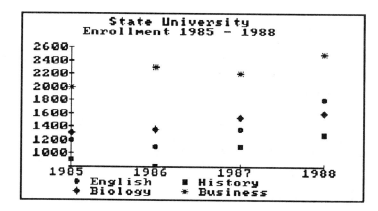

X-Y Charts: *Often called scatter diagrams, X-Y charts use pairs of numbers to plot points along the X and Y axes as coordinates. Data can be hard to understand when using this chart type, so use it carefully.*

Creating a Chart

To create a chart, the data must first be stored in an active spreadsheet. The X-axis labels are also stored in the spreadsheet (usually as titles), as are the legends. This concept can be seen in Figure 10.2; a spreadsheet used to store college enrollment levels for the years 1985 through 1988. Data is available for the departments of English, History, Biology, and Business.

Column A in Figure 10.2 contains the department names that will be used as the legends in the chart, while row 1 contains the year titles that will become the chart's X-axis labels. Each column contains data for that year and represents one *category* of data. Each row, on the other hand, will represent one series of data such as the enrollment for the Department of English. It is also possible to store the actual chart titles in the spreadsheet, although it is often easier to enter the titles using the Chart Titles option.

Figure 10.2

This is the spreadsheet data that was used to create all of the earlier charts.

File Print Data Format Options View Window Help

SHEET1.WKS

	A	B	C	D	E	F
1		1985	1986	1987	1988	
2	English	1200	1100	1350	1800	
3	History	900	800	1100	1275	
4	Biology	1300	1350	1540	1600	
5	Business	2000	2300	2200	2500	
6						
7						

After the data is entered into the spreadsheet, the chart can be created. Perhaps the fastest and easiest way to create the new chart is to select or highlight the desired data in the spreadsheet before entering the Chart module. Once the data is selected as a block and the New Chart option is selected, Works will automatically assign the Y-series data based on the shape of the blocked data.

➢ *Creating a Chart with More Rows than Columns* .

Before you select the Chart option, take a moment to examine the shape of the highlighted block of data. If the shape of the block is longer than it is wide (has more rows than columns), each *row* of data would become a different Y-series. For example, if you selected columns A, B, and C, and all five rows in the spreadsheet as a block shown in Figure 10.3, each row would become a Y-series and would be charted in a different color on a bar chart. This would cause a chart to be drawn that had four sets of bars; each set would then consist of two individual bars each. The data in the first cell of each Y-series would become the legend and the data in the left column, which is the department name, would become the X-axis labels.

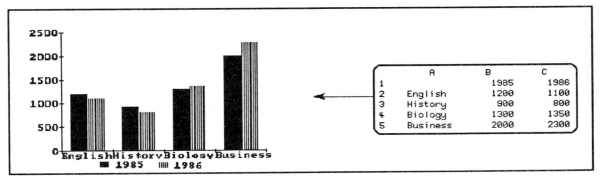

Figure 10.3 *Chart with rows forming the Y-Axis*

➢ *Creating a Chart with More Columns than Rows*

If the shape of the block selected in the spreadsheet is wider than it is long (more columns than rows), each *column* of data would become a different Y-series. In the spreadsheet shown in Figure 10.4, if rows 1, 2, 3, and 4 and columns A, B, C, D, and E were selected, each column becomes a Y-series and would be displayed in a different shade. This would provide for a graph consisting of four groups of three bars each. This time, each row, or department, would have a different shade. The first cell in each row would become the legend, and the first cell in each column would become the X-axis label.

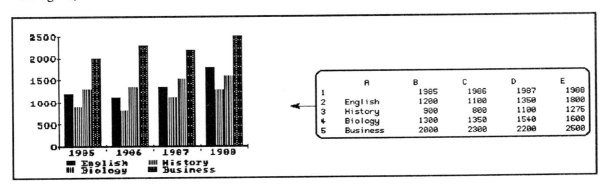

Figure 10.4 *Chart with columns as the Y-axis*

Drawing the Chart

Once the data to be included on the chart has been selected as a block, use the **New Chart** option from the **View** menu. This will cause the Works software to display the new chart and, after you press Esc to leave the displayed chart, will return you to the **Chart** module of the spreadsheet so that you may edit your new chart or create different charts. You can see that the chart module is active from the Works status line display as shown in Figure 10. 5.

Figure 10.5

The word Chart will appear on the status line in the Chart module.

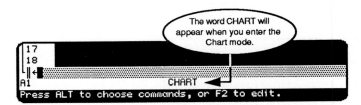

➢ *Viewing and Exiting the Chart*

After you press the Esc key to move to the **Chart** module, there will be no apparent change to the spreadsheet displayed, except that the menu bar now reflects charting options. The chart definition has been created according to your selection and is now identified as Chart1 in the **View** menu, as shown in Figure 10.6. You should note here that when the chart is displayed, you will not be able to access the menus or the spreadsheet to make changes.

Figure 10.6

The View menu is used to select the chart that you want to use. Choose Spreadsheet to exit the Chart module.

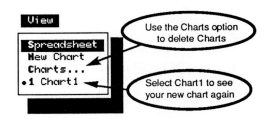

Changing the Chart Type

Frequently, you will want to view the chart using different chart types to determine which type seems most appropriate. This can be done through the options displayed on the **Format** menu shown in Figure 10.7. This menu displays each type of chart that is available. To choose a different type than the default bar chart, just move the highlight to the type of chart you want to use and press the Enter key. To see the new chart format, pull down the View menu and select the chart number (for example, **1** for Chart 1), and the chart will be displayed using its new format.

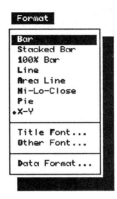

Figure 10.7

The options in the
Format menu allow you to
change the chart currently
in use.

Creating Chart Titles

To create titles for the new chart, select the **Titles** option from the **Data** menu shown in Figure 10.8. Each of the titles listed on the menu has an entry area that is contained on the Title dialog box, also shown in Figure 10.8.

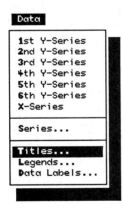

Figure 10.8

Titles are entered in the
Title dialog box which
appears after the Titles
option is selected.

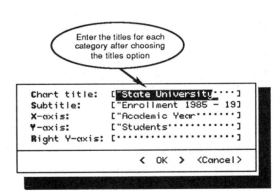

Titles can be entered in either of two ways:

1. You can enter the chart titles directly into the Title dialog box by using the **Tab** key to move the cursor to the title area desired, and then entering the title. Press the Tab key again to move to the next title, enter it, and so forth. Press the Enter key when all titles are entered. Titles can also be edited using the same process.

2. If the title you want to use is stored in a cell of the spreadsheet, you can enter the cell coordinate containing the title in the dialog area. If these coordinates were already defined, the cell coordinates will appear in the dialog area.

Specifying Legends

Chart legends allow you to identify important areas of the chart and can be altered as the need arises. For example, if you have created a chart by selecting and blocking data from the spreadsheet, the legends initially selected may need to be edited to provide further detail. To enter or change the legend data, select the **Legends** option from the **Data** menu. To change a legend, highlight the appropriate Y-series you want to change and then enter the new legend or cell coordinate. NOTE: To be sure that the new legend will be included in your chart, select the **Done** option in the Legends dialog box when you are finished. The Legends dialog box is shown in Figure 10.9.

Figure 10.9

Legends, which help describe the data shown in the chart, are entered in the Legends dialog box.

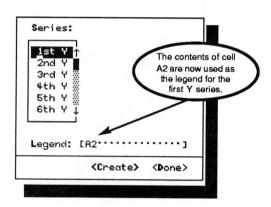

Creating and Deleting Data Labels

Data labels are values or text that is displayed above the bars on bar charts and next to the data points on line charts. When a chart is created, data labels are not included as a default value and therefore are not defined. To use the Data Labels option, select the cells in the spreadsheet that contain the values for the labels. Once these cells have been selected as a block, pull down the **Data** menu and select the **Data Labels** options shown in Figure 10.10. Next, identify the data series to be identified by the labels, and finally, select **Create** to finish creating the labels. Use the Done option after all labels have been assigned.

You can also delete existing data labels by using the Delete option after highlighting the label to be removed. The **Go To** option in the dialog box will cancel the operation, and your cursor will be placed on the data labels for the data series you have selected.

Figure 10.10

Data labels can help describe the Y-series in the chart.

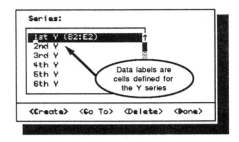

Changing the Default Data Format

Microsoft Works assigns a default color, or pattern, for each Y-series of data. This default can be changed to a wide variety of shades by using the **Data Format** option, shown in Figure 10.11, which is accessed through the **Format** menu.

Figure 10.11

*Use the **Data Format** option box to select how you want the colors or patterns in the chart to appear.*

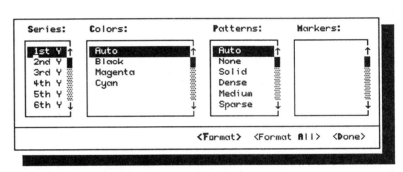

This dialog box consists of four distinct option boxes, with the first box titled as Series. This specification identifies which of the six possible (you might be using fewer than six) data series you want to change. Before you can change the chart colors or other attributes in the other areas of the Data Format box, you must highlight a data series in this series box. Once a data series has been selected, use the Tab key to move to the **Color** option box which allows you to specify the color for the highlighted series (NOTE: This will only work if you are using a color monitor).

The third option box is the **Patterns** box. The Patterns option is used to change the default shade or pattern of the data series highlighted in the Series box. This option is especially useful when working with a bar graph, as there are many different patterns available to choose from for this graph type. Be sure to use the arrow keys to scroll down in the Patterns box to see more available patterns. To select a specific pattern, simply highlight the pattern.

The last option box in this dialog is the **Markers**. The available markers will only be displayed if you have some type of a **Line** or an **X-Y** chart selected.

When you have finished with the option selections, choose the **Format** button which will enter the changes for the selected series. Continue this process until all series have been changed. When you have finished with the changes to all of the series, select the **Done** option.

Changing the Data for the Y-series

You will likely encounter situations in which you want to change the data coordinates for one or more of the six Y-series data groups. To change these coordinates, first highlight the new cells for the data series as a block in the spreadsheet. Then, pull down the **Data** menu, highlight the correct data series from the menu, and press Enter. The new coordinates will then be assigned to the graph.

Setting Graph Options

The Works charting software allows for the inclusion of many different options that can really improve the appearance of your chart. These options are found under the **Options** menu shown in Figure 10.12.

Figure 10.12

The Options menu displays many chart options in addition to the standard Works options.

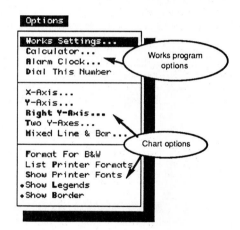

➤ *Setting X-and Y-Axis Grid Lines and Options*

The first option is called the **X-Axis** option, which allows you to specify that vertical **Grid Lines** be included in the chart. These vertical lines help to align points from the X-axis vertically onto the chart. This option also allows you to specify the frequency of the Grid Lines. An entry of a 1 prints a grid line for each bar grouping; 2 prints a grid line every second bar group; 3 every third, etc. This option box is illustrated in Figure 10.13.

The **Y-Axis** option allows you to specify the scaling of the Y-axis in place of the Works automatic scaling. You can specify the starting (minimum) point for the scale, the ending (maximum) point, and the interval for the scale. This menu, shown in Figure 10.13, also allows you to specify horizontal grid lines.

Figure 10.13

X-axis options will provide features for the X or horizontal axis of the chart. The Y-axis options will give options from the Y or vertical axis.

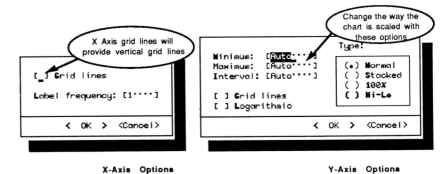

The other options, Right Y-Axis and Two Y-Axis, are not commonly used. For information on these options, refer to the Microsoft Works manual or the online help facility.

The **Mixed Line and Bar** option can be used to combine a bar and line chart into one chart, as shown in Figure 10.14. The Dialog box that is presented when the Mixed chart option is chosen, allows you to specify which Y-series will be shown in the line format and which will use the bar format. You should exercise some restraint when using this option, since too much information on a chart can easily become confusing.

Figure 10.14

You can select which data series will appear as a line chart and which will show as a bar chart.

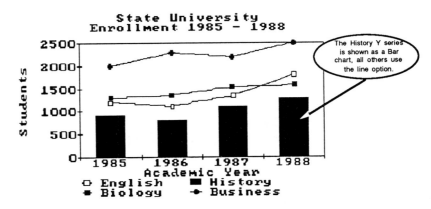

The final three options in the Options menu can be quite useful and act as toggles in that the option turns on when selected the first time and off when selected again.

Show Print Fonts:	This option will display any of the chart titles that have been assigned special print fonts and is helpful in editing your chart before it is printed.
Show Legends:	This option is to toggle the display of the legends on and off and allows you to turn off the legends without having to delete each one.
Show Border:	This option will draw a box around the graph if the option is turned on.

Setting Printer Fonts

The Works chart module supports many special print fonts. These fonts allow you to set up customized titles in your charts and are activated through the selection of options from the **Format** menu. There are two options that can be used to change the fonts when working with the chart module: the **Title Font** and the **Other Font** options, as seen in Figure 10.15.

The Title font is used to set the font for the chart title only, while the Other Font option is used to set the font for all other titles, legends, and labels. All of the titles, legends, and labels in a chart except the main chart title must use the same font.

Figure 10.15

The fonts for text shown on the charts can be changed using the Format Font options.

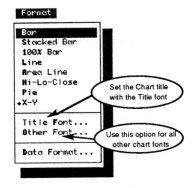

Printing the Chart

Printing charts usually takes longer than other print tasks, because the printer is operating at maximum resolution (its best quality). This means that you will want to be sure that the chart is set up correctly before you try to print it. The first thing to check is the **Page Setup & Margins** option of the **Print** menu, which determines how big the chart will be through entries in the Height and Width option blanks. This option also determines the position of the chart on the page through the settings of the Top and Bottom Margin values. No matter what Height and Width you use, Microsoft Works will try to scale or adjust the size of the chart to fit within the specified area.

The other important option in this dialog box is the chart **Orientation**. This option specifies whether the chart will be printed normally, across the page, or sideways, down the page. The **Landscape** mode prints sideways, while the **Portrait** mode prints in the normal, horizontal fashion. Figure 10.16 shows the Layout dialog box.

Figure 10.16

When the chart is printed, the size and orientation are determined by the entries in the Page Size and Margins dialog box found under the Print menu.

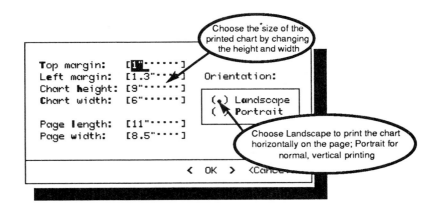

Naming, Saving, and Deleting Charts

Each chart is automatically assigned a default chart name as it is created. These names will be **Chart1, Chart2, Chart3,** etc. When you want to work with a different, existing chart, pull down the **View** menu, as seen in Figure 10.17, where you will see a list of all the charts you have defined for the spreadsheet. To make a chart **active,** highlight the chart's name on the View menu and press Enter.

To perform other operations on the chart, select **Charts** from the **Chart** menu to activate the Chart dialog box, as illustrated in Figure 10.17. This dialog box lists your charts and allows you to **Rename** or **Delete** a chart. This menu also allows you to **Copy** a chart. The Copy is a good way to duplicate the chart description and then change one feature to have two charts that are only slightly different.

Saving a chart is easy, as it is done automatically for you when the spreadsheet is saved. To work with a chart after it has been saved, load the spreadsheet and then enter the chart module by selecting the chart from the View menu.

Figure 10.17

Activate an existing chart from the View menu or choose the Charts option to edit existing chart names or to delete and copy charts.

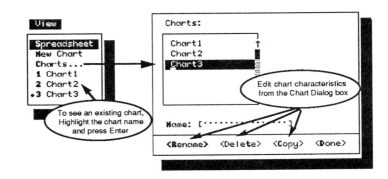

Conclusion

Presenting spreadsheet data in the form of charts is a powerful method of conveying information. As is the case with many things, the more you use the charting facilities, the better you will become at it. Therefore, feel free to experiment with the many different chart descriptions and options.

Chapter 10 Self Test

1.   Define the following Chart terms:

    X-axis

    Y-axis

    Scale

    Legend

    X-axis Label

    Data Labels

    Data Series

2.   List two ways to enter chart titles.

3.   How do you create a **legend** for a data series?

4.   What is a **grid line**? How do you specify that you want Grid Lines displayed?

5.   What do each of the following chart options do?

    a.   Show Printer Fonts:

    b.   Show Legends:

6.   How do you change the size of the printed graph?

7.   What is the difference between **Landscape** and **Portrait** printing?

8.   How do you change title fonts?

9.   How do you manually specify your Y-axis scale?

10.   How do you delete a chart?

Chapter 10 Tutorial

This tutorial allows you to practice charting techniques by creating several graphs based on data in an existing spreadsheet named TUT-CHRT.WKS. Begin the tutorial by starting Microsoft Works and opening this file.

❑   **Start Microsoft Works.**

❑   **Open Spreadsheet TUT-CHRT.WKS.**

This should provide you with the spreadsheet shown in Figure 10.18. Pay special attention to the years located in row 1 and notice that these years are used as labels, not as simple numeric entries.

Figure 10.18

The chart tutorial spreadsheet.

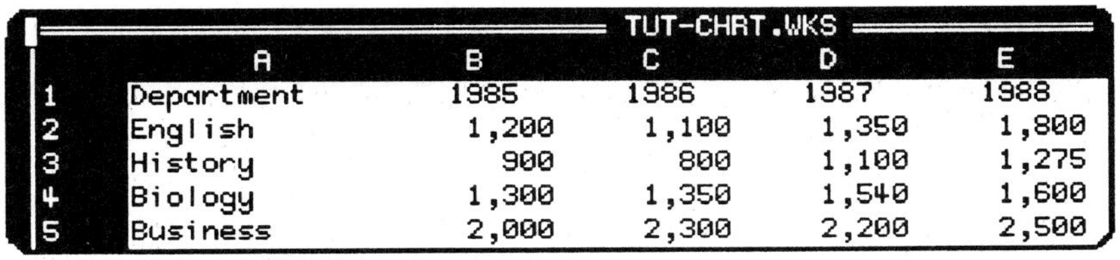

	A	B	C	D	E
				TUT-CHRT.WKS	
1	Department	1985	1986	1987	1988
2	English	1,200	1,100	1,350	1,800
3	History	900	800	1,100	1,275
4	Biology	1,300	1,350	1,540	1,600
5	Business	2,000	2,300	2,200	2,500

Creating the Chart

You can use the quick charting approach to create the first chart and see how fast and easy chart development can be. The Quick chart approach requires that you define the data to be charted as a block. You can also define the **Legends** and **X-axis Labels** at the same time if you want, a process described earlier in this chapter. For now, select the entire spreadsheet, rows 1 through 5 and cells A through E, as a block. This will define the data for the chart. Once you have selected the data, pull down the **View** menu and select **New Chart**.

❑   **Select the entire spreadsheet as a block.**

❑   **Select New Chart from the View menu.**

The Works Charting module will automatically define the new chart you have just created as **Chart1**, and it will be displayed as shown in Figure 10.19.

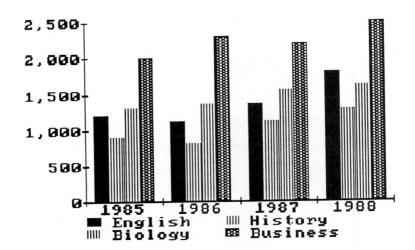

Figure 10.19

This is the chart that should be displayed after highlighting the tutorial spreadsheet as a block and choosing the New Chart option from the View menu.

Adding Titles to the Chart

Although your new chart does a good job of comparing data, it is difficult to understand, since no titles are included. To add titles to the chart, first press the Esc key to exit the chart display and then use the **Titles** option from the **Data** menu to add the titles. You will see in the Title dialog box shown in Figure 10.20, that five kinds of titles can be used; in this exercise, you will use the first four with the last title type, the **Right X-axis** title, being used for other types of charts.

Figure 10.20

The Title dialog box is used to add titles to the chart.

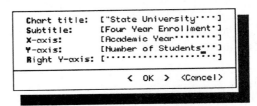

❑   **Press Esc to leave the chart display.**

❑   **Pull down the DATA menu and select the Titles Option.**

❑   **Enter the following titles and remember to use the TAB key to move from one title entry to the next.**

    Chart Title: **State University**

    Subtitle: **Four Year Enrollment**

    X-axis: **Academic Year**

    Y-axis: **Number of Students**

❑   **Press Enter.**

❑   **View the graph by selecting Chart1 from the View menu.**

The chart should now look like the one shown in Figure 10.21. Notice the new titles that are now a part of your chart. These titles can be enhanced, and you will have the opportunity to do so shortly. If you made a mistake or want to change the titles, you can use the **Titles** dialog to edit any or all of the titles.

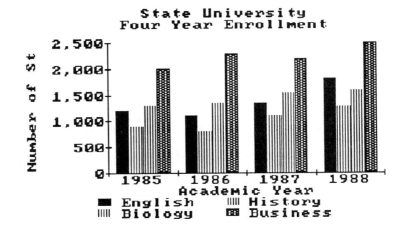

Figure 10.21

This is how your chart should look after the titles are added. Do not worry that the Y-axis title, Number of Students, has been truncated. You will fix this soon by changing the title font.

Special Note: Depending on your computer setup, it is likely that the Y-axis title *Number of Students* was truncated, and future graphs will show this condition. This *is not* a problem, and you will learn how to adjust this shortly. For now, just ignore this.

Adding Grid Lines

Grid lines help you locate a point on the chart and can be added in both the horizontal and vertical axis. Since you are working with a bar chart, horizontal grid lines would help align a point on a bar with a point on the scale. To set the horizontal grid lines on, use the **Y-axis** options under the **Options** menu. Pull down this menu and select **Grid Lines** by pressing the Tab key to advance to that dialog entry and pressing the space bar. An **X** should appear in the dialog box. Now, add grid lines to your chart as follows:

❑ **Press Esc to cancel the chart display.**

❑ **Select Y-axis from the Options menu.**

❑ **Select Grid Lines from the dialog boxes.**

❑ **Press Enter.**

❑ **View the chart.**

Your chart should now look like Figure 10.22.

Figure 10.22

The horizontal grid lines shown here are set by using the Y-axis options from the Options menu.

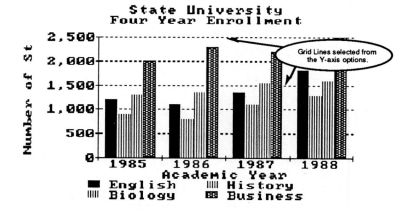

If you want to turn the grid lines off, repeat this same procedure and select the grid option again. This will remove the X in the option box and remove the lines. To create vertical grid lines, choose the **X-axis** option also located under the Options menu.

Setting Data Labels

Data labels, in the case of a bar graph, appear over each bar of a data series. These data labels can be anything that exists in your spreadsheet. In our case, assume that we are interested in knowing exactly what the enrollments are for the **English** department; we will use data labels to quickly display this.

Before labels can be assigned, you will have to cancel the block that you initially selected to draw the graph by pressing the **Esc** key to exit any chart currently displayed and then pressing the Esc key again to cancel the block of highlighted cells in the spreadsheet. Then, to set up the data labels, you will need to highlight a block of cells that contain the labels. For this example, the data for the English Department should be selected as a block which will consist of cells B2 through E2. Finally, pull down the **Data** menu and select **Data Labels**. Since English is charted as the **1st** data series, highlight that series and press Enter. Then view the graph.

- ❏ Press Esc twice to cancel the chart display and the highlighted cells.
- ❏ Select cells B2 through E2 as a block.
- ❏ Select Data Labels from the Data menu.
- ❏ Select 1st Y as the Series.
- ❏ Press Enter.
- ❏ View the chart.

Changing the Bar Patterns

The patterns that are currently used for the bars are the default patterns and can be changed to some pattern you would prefer. These patterns can be changed using the **Data Format** option of the **Format** menu. Pull this menu down now.

❑   **Press Esc twice to cancel the chart display and block of cells.**

❑   **Pull down the Format menu and select the Data Format option.**

To change a bar pattern, highlight the data series you want to change first. Next, tab to the **Patterns** box and highlight the pattern you want to use in the chart. You should note here that there are quite a few patterns available, with many additional patterns available by scrolling down in the Patterns box.

To go ahead and change patterns, follow this complete set of directions.

❑   **Highlight the 1st Y-series.**

❑   **Tab to Patterns box.**

❑   **Scroll down and highlight the backslashes "\ \ ".**

❑   **Press Enter to format the series.**

❑   **Press the Down arrow key to highlight the 2nd Y-series.**

❑   **Set the 2nd Y-series to the "XX" pattern in the same manner as for the first Y-series.**

❑   **Press Enter.**

❑   **Select Done.**

❑   **View the chart.**

❑   **When you are done, press Esc to exit the chart.**

Setting Borders

A border is a box around the chart. This option is set on or off by selecting **Show Borders** from the **Options** menu. Try this option now.

❑   **Select Show Borders from the Options box.**

❑   **View the chart.**

❑   **After comparing it with Figure 10.23, press ESC to exit the chart.**

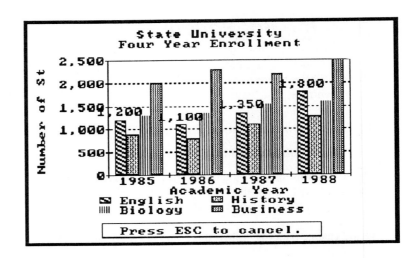

Figure 10.23

Your chart should now have data labels, different patterns for the first two Y-series, and a border. Do not worry if the labels are hard to read; this will be corrected when the chart fonts are altered.

Changing the Scale of the Chart

The scale is the numeric guide that runs along the left side or Y-axis of the chart. By default, Works automatically calculates this scale based on the data that is being charted, but there are times when this default scale is not appropriate. For instance, if you had numbers that ranged from 5,000 as the lowest to 5,500 as the highest, there would not be much difference in the bars using the default scale. You can change the scale to help show the difference more clearly.

To set the scale to something other than the default values, use the **Y-axis** option from the **Options** menu. This option dialog box provides three different points that must be set for the scale. The **Minimum** is the lowest point or bottom of the chart. The **Maximum** is the highest point or top of the chart, while the **Interval** is the difference between the numbers printed on the scale. To see how this can change the chart, adjust your chart to a Minimum value of 500, Maximum value of 2,500, and the increment to 400 using the following steps:

- ❏ Select Y-Axis from the Options menu.
- ❏ Set the Minimum to 500 and then press the Tab key.
- ❏ Set the Maximum to 2500 and Tab.
- ❏ Set the Interval to 400.
- ❏ Press Enter.
- ❏ View the chart.
- ❏ After viewing the chart, press Esc.

Changing Print Fonts

To change the print fonts for the titles of the chart, use the **Title** and **Other Fonts** options from the **Format** menu. The first of these options, the **Title Font**, is used to change the font of the Chart title only; while the **Other Fonts** option is used to alter all the other fonts in the chart. Since these font options are primarily used to print the chart, you must select the **Show Printer Fonts** option from the **Option menu** in order to display the new fonts on your screen.

NOTE: Due to the differences in some computer systems, not all fonts or font sizes may be available. Should a specified font not be available on your system, choose another font and a size that would approximate the size given in the tutorial.

- ❏ **Select Title Font from the Format menu.**

- ❏ **Select the Bold Modern B font.**

- ❏ **Select size 26.**

- ❏ **Press Enter.**

- ❏ **Select Other Fonts from the Format menu.**

- ❏ **Select the Modern B font.**

- ❏ **Select size 16.**

- ❏ **Press Enter.**

- ❏ **Select Show Printer Fonts from the Options menu.**

- ❏ **View the chart.**

- ❏ **Remember to press Esc to exit the chart display.**

Your chart should look like the one shown in Figure 10.24. Notice the **Y-axis** title, which had been truncated because there was not enough room in the Y-axis title area to display the entire title, is now visible. The data labels should now be easy to read as well.

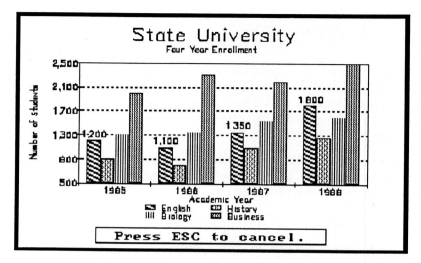

Figure 10.24

*The finished chart
showing title and other
fonts, border, and data
labels.*

Changing Chart Types

Once the data series has been defined as a block of cells and a New Chart created, other chart types can be quickly displayed with the same data specification. New chart types are selected by using the **Format** menu. Be sure to try several of the available types by selecting the chart type and then viewing it. You will also want to turn off the **Show Printer Fonts** before viewing the new charts.

❑   Select the Show Printer Fonts to turn the option off.

❑   Select the Stacked Bar chart from the Format menu.

❑   View the chart.

❑   Press Esc.

❑   Select the 100% Bar chart.

❑   View the chart.

❑   Press Esc.

❑   Select the Line chart.

❑   View the chart and then press Esc.

❑   Select the Area Line chart.

❑   View the chart and then press Esc.

❑   Select the Hi-Lo-Close chart.

❑   View the chart.

❑   Press Esc.

Creating a New Chart

Before you can display a chart, you must have at least one data series defined. For this example, you will create a pie chart using the 1985 data in the tutorial spreadsheet. Remember that to define the data for a data series, you need to select the desired data as a block and then select the data series option from the **Data** menu.

❏   **Select cells B2:B5.**

❏   **View the new chart using the New Chart option from the View menu.**

❏   **Press Esc.**

❏   **Select the Pie chart option from the Format menu.**

❏   **View the chart by pressing the number next to the most recent chart (in this case, it should be Chart2).**

Notice that in the pie chart, the pie slices are not identified by department. This identification can best be accomplished through the use of labels. Pie chart labels are defined as the X-axis labels, so you will need to select the X-axis cells that contain the labels as a block and then select **X Series** from the **Data** menu. Do this now and then view the chart.

❏   **Press Esc to return to the spreadsheet.**

❏   **Select cells A2 through A5.**

❏   **Select X Series from the Data menu.**

❏   **View the chart and then press Esc to move back to the spreadsheet.**

Now, further enhance the pie chart by adding the following titles:

❏   **Open the Titles dialog box from the Data menu.**

❏   **Enter Chart Title: Department Enrollments (Don't be alarmed when you see the word *Department* scroll past the title opening; it will still be there).**

❏   **Enter the Subtitle: (Place your name here) and press Enter.**

❏   **Open the Title Font dialog box from the Format menu.**

❏   **Set the Title Font to Decor A, Size 26, and press Enter.**

❏   **Again using the Format menu, set the Other Font option to Roman B, Size 22 and press Enter.**

❏   **Select Show Printer Fonts on from the Options menu.**

❏   **Set Show Border from the Options menu.**

❏   **View the chart.**

❏   **Press Esc after viewing.**

➤ *Exploding a Pie Slice*

You will often encounter a situation in which you would like to draw attention to a particular segment of the graph. This can be done by "exploding" a piece of the pie chart, which causes a piece of the pie to be separated from the remaining chart.

Assume that you want to explode the **Business** pie slice. This is done by selecting the **Data Format** option from the **Format** menu. When using the dialog box, select the slice you want to explode (count down from the first piece, English) and set the **Exploded** option on by tabbing down to the option and pressing the space bar.

❏   **Select Data Format from the Format menu.**

❏   **Highlight slice number 4, which represents the Business spreadsheet entry.**

❏   **Tab to the Exploded option.**

❏   **Press the space bar to set the option on.**

❏   **Press Enter.**

❏   **Tab so that the Done option is highlighted and press Enter.**

❏   **View the chart.**

Your chart should look much like Figure 10.25.

Figure 10.25

This is what the completed pie chart should look like.

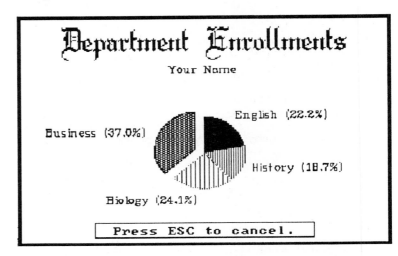

Printing the Chart

When you decide to print a particular chart, you must first be sure that it is assigned as the active chart under the **View** menu. Currently, you should have two charts assigned to your spreadsheet, with the pie chart being identified as the active chart. To print the original Bar chart, which is labeled Chart1, you must make it your active chart by activating the **View** menu and selecting Chart1. This will cause the bar chart, identified as Chart1, to appear. If you find that you left the chart as a **Hi-Lo-Close** chart, use the Format menu to set it back to a **Bar** chart.

❑   **Press Esc to exit the previous chart.**

❑   **Select Chart1 from the View menu.**

Next, pull down the **Page Setup & Margins** dialog box shown in Figure 10.26 from the **Print** menu. This menu determines where on the sheet the chart will print and how big the chart will be. Enter these settings for printing the chart:

❑   **Pull down the Layout options menu and set:**

> Top margin: 2.5"
>
> Left Margin: 1"
>
> Chart Height: 7"
>
> Chart Width: 5"
>
> Orientation: Landscape

❑   **Press Enter**

Figure 10.26

Position and size the chart using the Page Setup & Margins dialog box.

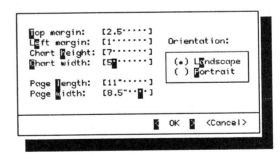

Once you have entered the options as shown, it is time to print the chart. To print the chart, just pull down the **Print** menu, select **Print,** and press Enter when you see the **Print** dialog box.

❑   **Pull down the Print options from the Print menu.**

❑   **Press Enter.**

Once you have printed the Bar chart, select the Pie chart, **Chart2**, and print this chart using the Portrait orientation.

Finishing the Tutorial

Once you have printed both of the charts, exit the **Chart** module by selecting **Spreadsheet** from the **View** menu. This will return you to the spreadsheet screen. You should now **Save** your spreadsheet to your disk. Remember that when the spreadsheet is saved, your chart definitions are automatically saved as well. Now **Exit** Works and turn your machine off.

Hands on Practice

In this exercise, you will be using the spreadsheet called HOP-CRT1.WKS. Using this spreadsheet, complete the following exercises. Be sure to include legends, chart title that shows the problem number, a subtitle with your name, and both X-and Y-axis titles for each chart. Print each chart.

A.   Create a bar chart that groups yearly salaries together by job title. Years should be printed along the X-axis, and job titles should be in the legend. Show data labels on this chart and use horizontal grid lines.

B.   Create a 100 percent bar using the same requirements as chart A.. Do not use data labels on this chart. Use a font of *Italic Roman B*-Size 26 for the chart title and a font of *Italic Modern C*-Size 15 for the other fonts.

C.   Create a stacked bar chart that stacks the job title salaries on top of each other. There should be one bar for each year in the spreadsheet. Use data labels and horizontal grid lines on this chart.

D.   Create a line chart that plots only the Database Admin., Security Admin., and Systems Analyst salaries. Years should be on the horizontal axis. Set the scale for a Minimum of 30,000, a Maximum of 70,000, and Interval to 5,000.

E.   Create an area line chart using the data listed in chart C. Scale your Y-axis with a Minimum of 30,000, Maximum of 170,000, and an Interval of 20,000. Use Y axis grid lines.

F.   Create an exploded pie chart that shows the salaries for Programmers. Explode the pie slice for 1988. Use the years as your X-axis data and use a border. Print this chart as a portrait.

G.   Create a Mixed Line & Bar chart. Use the same requirements a chart A above for your bars. Now create an average row for salary averages by year in your spreadsheet. Use this as your 5th data series. Chart this series as a Line in your Mixed Line & Bar chart. Print data labels on this series. Use a Title Font of *Decor A*-size 26, and Other Fonts of Modern B-size 12.

11

Introduction to Database

In this chapter, you will be introduced to the database management module of Microsoft Works. You will learn how to design the database and how to enter, delete, and modify data in the database. You will also learn how to protect your data from being edited, sort database records, and print the records in your database.

Database Concepts

Microsoft Works does not support the principles of a true database. In a true database, you can form relationships between records in multiple files. The database management module of Works is more like a file management system. These types of systems allow you to create, maintain, and organize only one file at a time. They do not allow relationships between files. However, to remain compatible with the terminology used by the Microsoft Corporation, we will use the term *database*.

A database is a structured, organized collection of information. The database management module allows you to create the database, sort the database records, generate queries, reports, and labels, and perform several other operations that help you maintain both the structure of, and the information in, the database.

➢ Records, Cells, and Fields

Databases are organized like spreadsheets. Each database is made up of a number of *rows* or *records*. A *record* is a group of information that is used to describe one particular entity. For example, all the information about one student would be a record. Each student would have his or her own record in the database. You can have a maximum of 4,096 records in a Works database.

Each record is made up of a number of *cells*. A cell is an area that stores one piece of information used to describe a particular entity. For example, the *social security number* of *Jake Jones* would be stored in a single cell. Likewise, the name *Jake Jones* might be stored in a single cell. This is similar to the concept of a cell in a spreadsheet. You can have a maximum of 256 cells in each database record.

A *field* is a group of cells that contain the same type of information and are referenced by the same *field name*. For example, all social security numbers would be stored in the social security number field. In a spreadsheet, this concept was called a column. There is one major difference between the spreadsheet column and the database field. In the database, all cells in a field must contain the same type of information and have the same format. This is not true in a spreadsheet. For example, in a database, if a column contains a student name, then each record is considered to contain a student name in that field, and the format must be the same for each student's name.

These concepts of records, cells, and fields are shown in Figure 11.1.

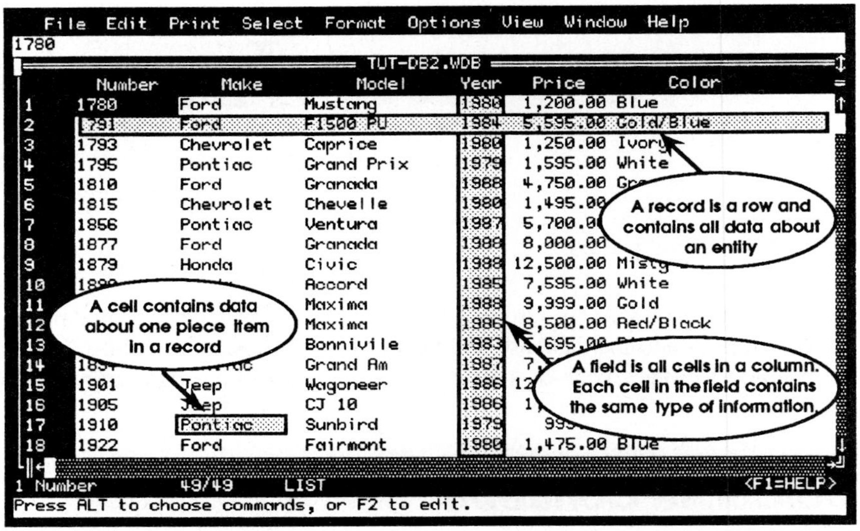

Figure 11.1

In a database, a cell contains a single piece of information, such as the make of a particular auto. A record contains all information about an entity, such as all information about a particular auto. A field contains the same type of data about all items, such as the production year of each automobile.

Database Phases

There are several phases that are used in the database module. These phases include *Design, View, Query,* and *Report.*

➤ Design Phase

The first phase of the database module is the *Design phase*. This phase allows you to define the fields that will be in each of the database records. Each field is named, and its format and width are defined. During this phase, you can create a form that can be used to enter or view the data.

➤ Entry and View Phase

This phase lets you enter, modify, and view the data in your database. The data can be viewed in either a *Form* format or a *List* format. These formats are shown in Figure 11.2. The List format will show as many records as the screen can hold at one time. The records are shown as rows and columns. In this view, you may not be able to view the entire record at one time. If the record is too long to fit on one line of the screen some of the data may be off the screen. You can scroll to the left or right to see the other fields in the record.

You can also view the database in Form view. This view will show only one record at a time using a form that you can create. This form can be up to eight pages (screens) long. You would use this view when you

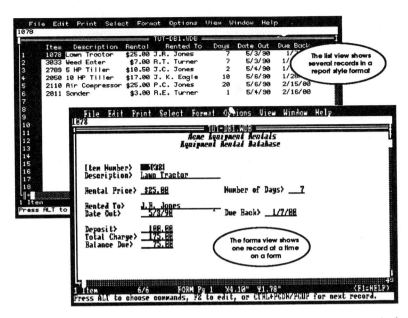

Figure 11.2

*The database has two different
views. The **List** view will show
several records in a report
style format. The **Form** view
shows one record at a time on
a form. You can use a default
form or you can design your
own form (see Chapter 12).
You can also style the data and
use different printer fonts.*

want to see the entire record at once. Since you can design the form any way you want to, you can design
this form to look like the printed form you may be using to enter the data.

➤ Query Phase

The query phase will let you specify which records you want to view or print. You do this by entering
conditions or sample data in certain fields. Works will then display only those records that contain data
that meets the conditions you have specified.

➤ Report Phase

This phase lets you define reports needed from the database. You can specify which fields you want on the
report, how you want the report sorted, and different totals that you may want based on three different
control levels, and you can print certain statistics about your data. Once a report is defined, it is stored with
the database so that it can be used at any time in the future.

Creating the Database

To create a database, you select *Create new file* from the **File** menu. Next you select *New Database* from
the application option box. This approach is shown in Figure 11.3.

Designing the Database

When you design a database, you specify the characteristics of each field or item of data you need to keep
for each record. By characteristics, we mean such things as the field's name, format, width, and origin.
Before you start the design of the database in Works, you should lay out all the data you think you will
need for each item. This preparation beforehand will save you a lot of time correcting and modifying a

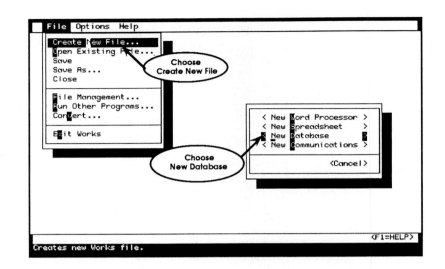

Figure 11.3

*To create a new database, choose the **Create new file** option from the **File** menu. When the application option box appears, choose New Database.*

database that has been designed poorly. If the data you need is not in the database, you will need to insert new fields and enter the new data for each record you have stored.

There are two different types of fields you will want to create. The first type of field is known as a *source* field. The data for this field will be entered from the keyboard. We say this type of field has its origin from outside the database. The second type of field is a *calculated* field. This field is calculated from data that is already in the database. Therefore, we say this data has its origin from within the database.

There are two ways to design a Works database. The first way uses the *Form* view. This is the view you are placed in when you first enter Microsoft Works to create a new database. Using this approach, you design the database by creating a *form* that can be used to enter the data into your database.

The second approach is to use the *List* view. This approach is somewhat easier and more natural to a new user. In this chapter, we will introduce you to creating the database from the *List* view.

No matter which view you create the database in, both views will be available to you. If you create the database in *Form* view, Works creates a *default List* view. If you create the database in *List* view, Works creates a *default Form* view for you.

Creating a Database Using List View

To create a database in *List* view, you must first change from *Form* view. To do this, you choose the *List* option from the **View** menu. This will provide you with a blank screen that is set up as a set of rows and columns, similar to a spreadsheet. Figure 11.4 shows a screen in *List* view.

➤ Adding a Field

When you enter List view, you will have a database, but it has no fields defined. Your first step will be to name your field. To name a field, you choose the *Field Name* option from the **Edit** menu. You will then be provided with a text box to enter the field name in. This is shown in Figure 11.5.

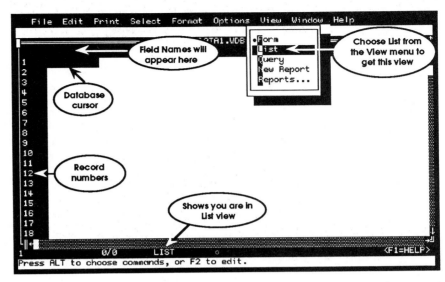

Figure 11.4

To change from Form view to List view, choose the List option from the View menu. The List view treats your database as a number of rows and columns. Field names will appear above the columns after you name the fields.

After you have named the field, the field name will appear at the top of the screen. You can then move your cursor to the next column and name that field, then move to the next column, name this field, and so forth.

➢ *Setting the Format, Font, Style, and Width of a Column*

After you have named your fields, you will need to set their format and width. You can also set the format and width as you name the fields. The order in which you do this is not important; it is more a matter of convenience.

When a format is set for any cell in the column, the format for all cells in that column will be set to that format. This is different from the spreadsheet module where you can set the format for individual cells. The width of a column will also be the same for all cells in the column. The width does work the same here as it does in the spreadsheet module.

To set the *format* of a column, you use the **Format** menu. The formats for the database columns are the same as the formats for the spreadsheet. You also use the **Format** menu to set the *width* of a column. Works automatically sets a field width of ten characters for each new field; however, you can change this width. When you set the width of a column that has a numeric format, you must consider the editing characters (commas, decimal point, dollar signs) that will be displayed in the field. You also have the

Figure 11.5

To name a field, choose the Field Name option from the Edit menu. You will be provided with the text box on the right. Enter a name for the field, and the name will appear above the column.

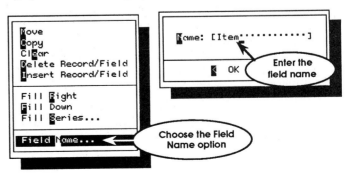

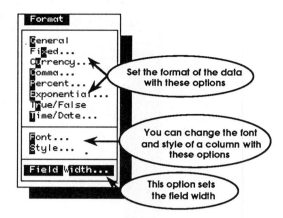

Figure 11.6

*Use the **Format** menu to set data formats like you do in the spreadsheet module. You can also change the **Font** and **Style** of a column with this menu. The last option on this menu allows you to set the column width.*

option of changing the *Font* and the *Style* of a column (see Setting Fonts and Styles in the word processing chapters). Once again, this is done using the **Format** menu. You must remember, any changes using the **Format** menu will affect an entire database column. The **Format** menu is shown in Figure 11.6.

Entering Data into the Database

Once you have defined the fields for your database, you can enter your data. The list view displays a screen with multiple records and columns. Using this view, you enter the data the same way that you enter data into a spreadsheet. You position your cursor on the cell and then type in your data. The tab key can be used to move from column to column within a record. Your arrow keys can be used to move from one record to another.

In the Works database, you can copy the contents of the cell from the previous record. For example, suppose you were entering a long list of names and addresses. Also assume that the most common state name in the addresses was *North Carolina*. When you enter the state name for the second record, you could enter *Ctrl/'* and the contents of the previous record's cell would be copied into the current cell. This would avoid typing *North Carolina* in each record.

➢ Using the Fill Options

The **Edit** menu has three fill options. These are the same options that are available in the *Spreadsheet* module. The *Fill Down* is used to copy the contents of one cell into the cells below it. The *Fill Right* is used to copy the contents of one cell into the cells to the right. The *Fill Series* option allows you to fill a set of cells with a series of numbers or dates. This option also allows you to specify an increment for the series (See these options in the Spreadsheet chapters).

➢ Editing a Record or Field

To edit the contents of a field within a record, you use your tab or arrow keys to move the cursor to the field you want to edit. Next, use your **F2** function key to edit the field. When you use the **F2** function key, the contents of the field are displayed on the *formula bar*. You can then use your arrow and delete keys to change the contents of the field. If you begin typing in a field without using the **F2** function key, the data you type will replace the data in the field.

➤ *Moving and Copying Fields and Records*

You can move a field by using the *Move* option from the **Edit** menu. You can also move an entire record if you select each field in the record before you choose the *Move* option. Copying a field or record uses the same approach. To copy a field, position your cursor in the field and choose *Copy* from the **Edit** menu. To copy a record, select each field in the record before you choose Copy.

➤ *Inserting and Deleting Fields and Records*

To insert a field, position your cursor in the field to the *right* of where you want the new field. Next choose the *Insert Record/Field* option from the **Edit** menu. You will be provided with a dialog box like the one shown in Figure 11.7. Choose *Field* in this dialog box. The new field will be inserted to the left of the field the cursor was in. To insert a record, position your cursor on a cell in the row *below* where you want the new record. Choose *Record* from the dialog box, and a blank record will be inserted. If you want to insert more than one field or record, highlight a series of cells, one for each row or record you want inserted, before you choose the *Insert Record/Field* option.

Figure 11.7

To insert a new field, position your cursor in the column to the right of where you want your new field. Choose Insert Record/Field from the Edit menu. Next choose Field from the option box. The new field will be inserted to the left of the cursor.

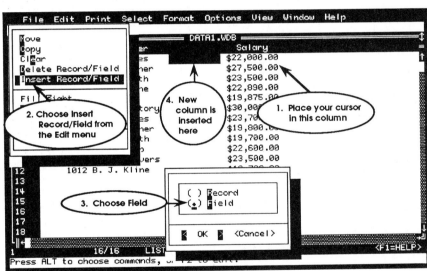

To delete fields or records, position your cursor on any cell in the field or record you want deleted. Next, choose *Delete Record/Field* from the **Edit** menu and choose either *Record* or *Field* from the dialog box. You can also delete several fields or records if you select them before you choose the *Delete Record/Field* option from the **Edit** menu.

Entering Database Formulas

You enter database formulas the same way that you enter spreadsheet formulas. Position your cursor in the column or cell where you want to calculate the value for a column, press the equals sign (=), and enter the formula. The database uses formulas differently than the way they are used in the spreadsheet. In a spreadsheet, a formula is assigned to a specific cell. It is considered local to that cell and would need to be copied to other cells in the column. In a database, a formula is assigned to an entire field or column. The formula is used to compute the value of every cell in that column or field unless a value has been entered into a specific cell. The formula is considered *global* to all blank cells in the field.

Because databases treat columns differently than the spreadsheet does, database formulas use the *field name* in the formula rather than a cell coordinate. For example, to compute the *Gross Pay* field by multiplying a field named *Hours* times a field named *Rate*, you would enter =*Hours*Rate* in the *Gross Pay* column. Ranges cannot be used in a field, since a formula works on records, not the entire database.

You can also enter formulas by using cursor pointing. This approach is similar to the way you use cursor pointing in the spreadsheet. To use cursor pointing, move your cursor to any cell in the column where you want the formula and press the equals (=) key. You can then use your arrow keys to move the cursor to the first cell used in the formula. As you move your cursor, the field name the cursor is on will be displayed on the formula line. Type any arithmetic symbol needed for the formula and then use your arrow keys to move to the next field in the formula. When you have completed the formula, press the Enter key.

A formula can include any field within the same record. If a formula contains the name of the field that contains the formula, Microsoft Works will use the value from the previous record for that field's value. For example, if you wanted to create a running total of a *Donations* field, you could enter the formula =*Donation+Running Total* in the field called *Running Total*. Works would add the value of the *Donation* field of the current record to the value of the field called *Running Total* from the previous record to compute the value of the *Running Total* field in the current record. This idea is shown in Figure 11.8

You can also use the functions described in Chapter 8 in a database formula. For example, to determine the payment from three fields, *Loan, Rate,* and *Term*, in a database record, you could enter the formula =*PMT(Loan, Rate,Term)*. If you have a field named the same as the function name, Works will use the field name in the formula unless you enclose the function name in single quotes (').

Another good use of a formula is to propose a *default* value for a field. For example, suppose your database had a field named *State* and you knew that most of your records would contain the value *NY* in the state field. You could use the formula =*"NY"* in the *State* field. All new records would automatically have this value for the *State*. If you had a record that should not use this value, simply type a different value in the field and the new value would replace the formula for that record only.

To remove a formula from a field, you can enter the equals sign and press Enter. This, in essence, places an empty formula in the field. You can edit a formula by placing your cursor in any cell in the field that contains the formula and pressing the **F2** function key. The formula will be displayed in the edit bar. You can then use any of your editing keys to change the formula.

Figure 11.8

Running totals can be used in a database field. The formula in the running total column must include the column name. Each cell in the column will add the contents of a field in its record to the contents of the field in the previous record to get the running total.

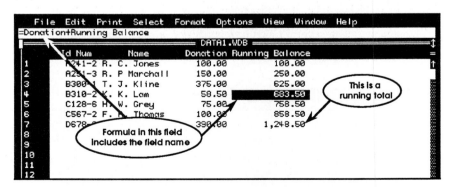

Protecting Fields

When you enter data into the fields of a database, there may be certain fields that you want protected from being changed. For example, if you have the contents of a field defined as a formula, you would not want someone to accidentally enter data into this field. If someone did enter new data into the field, the new data would destroy the formula. You can protect a field by using the *Protect* option of the **Options** menu. When database protection is turned on, you cannot change the data in the cell and many of the options cannot be changed. For instance, you cannot change the **Format** of a cell that is protected.

Setting protection takes two steps. The cells you want protected must be **Locked** first. Actually, Works locks all cells when the database is created, so you would need to set the *lock* off for cells that you do not want to protect. To *lock* or *unlock* cells, place your cursor in the column you want to change and then set the *Locked* option ON or OFF from the *Style* option of the **Format** dialog box. This dialog box is shown on the left of Figure 11.9.

The second step is to turn database protection **ON**. This is done by choosing the *Protect Data* option from the **Options** menu. This menu is shown on the right of Figure 11.9. When database protection is set ON, all cells that have the lock option set on are protected. All unlocked cells can be edited or changed. If database protection is OFF, all cells in the database can be edited or changed, even if they are defined as locked.

When you have protection set ON and you use the Tab key, or the Shift/Tab key to tab backwards, the locked cells are skipped and the cursor moves to the first unlocked cell.

Figure 11.9

To protect cells, you must first make sure the Locked option is set on for the cells. Next, set the Protect Data option ON in the Options menu.

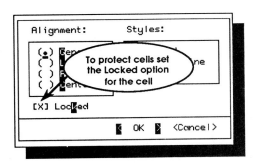

Sorting the Records in the Database

Records that have been stored in the database can be sorted in either an *ascending* or a *descending* sequence based on some key. A key is a field or combination of fields in the database. When you sort in an ascending sequence, the records are ordered with the record containing the lowest value of the key occurring first. The remaining records are ordered from low to high based on the contents of their sort key cells. When records are ordered in descending sequence, the record with the highest value of the sort key occurs first. Remaining records are ordered from high to low.

You can sort the records in a database using up to three sort key fields. When you use more than one sort key field, records are ordered based on a major, intermediate, and minor field. The major field is the most inclusive or outside sort field. The intermediate field is the next most inclusive, and the minor field is the least inclusive. As an example, assume you wanted to sort records where first names were sorted within

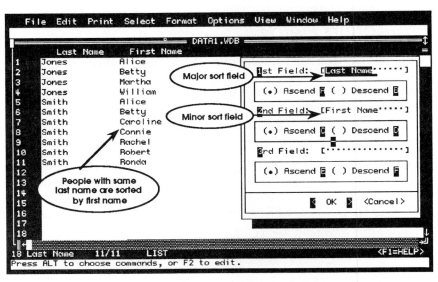

Figure 11.10

*To sort the records in the database, choose the **Sort** option from the **Select** menu. When sorting records, your major sort field should be the 1st Field, intermediate sort field is the 2nd Field, and your minor sort field is the 3rd Field.*

last names. This means that last names will occur in order, and people with the same last name would be in order based on their first name. In this case, you would perform the sort using the *Last Name* field as the major sort field and the *First Name* as the minor sort field. No intermediate field would be used in this case. This idea is shown in Figure 11.10.

If you wanted to sort people with the same first and last name in order by Pay Grade, the major sort field would be *Last Name*, the intermediate sort field would be *First Name*, and the minor sort field would be *Pay Grade*.

In the *Sort* dialog box, the major sort field is the 1st Field, the intermediate sort field is the 2nd Field, and the minor sort field is the 3rd Field. The *Sort* dialog box is also shown in Figure 11.10.

Printing the Database

Printing a database is similar to printing any other document in Microsoft Works. You use the **Print** menu. You can choose the *Print* option or the *Preview* option from this menu. The only additional option on the *Print* or *Preview* dialog box is the *Print Record and Field Labels* option. If this option is chosen, the field names will print over the columns and the record numbers will print on the left side of each record. For wide databases, those with many columns or very wide columns, the database prints like a spreadsheet. The leftmost columns print first with as many cells as will fit on a page. Then the columns to the right of those already printed will print.

Conclusion

This section has introduced some basic concepts of databases. If you are comfortable with spreadsheets, databases should seem familiar and easy to you. You should now complete the following self-test before you move on to the tutorial.

Chapter 11 Self Test

1.   Why would you not consider the database module of Microsoft Works to be a true database?

2.   Define the terms *record*, *cell*, and *field* as they apply to a Microsoft Works database.

3.   What is the primary difference between a database *field* and a spreadsheet *column*?

4.   How long can a database field name be?

5.   What is meant by the *origin* of a field?

6.   How do you name a field in the List view?

7.   How do you tell Works to copy the contents of a field from the previous record?

8.   How do you insert a new field into your database?

9.   Write the formula to compute a *Commission* field in a database. Assume the *Commission* is calculated by adding the fields named *Services* and *Contracts*, and then subtracting the field named *Cancels* and multiplying this answer by 10 percent.

10.   How would you specify a *default* value for a field in a database?

11.   What is a *running balance* or *running total*?

12.   What happens if you use the name of a field that contains a formula in the formula for the field?

13.   What is the difference between setting database *Protection* ON and setting the *Lock* option *ON* for specific cells?

14.   How would you delete records 1 through 5 from a database?

15.   Assume that you wanted to sort database records so that *Zip Codes* were sorted in ascending order by *City*, city was sorted in ascending order by *State*, and states were sorted in ascending order. What would be the major, intermediate, and minor sort fields?

16.   What does the *Print Record and Field Labels* option of the Print menu do?

Chapter 11 Tutorial

In this tutorial, you will create a database that contains information about equipment rentals for a rental company. You will design the database using *List* view, enter records using both *Form* and *List* view, sort, and print the database.

Starting the Tutorial

To start the tutorial, you should start Microsoft Works. When you get the opening *File* menu, choose *Create New File*, then *New Database* from the selection box.

- ❑ **Start Microsoft Works.**
- ❑ **Select** *Create New File* **from the File menu.**
- ❑ **Choose** *New Database.*

Once you complete these steps, you will be provided the *Form* design screen. This is the default mode for creating a Works database. To change to *List* view to create a database, choose the *List* option from the **View** menu. This process is shown in Figure 11.11.

- ❑ **Choose** *List* **from the** *View* **menu.**

Once you are in *List* view, your screen will be treated as a set of columns, much like a spreadsheet. Your cursor will be like a spreadsheet cursor. That is, it will be a block as large as one database cell. Your cursor should be in the first column of the first record. If it is not, move your cursor there.

- ❑ **Move your cursor to the leftmost column of the first record.**

Creating the Database

To demonstrate how Works creates your database, enter the number *2058* in this cell. This will eventually be your first item in your database.

Figure 11.11

*When you create a new database, you are placed in the **Form** view of the database. To change to **List** view, choose the **List** option from the **View** menu.*

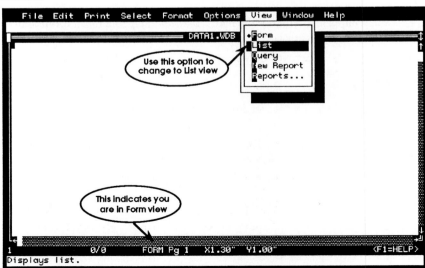

Figure 11.12

Works assigns default names of Field1, Field2, Field3, etc., to any column that contains data but has not been named by the user.

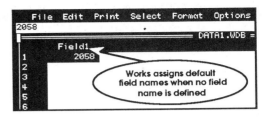

❏ **Enter *2058* in the first cell and press the Enter key.**

You should now have a field name of *Field1* over your first column like the one shown in Figure 11.12. When you enter data in a field but do not name the field, Works automatically assigns field names of *Field1*, *Field2*, *Field3*, etc.

➢ *Naming Fields*

Assume that the first field in your database records will contain *Item numbers*. To name the field, you need to position your cursor in the column and choose the *Field Name* option from the **Edit** menu. When you choose this option, you will be provided with a text box to enter the name of the field. This process is shown in Figure 11.13. Name your first column *Item* now.

❏ **Choose the *Field Name* option from the *Edit* menu.**

❏ **Enter *Item* in the Name text box.**

❏ **Choose the *OK* button.**

If your screen does not look like this, move your cursor to the field or text that is incorrect, choose *Delete* from the **Edit** menu, and redo these steps.

Figure 11.13

*To name a field, choose the **Field Name** option from the **Edit** menu and enter the name of the field in the **Name** text box.*

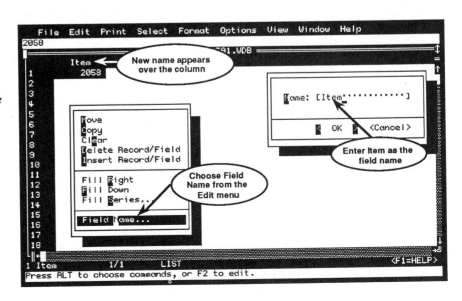

➤ *Formatting Columns*

Remember that the default width of your field is 10 characters. Assume that you wanted to limit the *Item* number to 6 characters. To do this, you would need to set the field width to 6 characters. This is done with the *Field Width* option of the **Format** menu. Set your field width now.

❏ Choose *Field Width* from the *Format* menu.

❏ Enter 6 in the *Field Width* dialog box.

❏ Choose OK.

Your *Item* field should now be smaller.

We will step you through the creation of one more field and then let you try a few on your own. We now want a field for the description of the item. To create this field, do the following:

❏ Tab to the second column.

❏ Choose *Field Name* from the *Edit* menu.

❏ Enter Description as the field name.

❏ Choose *Field Width* from the *Format* menu.

❏ Enter 15 for the width.

You should now have the field name *Description* over the second column, and the width of the description should be set to 15 characters. This will be your second database field.

➤ *Completing the Database Design*

Now continue designing your database. Remember to tab to the next column before you name a column. If you enter the wrong name for a column, you can rename it exactly the way you originally named it. Use the **Format** menu to set the formats for fields that require them. Use the following field names, widths, and formats for your new fields.

Field Name	Width	Format	
Rental	7	Fixed	2 decimals
Rented To	15	General	
Days	4	Fixed	zero decimals
Date Out		Date	month, day, year, short
Due Back		Date	month, day, year, short
Deposit	8	Comma	2 decimals
Total	8	Comma	2 decimals
Balance	9	Currency	2 decimals

After you have completed designing the database, press the **Home** key. Your screen should be like the one shown in Figure 11.14.

❏ Press the *Home* key.

➤ *Entering the data*

Now that you have your columns named and their formats set, you can begin entering your data. You can enter the data in either the *List* view or the *Form* view. We will begin by having you enter four of your records in *List* view; the others will be entered in *Form* view.

Figure 11.14

After you have completed naming your fields, the field names will be displayed above their respective columns.

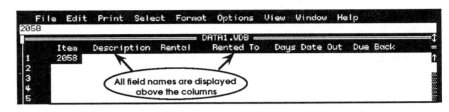

Before you begin, you must know that you will be using formulas to compute the data for the *Due Back, Total,* and *Balance* fields. Because of this, you need to be careful not to enter data in these fields. You have already entered the *Item* number for your first record. Now tab to the second column, *Description,* and enter the following fields. Remember to press the Tab key each time you want to move to the next field.

> ❑ **Enter the following data in record one:**

Item	Description	Rental	Rented To	Days	Date Out	Due Back	Deposit
	Lawn Tractor	25	J. R. Jones	7	5/3/90	tab past this field	100

This should complete your first record. Now use your arrow keys to move to the first field of the second record and enter the following three records.

> ❑ **Press *Home* and Down arrow.**

> ❑ **Enter the following data in records 2, 3, and 4:**

Item	Description	Rental	Rented To	Days	Date Out	Due Back	Deposit
3033	Weed Eater	7.	R.T. Turner	7	5/3/90	Tab past this field	20
2789	5 HP Tiller	10.5	J.C. Jones	2	5/4/90	Tab past this field	0
2050	10 HP Tiller	17.	J.K. Eagle	10	5/6/90	Tab past this field	75

Your screen should now look like Figure 11.15.

➤ *Entering Formulas in Fields*

There are three formulas that need to be entered. These formulas compute the *Due Back* date, *Total,* and *Balance* fields. We will begin with the *Due Back* date. This should be the *Date Out* field plus the *Days* rented field. To enter this formula, all you need to do is add the two fields together. Enter the formula in this column now. You can enter the formula in the *Due Back* field of any record.

> ❑ **Tab to the Due Back column.**

> ❑ **Enter: =Date Out + Days**

> ❑ **Press Enter to complete your formula.**

Figure 11.15

Your database should now have four records in it.

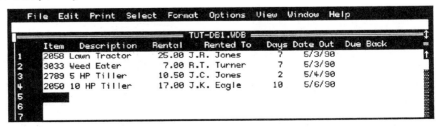

You should now have computed dates in the *Due Back* column of all four of your records. Remember, if you make a mistake, press the **F2** formula edit key and correct your formula.

The next formula to enter will be for the *Total* field. This field will contain the total charges for the rental, so it should be the *Rental* fee times the *Days* rented. Enter this formula now.

❏ **Tab to the *Total* column.**

❏ **Enter: =Rental * Days as your formula.**

The last formula will be for the *Balance* field. This should be the *Total* field minus the *Deposit* field. We will leave this formula for you to develop.

❏ **Enter the *Balance* formula.**

The right hand side of your database should look like the one shown in Figure 11.16. If it does not, examine your data and formulas and correct them. Remember, if you have accidentally entered data in a cell of a column that has a formula, the data replaces the formula. To correct this error, place your cursor in the cell that contains the data and choose the *Clear* option from the **Edit** menu.

Entering Records Using FormsView

As mentioned earlier, when you create a database a *default* form is created for you. You will enter three more records using this form. To change to *Form* view, you choose the *Form* option from the **View** menu. Before you change to this view, move your cursor to the first field of the first record.

❏ **Enter *Ctrl/Home* to move to your first cell.**

❏ **Choose *Form* from the *View* menu.**

You should now have a form like the one shown in Figure 11.17. The default form assigns a field width of 20 characters to each field. This may not be the same width as you assigned the fields in the *List* view, but will be fine for now. For this reason, your form does not look as neat as it should. You will work with

Figure 11.16

After you have entered your formulas, all the records in the database should have the values for the computed fields.

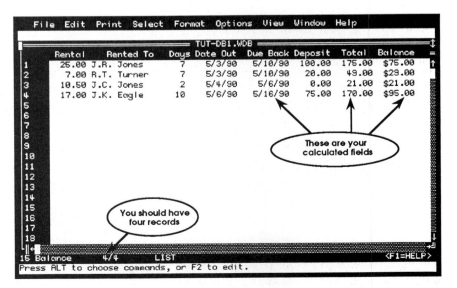

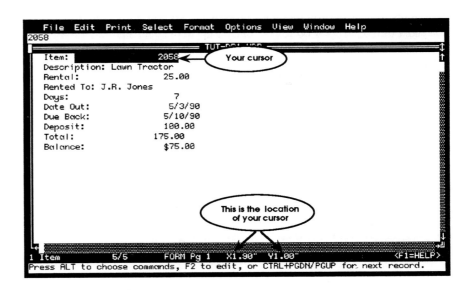

Figure 11.17

Works creates a default form for each database. Each field in the default form has a width of 20 characters. This may be different from the width defined in the List view.

form design more in Chapter 12. You can also use this form to edit, view, or add records. To see your remaining records, use your *Ctrl/PageDown* key.

❏ **Use your *Ctrl/PageUp* and *Ctrl/PageDown* keys to review your records.**

To add records to your database, you need to make sure you are on your first blank record. The bottom of your screen should indicate that you have four records stored. Use your *Ctrl/PageUp* or *Ctrl/PageDown* key to move to record number five. The record number you are viewing will be indicated in the lower lefthand corner of your screen.

Now enter the following records. Remember to use the Tab key to move to the next field.

❏ **Enter the following records**

2110	**2011**	**1890**
Sander	**Weeder**	**Jack Hammer**
2.5	**3**	**15**
Y. C. Hackett	**R.R. Miller**	**P. S. Hayes**
3	**2**	**25**
5/16/90	**5/16/90**	**5/22/90**
Tab past this field	Tab past this field	Tab past this field
0	**0**	**200**

This should complete the data for your database. To complete the last few steps, change back to *List* view.

❏ **Choose *List* from the *View* menu.**

Protecting Cells

Because a value will destroy a formula in a field, you may want to protect certain fields, especially those with formulas. When a field is protected, you cannot change the contents of any cell in the field.

Setting up your protection requires two steps. First you must specify the *Locked* option for the field; then, you must turn protection on for the database. Remember that the *Locked* option deals with a single field, while the *Protect Data* option deals with the entire database.

When you initially create a field, the *Locked* option is set on. If there are any fields you do not want locked, you must turn the *Locked* option off. To demonstrate how protection works, we will turn the Locked option off for the *Item, Description, Rental, Rented To, Days, Date Out,* and *Deposit* fields. Doing this would allow you to continue to use the database to add or change records. Having the fields with formulas protected would guarantee that you do not accidentally destroy a formula.

To set protection off for these fields, you will need to select the fields as a block and then choose the *Style* option from the **Format** menu. You should get the dialog box shown in Figure 11.18. Next tab to the *Locked* option and set it off.

❑   **Use *Ctrl/Home* to move to your first field.**

❑   **Select the first six fields as a block.**

❑   **Choose *Style* from the Format menu.**

Notice that the *Locked* option is marked. To turn the option off, you must tab to the option and use your space bar to remove the X. Do this now.

❑   **Tab to the *Locked* option and press the space bar to set this option off.**

❑   **Press the Enter key.**

This will set the Locked option off for the selected fields. You must also set the Locked option off for the *Deposit* field.

❑   **Tab to the *Deposit* field and set the Locked option off for this field.**

The next step is to set the *Protect Data* option on for the database. You do this from the **Options** menu. Set the *Protect D*ata option on now.

❑   **Choose *Protect Data* from the *Options* menu.**

Figure 11.18

When fields are created, they are defined as locked fields. To allow you to edit or enter data in the fields when protection is set on, you must set the protection off for the fields.

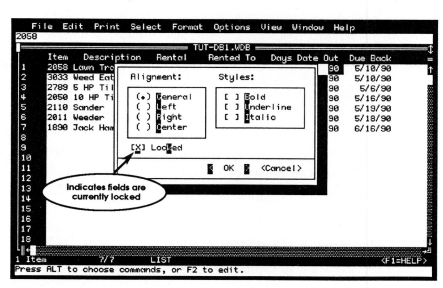

Protection should now be set on for the *Due Back, Total,* and *Balance* fields. All other fields should have protection set off. To see if the protection works, use your Tab key to tab through the database. Your cursor should skip the protected fields.

❑ **Use your Tab key to try to tab into protected fields.**

Now use your arrow keys to move to different cells that are locked, and try to enter data into these fields. When you press the Enter key after changing any of these fields, you should get the check box shown in Figure 11.19.

Figure 11.19

You get this Error box when you try to change the contents of a protected field.

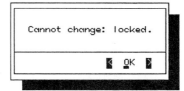

❑ **Use your arrow keys to move to a locked field and change the value for the field.**
❑ **Press the Enter key when you get the Error box.**

When cells are protected, you cannot change their contents or format. If you pull down the **Format** menu, the options on the format menu cannot be accessed.

If you want to change the contents of any locked cell, you must first use the **Options** menu to set the *Protect Data* option off. Remember that all cells will then be unprotected.

Sorting the Database

The records in your database are currently in no particular order. This is because they are listed the way you entered them. Normally you want your records arranged based on the value of some field. In our case, we will assume that we want our records sorted in ascending sequence based on the *Item* field. To arrange the records, you must *Sort* them.

To sort records, you select the *Sort records* option from the **Select** menu. The *Sort records* option dialog box is shown in Figure 11.20. The *Sort records* option assumes you want to sort on the first field of your database and will have this field name in the *1st Field* text entry. If this is not the field you want to sort on, you must enter your field name here.

Figure 11.20

When you first access the Sort records option, the first field in your database will be defined as the 1st Field. You can change this sort field by entering a different field name in this text entry area.

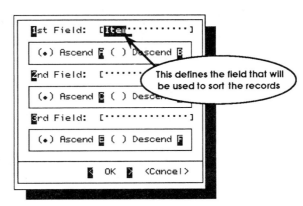

Figure 11.21

Any time you access the Sort option and choose the OK button, the records are sorted according to the sort fields defined. If you add new records, they will not be sorted until you choose the Sort records option again.

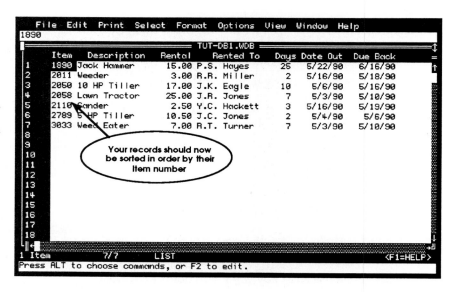

Since you want the records sorted on the first field, all you need to do is select the *Sort records* option from the **Select** menu, check the 1st Field option to see that it contains the correct field name, and then press the Enter key. Do this now.

❏ **Choose** *Sort records* **from the** *Select* **menu.**

❏ **Press the Enter key when you get the** *Sort records* **dialog box.**

Your records should now be sorted in ascending sequence based on the contents of the *Item* field. Figure 11.21 shows the records in the new sorted order.

There may be times when you want to sort on more than one field. For instance, assume that you want the records sorted by the *Item* number field within the *Due Back* field. This means that you want the *Due Back* field to be the major sort field so that all items due back on the same day would be together. Then, for each day that items are due back, items would be sorted by the *Item* number. To do this, you would need to enter *Due Back* in the *1st Field* area and *Item* in the *2nd Field* area. The 3rd Field area would be left blank, since you do not have a third field to sort on. Sort your records this way now.

❏ **Select** *Sort* **from the** *Select* **menu.**

❏ **Enter** *Due Back* **in the** *1st Field* **entry.**

❏ **Select** *Ascend* **as the sort order.**

❏ **Enter** *Item* **in the** *2nd Field* **entry.**

❏ **Select** *Ascend* **as the sort order.**

❏ **Press the Enter key.**

Check your records now to make sure they are sorted by *Item* number within the *Due Back* field. Your database should look like the one shown in Figure 11.22.

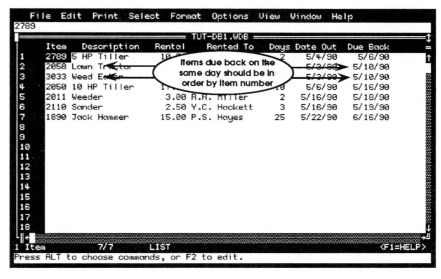

Figure 11.22

When two fields are used to perform a sort, the 1st Field is used as the major sort field and the 2nd Field is used as the minor sort field.

Printing the Database

Printing a database is like printing any other document. You select the *Print* or *Preview* option from the **Print** menu. When the database is printed, the records are printed according to the way they are sorted when you execute the print option.

Now select *Preview* from the **Print** menu. You should get the *Preview* dialog box shown in Figure 11.23.

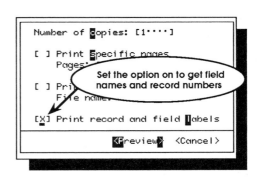

Figure 11.23

*To get the record numbers and field names printed with your database data, you must set the **Print record and field labels** option ON.*

Since you want the field names and record numbers printed when you print the database, you must make sure the *Print Record and Field Labels* option is set on. If this is not set on, you will get only the data in your records. Tab to the *Print Record and Field Labels* and turn this option on. To print the database, choose the Print button from the Print dialog box.

- ❑ Select *Preview* from the *Print* menu.
- ❑ Tab to the *Print Record and Field Labels* option and set this option on.
- ❑ Preview your database.
- ❑ Print your database.

Saving the Database

When the database completes printing, you should save your database. Since you have just created the database, you should use the *Save As* option from the **File** menu.

Conclusion

This completes your first database tutorial. You should remove your printout from the printer and *Exit* Microsoft Works. Remember to turn off your machine.

Hands on Practice

Exercise 1

Create a database that contains information about members in an organization. Assume that the organization is a bowling league. Create the database using the following fields and field definitions:

First Name	General	10
Last Name	General	10
Phone	General	9
P.O.	Fixed	5
City	General	15
ST (state)	General	2
Score	Fixed	5

Enter the following records in the database:

Robert	Wilson	433-4001	2123	Fairfax	VA	220
Mary	Wilson	434-5678	5613	Fairfax	VA	195
Phyllis	Miller	783-7856	1082	Baltimore	MD	210
Tina	Miller	433-8910	6661	Virginia Beach	VA	215
Alice	Miller	433-8911	1195	Baltimore	MD	210
Mark	Wilson	434-0001	6557	Landover	MD	207

Sort your database on First Name within Last Name and print your database with record and field labels.

Hands on Practice

Exercise 2

Create a database that contains information about employees in a company. Create the database using the following fields and field definitions:

```
First Name        General    10
Initial           General     1
Last Name         General    10
Title             General    15
Office            General     5
Phone             General     8
Birth Date        Date       15      Month, Day, Year  Long
Retirement Date   Date       15      Month, Day, Year  Long
Annual Salary     Currency   12      2 decimals
Monthly Salary    Currency   10      2 decimals
```

Enter the following records. Leave the Retirement Date and Monthly Salary blank.

Name	Title	Office	Phone	Birth Date	Annual Salary
Francis T Turner	Treasurer	102	790-4567	10/02/48	$39,000.00
Robert J Smith	Auditor	107	790-7777	10/01/50	$28,000.00
Sarah D McDonald	Auditor	224	790-9901	01/15/35	$26,000.00
Phyllis K Eble	Clerk	105	790-8811	01/30/55	$15,500.00
Michael D Carver	Secretary	119	790-4444	02/16/61	$18,750.00
Wesley M Smith	Analyst	340	790-1111	08/12/68	$41,000.00
Carol H Miller	Auditor	214	790-8812	08/13/65	$31,000,00
Robert J Smith	Clerk	235	790-2222	06/21/66	$14,800.00

Use a formula to compute the retirement date. The retirement date should be 65 years after the birth date. To do this, you will need to add the number of days in 65 years (65 * 365.25) to the birth date. Do this in your formula (the .25 will help consider leap years).

Compute the monthly salary as one twelfth of the annual salary.

Sort and print your database in each of the following orders. When you print the database set your field labels on.

a. Sort and print in ascending sequence by *Office* number.

b. Sort and print your database in ascending sequence by *first name* within *last name*. Sort by *Annual Salary* in descending sequence as your third sort field.

c. Sort and print your database in descending sequence by *Retirement Date* within ascending *Title*.

12

Form Design and Database Queries

In the previous database chapter, you created a database using the List view. When you use this view to create a database a default database *form* is automatically created for you. This form is normally used to enter records into your database or to view records one at a time. The form that is created for you is sufficient for most of your needs; however, you may want to change this form to make it easier to use or to make it look like a document you are copying from. You may also want to print records from your database in the format that the form uses. Figure 12.1 shows the default form and a customized form for a sample database.

One way to create a customized form is to create your database in List view, let Works generate a default form, and then modify the default form. This is the approach we will use in this text.

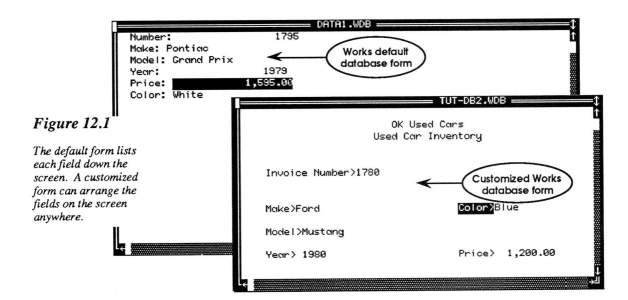

Figure 12.1

The default form lists each field down the screen. A customized form can arrange the fields on the screen anywhere.

Before we discuss changing the form, we need to explain two general concepts.

When Microsoft Works creates the default form, two items are created for each column or field in the database. The first item is the field name. This item is treated as a field and can be moved as a unit. You can also *hide* this field name and enter other text that better explains the data in the field. In fact, text can be entered anywhere on the form.

The second item is the actual database field. Works assigns a default width of 20 characters to all fields in the form. This default width can be changed with the *Format* menu. To arrange the form the way you want it, you can use the *Move* option from the **Edit** menu to move this field entry area.

Altering the Default Form

To alter a form, you must use the *Form* view. Once you are in the Form view, you can use your menu options to move items on the form to different areas on your screen. To move a field, use your Tab key or arrow keys to position the cursor on the field you want to move, choose the *Move* option from the **Edit** menu, use your arrow keys to move the field, and press the Enter key.

As you move a field, the status line will indicate the position of the field or cursor on the form. This is shown as X and Y coordinates in the center of the status line. You can use these coordinates to position a field or text exactly where you want it on the form. Figure 12.2 shows these coordinates.

To change the text that indicates a field, you must first *hide* the field name. This is done using the *Show Field Name* option from the **Format** menu. When this option is set off, the field name is not displayed. You can then enter the text you want to use to identify the field. When you enter this text, it cannot *flow* into the field area.

By moving fields and changing the text used to identify the field, you can create a form that is customized to your individual needs.

Database Queries

The function of a database is to store information about objects. These objects are things that you need to know about at some later time. The database will usually contain information about more objects than you want to know about at any one point in time. One of the primary advantages of storing information in a database is that the database will allow you to ask questions about the data within it. These questions are referred to as **Queries**. When you query a database, you normally want to find specific records that meet some type of condition. For example, assume you were a used automobile dealer and you had a customer that wanted to purchase a 1980 Ford Escort. You could query the database to see if you had any of these automobiles and, if you did, view the information about the automobiles.

Figure 12.2

The X and Y coordinates help you position fields and text on your form.

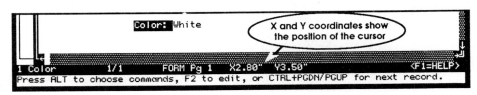

Figure 12.3

To define a Query, choose the ***Query*** *option from the* ***View*** *menu.*

Queries can be as simple and straightforward as the one just described, or they can be complex. For example, you could ask for all automobiles that were made after 1985, cost between $5,000.00 and $6,500.00, and were not blue. In either case, Microsoft Works would search through the database and display only those records that met the conditions you specify.

➤ Defining a Query

Remember that there are two ways to view the database: the *List* view and the *Form* view. You can begin a query from either view. Exactly how the query displays the selected records depends on which view you are using at the time you define the query. If you are in Form view, records will be displayed one record at a time. If you are using the List view, all records are displayed as a listing. Once the query has been completed and the records have been selected, you can switch between views of the database.

To define a query, you must first open the database that you want to query. When the database is opened, you will be placed in *List* view. Next, you select the *Query* option from the **View** menu. The **View** menu is shown in Figure 12.3.

When you choose this option, the database form is displayed. This form is used to define your query.

➤ Defining Queries by Example

Microsoft Works uses a query concept referred to as *Query By Example* (QBE). To use this approach to make a query, you simply fill in the fields of the form with example data that you are using as your query criteria. If you specify data in any field, the database will be searched and all records that contain that value in the field will be displayed. If a field is left blank, Works assumes that you will allow any value in that field. For example, suppose you wanted to list all automobiles that were *1988 Red* automobiles. To form this query, you would fill in the Year field with the value *1988* and the *Color* field with the word *Red*. Since you have filled in more that one field, Works assumes that you want both criteria to be met when the search is performed. Once you have completed the query form, you must select *List* or *Form* from the **View** menu or press the **F10** function key. The example query just described is shown in Figure 12.4.

When you enter the value of a field as text, capitalization in the text is not significant. Works will check for both the uppercase and lowercase for any letters in the text. This means the words RED, red, ReD and Red will all be considered equal. When you enter numbers in a field, Works assumes that the number is positive. If you want to search for a negative, you must precede the number with a minus sign.

➤ Changing a Query

Microsoft Works will allow you to have only one query form. Once you make a query, the values used in the query remain in the query form. To make a different query, you must change the values in the form.

Figure 12.4

When you want to search your database for records that meet two or more conditions, you must enter a value in each of the fields. This query will find all automodibles that are Red and were manufactured in 1988.

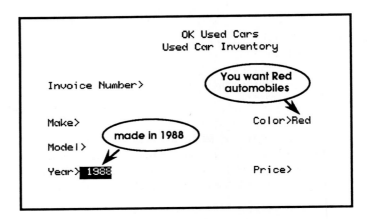

If you want to make simple changes to the query, you can tab to the fields you want to change and enter new values into these fields. Any new value will replace the old value stored in the form. You can also use the **F2** formula edit key to change a field value. When you use the **F2** formula edit key, the contents of the field your cursor is on are displayed on the formula line. You can then use your arrow and delete keys to modify the contents of the field. When you have completed changing the data in the field, you must press the Enter key to complete the change.

If you want to remove a value from a query field, there are two ways to do this. The first way is tab to the field, press the Delete key, and then press the Enter key. The second way is to tab to the field and then select the *Clear Field Contents* option from the **Edit** menu. This will remove anything in the field. The **Edit** menu is shown in Figure 12.5.

If you want to remove entries from all fields in the form, you can select the *Delete Query* option from the **Edit** menu. Using this option is the same as using the *Clear Field Contents* option on each field.

When you enter data in a field, Works will assume that you are searching for an equal condition. If you are looking for a greater than or less than condition, you must precede the data you enter with the > or < sign.

Using Wild Cards in Query Criteria

Wild cards can be used when you specify the criteria for a query. Works uses wild cards in the same way that MS-DOS uses wild cards. The first type of wild card is the asterisk (*). This wild card can take the

Figure 12.5

*You can use the **Clear Field Conctentys** of the **Edit** menu to clear data from a field or use the **Delete Query** option to clear the entire query.*

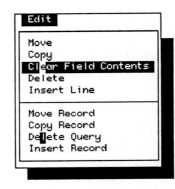

place of any number of characters. For example, if you wanted any model of car that began with the letter C, you could use the criterion **C***. Now suppose that you wanted to find all cars that have a color of blue. The color might be *dark blue, misty blue, royal blue*, or *blue/green*. Since blue can occur anywhere in the color, you would use the criterion ***Blue***.

You can also use the question mark (**?**) to substitute for a single character. For example, suppose you had F100, F150, F1000, and F1500 model Fords and you only wanted to find the automobiles that were numbered in the hundreds, F100 and F150. You could not use the criterion **F1***, because this would find all the automobiles. You could use the criterion **F1??**. Since the question mark will only substitute one character, the F1000 and F1500 would not be selected. This criterion would find all numbers between 100 and 199. You should also realize that if you had a model F1AB, it would also be found, since the wild card will not distinguish between letters and numbers.

Querying Using Ranges

A query criterion can also be used to select a range of values. A range specifies a lower and an upper limit for the values you are searching for. The simplest concept of a range uses the following relational operators:

>	**is greater than**
>=	**is greater than or equal to**
<	**is less than**
<=	**is less than or equal to**
<>	**is not equal to**

Suppose you wanted to find all automobiles that were made after 1985. You could specify the criterion **>1985** in the Year field. Recognize that this is the greater than symbol. If you also wanted to find the automobiles made in 1985, you would need to rephrase the query so that you would include these. For this query, you would need to use **>=1985**.

Now suppose that you wanted to find all automobiles that were **not Fords**. In this query, you are looking for character or text type data. When you search a range using text data, you must enclose the text in double quotes. This query would be phrased as **<>"Ford"**.

Earlier we said that a range specifies an upper and a lower limit. The aforementioned queries have specified only one limit in the range. The first query, **>=1985**, uses an *implied* upper limit that is infinite. That is, any number greater than 1985 will match. The lower limit is 1985.

When alphabetic characters are used in the criterion, only the number of characters enclosed in the quotes must match. For example, suppose you wanted to find all automobiles whose model started with the letter **P** or any letter after **P**. This criterion could be written as **>="P"**. Likewise, if you were searching for all last names that began with Smith, you could use the criterion **>="Smith"**. This query would find *Smith, Smithfield, Smithsonian,* and *Smithers.*

Works will also allow you to specify calculated data as the search criterion. Assume that, for a sale, you reduced all automobiles by 15 percent. Now you want to find all automobiles that had a sale price of less than $5,000.00. You could phrase this query as **=*.85<5000**. Generally stated, if you use a formula in a cell for a query criterion, you must precede the formula with the equals sign. If the criterion is entered in the field that you are applying the formula to, the field name does not need to be specified. You need only specify the formula after the equals sign, then specify a relational operator and the data that you are comparing with the results of the formula.

Using the AND (&) Connector

There are times when you want more than one condition to be met on a single field. This type of query is referred to as an **AND** query. AND queries must meet all conditions of the query in order to be selected. For example, assume that you wanted to list all automobiles that cost more than $5,000.00 and less than $8,000.00. You would need to phrase the query as >5000.00 & <8000.00. Notice that the two criteria are connected by the *ampersand* (&) rather than the word AND. In Microsoft Works, the ampersand means AND.

The natural form of a query is an AND. If you enter criteria in two or more fields, all criteria must be met before the records are selected. This is precisely the idea of the AND. For example, if you wanted to see all Fords that had a Price between $5,000.00 and $8,000.00, you are using three AND conditions. The make, Ford, is your first condition. This is a simple condition on the Make field. It would be entered in the Make field as =**"Ford"**. The Price field has a compound condition. This would be entered in the Price field as >=**5000&<=8000**. Used together, all three conditions must be met before the records are selected. The results of this query are shown in Figure 12.6.

Figure 12.6

When & connectors are used, all criteria must be met.

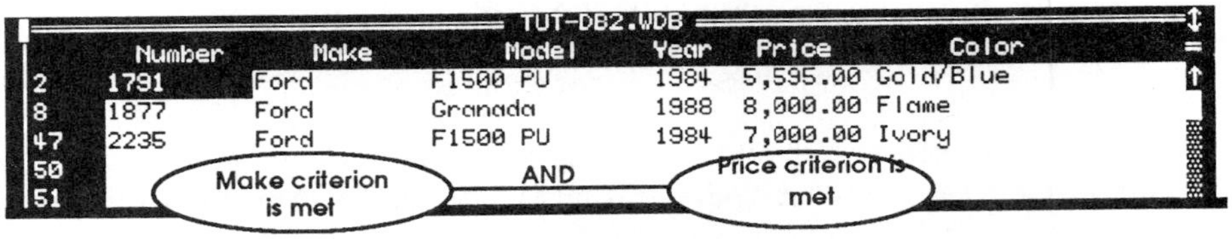

Using the OR (:) Connector

Note: *The OR connector is not the colon. It is an OR symbol. It looks like a colon, except that it is composed of two small bars rather than two dots. It is on the same key as the backslash (\) on most keyboards. To help distinguish this from the colon, we will use the bar (/) in this text.*

You may also want to specify an **OR** operation in a query. In an OR operation, if either condition of the OR is met, the record is selected. For example, suppose you wanted to list one of the following models: Accord, Maxima, or Civic. You would phrase this criterion as ==**"Accord"|="Maxima"|="Civic"** (equal Accord or equal Maxima or equal Civic). Since you are not specifying the field name in the comparison, this formula must be entered in the **Model** field. The results of this query are shown in Figure 12.7.

There are times when you may want to specify an OR operation using more than one field. For example, suppose you want to find all Fords or all automobiles that cost less than $8,000.00. You cannot place the criterion in the different fields (Fords in the Make field and <8000 in the Price field) because it would be treated as an AND query. This query would be interpreted as Make=Ford and Price<8000. To phrase this OR query, you should enter the criterion in either the Make or Price field. If you place the criterion in the Make field, the query would be phrased as =*"Ford"|Price<8000*. If you placed the criterion in the Price

Figure 12.7

When an OR connector is used, either condition in the OR can be met.

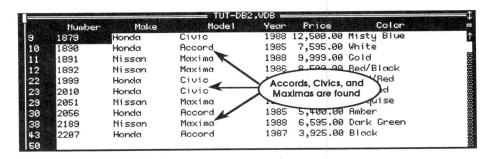

field, it would be phrased as *<8000/Make="Ford"*. Notice that you do not need to specify the field name for the field that the criterion is entered in, but you must specify the field name for any comparison that does not use the field name that contains the criterion.

Using the NOT (~)

The **NOT** condition can be used to select all records that are outside a range or that do not meet a specific condition. For example, suppose you are opposed to owning a Ford, so you want to see all automobiles that are not Fords. You could phrase the query criterion as =~="**Ford**" (not equal Ford). Any record that did not contain the value Ford in the Make field would be displayed. You can also use the NOT condition with operators other than the equal. For example, suppose you wanted to list all automobiles that cost $8,000.00 or less. You could use =~>8000. You should realize that the results of this query would be exactly the same as phrasing the query as <=8000.

Combining ANDs, ORs, and NOTs

You can combine any of the operators together in a single Query. Suppose you had the following criteria for a query. You wanted to list all automobiles that have a price between and including $4,000.00 and $5,000.00 or a price between and including $8,000.00 and $10,000.00. This means that you do not want to list automobiles less than $4,000.00 or greater than $10,000.00 or any automobile between $5,000.00 and $8,000.00. To phrase the query, you would need to use both an AND and an OR in the query. This query would be phrased as *>=4000&<=5000/>=8000&<10000*. This would be read as (greater than or equal to 4,000 and less than or equal to 5,000) or (greater than or equal to 8,000 and less than or equal to 10,000).

You can use parentheses in a search criterion to change the order of evaluation. When parenthsis are used, the order of evaluation is from the inner most prenthsis to the outer most parenthisis. For example, you could phrase a query as *=Make="Ford" /Make="Pontiac"&Price<8000*. This would list all Fords and Pontiacs that have a price less than $8,000.00. You could rephrase the query as *=Make="Ford": (Make="Pontiac"& Price < 8000)*. This would list all Fords, but only those Pontiacs that have a price less than $8,000.00.

Writing a Query in Any Field

You can define any query in any field. If the field you are comparing with is also the field that contains the query criterion, you do not need to specify the field name in the comparison. If the field used in the comparison is not the field that contains the query criterion, you must specify the field name in the criterion. Two examples will help clarify this.

If you want all automobiles that have a price less than $8,000.00 and you enter the criterion in the Price field, you would enter it as *<8000*.

The criterion could also be entered in the Make field. In this case, you would enter *=Price<8000*.

Applying a Query

To create a query, you must choose the *Query* option from the **View** menu. After you have entered your query criterion, you must press the **F10** key or select *List* or *Form* options. When you do this, the criterion in the query is automatically evaluated and applied to your database. All records that meet the criterion are displayed and made available to you. All records that fail the criterion are hidden. When these records are hidden, they are not available to you or to any operation that you may perform on the database, such as sorting, reporting, or printing.

If you want to see all of your records, you must select the *Show All Records* from the **Select** menu. This menu is shown in Figure 12.8.

If you want to apply the current query to the database after you have set the *Show All Records* option on, you can choose the *Apply Query* option from the **Select** menu.

Switching Hidden Records

There may be times when you want to see all the records that do not meet the criterion in a query. You can view these records by choosing the *Switch Hidden Records* option from the **Select** menu. This option will hide all displayed records and display all hidden records. If you choose this option a second time, the records are switched again, and you will see the results of your query and hide all records that do not meet the query criterion.

You can use the *Switch Hidden Records* option to make a **NOT** query. For example, suppose you wanted to see all automobiles that were not Fords. You could form a query as *="**Ford**"* and then use the *Switch Hidden Records* option to view all automobiles that did not meet the criterion (are NOT Fords).

Figure 12.8

*The **Select** menu has options to apply existing queries, hide records, and switch hidden records. All of these options are used in conjunction with query operations.*

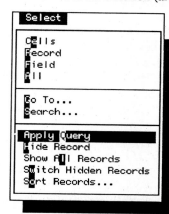

Printing Query Results

Once a query has been applied to a database, those records that do not meet the criterion of the query are hidden. When the database is printed, only those records that can be viewed are printed. To print selected records from the database, you must first define your query so that only the records you want printed are displayed. Once you have done this, you can use your *Print* option from the **Print** menu to print the records that are displayed.

Conclusion

This completes our discussion of Query concepts. You should complete the following *self-test* before moving on to the tutorial.

Chapter 12 Self Test

1. Explain how the concept of Query by Example works.

2. How do you remove all entries from a database query so that you can start a new query?

3. Write a query to list all book titles that contain the word WORKS using wild cards.

4. Write a query to list all books costing more that $20.00 but less than $30.00.

5. Write a query to list a book that was the first edition (1Ed) or the third edition (3Ed) of a book.

6. Write a query to list all books that were not the first edition (1Ed).

7. Write a query that will list all books that have a price between $20.00 and $30.00 and have a Title that contains the word Works.

8. When must you specify a field name in a comparison in query criteria?

9. How do you view all records after you have applied a query?

10. What does the Switch Hidden Records option of the Query menu do?

11. How does Works determine what to print when you print a database?

Chapter 12 Tutorial

In this tutorial, you will be using a database that has already been created. This file will be on your tutorial files disk. You will first modify the database form and then you will make several queries on the database and print the results of your queries.

Starting the Tutorial

Start the tutorial by starting Microsoft Works and loading the database named **TUT-DB2.WDB**.

❑ **Start Microsoft Works.**

❑ **Open the database named TUT-DB2.WDB from your tutorials disk.**

When you have completed loading the database, you should have a list of automobiles and prices on your screen. This will be the database that will be used in this tutorial.

Modifying the Form

To begin this tutorial, you will need to change to the *Form* view of the database. The easiest way to do this is by using your **F9** function key. Press this key now.

❑ **Press the *F9* function key to change to Form view.**

You should now have the form shown in Figure 12.9. Note that most of the form has been customized. To keep this tutorial simple, you will only need to change two of the fields on the form. These will be the *Year* and the *Price* fields.

To begin, tab to the *Year* field.

❑ **Tab to the *Year* field.**

Figure 12.9

For this tutorial, you will be moving the Year and the Price fields. These fields are at the bottom of your current form.

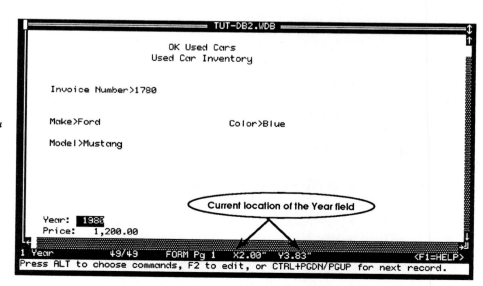

Notice the middle of the status line. It indicates that this field is currently 2.50 inches from the left margin and 3.83 from the top margin. You want this field moved up so that it is with the rest of the fields on the form. As you move the field, watch the status line to make sure you have moved it to the correct location on the form.

- ❑ **Choose** *Move Field* **from the Edit menu.**
- ❑ **Use your arrow keys to move the field to X coordinate 2.5 and Y coordinate 3.00.**
- ❑ **Press your Enter key to complete the move.**

You should have noticed that both the field name and the field area were selected and moved when you chose the *Move Field* option from the **Edit** menu. This is because the *Show Field Name* option was turned on.

You will now change the caption by the field name. To do this, you must first turn off the *Show Field Name* option then enter your new caption.

- ❑ **Make sure you have the *Year* field highlighted and choose the *Show Field Name* option from the *Format* menu.**
- ❑ **Move your cursor to coordinates X1.50 and Y3.00.**
- ❑ **Enter** Year Made> **and press the Enter key.**

Your caption should now be changed.

To see how well you have understood what you have done, we will leave the next change for you to complete. This change will move the *Price* field and change its caption.

- ❑ **Move the *Price* field to coordinates X5.30 and Y3.00.**
- ❑ **Change the caption to** Sales Price>.

Your form should now look like the one in Figure 12.10.

Remember, the reason for modifying the default form is to lay out the form so that it looks like a document that you want printed or to make the form clearer and more understandable to a user.

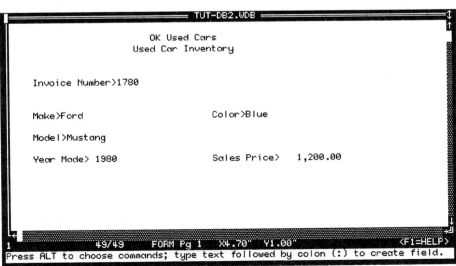

Figure 12.10

Your database form should be like this one after you have completed modifying the form.

Making Queries

Before you begin to make queries, you should shift back to the *List* view. This will allow you to see the results of your queries more clearly.

❑ **Press F9 to move back to *List* view.**

To make a query of the database, you select the *Query* option from the **View** menu. Do this now.

❑ **Select *Query* from the View menu.**

You should now have a blank database form. To make a simple query, you fill in the value of a specific field. For example, assume you wanted to see all automobiles that were *Pontiacs*. You would use your Tab key to tab to the *Make* field and enter the value *Pontiac* as the query criterion. Make this query now.

❑ **Tab to the *Make* field and enter *Pontiac* and press Enter.**

This will define the query. To see the records that are selected by the query, you need to exit the Query routine. To do this, press the **F10** function key.

❑ **Press the *F10* key to view your records.**

Your screen should now be similar to the one in Figure 12.11. You should only have Pontiacs displayed.

Notice a few things on your status line. The status line is above the last line at the bottom of your screen. In the left corner of the status line, the record number and field name of the field that the cursor is positioned on are displayed. Also notice that the status line shows that you have 6 of 49 records displayed (6/49) and that you are in List view.

Next, notice the record numbers down the left side of the screen. These indicate the actual record numbers for the records displayed (4, 7, 14, 17, 32, and 46).

➤ *Defining a Query on Multiple Fields*

You can also specify a query that tests multiple fields. This form of a query works like an AND statement. For example, suppose you wanted to see all automobiles that were 1987 Fords and cost under $10,000.00.

Figure 12.11

Query of all
***Pontiacs** in the*
database.

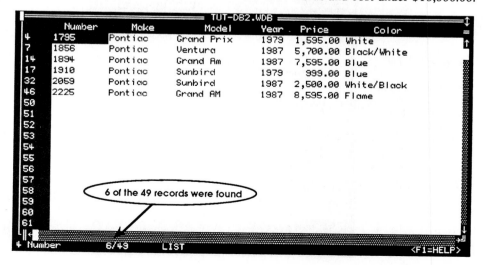

6 of the 49 records were found

You want all three conditions to be met. To define this query, you would fill in multiple fields in the query form. Define this query by completing the following instructions:

- ❑ Select *Query* from the *View* menu.
- ❑ Select *Delete Query* from the *Edit* menu to clear your old query.
- ❑ Enter: Ford in the *Make* field.
- ❑ Enter: 1987 in the *Year* field.
- ❑ Enter: <10000 in the *Price* field and press Enter.
- ❑ Press F10 to apply the query.

You should now have the screen shown in Figure 12.12. Only one record should be found.

Figure 12.12

Results of query for 1987 Fords under $10,000.

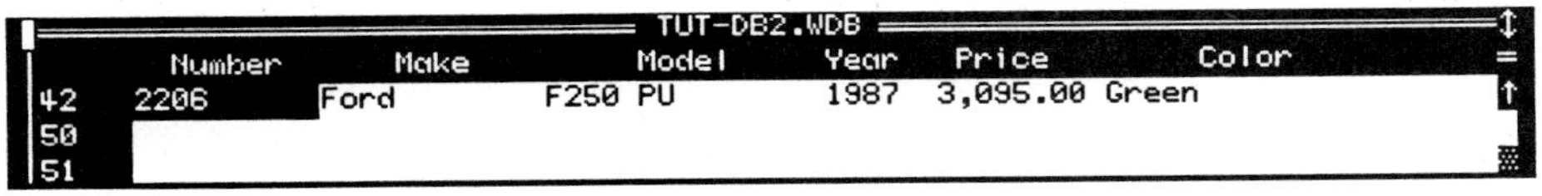

```
============================ TUT-DB2.WDB ============================
      Number        Make          Model       Year    Price        Color
  42  2206        Ford          F250 PU       1987   3,095.00 Green
  50
  51
```

➤ *Defining AND Queries*

The query that you just entered is a form of an AND query because the criteria in all three fields had to be satisfied before a record was displayed. There are times when you may want to satisfy multiple conditions on a single field. For example, assume that you wanted to list all automobiles that cost between $6,000.00 and $10,000.00. You want any price that is greater than $6,000.00 AND less than $10,000. To phrase this query, you would need to use an AND in the *Price* field. Remember that the AND is the & sign in a Microsoft Works database. Try phrasing the query now by doing the following:

- ❑ Select *Query* from the *View* menu.
- ❑ Select *Delete Query* from the *Edit* menu.
- ❑ Enter >6000 & <10000 in the *Price* field and press the Enter key.
- ❑ Press the F10 function key.

Your screen should now look like the one shown in Figure 12.13 with 16 records displayed. You should examine the *Price* field and make sure none of the automobiles are outside of your selected price range.

Remember that AND queries are used when you want two or more conditions met. For a record to pass the AND query criterion, all conditions in the criterion must be true.

➤ *Defining OR Queries*

There are times when you will need to make OR queries. Assume that you wanted to see all Ford Escorts and all Ford Mustangs. Initially you may think this is an AND query. When you look at it closely you see that a model cannot be an Escort and a Mustang. An automobile is either an Escort or a Mustang but not both. Part of the query is an AND query. Since the automobile Make must be a Ford and the Model must be Escort OR Mustang, you will need to force the AND by entering Ford in the Make field and force the OR by entering it in the Model field. Remember that the OR is the | (this may look like a colon on many keyboards but it is not, it is the character above the backslash) on some keyboards. To make this query complete, the following set of instructions:

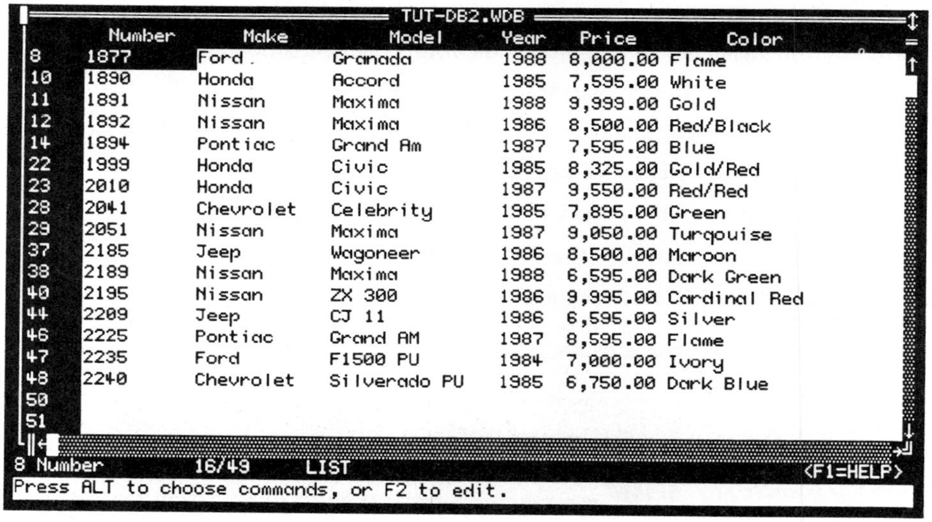

Figure 12.13

*Query of all autos
with a price between
$6,000 and $10,000.*

```
═══════════════════════ TUT-DB2.WDB ═══════════════════════
       Number     Make        Model      Year    Price       Color
8     1877    Ford .      Granada       1988   8,000.00 Flame
10    1890    Honda       Accord        1985   7,595.00 White
11    1891    Nissan      Maxima        1988   9,999.00 Gold
12    1892    Nissan      Maxima        1986   8,500.00 Red/Black
14    1894    Pontiac     Grand Am      1987   7,595.00 Blue
22    1999    Honda       Civic         1985   8,325.00 Gold/Red
23    2010    Honda       Civic         1987   9,550.00 Red/Red
28    2041    Chevrolet   Celebrity     1985   7,895.00 Green
29    2051    Nissan      Maxima        1987   9,050.00 Turqouise
37    2185    Jeep        Wagoneer      1986   8,500.00 Maroon
38    2189    Nissan      Maxima        1988   6,595.00 Dark Green
40    2195    Nissan      ZX 300        1986   9,995.00 Cardinal Red
44    2209    Jeep        CJ 11         1986   6,595.00 Silver
46    2225    Pontiac     Grand AM      1987   8,595.00 Flame
47    2235    Ford        F1500 PU      1984   7,000.00 Ivory
48    2240    Chevrolet   Silverado PU  1985   6,750.00 Dark Blue
50
51
8 Number        16/49     LIST                        <F1=HELP>
Press ALT to choose commands, or F2 to edit.
```

- ❑ Choose *Query* from the *View* menu.
- ❑ Choose *Delete Query* from the *Edit* menu.
- ❑ Enter Ford in the *Make* field.
- ❑ Enter =="Escort" | ="Mustang" in the *Model* field and press Enter.
- ❑ Press F10 to apply the query.

You should now have one Mustang and five Escorts displayed, as shown in Figure 12.14.

Part of the query above needs to be explained. The criterion in the Model field is considered a formula. The first equals sign (=) starts the query. The second equals sign indicates that the criterion is to equal *Escort (="Escort")*. The | symbol defines the OR condition and the last part of the query, =*"Mustang"*, is the other OR criterion.

There may be one other case where you need an OR condition. Assume that you wanted to find any 1987 automobile or any Honda. You could not enter this type of Query by entering Honda in the Make field and 1987 in the Year field. This would be an AND, and you would only get the 1987 Hondas. You need to enter it as an OR condition in a single field. Generally stated, if you enter a condition for a field and the condition is not entered in the field's entry area, you must specify the field name in the condition. Try testing this query by entering the following:

- ❑ Select *Query* from the *View* menu.
- ❑ Select *Delete Query* from the *Edit* menu.

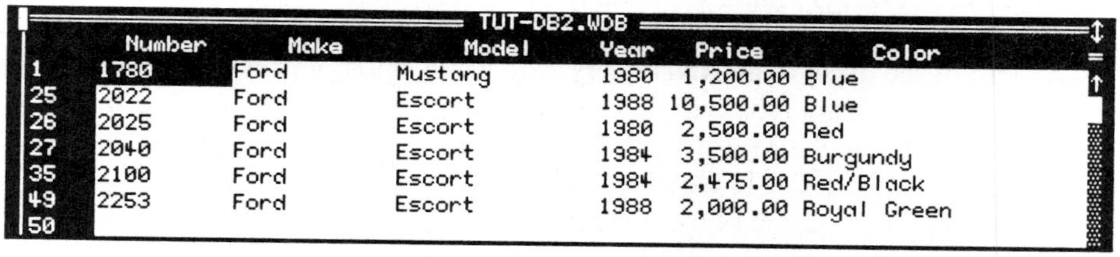

Figure 12.14

*Query of all Escorts
or Mustangs.*

```
═══════════════════════ TUT-DB2.WDB ═══════════════════════
       Number     Make        Model      Year     Price       Color
1     1780    Ford        Mustang       1980    1,200.00 Blue
25    2022    Ford        Escort        1988   10,500.00 Blue
26    2025    Ford        Escort        1980    2,500.00 Red
27    2040    Ford        Escort        1984    3,500.00 Burgundy
35    2100    Ford        Escort        1984    2,475.00 Red/Black
49    2253    Ford        Escort        1988    2,000.00 Royal Green
50
```

❏ **Enter:** = ="Honda" | Year=1987 **in the** *Make* **field and press Enter.**

❏ **Press the F10 function key.**

You should now have 12 records displayed, all of the Hondas and all of the 1987 automobiles.

➤ *Defining NOT Queries*

You can also define NOT types of queries. Suppose you had something against owning a Ford and you wanted to see all automobiles that are not Fords. You could use an OR and define an OR condition for every possible automobile. This would be very cumbersome, and you would probably never figure out all possible automobile makes. An easier way would be to define a NOT condition. Remember that the NOT symbol in the Microsoft Works database is the ~ symbol. Try the NOT by doing the following:

❏ **Select** *Query* **from the** *View* **menu.**

❏ **Select** *Delete* **Query from the** *Edit* **menu.**

❏ **Enter:** =~="Ford" **in the** *Make* **field and press Enter.**

❏ **Press the F10 function key.**

You should now have all automobiles except Fords displayed. Scan your screen and make sure there are no Fords displayed. There should be 34 records found. The results of this query are shown in Figure 12.15.

➤ *Defining Combination AND and OR Queries*

There are times when you may want to combine AND and OR queries. For example, assume you wanted to list all 1980 automobiles and all automobiles made between 1985 and 1988. You could phrase the query as: =1980|=1985|=1986|=1987|=1988; however, this would be very cumbersome for many queries. You can combine this query by using both AND and OR in the same query. Try this query by doing the following:

❏ **Select** *Query* **from the** *Edit* **menu.**

❏ **Select** *Delete Query* **from the** *View* **menu.**

❏ **Enter:** >=1985&<=1988 | =1980 **in the** *Year* **field and press Enter.**

❏ **Press the F10 Function key.**

Figure 12.15

Query results of all autos that are not Fords.

	Number	Make	Model	Year	Price	Color
3	1793	Chevrolet	Caprice	1980	1,250.00	Ivory
4	1795	Pontiac	Grand Prix	1979	1,595.00	White
6	1815	Chevrolet	Chevelle	1980	1,495.00	Blue
7	1856	Pontiac	Ventura	1987	5,700.00	Black/White
9	1879	Honda	Civic	1988	12,500.00	Misty Blue
10	1890	Honda	Accord	1985	7,595.00	White
11	1891	Nissan	Maxima	1988	9,999.00	Gold
12	1892	Nissan	Maxima	1986	8,500.00	Red/Black
13	1893	Buick	Bonneville	1983	5,695.00	Black
14	1894	Pontiac	Grand Am	1987	7,595.00	Blue
15	1901	Jeep	Wagoneer	1986	12,500.00	Burgundy
16	1905	Jeep	CJ 10	1986	1,300.00	Gold/Black
17	1910	Pontiac	Sunbird	1979	999.00	Blue
19	1977	Chevrolet	Celebrity	1985	3,795.00	Flame
20	1988	Chevrolet	Celebrity	1985	3,950.00	Misty Blue
21	1993	Jeep	Wagoneer	1986	13,450.00	Red
22	1999	Honda	Civic	1985	8,325.00	Gold/Red
23	2010	Honda	Civic	1987	9,550.00	Red/Red

TUT-DB2.WDB

3 Number   34/49   LIST   <F1=HELP>

You should now have 37 of the 49 records displayed. Scan your database to make sure you do not have records with years between 1981 and 1984 displayed.

➤ Using Wild Cards

Remember, you can use wild cards in the query criterion. Microsoft Works has two wild card characters. Assume that you want a blue automobile, but you do not care about the make, model, year, or price. You also do not care what color blue it is. If you enter the criterion as =*"Blue"*, you would only get the blue automobiles. You would not get royal blue, navy blue, or the other blues. You would need to use the wild card to search for the other blues. Since the color may be navy blue or blue/green, you would need to use the wild card on each side of the word *blue*. Try this query now.

- ❑ Select *Query* from the *View* menu.
- ❑ Select *Delete Query* from the *Edit* menu.
- ❑ Enter: ="*Blue*" in the *Color* field and press Enter.
- ❑ Press the F10 function key.

Your screen should now display only the records that have blue in their color. Your screen is shown in Figure 12.16. You should have found 14 of the records.

Figure 12.16

Query of all autos that have blue in their color.

	Number	Make	Model	Year	Price	Color
1	1780	Ford	Mustang	1980	1,200.00	Blue
2	1791	Ford	F1500 PU	1984	5,595.00	Gold/Blue
6	1815	Chevrolet	Chevelle	1980	1,495.00	Blue
9	1879	Honda	Civic	1988	12,500.00	Misty Blue
14	1894	Pontiac	Grand Am	1987	7,595.00	Blue
17	1910	Pontiac	Sunbird	1979	999.00	Blue
18	1922	Ford	Fairmont	1980	1,475.00	Blue
20	1988	Chevrolet	Celebrity	1985	3,950.00	Misty Blue
25	2022	Ford	Escort	1988	10,500.00	Blue
36	2180	Chevrolet	Caprice	1982	2,795.00	Blue/Green
39	2190	Ford	F150 PU	1984	4,500.00	Royal Blue
41	2205	Chevrolet	Celebrity	1982	3,150.00	Blue
45	2215	Buick	Regal	1983	3,200.00	Misty Blue
48	2240	Chevrolet	Silverado PU	1985	6,750.00	Dark Blue
50						

(TUT-DB2.WDB)

Microsoft Works' second wild card character is the question mark. This wild card character replaces only one character.

➤ Using Formulas in Queries

Microsoft Works will also allow you to compute values in your query criteria. Assume the following: You are ready to trade automobiles, and the salesperson will allow $2,500.00 on a tradein for your old automobile. You know that you can only afford to finance another $5,000.00. Therefore, you want to see any automobile where the Price minus your trade-in ($2,500.00) is less than or equal to $5,000.00. This should list 31 of the 49 automobiles. You can make this query by doing the following.

- ❑ Select *Query* from the *View* menu.
- ❑ Select *Delete Query* from the *Edit* menu.
- ❑ Enter: =Price-2500<=5000 in the *Price* field and press the Enter key.
- ❑ Press the F10 function key.

Figure 12.17

Query results after using the Switch Hidden Records option.

```
═══════════════════════ TUT-DB2.WDB ═══════════════════════
       Number     Make        Model      Year    Price       Color
 8     1877    Ford        Granada       1988    8,000.00  Flame
 9     1879    Honda       Civic         1988   12,500.00  Misty Blue
10     1890    Honda       Accord        1985    7,595.00  White
11     1891    Nissan      Maxima        1988    9,999.00  Gold
12     1892    Nissan      Maxima        1986    8,500.00  Red/Black
14     1894    Pontiac     Grand Am      1987    7,595.00  Blue
15     1901    Jeep        Wagoneer      1986   12,500.00  Burgundy
21     1993    Jeep        Wagoneer      1986   13,450.00  Red
22     1999    Honda       Civic         1985    8,325.00  Gold/Red
23     2010    Honda       Civic         1987    9,550.00  Red/Red
24     2013    Nissan      ZX 300        1988   14,500.00  Black
25     2022    Ford        Escort        1988   10,500.00  Blue
28     2041    Chevrolet   Celebrity     1985    7,895.00  Green
29     2051    Nissan      Maxima        1987    9,050.00  Turquoise
31     2058    Ford        Lariet PU     1988   14,575.00  White/Red
37     2185    Jeep        Wagoneer      1986    8,500.00  Maroon
40     2195    Nissan      ZX 300        1986    9,995.00  Cardinal Red
46     2225    Pontiac     Grand AM      1987    8,595.00  Flame
8 Number        18/49       LIST                          <F1=HELP>
```

➤ *Using the Switch Hidden Records Option*

You can choose the *Switch Hidden Records* option from the **Select** menu to view all the records that are not displayed. You can use this option to form a NOT condition. For example, assume that you wanted to see all automobiles that you cannot afford in the preceding query. You have just completed a query for this. Now you can choose the *Switch Hidden Records* option from the **Select** menu to see the **NOT** of this query. Do this now.

❑ Choose the *Switch Hidden Records* option from the *Select* menu.

You should now have all the automobiles that did not meet the original query. This would be the other 18 automobiles out of the 49 that are available in the database. These autos are shown in Figure 12.17.

Printing Query Results in List View

When you print a database, only those records that are displayed are printed. If you have a query applied to the database, only those records that satisfy the query criterion are displayed. When you are in *List* view, your queries will print in a column format. Before you print your query, you should select a small *Font* so all records will print on a single page. First, change your font, then print the results of your last query by selecting *Print* from the **Print** menu. (You may want to use the *Preview* option to make sure your records will fit on one page before you print.)

❑ Choose *Font* from the *Format* menu and select a small font. Use *Elite 12* if you have it.

❑ Make sure your printer is turned on and online.

❑ Select *Print* from the *Print* menu.

❑ Set on the *Print Record and Field Labels* option.

❑ Select *Print*.

Printing from Form View

You can also print your query results as forms if your are in *Form* view. This option is especially handy if you need to provide individual copies of records to different people. Before you print from *Form* view, create the following query so you will not have many pages to print. This query should give you three records to print.

❑ Choose *Query* from the *View* menu.

❑ Choose *Delete Query* from the *Edit* menu.

❑ Enter Ford in the *Make* field and Blue in the *Color* field and press Enter.

❑ Press F10 to exit the query.

❑ Choose *Form* from the *View* menu.

❑ Choose *Print* from the *Print* menu.

❑ Set the *All Records* option on in the *Print which records* option box.

❑ Choose *Print* to print your results.

Conclusion

This chapter has shown you how to modify a form. Forms are used to make data entry easier and to allow you to print the records in your database as if they were on preprinted forms. This chapter has also shown you how to make queries of the database. Queries are used to help eliminate from view records that are not important to you. You should review the material in this chapter and then complete the Hands on Practice exercises that follow.

Hands on Practice

Exercise 1

For this practice set, you will be using the the file named **HOP-D121**. This file is on your tutorials diskette. The file contains records about property listed by a real estate agency. You should open this file now.

Part 1

1. Modify the default form so that it looks like the one shown on the below. Use your name for the name of the Real Estate Agency.

Part 2

Make the following queries. Print the results of each query with record and field labels as you make the query.

1. Write a query that will display all property that is Zoned *B1*.

2. Write a query that will display all property that is Zoned *B1* and in the city of *Augusta*.

3. Write a query that will display all property that is Zoned *B1* or *B2*.

4. Write a query that will display all property that is *NOT* in the city of *Harrisonburg*.

5. Write a query that will display all property that has more than *10,000* feet but less than *30,000* feet.

6. Write a query that will display all property that has a Zone of *R1* or *R2*, is in the City of *Harrisonburg*, has less than *3,000* feet, and has an asking price between *$30,000.00* and *$60,000.00*.

7. Write a query that will list all property where the *Asking Price* is more than 10 percent above the *Appraisal Price*.

8. Write a query that will display all property where the *Asking Price* is less than *$20.00* per square foot.

```
┌──────────────────────────── HOP-D121.WDB ─────────────────────────────┐
│                        (your name) Real Estate Company                 │
│                                                                        │
│                              Current Listings                          │
│                                                                        │
│                          Contract Number>  ...........                 │
│                                                                        │
│         City>  ............................                            │
│                                                                        │
│         Property Zoning>  ..........................                   │
│                                                                        │
│         Square Footage> ...........Sq. Ft.                             │
│                                                                        │
│         Appraised Value> ....................   Asking Price> ████████ │
│                                                                        │
└────────────────────────────────────────────────────────────────────────┘
```

Exercise 2

For this practice set, you will be using the file named **HOP-D122**. This file is on your tutorials diskette. The file contains records about books in a bookstore. You should open this file and complete this exercise. Print the results of each query with record and field labels.

1. Write the query to find the book with the title *Kings and Queens.*

2. Write the query to find the book with ISBN number *656-0000-22.*

3. Write the query to find all books where the author is *Karen King.*

4. Write the query to find all books that are in *Edition 3.*

5. Write the query to find all books that have a copyright between and including *1988* and *1990.*

6. Write the query to find all books that have a copyright date before *1987* and are in *Edition 1.*

7. Write the query to find all books where the Number On Order is greater than the Number On Hand.

8. Write the query to find all books that have a subject about *Computer.* The Subject field may contain several subjects, so you will need to use wild cards when you search on this field.

9. Write the query to find all books that have a subject that contains *Tax* or *Income.*

10. Write the query to find all books where the Number On Hand and and the Number On Order are zero.

11. Write the query to find all books where the Number On Order is more than twice the Number On Hand.

12. Write the query to find all books about *computers* and *programming.*

13

Creating
Database Reports

This chapter will introduce you to the Report routines of the Database module of Microsoft Works. These routines will allow you to create reports that contain all the records and fields in the database, or you can specify that only certain fields and records are to be used. You can also specify new fields that do not exist in the database as long as the new data can be derived from existing data. You can specify the order that the records are to be sorted, calculate totals, calculate averages, count the number of records, and perform several other functions. These functions can be performed for all records in the report, or they can be performed on certain groups of records. You can also view your report on your screen before printing it.

Report Concepts

As we discuss how to generate reports in the following sections, we will use a **United Way Contributions** database. This database will contain eight fields. They will be the *Contributor ID, First Name, Initial, Last Name, City, State, Contribution Last Year,* and *Contribution This Year.*

Reports are more formalized than queries. Normally, queries are used by an individual to examine a database. Reports are used when a formal copy of the database is needed that indicates totals or other statistical information. These reports may be used by managers to analyze data, or they may be used as copies to be distributed to members of a team. Since reports can contain information that may not be in the database, a report may need to be generated to get this new information.

In Microsoft Works, you do not actually create a report. You create a *report format*. When the report is printed, it uses this report format and the data that is currently in the database to generate the report. This technique allows you to change the data in the database and generate a new report without changing the report format.

You can create and save up to eight report formats for each database. A report format is always saved with the database when the database is saved. This makes it available for future use.

➤ *Report Lines*

Reports are composed of several different types of lines or rows. Each type of line or row on the report performs a different function. Before we look at how to create a report, we need to examine the different types of lines that appear on a report. Examine the sample report in Figure 13.1.

Works supports six different types of report lines.

Intr Report: These are the *Introductory Report* lines. These lines are printed one time, on the first page of the report only. This type of line is normally used to specify report titles, run dates, times, or any other information that you only want printed on the first page of a report. There can be any number of *Intr Report* lines for a given report. On the sample report in Figure 13.1, there are two Intr Report lines. A report title is the first line, and a line that contains the date and time is the second line.

Intr Page: *Page Introductory* lines are printed on each page of the report. They are often referred to as page heading lines. Normal items for this type of line are column headings. There can be any number of *Intr Page* lines for a report. Notice in the sample report in Figure 13.1 that these lines occur on both pages, but the *Intr Report* lines are only on the first page.

Intr Break: This is an *Introductory Break* line. These lines are printed when Works encounters a change in the data of a specified field. Works will support three different levels of breaks with any number of these lines for each break. The sample report in Figure 13.1 uses a break for each state that is in the report. These are the *Intr State* lines. This Intr Break line is printed before any records for a state are printed. Breaks are discussed in more detail later in this chapter.

Record: These are *record* lines. Works prints one of each of these lines for every record in the database. This type of line is used to print the data in the database. You can have any number of record lines in a report.

Summ Break: These are *Summary Break* lines. Break lines are similar to subtotal lines. These lines are printed at the end of each group of records that contain the same value for the break field. Microsoft Works will support up to three different levels of breaks or groups. The sample report in Figure 13.1 has two levels of breaks, the first break is on the *City* field. Notice that there is one of these break lines for each city in the report. The second break is on *State*. Groups and Breaks are discussed more fully later in this chapter.

Summ Report: These lines print one time at the end of the entire report. They are normally used to print report totals and other statistics that deal with the entire report.

Customizing a Report

To create a report, you select the *View New Report* option from the **View** menu. When this option is selected, a default report is created and you are placed in the **Report** phase of the database. The default report will be displayed on your screen. To cancel the display of the report and move to the phase that allows you to customize the default report, you press the **Esc** key. The default report will contain two *Intr*

Figure 13.1

*A database report can contain several different types of lines. These lines can be printed at the top of the report (**Intr Report**), once at the top of each page (**Intr Page**), once at the begin-ning of a group of records (**Intr break**), once for each database record (**Record**), once at the end of a group of records (**Summ break**), and once at the end of a report (**Summ Report**).*

Label		First Name	I	Last Name	City	State	This Year	Last Year	Amount Change
Intr Report						Contribution Listing			
Intr Report		3/11/88							11:26 PM
Intr Page		First		Last			This	Last	Amount
Intr Page		Name	I	Name	City	State	Year	Year	Change
Intr State		State: MD							
Record		Marcia	K	Smith	Baltimore	MD	225.00	200.00	25.00
Record		Thomas	J	Smith	Baltimore	MD	150.00	150.00	0.00
Record		Mary	C	Smith	Baltimore	MD	500.00	500.00	0.00
Record		Karen	L	Smith	Baltimore	MD	60.00	50.00	10.00
Summ City		Total For Baltimore					935.00	900.00	35.00
		Phillip	M	Jones	Silver Springs	MD	410.00	500.00	(90.00)
		Gayle	R	Jones	Silver Springs	MD	50.00	0.00	50.00
		Carol	T	Jones	Silver Springs	MD	25.00	25.00	0.00
		Everett	A	Kline	Silver Springs	MD	1,500.00	1,000.00	500.00
Summ City		Total For Silver Springs					1,985.00	1,525.00	460.00
Summ State		Total For MD		8 Contributions			2,920.00	2,425.00	495.00
Intr State		State: PA							
		Jason	D	Miller	Philadelphia	PA	10.00	10.00	0.00
		Samuel	U	Miller	Philadelphia	PA	50.00	55.00	(5.00)
		Anne	B	Miller	Philadelphia	PA	100.00	75.00	25.00
Summ City		Total For Philadelphia					160.00	140.00	20.00
Intr Page		First		Last			This	Last	Amount
Intr Page		Name	I	Name	City	State	Year	Year	Change
		Donald	Q	Applebaum	Pittsburgh	PA	50.00	75.00	(25.00)
		Alice	A	Applebaum	Pittsburgh	PA	500.00	210.00	290.00
		Jim	G	Jacobs	Pittsburgh	PA	175.00	275.00	(100.00)
		William	C	Jacobs	Pittsburgh	PA	150.00	150.00	0.00
		Gary	W	Jacobs	Pittsburgh	PA	1,000.00	500.00	500.00
		Henry	Z	Kline	Pittsburgh	PA	225.00	200.00	25.00
		Carl	M	Smith	Pittsburgh	PA	120.00	100.00	20.00
		Calvin	S	Smith	Pittsburgh	PA	25.00	25.00	0.00
Summ City		Total For Pittsburg					2,245.00	1,535.00	710.00
Summ State		Total For PA		11 Contributions			2,405.00	1,675.00	730.00
Intr State		State: VA							
		Kimberly	F	Martin	Richmond	VA	550.00	500.00	50.00
		Frank	B	Martin	Richmond	VA	95.00	100.00	(5.00)
		Larwrence	K	Martin	Richmond	VA	750.00	600.00	150.00
		Marion	S	Martin	Richmond	VA	100.00	85.00	15.00
		Jane	C	Martin	Richmond	VA	150.00	0.00	150.00
		Victor	L	Martin	Richmond	VA	350.00	700.00	(350.00)
		Betty	T	Smith	Richmond	VA	250.00	0.00	250.00
Summ City		Total For Richmond					2,245.00	1,985.00	260.00
Summ State		Total For VA		7 Contributions			2,245.00	1,985.00	260.00
Summ Report		Grand Totals		26 Contributions			7,570.00	6,085.00	1,485.00
Summ Report		Average Contribution:					291.15		
Summ Report		High Contribution					1500.00		
Summ Report		Low Contribution					10.00		

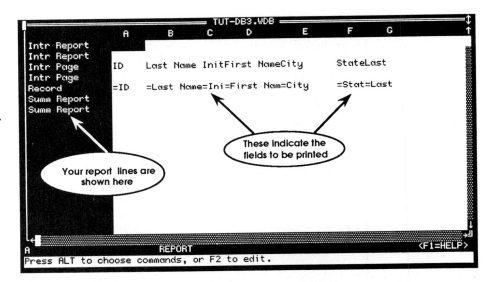

Figure 13.2

*The default report contains several **Intr Report** and **Page** lines, a **Record** line, and two report **Summary** lines.*

Report lines, two *Intr Page* lines, one *Record* line, and two *Summ Report* lines. An example of this default report format is shown in Figure 13.2. This example report form is the default form for the *United Way Contributions* report used in this chapter.

The left-hand side of the report format shows the type of line for the line displayed to the right. The right side of the report shows the fields for each line type and the contents of the fields. In the case of most of the lines the fields are blank. This approach of leaving fields blank is used to print blank lines at various places in the report.

The report form has several things in common with a spreadsheet. First, the columns on the report are lettered rather than named. The column letters start with an **A** and will continue up to **IV** to allow up to 255 columns in a report. Next, most formulas in the cells cannot be displayed completely. The cells show only what will fit within the width of the cell. This width is the same as that defined in the width of the *View* form of the database. The complete contents of the cell are displayed in the *Formula* line.

The two first lines in Figure 13.2 are *Intr Report* lines. The first line is normally used to specify a report title, a date, and a page number. These would be entered as text or formulas in a cell of one of the columns. The second *Intr Report* line is normally left blank to provide a blank line between the report title and the column headings.

The next two lines on the default report are *Intr Page* lines. On the first of these lines, the default report will use the field names of each field in the database to generate column headings for each page. The second *Intr Page* line places a blank line between the column headings and the first detail or record line on a page.

The fifth line is a *Record* line. In the default report shown, each field in the database is to be printed. Notice that the entries in the columns of the record line are preceded by the equals (=) sign. In essence, these entries are formulas. If the equal sign were not included, Works would treat these entries as labels rather than fields. The entry in the first column, *=ID*, indicates that the value of the ID field in the record is to be printed here. You can enter any formula in these columns. For instance, if you wanted to print the contribution this year minus the contribution last year, you could enter this as a formula in a new field.

The last two lines on the default report are the *Summ Report* lines. These lines print one time at the end of the report. These lines would be used to enter formulas to calculate report totals, averages, and other statistics that deal with all of the records in the report.

If you printed the default report as it now exists, the report would look like a printing of the database from *List* view with the *Print record and field labels* option set on. Normally you would want to modify the report by adding report titles and summary statistics.

➤ *Changing Entries in Report Lines*

To change any entry in a report line, you must first position your cursor on the entry you want to change. Once you have your cursor positioned, you can either use the F2 formula edit key to edit the current contents of the entry, or you can enter new contents by typing them in. You could use this idea to enter a report title in one of the fields on the first *Intr Report* line. You could also enter some of the special characters to get the *Current Date* and *Page Numbers* to print with the report title.

For other types of changes, you can use the **Edit** menu. This menu is shown in Figure 13.3.

To move an entry from one location to another, you select the *Move* option from the **Edit** menu. To copy an entry, you use the *Copy* option. In both cases, you position your cursor on the field you want moved or copied then select the desired option. Next, you need to move your cursor to the new location and press the Enter key.

The *Clear* option is used to blank out an entry, row, or column. To clear an entry, you must position your cursor on the entry before you select the *Clear* option. To clear a column or row, you must first select the entire column or row and then select the *Clear* option from the menu. You can also clear multiple entries, rows, and columns by selecting them as a block before you choose the *Clear* option from the **Edit** menu.

➤ *Inserting and Deleting Report Lines*

The *Delete Row/Column* option is used to delete a line or column from the report. To use this option, position your cursor on any cell in the line or column you want deleted. Next, select the *Delete Row/Column* option. You will be provided with a check box to indicate what you want deleted, a row or a column. Select the appropriate choice and press the Enter key.

The *Insert Row/Column* option is used to insert either a new row or a new column. When you insert a new column, the new column will be inserted to the left of the cursor. To insert a column, you use the same approach you used to insert a column into the List view of the database. When you insert a new row, the

Figure 13.3

*The **Edit** menu can be used to move, copy, and clear fields. This menu also has options for inserting and deleting rows and columns.*

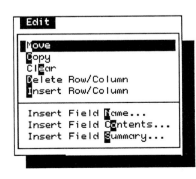

Figure 13.4

*The Fields dialog box is used to specify which field name or field content you want displayed in a report line column. You get this dialog box when you choose **Insert Field Name** or **Insert Field Contents** from the Edit menu.*

new row will be inserted above the cursor. Each row must be one of the types discussed earlier. Inserting rows will be covered in detail later in this chapter.

➤ Entering Field Contents

The bottom part of the **Edit** menu can be used to enter the contents of the field entries. These options allow you to select data or field names from the database. If you select either *Insert Field Name* or *Insert Field Contents*, you will be provided with a dialog box similar to the one shown in Figure 13.4. The dialog box will list all the field names in your database. You can then select one of the fields displayed. If you have selected *Insert Field Name,* the field name is placed in the cell. If you select *Insert Field Contents*, the formula to print the contents of the field is placed in the cell.

The last option on the **Edit** menu is the *Field Summary* option. This option allows you to select statistical functions for the cell. These functions should only be used in summary lines. When the *Insert Field Summary* option is selected, you are provided with the dialog box shown in Figure 13.5. You must then select one of the fields on the left side of the dialog box and one of the functions shown on the right side of the dialog box. This function will then be inserted into the cell. The function inserted will be applied to the field that you select from the left side of the dialog box.

Each of the functions provided in the Field Summary box is described in Figure 13.6.

You can also insert these field names, field values, and field summaries by entering them into the cells rather than choosing them from the dialog boxes. If you want to enter a field name, you simply type the

Figure 13.5

*When you choose the **Insert Field Summary** option from the Edit menu you are provided with this dialog box. You must first choose the field you want to apply the statistic to, then choose the statistic. When you choose the OK button, a formula to compute the statistic is inserted into the report.*

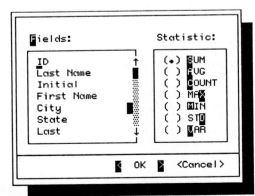

SUM:	This function provides a total of the field for the group or report.
AVG:	This function provides the average of the field for the group or report.
COUNT:	This function counts the number of occurrences of the field for the group or report.
MAX:	This function displays the largest value in the field for the group or report.
MIN:	This function provides the smallest value in the field for the group or report.
STD:	This function provides the standard deviation of the values in the field for the group or report.
VAR:	This function provides the variance of the values in the field for the group or report.

Figure 13.6

*Statistics can be computed on fields in **Summary** lines. These statistics can provide data that is calculated from data in a column. The statistic can be applied to all records in a report summary line or to groups of records if it is placed in a summary break line.*

field name into the cell. If you want to enter a field value, you must enter the field name as a formula by preceding the field name with an equals (=) sign. If you want to enter a field summary by typing it, you must precede the summary statistic name by the equals sign (=) to indicate it is a formula, then enter the statistic name followed by the field name enclosed in parentheses.

➤ Inserting Lines in the Report

To insert a new line in a report, you select the *Insert Row/Column* option from the **Edit** menu. Next, you select the *Row* option from the diaiog check box provided by the *Insert Row/Column* option. This will provide you with a selection box similar to the one shown in Figure 13.7.

This selection box may differ in one major way from report to report depending on how you have sorted the database. This difference deals with the number of *Intr* and *Summ* lines shown in the selection box. An

Figure 13.7

*When you choose the **Insert Row/Column** option from the Edit menu and choose **Row** from the check box, you must specify what kind of row (line) you want to insert. The types available are determined by what you have specified in the Sort routine of the report procedure.*

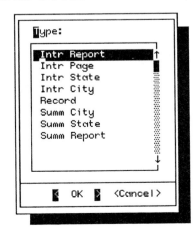

Intr and *Summ* line will be shown for each field that has been specified as a sort field with a *Break* option. In the example shown in Figure 13.7, the database has been sorted by *City* within *State* before the insert option was selected. Therefore, there are two options for Intr group lines, *Intr City* and *Intr State*. There are also two options for *Summ* group lines. These are the *Summ City* and *Summ State* lines.

Microsoft Works will only allow *Intr* and *Summ* lines for fields that have been defined in the **Report** phase as sort fields with breaks. When you get the insert row dialog box, you select the type of line you want inserted. Once you press the Enter key, the line will be inserted. You can then enter the text or data that you want printed on the line. Lines will be inserted in a specific order. This order is:

> **Intr Report**
> **Intr Page**
> **Intr 1st break field**
> **Intr 2nd break field**
> **Intr 3rd break field**
> **Record**
> **Summ 3rd break field**
> **Summ 2nd break field**
> **Summ 1st break field**
> **Summ Report**

The only exception to the preceding order occurs when you insert a line type that already exists. For example, assume you insert a new *Intr Page* line and you already have one of these line types. If your cursor is below the first line of the line type, the new line is entered below the existing line of the same type. If your cursor is above or on the existing line of the same type, the new line is inserted above the existing line of the same type. If you have two lines of the same type and your cursor is positioned on one of the lines, the new line is inserted directly above the cursor. If you insert a line type that does not exist, the line is inserted in the order just described.

Sorting Records for a Report

In order to sort the database records, and most importantly to specify fields for summary lines, you must choose the *Sort* option from the **Select** menu. When you choose this option, you will be provided with the Sort dialog box shown in Figure 13.8.

Figure 13.8

*When you are in the Report phase and choose the Sort option, the sort dialog box has several entries that are used only with reports. The **Break** option will allow you to insert **Intr** and **Summ** lines for the sorted fields. The 1st letter option will force printing of these **Intr** and **Summ** lines when the first letter of the sort field changes.*

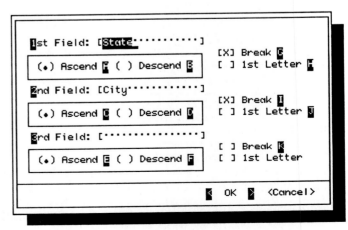

This dialog box is similar to the dialog box you get when you sort records in the *List* or *Form* view of the database. You must enter the sort fields in the *Field* text entries. You must specify the most inclusive or major sort field as the 1st Field, the intermediate sort field as the 2nd Field, and the minor or least inclusive field as the 3rd Field. You also have the option to specify that the field is to be sorted in either ascending or descending order.

Notice that there are two entries to the right side of each sort field entry. These entries are used to specify that the field is to be used as a control break field. If the *Break* option is selected, you will be allowed to specify introductory and summary lines for the field. If the Break option is not selected, no introductory or summary lines can be specified for the field.

The last option for each field is the *1st Letter* option. If this option is selected, a break will occur when the first letter in the field changes. The difference between the *Break* and the *1st Letter* options is that if the *Break* option is chosen and the *1st Letter* option is not chosen for the *State* field, a break will occur when the state changes from *Alabama* to *Alaska*. If the *Break* and *1st Letter* options are chosen, no break would occur until the first letter in the state changes from A to B or some other letter. No break would occur between *Alabama* and *Alaska*.

Multiple-Level Breaks

Works will allow you to define reports that have up to three levels of breaks. A break occurs when the value of some cell changes as the report is printed. For instance, assume that you wanted a report that listed United Way contributions sorted by last name with a total for contributors that had the same last name. Next, assume you wanted all people from the same city together with a total for the city. Finally, assume you wanted all cities together within a state and a total for the state. This would mean that all contributions from any Jones from Baltimore, Maryland, would be together with a total, and then all contributions for any Smith from Baltimore, Maryland, would be together with a total. After you had listed all contributions from Baltimore, Maryland, a total for Baltimore would be printed. You would then list all contributions from Silver Springs, Maryland, with a total for that city and then a total for Maryland. Next, you would begin listing contributions from the first person in the first city of the next state.

Since a break occurs when the value of a cell changes, the records for the report must be sorted in the appropriate order before the report is printed. In the case just described, this order would be to sort by *Last Name* within *City* within *State*. This would put the records in the correct order to perform the control breaks on Last name, City, and State. A report like the one just described in shown in Figure 13.9.

The first two lines in the report are *Report Intr* lines. The next two lines are *Page Intr* lines. The next three lines are *Intr* lines for the control breaks. The first or most inclusive break is on the State field. The next most inclusive or second break is on the City field. The least inclusive or third-level break is on the Last Name field. Notice that these lines are printed at the beginning of the first group. Now notice that there is a set of detail lines for contributions from people named Jones and then a total line for the Joneses. This is the third-level summary line. After the Joneses' total line comes the next group of contributions for the Smiths and then a third-level summary line for contributions from Smiths.

When the City changes from Baltimore to Silver Springs, a second-level control break occurs. Anytime a higher-level break occurs, it automatically forces all lower-level breaks to occur. This change in City forces a summary line for the Last Name on Smiths and then the summary line for the City, Baltimore. After the summary lines are printed, the introductory lines for both the second-level and third-level control breaks are printed.

```
                                          Contributions Listing
                          3/11/88                                        11:26 PM

                          First      Last
                          Name       I    Name        City       State   Contribution

        1st-Level Intr    State:          MD
        2nd-Level Intr    City:           Baltimore
        3rd-Level Intr    Last Name:      Jones
                          Phillip    M    Jones       Baltimore  MD        410.00
                          Gayle      R    Jones       Baltimore  MD         50.00
                          Carol      T    Jones       Baltimore  MD         25.00

        3rd-Level Summ    Total for:      Jones                            485.00

        3rd-Level Intr    Last Name:      Smith
                          Marcia     K    Smith       Baltimore  MD        225.00
                          Thomas     J    Smith       Baltimore  MD        150.00

        3rd-Level Summ    Total for:      Smith                            375.00
        2nd-Level Summ    Total For:      Baltimore                        860.00

        2nd-Level Intr    City:           Silver Springs
        3rd-Level Intr    Last Name:      Jones
                          Karen      L    Jones       Silver Springs  MD    25.00
                          Linda      P    Jones       Silver Springs  MD   100.00
                          Marsha     W    Jones       Silver Springs  MD    50.00

        3rd-Level Summ    Total For:  Jones                                175.00
        2nd-Level Summ    Total For Silver Springs                         175.00
        1st-Level Summ    Total For MD              8 Contributions       1,035.00

        1st-Level Intr    State:          PA
        2nd-Level Intr    City:           Philadelphia
        3rd-Level Intr    Last Name:      Miller
                          Jason      D    Miller      Philadelphia  PA     10.00
                          Samuel     U    Miller      Philadelphia  PA     50.00
                          Anne       B    Miller      Philadelphia  PA    100.00

        3rd-Level Summ    Total For:      Miller                          160.00
        2rd Level Summ    Total For       Philadelphia                    160.00
        1st-Level Summ    Total For:      PA         3 Contributions      160.00
        Report Summ       Grand Totals              11 Contributions    1,195.00
```

Figure 13.9

A multiple-level control break report will print Intr and Summ lines when a sort field changes. These lines are used to break the report at specific areas during the printing of the report.

When the state changes from MD to PA, a first-level control break occurs. This forces the summary lines for all three levels to be printed. Notice that the total lines are printed with the minor or lowest level control break first. Summary lines always print with the lowest level occurring first and then moving to the highest-level break.

At the very bottom of the report are all three summary break lines and a Report Summary line. When the last record of the database is printed, all summary lines are printed.

The important things to remember about control breaks are the following:

1. The database must be sorted in the correct order before control breaks will work properly. The sort fields must be specified using the Sort option from the Query menu in the Report phase of the database.

2. The sorting order must specify that the most inclusive field is the 1st sort field, the middle-level control break is the 2nd sort field, and the least-inclusive group is the 3rd sort field.

Figure 13.10

To view a report before you print it, choose the report name from the **View** *menu. Each report that has been created for the database will be listed in the* **View** *menu. When the report name is selected, the report will be displayed on your screen.*

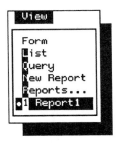

3. You must choose the *Break* option in the *Sort* dialog box.

4. You must include summary break lines in your report definition.

Viewing a Report

When reports are created, they are assigned a default name. These report names will be *Report1*, *Report2*, *Report3*, *etc.* You can view a report from the Form view, List view, or Report phase of the database. To view a report, choose the name of the report you want to view from the **View** menu. This menu is shown in Figure 13.10.

Before you view a report, you must choose the correct report from this menu. Choosing the report makes that report the active report. The active report will be marked with an asterisk.

When you view the report, as much of the report as will fit on a single screen will be displayed. If you press the Enter key, an additional screen will be displayed. When the entire report has been displayed, you will be returned to the *Report* view.

If you press the Esc key while viewing a report, the report will be canceled and you will be returned to the *Report* view.

Printing a Report

To print a report, you choose the *Print* or *Preview* option from the **Print** menu from the *Report* phase. If you are in the *List* or *Form* phase, you must first move into the *Report* phase by choosing the report name from the **View** menu. You can then press the *Esc* key and choose the *Print* option from the *Print* menu.

Printing Summary Reports

Summary reports contain summary lines but no record lines. You print this type of report when you need to see the totals but are not interested in the detail or record lines.

To print this type of report, you must set the *Print all but record rows* on from the **Print** dialog box. This dialog box is shown in Figure 13.11.

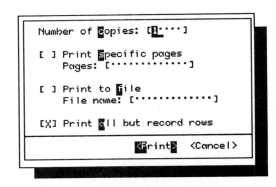

Figure 13.11

To print a summary report, you must set on the Print all but record rows from the Print option of the Print menu. A summary report will print summary lines but not detail lines.

Using Queries in Reports

You can also apply a query to the database before the report is printed. If you do this, only the records that meet the query requirements are printed on the report.

To define a query for the report, you must define the query conditions before you print the report. First, choose the *Query* option from the **View** menu. Next, define the query using the approach discussed in Chapter 12. From the *Query* routine, choose the report name from the **View** menu. You can then print the database from the *Report* phase.

Naming, Deleting, and Copying Reports

When you first create a report, Microsoft Works names the report Report1, Report2, Report3, etc., depending on the number of reports defined for the database. If you want to rename a report, you must choose the *Reports* option from the **View** menu. When you choose this option, you will be provided with a dialog box similar to the one shown in Figure 13.12.

To rename a report, you use your arrow keys to choose the report you want to rename. Next, tab into the *Name* text box and enter the new name for the report. Finally, you must tab to the *Rename* button and press the Enter key.

To delete a report, you must first use your arrow keys to select the report you want to delete and then choose the *Delete* button. You cannot recover a report that has been deleted.

Figure 13.12

To rename, copy, and delete reports, you choose the Reports option from the View menu. The dialog box for this menu lists each report you have defined for the database.

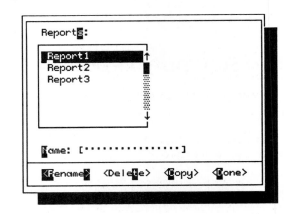

To copy a report, you must use your arrow keys to select the report you want to copy. Next, tab to the *Name* text box and enter a name for the new report. Finally, tab to the *Copy* button and press the Enter key. Copying a report is an easy way to initially begin a new report. You can make a copy of an existing report and then edit the report form to create a totally different report.

Saving a Report

To save a report, you must save the database. All reports that are defined for the database are saved when the database is saved.

Conclusion

This completes the report concepts section of this chapter. You should review the chapter and then complete the selftest before moving on to the tutorial.

Chapter 13 Self Test

1. Distinguish between an Intr Report line and an Intr Page line.

2. In a database report, when does an Intr Report line print?

3. In a database report, when does a Record line print?

4. What is the purpose of Summ lines?

5. How would you get a blank line to print between a Record line and the next Summ line?

6. How do you change an entry in a field of a report line?

7. What is the difference between the Insert Field Name option and the Insert Field Contents option of the Edit menu?

8. How do you insert statistics in a report?

9. What option is used to insert a new line in a report?

10. If you insert a new Intr Report line and your cursor is on the last line of the report definition, where will the new Intr Report line be inserted?

11. Sorting database records using the Sort Records option in the Report phase serves two purposes. The first purpose is to sort the records. What is the second purpose?

12. What is the difference between the Break option and the 1st Letter option in the Sort menu?

13. Explain what causes a control break.

14. How do you print a report if you are in the List or Form phase of the database?

15. What is a Summary report? How do you print a Summary report?

16. How do you name a report?

17. How do you delete a report?

18. How do you save a report?

Chapter 13 Tutorial

In this tutorial, you will be using a database that has already been created. You will use the database to generate a report without control breaks and a report that contains several level breaks.

Starting the Tutorial

Start the tutorial by starting Microsoft Works and loading the database named **TUT-DB3.WDB**.

❑ **Start Microsoft Works.**

❑ **Open the database named TUT-DB3.WDB.**

When you complete loading the database, you should have a list of names, addresses, and contributions on your screen similar to those in Figure 13.13. This will be the database that will be used in this tutorial.

Creating Reports

We will begin this tutorial by creating a default report. To create this report, choose the *New Report* option from the **View** menu. This menu is shown in Figure 13.14.

❑ **Pull down the *View* menu.**

❑ **Choose the *New Report* option.**

❑ **Press the Enter key.**

After you choose this option, Works will display a report of the records in your database. These will be the same records you see in the *List* view. To cancel the display of the report and change to the report phase, you must press the *Esc* key.

❑ **Press the *Esc* key to cancel the report display and change to the report phase.**

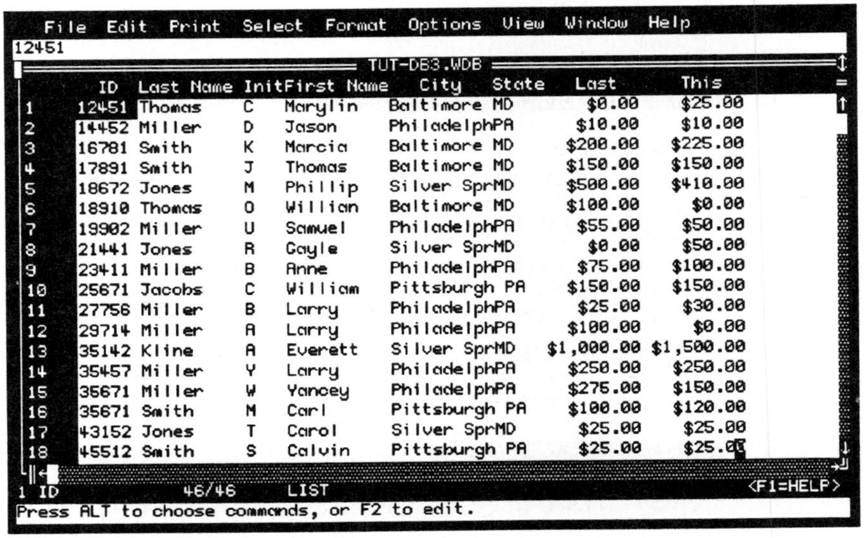

Figure 13.13

The tutorial file for this chapter will be a list of contributors and their contributions for the United Way.

```
  File  Edit  Print  Select  Format  Options  View  Window  Help
 12451
═══════════════════════════════ TUT-DB3.WDB ═══════════════════════════════
        ID  Last Name Init First Name  City      State    Last        This
  1    12451 Thomas    C    Marylin    Baltimore  MD       $0.00       $25.00
  2    14452 Miller    D    Jason      PhiladelphPA        $10.00      $10.00
  3    16781 Smith     K    Marcia     Baltimore  MD       $200.00     $225.00
  4    17891 Smith     J    Thomas     Baltimore  MD       $150.00     $150.00
  5    18672 Jones     M    Phillip    Silver SprMD        $500.00     $410.00
  6    18910 Thomas    O    William    Baltimore  MD       $100.00     $0.00
  7    19902 Miller    U    Samuel     PhiladelphPA        $55.00      $50.00
  8    21441 Jones     R    Gayle      Silver SprMD        $0.00       $50.00
  9    23411 Miller    B    Anne       PhiladelphPA        $75.00      $100.00
 10    25671 Jacobs    C    William    Pittsburgh PA       $150.00     $150.00
 11    27756 Miller    B    Larry      PhiladelphPA        $25.00      $30.00
 12    29714 Miller    A    Larry      PhiladelphPA        $100.00     $0.00
 13    35142 Kline     A    Everett    Silver SprMD    $1,000.00   $1,500.00
 14    35457 Miller    Y    Larry      PhiladelphPA        $250.00     $250.00
 15    35671 Miller    W    Yancey     PhiladelphPA        $275.00     $150.00
 16    35671 Smith     M    Carl       Pittsburgh PA       $100.00     $120.00
 17    43152 Jones     T    Carol      Silver SprMD        $25.00      $25.00
 18    45512 Smith     S    Calvin     Pittsburgh PA       $25.00      $25.00
 1 ID              46/46      LIST                              <F1=HELP>
 Press ALT to choose commands, or F2 to edit.
```

Figure 13.14

To create a new report, choose the
New Report *option from the View*
menu. This option will create a
default report format that can be
modified or customized.

You need to realize that using the *New Report* option from the **View** menu creates a new report with default lines. Since you do not have the database sorted at this time, no break lines are included in the new report. If you did have the database sorted, there would be a summary line for each field defined as a sort field.

Your new report format should look like the one shown in Figure 13.15.

Figure 13.15

The default report has
Intr Report *lines,* ***Intr***
Page *lines, a* ***Record***
line, and ***Summ***
Report *lines. These*
lines are provided to
make customizing of
the report easy.

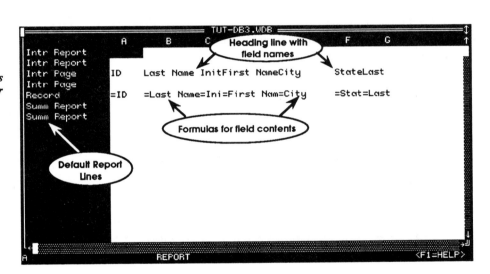

This report contains two *Intr Report* lines, two *Intr Page* lines, one *Record* line, and two *Summ Report* lines. The first *Intr Page* line contains the names of the fields within your database. These are used as the report's column headings. The second *Intr Page* line is used to produce a blank line between your headings and your first database record.

The *Record* line contains a formula to print each of the fields in the database. These formulas only contain the name of the field that will be printed in the columns.

Both the *Intr Report* and the *Summ Report* lines are blank.

Before you begin modifying the report format you need to view the report again to understand how the default report has been set up with field widths and headings. To view the report, choose the report name from the **View** menu.

    ❑ **Choose *Report* 1 from the *View* menu.**

Your first screen should look like the one in Figure 13.16.

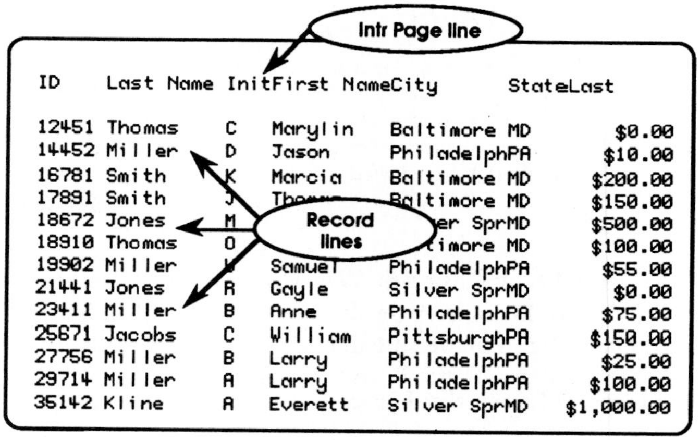

Figure 13.16

*The default report provides field names for column headings. These are printed using an **Intr Page** line. The records are printed using a **Record** line. The fields on the Record line have the same width as they have in List view.*

Notice several important problems with the report. The first problem is that the city name for some cities is truncated. The city *Silver Springs* printed as *Silver Spr*. Notice also that the City and the State are run together as one word, for example, *PhiladelphPA*. The last problem is that the last column is not displayed. It will print by itself on a separate page. This is because the page is not wide enough to print all the columns.

➤ Setting the Field Width

We will correct the first two problems by changing the field width for the City and by changing the alignment for the State. You change field widths, and change all field formats, with the **Format** menu. To change a field width, you need the *Column Width* option.

- ❑ Press the *Esc* key to cancel viewing of the report.
- ❑ Place your cursor in the *City* field (column E) of any row.
- ❑ Choose *Column Width* from the *Format* menu.
- ❑ Set this width to 15.
- ❑ Place your cursor in column F of the *Record* line.
- ❑ Choose *Style* from the *Format* menu.
- ❑ Choose *Center* from the *Style* dialog box.
- ❑ Press the Enter key to complete your change.

This should correct the first two problems.

➤ Setting the Report Margins

To correct the last problem, printing the last column on a separate page, you will need to change your left and right margins. Do this now by using the *Page Setup & Margins* option of the **Print** menu.

- ❑ Choose *Page Setup & Margins* from the *Print* menu.
- ❑ Tab to the *Left Margin* entry and set this to 0".
- ❑ Tab to the *Right Margin* entry and set this to 0".
- ❑ Press the Enter key.

This should correct the problems you had with the last two columns. To check this, view your report again.

❑ **Choose** *Report1* **from the** *View* **menu and view your report.**

If the problems mentioned earlier are not corrected, you should redo the steps setting the field widths and report margins.

➤ *Creating the Report Title*

You have two **Intr Report** lines in your default report. As mentioned earlier, these two lines will print one time at the beginning of your report. You can use these lines to create report titles. To create a report title, all you need to do is enter the title in one of the fields. Do this now.

❑ **Tab to column D on the first** *Intr Report* **line.**

❑ **Enter:** United Way Contributions.

❑ **Press the Enter key.**

It is also customary to place the current date in the report heading. The date could be on either the left side or the right side of the report title. We will place the date on the left hand side of the report title line in column A, the ID field. To enter your report date, use your control keys (Ctrl/;).

❑ **Place your cursor in column A of the first** *Intr Report* **line.**

❑ **Enter** Cntl/; **and press Enter.**

Notice that the date is displayed as pound signs, #####. This is because the column is not wide enough to store the entire date. You will need to change the width of this column to 8 characters so it can display the entire date.

❑ **Use the** *Format* **menu to change the width of column A to 8 characters.**

Your screen should now look like the one shown in Figure 13.17.

View your report now to see that the report headings are included.

❑ **Select** *Report1* **from the** *View* **menu and view your report.**

➤ *Changing the Column Headings*

The report looks much better, but the column headings on the first **Intr Page** line are not aligned properly. Also, since some of the column headings run together, the field names may not be the best headings for some column. You will now change the column headings so they look better on the report.

Figure 13.17

The **Intr Report** *lines can be used to create report titles and report dates for the first page of a report.*

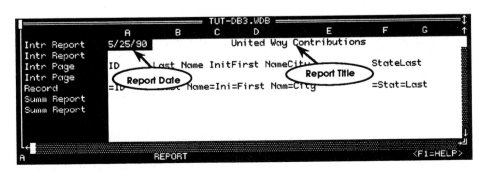

The first thing to do is to align all of the column headings over the columns. It is standard practice to center headings over fields that contain text (alphabetic data). Normally, headings over columns that contain numeric data are aligned to the right. We will consider the first six columns as text data. The last two columns contain numeric data. Align your headings now.

❑ **Select the first six cells of the first** *Intr Page* **line.**

❑ **Choose** *Style* **from the** *Format* **menu.**

❑ **Choose** *Center* **for your style.**

❑ **Select the last two cells of the first** *Intr Page* **line.**

❑ **Choose** *Style* **from the** *Format* **menu.**

❑ **Choose** *Right* **as your style.**

This should align your headings, but some of them still appear to run together. For example, the First Name, Initial, and Last Name run together. To correct this, you will change some of the headings. To change a heading, simply tab to the cell and enter your new heading. Make the following changes:

❑ **Change the heading for column B to** Last.

❑ **Change the heading over column C to** MI.

❑ **Change the heading over column D to** First.

Now view your report. It should look like the one in Figure 13.18.

➢ *Creating Summary Statistics*

The Microsoft Works report phase has several summary statistics that are available. These statistics are placed on the summary lines. Assume that you wanted a total of both the *Last* and *This* (last year's and this year's contributions) columns. Assume you also wanted an average of these contributions. You can use the statistics to get these figures.

To insert a summary statistic, you must first place your cursor in the cell where you want the statistic to appear. Next choose the *Insert Field Summary* option from the **Edit** menu. Assume you want the totals for the *First* and *Last* fields on the last *Summ Report* line. Do the following.

Figure 13.18

The default report provides an **Intr Page** *line with column headings; however, they are not always the best headings for the reports. Many times you must modify the column headings to get the report to look clearer.*

```
5/25/90              United Way Contributions

   ID    Last    MI   First      City         State    Last      This

  12451 Thomas   C    Marylin    Baltimore     MD      $0.00     $25.00
  14452 Miller   D    Jason      Philadelphia  PA      $10.00    $10.00
  16781 Smith    K    Marcia     Baltimore     MD      $200.00   $225.00
  17891 Smith    J    Thomas     Baltimore     MD      $150.00   $150.00
  18672 Jones    M    Phillip    Silver Springs MD     $500.00   $410.00
  18910 Thomas   O    William    Baltimore     MD      $100.00   $0.00
  19902 Miller   U    Samuel     Philadelphia  PA      $55.00    $50.00
  21441 Jones    R    Gayle      Silver Springs MD     $0.00     $50.00
  23411 Miller   B    Anne       Philadelphia  PA      $75.00    $100.00
  25671 Jacobs   C    William    Pittsburgh    PA      $150.00   $150.00
  27756 Miller   B    Larry      Philadelphia  PA      $25.00    $30.00
  29714 Miller   A    Larry      Philadelphia  PA      $100.00   $0.00
  35142 Kline    A    Everett    Silver Springs MD   $1,000.00 $1,500.00
Page 1                    REPORT
Press ENTER to continue, ESC to cancel.
```

Figure 13.19

*To insert a summary statistic, you choose the **Insert Field Summary** from the **Edit** menu. You must then select the field you want the statistic applied to and the statistic you want from the **Insert Field Summary** dialog box.*

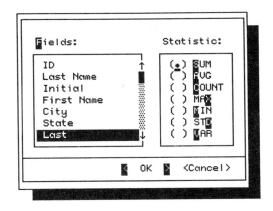

❑ **Move your cursor to the *Last* field of the last *Summ Report* line (row 7, column G).**

❑ **Choose *Insert Field Summary* from the *Edit* menu.**

You should now have the dialog box shown in Figure 13.19.

To insert the statistic, choose the field name you want the statistic applied to and the statistic you want to use. In this case, the field name would be *Last* and the statistic would be *Sum*. Insert the statistic now.

❑ **Choose *Last* from the *Fields* entry.**

❑ **Choose *Sum* from the *Statistic* area.**

❑ **Press the Enter key.**

The formula for your statistic should now be inserted into the column. Now insert the statistic to sum the *This* field (column H).

❑ **Insert the statistic to sum the *This* field (column H). Place this statistic in the cell at row 7 (column H).**

Now you should place a label on the summary line to indicate that these are totals for the report.

❑ **Enter: Report Totals in the *City* field (column E) of the summary line.**

Your Summary line should look like the one in Figure 13.20.

Figure 13.20

Summary statistics and labels can be placed in cells on the summary lines.

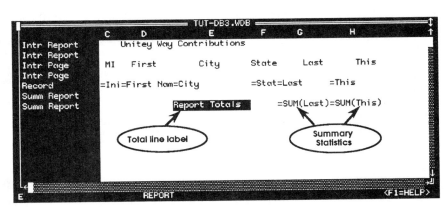

➣ _Inserting New Lines (Rows) in the Report_

You now want to compute the _average_ contribution for the two contributions. You want these averages to be below your totals, but there is no line to place them on. You don't want to use your first _Summ Report_ line because you want a blank line between your detail lines and your totals. To get these averages in your report, you will need to insert a new summary line. To insert a new line type in your report format, you use the _Insert Row/Column_ option of the **Edit** menu. Before you insert the new row, you will need to move your cursor below your last _Summ Report_ line.

❑ **Move your cursor to a cell below your last _Summ Report_ line.**

❑ **Choose _Insert Row/Column_ from the Edit menu.**

You should now have the selection box shown on the left in Figure 13.21.

To insert a row, choose _Row_ from the selection box.

❑ **Choose _Row_ from the selection box.**

You should now have the list box shown on the right of Figure 13.21. Your choice from this list box determines the type of row inserted. Since you want your totals printed at the end of your report, you will need a _Summ Report_ row type. Choose the _Summ Report_ row type.

❑ **Choose the _Summ Report_ row.**

You should now have the new row inserted at the bottom of your report format. You will now need to insert a message to indicate that these are averages. You will also need to insert the statistics for your averages. Remember, to insert a message or label, simply move to the cell and type in the label. To insert a statistic, choose _Insert Field Summary_ from the **Edit** menu. Next, choose your field name and statistic from the field summary dialog box.

❑ **Place the message** Report Averages **under the message _Report Totals_.**

❑ **Insert the statistic to average the _Last_ field of your database.**

❑ **Insert the statistic to average the _This_ field of your database.**

Your summary lines should look like the ones shown in Figure 13.22.

Figure 13.21

To insert a new column or row into a report format, you choose the Insert Row/Column from the Edit menu. This will provide you with the selection box on the left. Choose the item you want inserted. If you insert a row you will be provided with the list box on the right. Choose the appropriate row type form this box. The row will be inserted in your report format.

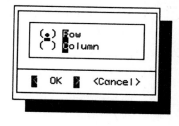

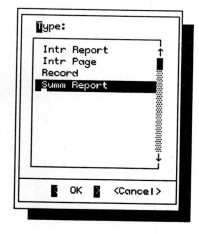

Figure 13.22

*When you have completed
your summary lines, you
should have one summary
line for the totals and one
summary line for the
averages.*

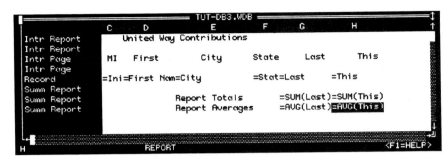

Now view your report. You will need to view each screen until you reach the end of the report to see that your total and average summary lines are correct.

❏ **View your report by choosing *Report1* from the *View* menu.**

Notice that the totals and averages are not formatted. When a statistic is inserted, it is assigned a *General* format. To complete the report, you will need to format the total and average cells. You will also need to reset the width of these two columns to allow for dollar signs, commas, and decimal points. Format your cells now and view your report totals.

❏ **Set the format for your total and average cells to *Currency*.**

❏ **Set the width of your total and average cells to 12.**

❏ **View your report summary lines.**

Printing Your Report

To print a report, you must be in the *Report* phase of the database. Since you are in the report phase you can print the report from either the *Print* option or the *Preview* option. Print your report now.

❏ **Print your report.**

Creating Control Break Reports

You will now create a report that contains control break totals. Before you begin this report format you will copy the report format that you just created. This will allow you to keep the report format you just created and have a new report format that can be customized for the new control break totals report.

➤ Copying a Report Format

To copy a report format, you use the *Reports* option of the **View** menu. Select this option now.

❏ **Choose *Reports* from the *View* menu.**

You should now have the dialog box shown in Figure 13.23.

Since you only have one report at this time you will have only have one report shown in the list box, *Report1*. To copy this report, make sure it is highlighted and choose the *Copy* button.

❏ **Choose *Copy* button.**

Figure 13.23

The Reports option of the View menu will allow you to Rename, Delete, and Copy report formats. To copy a report, highlight the report name you want to copy and choose the Copy button. Next choose the Done button.

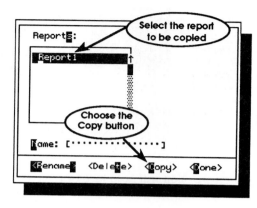

You should now have two reports in your list box, *Report1* and *Report2*. To make your second report, *Report2*, the active report, you will need to select it before you exit the dialog box.

❑ **Select *Report2*.**

❑ **Select the *Done* button.**

➤ Sorting the Database

In order to specify control breaks, you must sort the database. To sort the database, you use the *Sort Records* option from the **Select** menu. Each sort field has three areas that need to be set. The first is the sort field name. You enter the name of the sort field in this area. The second area is the sort sequence area. You need to specify whether the sort is to be *ascending* or *descending* in this area. The last area is the *Break* area. This option is set on so you can specify *Intr* and *Summ* lines for the field. This area will also allow you to specify that a break occurs only when the first letter in the field changes.

Before you sort the database, visualize how you want report totals and statistics printed. For this tutorial, we will assume the following: You want the database sorted in ascending order by last name within each city within each state. You also want a total line that contains the total of the contributions this year and a total of all contributions last year for each city. You want these same totals for each state.

In order to produce these totals, you will need to define the *State* field as your major or first-level sort field. The *City* field will need to be defined as the second sort field. This will sort cities within each state. Since you want to produce totals when these fields change, you will need to specify that you want a break on these fields.

The third sort field needs to be the *Last Name* field. Using this as the third sort field will sort by last name within each city. Since you do not want to produce totals on this field, you do not want to specify a break for the Last Name field. Sort your database now by doing the following. When you finish, your *Sort Fields* dialog box should look like the one in Figure 13.24.

❑ **Choose *Sort Records* from the *Select* menu.**

❑ **Enter *State* as the 1st sort Field.**

❑ **Tab to the *Break* option on the right of the text entry box and set this option on.**

❑ **Tab to the 2nd Field entry.**

❑ **Enter *City*.**

Figure 13.24

*In order to define Intr and Summ lines in a report, you must sort the records. Each field must specify a sorting sequence, ascending or descending. For any field that you want **Intr** and **Summ** lines, you must specify the **Break** option.*

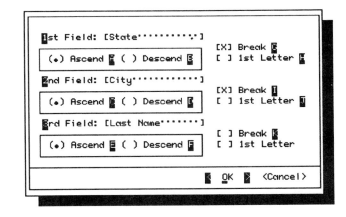

- ❏ Tab to the *Break* option and set this option on.
- ❏ Tab to the 3rd Field entry and enter *Last Name.* Leave the *Break* option off for this field.
- ❏ Press Enter.

You should now have two additional summary lines in your report format, one for the *City* field and one for the *State* field. These lines should also have formulas in each field. When you sort your records and specify a break on the sort fields, Works inserts a summary line for each break field. The fields in the summary lines will contain either a formula to count the fields or a formula to sum the field depending on the type of data in the field. If the field contains text data, a formula for counting is inserted. If the field contains numeric data, a formula to sum the field is inserted.

To see how the level breaks work, view your report.

- ❏ Choose *Report2* from the *View* menu and view your report.

After your first screen appears, notice the two new total lines. There should be one total line after the last record for *Baltimore* and one total line after the last record for *Silver Springs*. Your first screen should be similar to the one shown in Figure 13.25. Also notice that there are two total lines when the state changes from *MD* to *PA* and from *PA* to *VA*. Finally, notice that you have four total lines at the end of your report, one for the last city, one for the last state, and two for the entire report. You should get two pages for the report now. Notice there is no date or report title for the second page.

Figure 13.25

*When the database records are sorted, **Summary** lines are inserted for each sort field that is defined as a break field. The summary lines count text fields and sum numeric fields.*

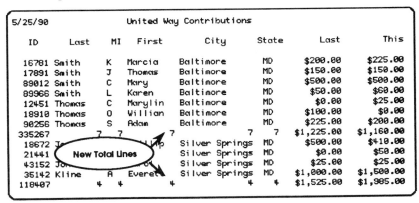

➤ *Correcting the Summary Break Lines*

You currently have four summary lines. These are the *Summ City*, *Summ State*, and two *Summ Report* lines. When you view the report, you get the number of records in each group several times across the line and a total for the *Last* and *First* fields. We now want to make the appearance of your new summary lines a little better.

The first step we will take is to delete the majority of the formulas in the line. The formula in the first column, ID, sums the values of the ID field. The next five formulas count the number of values printed in the group. We will delete these formulas. Do this now.

❑ Move your cursor to the first cell in the *Summ City* line.

❑ Hold down the Shift key and use your arrow keys to select all the cells from *ID* to *State* for the *Summ City* and the *Summ State* lines.

❑ Choose *Clear* from the *Edit* menu.

❑ Press the Esc key to cancel your selection.

This should delete the formulas. View your report now to see the effect on your report.

❑ View your report.

Assume that you want to print the number of contributions for each group with a message that indicates the number of contributions. You can enter the message in one cell and use a formula to count the contributions in a second cell. First, enter your message in the column B of the summary line and then use your *Insert Field Summary* option from the **Edit** menu to insert the count formula. We will do this for the *Summ City* line first.

❑ Move your cursor to column B in the *Summ City* line.

❑ Enter: Number of Contributions =.

❑ Tab to column F.

❑ Choose *Insert Field Summary* from the *Edit* menu.

❑ Select *Last Name* from the *Fields* entry.

❑ Tab to the Statistic entry and select *Count*.

❑ Press the Enter key.

You will need to place the same text and statistic in the *Summ State* line. You can use the *Copy* option from the **Edit** menu to copy the statistics.

❑ Select the cells from column B through column F of the *Summ City* line.

❑ Choose *Copy* from the *Edit* menu.

❑ Move your cursor to column B in the *Summ State* line.

❑ Press Enter.

Now view your report. The last page's total lines should look like those shown in Figure 13.26.

Figure 13.26

Your new total lines should contain a count of the records in a group and the subtotals of all records in the group.

```
 ID    Last   MI   First      City      State     Last        This

78915 Smith   P    Bosco    Richmond     VA       $0.00      $200.00
97810 Smith   G    Benny    Richmond     VA    $2,500.00   $2,500.00
             Number of Contributions      13    $5,535.00   $5,955.00
             Number of Contributions      13    $5,535.00   $5,955.00

                               Report Totals   $11,620.00  $13,080.00
                               Report Averages    $252.61     $284.35
```

➤ Inserting an Introductory Break Line

Introductory break lines print before a group of records print. Assume that you wanted a line at the beginning of each group of states that would indicate the state that followed. You would need an introductory line to do this. Since you specified that you wanted breaks on the *State* field, you can insert an introductory line for this field. Insert an introductory line now.

- ❑ Choose *Insert Row/Column* from the *Edit* menu.
- ❑ Choose *Row* from your first insert check box.
- ❑ Choose *Intr State* from your second insert list box.

You should now have a new line in your report format. Notice that it comes after your *Intr Page* line. This is where Works inserts Intr break lines. The line is currently blank, so you will need to enter the text or field names that you want printed on this line.

You want your introductory line to read:

Contributions from State: XX

To get this, you will need to enter some text and one field name. The text for the message *Contributions from State:* should be entered starting in the column A. Do this now.

- ❑ Move your cursor to column A of the *Intr State* line.
- ❑ Enter: Contributions from State:
- ❑ Press the Enter key.

Now you want the report to contain the state name. You can use the *Insert Field Contents* option from the **Edit** menu or you can type the formula for the value directly into the cell. We will use this last approach.

- ❑ Move your cursor to the *City* field on the *Intr State* line.
- ❑ Enter: =State

You should now have your introductory line in your report. View your report now. Each time a state changes, look for your introductory state line. Figure 13.27 shows the first *Intr State* line.

- ❑ View your report.

➤ Inserting Blank Lines

Your report looks better, but it can be improved if you place some blank lines between your summary lines. Assume you want a blank line before and after your *Summ City* line. Also assume you want blank lines

Figure 13.27

Intr State lines will print at the beginning of each group of lines for each state.

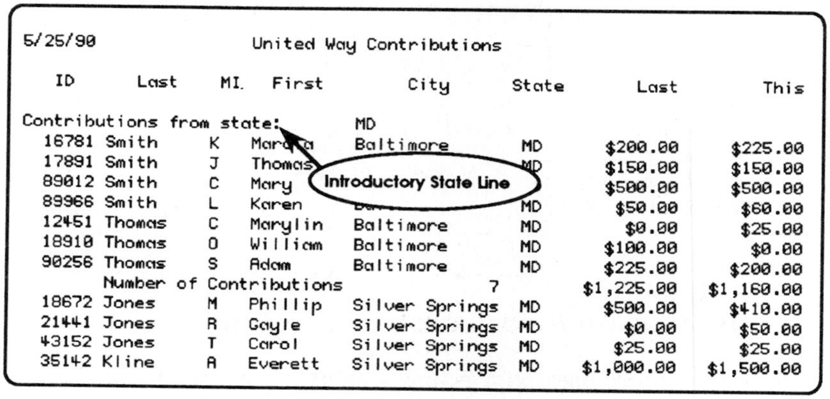

```
5/25/90              United Way Contributions

   ID    Last    MI.   First       City       State    Last         This

Contributions from state:          MD
   16781 Smith    K    Mar␣␣a    Baltimore      MD     $200.00      $225.00
   17891 Smith    J    Thomas                   MD     $150.00      $150.00
   89012 Smith    C    Mary     Introductory State Line $500.00     $500.00
   89966 Smith    L    Karen                           $50.00       $60.00
   12451 Thomas   C    Marylin   Baltimore      MD     $0.00        $25.00
   18910 Thomas   O    William   Baltimore      MD     $100.00      $0.00
   90256 Thomas   S    Adam      Baltimore      MD     $225.00      $200.00
          Number of Contributions           7        $1,225.00    $1,160.00
   18672 Jones    M    Phillip   Silver Springs MD     $500.00      $410.00
   21441 Jones    R    Gayle     Silver Springs MD     $0.00        $50.00
   43152 Jones    T    Carol     Silver Springs MD     $25.00       $25.00
   35142 Kline    A    Everett   Silver Springs MD    $1,000.00    $1,500.00
```

between the *Summ City* and the *Summ State* and between the *Summ State* and the *Summ Report* lines. Since a State summary line never prints unless a City summary line prints, and you have a blank line after a City summary line, you will not need to place a blank line before the State summary line. This is also true of the Report summary line.

When you insert a new line, and a line of the same type already exists, the new line is placed above the cursor. You must be aware of this to get the blank lines in the right place. To get a blank line before the summary line for the city, the cursor must be on the *Summ City* line before you insert the new line. To get a line after the *Summ City* line, your cursor must be below the *Summ City* line before you insert the new line.

Insert your blank lines now.

❑ Place your cursor on the *Summ City* line.

❑ Choose *Insert Row/Column* from the *Edit* menu.

❑ Choose *Row* from the first check box.

❑ Choose *Summ City* from the list box.

❑ Move your cursor to the *Summ State* line.

❑ Insert a *Summ City* line.

❑ Move your cursor to the *Summ Report* line.

❑ Insert a *Summ State* line.

Your report format should now look like the one shown in Figure 13.28. View your report now to see the effects of your new lines.

❑ Select Report2 from the *View* menu and view your report.

Printing the Report

To print the report, you can choose *Print* or *Preview* from the **Print** menu. Use the *Preview* option to preview your report before you print it.

❑ Choose *Preview* from the *Print* menu.

❑ Print your report.

Figure 13.28

When you have completed the report format, you should have eight summary lines. Four of these lines are used to provide spacing between the summary lines.

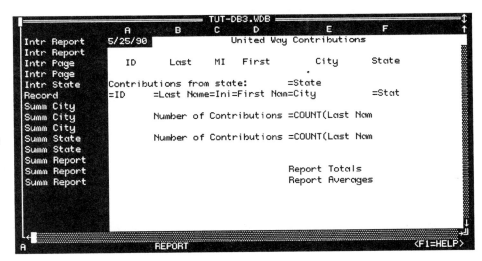

Using Queries with Reports

You can apply a query to the database and print your report. When the query is applied to the database and a report is printed, only those records that are shown by the query are reported. For example, suppose you wanted a report of only those records where the contribution was lower this year than it was last year. You could apply that query and then print your report.

To do this you would need to choose the *Query* option from the **View** menu and define your query. Next select your report name from the **View** menu, enter the report phase, and print your report.

Printing Summary Reports

Summary reports are reports that only print introductory and summary lines. These reports can easily be printed using the same report format as a standard report. To print a summary report, you must choose the *Print all but record rows* from the **Print** dialog box before you print the report.

Saving the Report

When you save the database, you also save your report format. To save the report, you use the *Save* or *Save As* option from the **File** menu.

Conclusion

This chapter has introduced you to the creation of database reports. By using the material learned in this chapter, you can create almost any style report you need from a Works database.

Hands on Practice

Exercise 1

For this practice problem, use the database named **HOP-D131.WDB**. This database is on your tutorials disk.

1. Print a report of all the records in the database. The report should be similar to the one shown in Figure 13.29, however, it should include all records in the database.

    a. Use Introductory Report lines like the first two lines on the report in Figure 13.29.

    b. Take level breaks on Zone within City. Have the property listed by contract number within each Zone.

    c. Use an Introductory line to print the name of the city prior to listing the records for a given city, as shown on the report.

    d. Count the number of records and sum the Appraisal and Asking prices for each total line. Also print the words 'Zone Totals:', 'City Totals:', or 'Grand Totals:', depending on which total line it is.

    e. Have the report print blank lines where they are shown on the report.

    f. Print your report.

2. Write a query for your report that will list only the property that has an appraisal value between $70,000.00 and $200,000.00. Print your report with this query applied.

Figure 13.29

Your report will have more data than this. Use this as a model for the report form you create in Exercise 1.

Contract	Zone	City	Sqr. Ft.	Appraisal	Asking
\multicolumn{6}{l}{Harrisonburg Real Estate Company}
\multicolumn{6}{l}{(Your Name Here)}
City of:	Augusta				
20100	B1	Augusta	4,000	142,000.00	155,000.00
26781	B1	Augusta	4,590	120,000.00	125,500.00
34000	B1	Augusta	30,000	200,000.00	10,500.00
55001	B1	Augusta	1,200	15,000.00	17,900.00
Zone Totals:	4			477,000.00	308,900.00
12333	B2	Augusta	22,000	250,000.00	300,000.00
34500	B2	Augusta	4,571	110,000.00	155,000.00
55002	B2	Augusta	1,350	46,780.00	65,000.00
Zone Totals:	3			406,780.00	520,000.00
15671	R1	Augusta	5,500	110,000.00	125,000.00
20981	R1	Augusta	10,000	145,000.00	150,500.00
26711	R1	Augusta	2,430	55,000.00	58,000.00
43091	R1	Augusta	3,000	87,550.00	91,250.00
Zone Totals:	4			397,550.00	424,750.00
City Totals:	12			1,281,330.00	1,253,650.00
Grand Total:	12			1,281,330.00	1,253,650.00

14

Integrating Between Applications

Integration refers to the ability to copy information from one of the Microsoft Works' applications into another Works application. Examples of integration are the ability to copy data from a spreadsheet into a database or from a database into a word processing document. Further, you will find that you can create a chart from a spreadsheet and copy the chart into a word processing document. In order to do this, you must use *windows* and place each of the documents you want to integrate in a separate window. Microsoft Works will allow you to do this easily. In this chapter, you will learn how to move from one window to another and copy information between four of the Works tools - the word processor, spreadsheet, charts, and database.

Integration Concepts

The concept of *windows* is the foundation for integration between the Works applications. Before we cover how to perform the integration steps, you will need to know how to use windows.

➤ Using Windows

To Microsoft Works, any opened document, spreadsheet, or database is considered a window. Works will allow you to open several windows at one time. The limitation on the number of windows that can be opened at one time depends upon the amount of memory you have in your computer system. This is because each window is a file that has been loaded into memory. Each different window can contain a different kind of application. For example, one window may contain a word processing document while another window contains a spreadsheet with still a third window containing a database. When you have several windows opened at one time, windows will be *hiding* behind one another. That is, one of the windows will be visible while the others are covered by the window that is visible. This idea is shown in Figure 14.1.

If you want to work in a particular window you must make that window the active window. When the window is activated, it comes to the front and the previously active window moves to the back. You make

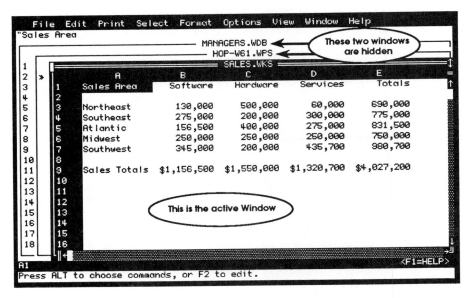

Figure 14.1

When you have multiple windows open, only one of the windows is active, the others are normally covered by the active window. To move between windows you can use the Window menu.

a window active by selecting the appropriate file name from the **Window** menu. This menu is shown in Figure 14.2.

The window menu shown in Figure 14.2 shows that three windows are available. To select a window and make it active, you can enter the window number, use your cursor to highlight the window name, or drag your mouse to highlight the window name. Once you have selected the window, it immediately moves to the front of your screen and becomes the active window.

➤ Opening an Additional Window

Although you have used windows for all of your work thus far, you have usually had only one window open at a time. To open an additional window, you open a file. When the file is loaded into memory, it is placed in a window and automatically becomes the active window.

To open an additional file (and window), select the *Open Existing File* option from the **File** menu. When you select this option, a list of available files will appear on the screen just as if it were the first file you were opening. If you wanted to create a new window, you would select *Create New File* from this menu. This would give you the applications screen as usual.

Figure 14.2

The Window menu is used to move between windows. To make a window active and bring it to the front, select the window's name from the Window menu.

Copying Between Windows

➣ Copying Between Two Word Processing Windows

To copy from one word processing document to another, both of the documents must be open in windows. To begin the copy, move to the document that contains the text that you want to copy. Next, select this text by using your *Shift/Arrow* keys, the F8 function key, or your mouse. Now select the *Copy* option from the **Edit** menu. You should then see the message:

```
Select new location and press ENTER or press Esc to cancel.
```

Next, pull down the **Window** menu and choose the document name that you want the text copied to. The new window containing the *target* document will move to the front and be the active window. Next, move your cursor to the location where you want the text copied to and press the Enter key. The new text will be inserted at the cursor. This process is shown in Figure 14.3.

When you copy text from one word processing document to another, the original formatting is also copied. This includes any special character fonts, paragraph formats, underlines, bold, italics, tab markers, and so forth.

➣ Copying from a Spreadsheet or Database into the Word Processor

The procedure for copying information from a spreadsheet or database into a word processing document is similar except that the data is copied into the word processing document as a series of rows and columns. Works will place a *tab marker* between each column and a paragraph marker at the end of each row. The distance between each tab setting is determined by the field width that was used in the database or spreadsheet. This makes the text in the word processor look identical to that in the original database or spreadsheet. Once you have copied the data, you can use the *Tabs* option from the **Format** menu to change the tab alignment.

Figure 14.3

To copy text between word processing windows, start the copy as if you were copying within the same document. When you need to select your new location, change to the window you want the text copied to before pressing the Enter key.

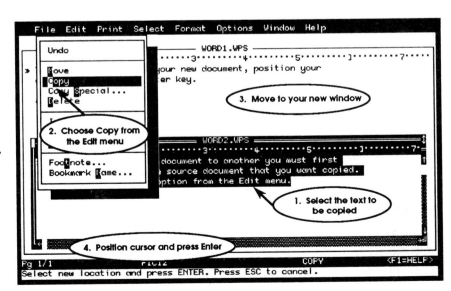

To copy from a spreadsheet or database to a word processing document, you must open both of the documents as windows. Next, move to the spreadsheet or database that contains the data you want to copy and make that window active. Select your data by using your F8 key, *Shift/Arrow* keys or the mouse and then choose the *Copy* option from the **Edit** menu. You will again get the message:

```
Select new location and press ENTER or press Esc to cancel.
```

At this point, pull down the **Window** menu and select the document that you want the text copied to. This window will then become the active window allowing you to move the cursor to the location you want the text placed. Complete the copy by pressing the Enter key. The new data will be inserted after the cursor.

➤ *Inserting a Chart into a Word Processing Document*

Inserting a chart into a word processing document is a little different than copying text. To insert a chart into a document, you must first open a window that contains the spreadsheet and the chart (recall that the chart is automatically opened with the spreadsheet). Next, make the word processing document the active window and position your cursor where you want the chart inserted. Now select *Insert Chart* from the **Edit** menu. A dialog box similar to the one in Figure 14.4 will appear.

To determine what charts are available with each spreadsheet, use your arrow keys to select the spreadsheet. The *Charts* list box will then show any corresponding charts available for the selected spreadsheet. You can then select the desired chart from the *Charts* list box and press the Enter key.

The chart itself will not appear in the document. Only a *placeholder* for the chart will appear. A placeholder will look like the following:

```
*chart  SALES.WKS:Region Sales*
```

This example shows that *SALES.WKS* is the name of the spreadsheet file and *Region Sales* is the name of the chart. You can now select and move the chart placeholder as needed in the same way you would move any other text. To delete the chart, select the placeholder as a block and then select *Delete* from the **Edit** menu.

You should be aware that there may be no entries in the *Charts* portion of the *Insert Chart* dialog box. This can occur if there are no charts associated with a particular spreadsheet.

Figure 14.4

The Insert Chart dialog box has two areas. The first area lists all spreadsheets that are open. The second area lists the charts available for the selected spreadsheet. To insert a chart, select the spreadsheet that contains the chart, then select the chart and choose the OK button

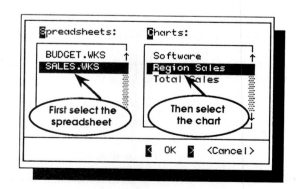

Figure 14.5

When you have a placeholder for a chart selected and choose the **Indents & Spacing** *option from the Format menu, you get the Chart dialog box. You use this dialog box to specify the size, horizontal location, and orientation of the chart.*

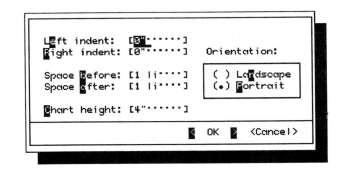

➣ Sizing the Chart

When you initially insert the chart, the size of the chart is the same as it is in the spreadsheet. This will probably be larger than you want it to be in the document. Works will allow you to change the size and orientation of the chart. To make these changes, select the chart's placeholder and then select *Indents & Spacing* from the **Format** menu. The **Chart** dialog box in Figure 14.5 should appear.

You can now tab to the appropriate entry to change the left and right margins, spacing before and after the chart, chart height, and orientation. When you change the left and right margins for the chart, you are changing the width of the chart. The chart will be printed between your left and right margins.

Charts have two types of *Orientation*. The *orientation* determines how the chart is printed. The *Portrait* orientation prints the chart on the page vertically. The *Landscape* orientation prints the chart sideways.

➣ Printing a Document That Contains a Chart

Before you print a document that contains a chart, you must make sure both the word processing document and the spreadsheet that contains the chart have been opened as windows. You should use the *Preview* option to preview your document before you print it. The chart will not display on your screen in the word processor's editing mode, but it will be displayed in its proper location and with its defined size, in the *Preview* mode. Once you know the document is correct, you can print the document from the preview mode.

➣ Copying from the Word Processor to a Database or Spreadsheet

You can also copy from a word processing document into a spreadsheet or database. To avoid confusion, you will need to organize your word processing data in a row and column format, tabbing between each column and pressing the Enter key at the end of each row. Each tab mark will be used to separate the data into cells in a row, and each paragraph marker will be used to specify a new row. The data will be copied into the spreadsheet or database with each paragraph becoming a row in the spreadsheet or database.

To make the copy, you must first select the data in the word processor that you want copied. Next, select the *Copy* option from the **Edit** menu. Now make the spreadsheet or database that you are copying to the active window. Position your cursor, in the spreadsheet or database, in the upper-left corner of the area you want the word processing data copied into and press the Enter key.

You should be aware that the new data will replace any data in the spreadsheet or database cells. For this reason, if you do not want to lose any data that may be in the spreadsheet or database cells, you should copy the data to the end of the spreadsheet or database and then use the *Move* option of the spreadsheet or database to move the data to the appropriate rows. You should either do this or insert enough blank rows before the *Copy* to hold the new data. Once the data is copied, you can format the data as if you had entered it directly into the spreadsheet or database.

➤ Copying Between Spreadsheets and Databases

Copying between spreadsheets and databases is pretty direct because they are both formatted as columns and rows. When data is copied, each row in the spreadsheet becomes a row in the database and each cell in the spreadsheet becomes a field in the database, or vice versa if you are copying from the database to the spreadsheet.

To perform the copy, make the window containing the data you want copied the active window. Next, select the data that you want copied. Now make the *target* window the active window. Position your cursor in the upper-left cell of the area where you want the new data and press the Enter key. Like copying from a word processing document, the new data will replace any existing data. You should make room for the new data by inserting empty rows before you make the copy.

You should be aware that when you copy data from a spreadsheet to a database, or in the other direction, only the **values** of the cells are copied. The formulas are not copied. Therefore, if you copy the spreadsheet data to a database and sort the database, and then copy the database data back to the spreadsheet, you will lose all the formulas you had in the spreadsheet. You will still have the values, but you will not have the formulas used to compute the values.

Creating Customized Form Letters

One of the advantages of integrating information from different Works modules is the ability to create form letters or mailing lists. Form letters can be created by merging data from a database with a letter created in the word processing module. A customized form letter is simply a letter that contains standard text in most of the letter, but specified parts of the letter are tailored for a particular person or event. For example, you may want to mail a personalized letter to all of your customers informing them of a special sale. The body of the letter, which describes the sale, is the same for every customer, but the name and address are changed to reflect the individual receiving the letter. The contents of the letter are typed as a standard word processing document, but the names and addresses are inserted from a database.

The body of the letter is created as a normal word processing document with special *field placeholders* inserted where you want individualized data printed. These *field placeholders* refer to data held in a specific database. When you want to insert a *field placeholder,* you select the *Insert Field* option from the **Edit** menu. This menu will provide a list of databases that are currently available in open windows. Figure 14.6 shows an *Insert Field* dialog box.

The database that contains the data you want inserted is selected first. Works will then provide a list of all the fields in the selected database. When you select a field name from the *Fields* list box, Works will insert a *placeholder* for the field. For example, if you choose the field named "Lname," the placeholder would appear as:

`«Lname»`

Figure 14.6

To insert field placeholders in a document, you choose the Insert Field option from the Edit menu. When the Field dialog box appears, select the database that contains the data and the field name for the data you want inserted.

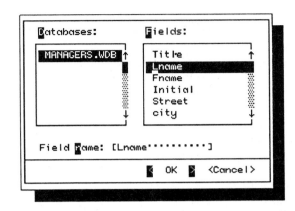

The two « and » symbols show that this is a placeholder for the database field with the word inside the symbols being the name of the field in the database. The placeholder will be replaced by the data from the database when the form letter is printed. You can insert as many placeholders in a document as you want, but all placeholders must come from a single database. If all your data is not in a single database, you can copy needed fields from one database into another using the procedures discussed earlier. You may also want to copy spreadsheet data into a database in order to create a customized form letter.

Once the placeholder is inserted, it can be moved or copied by selecting it and using the *Move* or *Copy* options from the **Edit** menu.

➤ Printing a Customized Form Letter

After you have inserted the *field placeholders* in the form letter, you will want to begin printing. To print the customized form letter, you must select the *Print Form Letters* option from the **Print** menu. This menu is shown on the left side of Figure 14.7. Works will present you with a list of the databases that are in open windows, as shown in the dialog box on the right side of Figure 14.7. After selecting the database that you used to create the form letter, you are ready to print the letters. You can then print the letters from the **Print** dialog box. Works will print one copy of the document for each record that is available in the database. You can control which records have a letter printed by applying a *Query* to the database or hiding specific records before printing.

Figure 14.7

To print your form letters, choose the Print Form Letters option from the Print menu. Next, select the database that contains the data to be used in the form letters and choose the OK button.

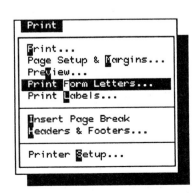
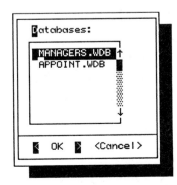

➤ *Creating Mailing Labels*

Mailing labels can also be created from the data in a database. Labels are developed through a customized mailing labels form in the word processor, much the same way you set up a customized form letter. The primary difference is that there is usually no standard text in the form letter, only field markers and punctuation. The customized label form, or *template*, consists of one field marker for each field from the database that you want printed on the labels. To insert the field labels, you would use the *Insert Field* option from the **Edit** menu the same way you do for a customized form letter. An example of a labels form is shown in Figure 14.8. The words inside the « and » symbols are the names of the database fields that you want printed on the labels.

Figure 14.8

A customized labels form contains the names of the database fields that are to appear on the labels.

«Title» «Fname» «Initial». «Lname»
«Street»
«City», «State» «Zip»

Since mailing labels are available in several sizes and styles, your next step is to define the size and type of label to be used. Mailing labels are normally printed on continuous forms. The labels can be purchased with as few as one label per row, called *One Up* labels, or as many as five labels per row, called *Five Up* labels. An example of the continuous forms mailing labels is shown in Figure 14.9.

To specify the size and style of your labels, you choose the *Print Labels* option from the **Print** menu. This will provide you with the *Labels* dialog box shown in Figure 14.10.

You would complete the *Labels* dialog box by first selecting the database that contains the data needed for the labels. Next, specify the size of the labels in the *Vertical spacing* and *Horizontal spacing* text boxes. The vertical spacing is the distance from the top of one label to the top of the next label. The horizontal spacing is the distance from the left edge of one label to the left edge of the label to the right. If you are using standard *one up* labels, you would enter the width of that label here. Your final entry is for the number of labels per row on the mailing labels.

Figure 14.9

Mailing labels are available in several different styles. They are normally on continuous forms and are available from one up to five up styles.

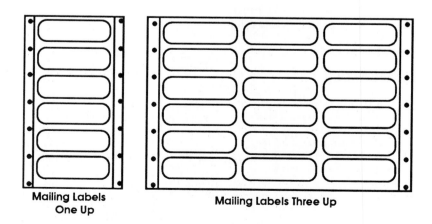

Mailing Labels
One Up

Mailing Labels Three Up

Figure 14.10

The Labels dialog box is used to specify the database that contains the data for the labels. You also specify the size and number of labels per row in this dialog box. You can use the Test button to test print your labels.

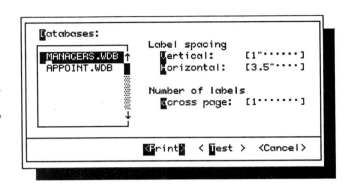

➤ *Testing the Labels*

When the specifications have been completed, you should test print your labels. To test print the labels, you select the *Test* button. This will print your first row of labels. You would do this to make sure that you have the labels positioned correctly in the printer and to make sure that you have the correct label sizes in the vertical and horizontal spacing. You could then make any changes necessary in the *Labels* dialog box and test again or choose *Print*. When you choose *Print*, Works will display the Print dialog box. You then select the desired print options and finish printing the labels. You will get one label for each record available in the database.

Remember that you are getting the data for your labels from a database. If you do not want to print a label for each record in the database, you could use a query to restrict the database records before printing.

Closing Windows

You can use the **File** menu to *Close* windows that you are through using. Closing a window will not save any changes you have made to the contents of the window. If you do try to close a window that has been changed, Works will ask you if you want to save your changes before closing the window. If you try to exit Works with windows open, Works will check each window for changes. If any changes have been made to a window, you will be asked if you want to save the changes before Works will close the next window.

Conclusion

This chapter has introduced you to the techniques used to integrate the applications in Microsoft Works. It is this ease of integration that makes Microsoft Works superior to most other packages. You should complete the following self-test and then work through the integration tutorial.

Chapter 14 Self Test

1. Explain the concept of a window as it applies to Microsoft Works.

2. How do you open a new window in Microsoft Works?

3. How do you switch between windows in Microsoft Works?

4. List the steps required to copy a block of text from one word processing window to another word processing window.

5. How do you insert a chart into a word processing document?

6. How do you change the size of a chart once the chart has been placed in the word processing window?

7. What is the orientation of a chart?

8. Explain exactly how Microsoft Works determines what data is placed in which cells of a spreadsheet when the data is copied from a word processing document into a spreadsheet.

9. When a spreadsheet is copied into a database, exactly what is copied from the spreadsheet?

10. Explain how you create a customized form letter.

11. In the field placeholder «INVENTORY:Price», what is the name of the database that contains the data? What is the name of the field in the database?

12. How do you print a customized form letter so that the database placeholders will be replaced by the database data?

13. How can you restrict the database data that will be printed when you print a customized form letter?

14. How do you calculate the *vertical* spacing for labels?

15. Where do you specify the size and number of mailing labels that you are going to print?

Chapter 14 Tutorial

In this session you will create a customized form letter and print a copy of the form letter for a selected set of sales managers. The form letter will contain data from a spreadsheet, a chart from the same spreadsheet, and data from a database. You will also print mailing labels for each sales manager in the database.

Getting Started

Start Microsoft Works. From the **File** menu, select *Create New File* and select *New Word Processor* from the applications menu.

❑ **Start Microsoft Works.**

❑ **Select** *Create New File* **from the** *File* **menu.**

❑ **Select** *New Word Processor* **from the applications menu.**

➤ *Entering the Letterhead*

Begin the form letter by entering the following letterhead and print date code. Remember to press the Enter key after each heading line in the letterhead.

❑ **Select** *Center* **from the** *Format* **Menu.**

❑ **Enter:** High Tech Computer Center

❑ **Enter:** 109 East Main St.

❑ **Enter:** Blissville, VA 22801

❑ **Select** *Right* **from the** *Format* **menu.**

❑ **Select** *Insert Special* **from the** *Edit* **menu.**

❑ **Select** *Print Date* **from the** *Insert Special* **selection box and press the Enter key.**

❑ **Press the Enter key again.**

❑ **Select** *Left* **from the** *Format* **menu.**

A professional letterhead would have the company name highlighted in some way. This highlighting makes the company name stand out and makes the letter look more professional. You can highlight your company name by changing its font's size and style. To change the font and style, you use the *Font & Style* option from the **Format** menu. Move your cursor up to the first line in the letterhead and format the company name now.

❑ **Select the company name from the first line you entered.**

❑ **Select** *Font & Style* **from the** *Format* **menu.**

❑ **Set** *Bold* **and** *Italic* **on.**

❑ **Select** *PICA* **for the font and** *16* **for the font size. If you do not have this font or size, select some other font with a large size.**

Your document should now look like the one in Figure 14.11.

Figure 14.11

A professional letter has a letterhead that contains the company name and address. The date is normally placed on the righthand side of the letter.

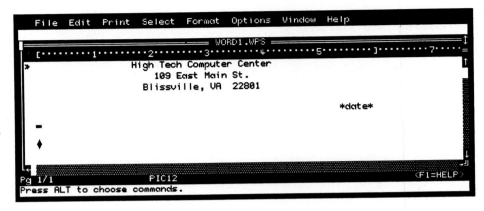

Entering the Mailing Address

Since you are developing a form letter, you will want the mailing address of each letter individualized for the person receiving the letter. The names and addresses for these letters are stored in a database. This means that you need to insert a placeholder for each field. Before you can insert the placeholder for the database data, you must open the database.

➤ Opening the Database

To open the database, you use the **File** menu and choose the *Open Existing File* option. Open your database now.

❏ Select *Open Existing File* from the *File* menu.

❏ Select *MANAGERS.WDB* from the *Files* dialog box.

This will open the *Managers* database and make it the active window. Notice that the database window is in front of the word processing window. You can see the word processing window on the left and above your database window.

Once you have the database in an open window, you will need to move back to the word processing document you just created and insert the field placeholders.

❏ Select *WORD1.WPS* from the *Window* menu.

❏ Enter *Ctrl/END* to move to the end of your document.

❏ Press the Enter key to provide a blank line.

➤ Inserting the Field Placeholders

The field placeholders will be inserted at the position of the cursor when the placeholder is inserted. Your cursor should now be located on the left side of the screen, one line below your date.

To insert the field placeholders, you select the *Insert Field* option from the **Edit** menu. This will display the *Insert Field* dialog box. Next, you select the database that contains your data.

❏   Choose *Insert Field* from the *Edit* menu.

❏   Select the *Managers* database.

Figure 14.12

The **Insert Field** *dialog box will list each database that is open. To insert a field marker, you first select the database and then select the name of the field you want inserted in the document.*

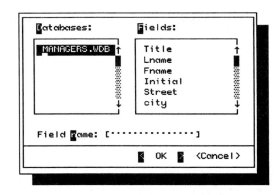

Your dialog box should look like the one shown in Figure 14.12.

To insert a specific field placeholder in your document, you must tab into the *Fields* list box and use your arrow keys to select the name of the field you want inserted. The first field you want inserted will be the *Title* field. Insert this field placeholder now.

❑ Tab to the *Fields* list box and select the *Title* field.

❑ Choose the *OK* button.

You should now have the *Title* field placeholder in your document.

For the first line of the address, you want the person's title, first name, middle initial, and last name. Example: **Mr. Francis T. Robertson**. Note that you want a period after the middle initial. Since the period is not in the database, it must be entered between the middle initial and the last name field placeholders. To complete the first line of the address, do the following:

❑ Press the space bar one time to place a space between the title and the first name.

❑ Select *Insert Field* from the *Edit* menu.

❑ Select *Fname* from the *Fields* box.

❑ Press space bar one time.

❑ Select *Insert Field* from the *Edit* menu.

❑ Select *Initial* from the *Fields* box.

❑ Enter a period and one space.

❑ Select *Insert Field* from the *Edit* menu.

❑ Select *Lname* from the *Fields* box.

❑ Press the Enter key.

This should create the first line of the mailing address. The line should appear as:

```
«Title» «Fname» «Initial». «Lname»
```

Now complete the address and introduction by inserting lines for the Street address, City, State, Zip, and the introduction line. Don't forget that you want a comma between the City and State. You also want the word *Dear* to start the introduction and a comma at the end of the line. When you complete the lines, they should look like Figure 14.13.

Figure 14.13

The mailing address consists of three lines - the name line, street line, and city state zip line. The introduction should have the word Dear, the title, and last name.

```
«Title» «Fname» «Initial». «Lname»
«Street»
«City», «State»    «Zip»


Dear «Title» «Lname»,
```

Starting the letter

The database field entries are now complete. Next, enter a few introductory sentences for the body of the letter. Enter the following :

❑ **Press the Enter key twice to get one blank line.**

❑ **Enter the following sentences:**

This is the sales data we discussed at the last regional meeting. The data for each region is shown below in table form. The totals for regions and sales categories are also shown.

❑ **Press Enter twice to get a blank line.**

Copying the Spreadsheet Data

You are now ready to copy data from the sales spreadsheet into the document. Before you can copy the data, the spreadsheet must be opened and placed in a window. You can now open the *Sales* spreadsheet.

❑ **Select *Open Existing File* from the *File* menu.**

❑ **Select the *SALES.WKS* spreadsheet.**

The *Sales* spreadsheet should now be visible in the active window. Since you want to copy the entire spreadsheet, you should select all cells from cell **A1** through cell **E9**. Once you have your data selected, you need to select the *Copy* option from the **Edit** menu. This will place you in copy mode. Next, you can move back to your document and complete the copy.

❑ **Select cells A1 through E9 as a block.**

❑ **Select *Copy* from the *Edit* menu.**

❑ **Select *WORD1.WPS* from the *Window* menu.**

❑ **Press the Enter key to complete the copy.**

You should now have the spreadsheet data in your word processing document. Remember that the ruler to align the data is also copied into the document and can be seen at the top of the screen. You will need to set the *Justified* margin back on.

❑ **Select *Justified* from the *Format* menu.**

The next step is to enter an introductory paragraph for the chart you are about to insert. Insert this paragraph now.

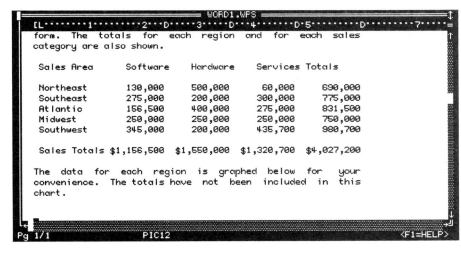

Figure 14.14

You should now have the spreadsheet data and several paragraphs in your word processing document.

❏ **Enter Ctrl/End then press the Enter key twice.**

❏ **Now enter the following sentences:**

    The data for each region is graphed below for your
    convenience. The totals have not been included in
    the chart.

❏ **Press the Enter key twice.**

Your screen should now look like Figure 14.14.

Inserting the Chart

It is now time to insert the chart. The chart has already been created and is in the **SALES** spreadsheet. To insert the chart, you need to select *Insert Chart* from the **Edit** menu. The dialog box for this option is shown in Figure 14.15.

❏ **Select *Insert Chart* from the *Edit* menu.**

You now must select the spreadsheet that contains the chart. Once you have the spreadsheet selected, all of the charts in the spreadsheet will be displayed in the chart box. Next, tab to the *Charts* list box and select the *Region Sales* chart.

❏ **Select *SALES.WKS* from the spreadsheets box.**

Figure 14.15

*The **Insert Chart** dialog box will display all the open spreadsheets. When you select a spreadsheet, the available charts for that spreadsheet are displayed. To insert a chart, select it and choose the **OK** button.*

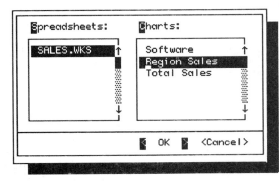

❑ **Tab to the *Charts* list box and select the *Region Sales* chart.**

❑ **Choose the *OK button*.**

The following chart placeholder should now appear in your document:

```
«chart SALES.WKS:Region Sales»
```

The chart will not display in your document; however, it will be printed when you print the document.

Completing the Letter

Now complete the document by entering the following closing.

❑ **Press the Enter key once.**

❑ **Enter the following closing:**
```
As you can see, sales continue to be strong in all
regions. We will discuss these figures at our next
managers meeting.

                              Sincerely,
                              (your name here)
```

Resizing the Chart

You have completed creating the form letter; however, you have one problem. Notice the page marker (») by the chart placeholder. This indicates that the chart will be printed on the second page of the letter, but you want the letter to fit on a single page. To correct this problem, you will need to make your chart smaller. You size a chart by selecting the placeholder as a block and then selecting the *Indents & Spacing* option from the **Format** menu. Do this now.

❑ **Select the chart place holder as a block.**

❑ **Select *Indents & Spacing* from the *Format* menu.**

You should now have the dialog box shown in Figure 14.16.

To change the chart, you will need to decrease its height. A height of 2.5 inches should be small enough to keep the entire document on one page. Since you are changing the height of the chart, you should also change the left and right indents to keep the chart somewhat proportional. Change the height of the chart and the margins now.

Figure 14.16

For a chart you use the Indents & Spacing option from the Format menu to change the chart's size and orientation.

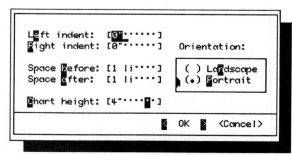

❑ Change the *Left Indent* to .5.

❑ Change the *Right Indent* to .5.

❑ Tab to the *Chart Height* entry and enter 2.5".

❑ Press the Enter key.

You will also need to change your page margins to 1 inch.

❑ Choose *Page Setup & Margins* from the *Print* menu.

❑ Set the left and right margins to 1 inch.

Check the position of the page marker now. If it is not below your name, make the chart a little smaller. Keep changing the size of the chart until it is small enough for the entire document to fit on one page.

Previewing the Letter

You can now preview your letter to see that it appears on the page correctly. When you preview a document that has a chart in it, the chart is also displayed. You can use the *Preview* option to determine whether the document is correct before you try to print it. Preview your document now. It should look like the one in Figure 14.17.

❑ Choose *Preview* from the *Print* menu.

❑ Press the Enter key to bypass the *Preview* dialog box.

Printing the Letter

The last step in completing the letter is to query the database to get only the managers you want. Assume you only want to send this letter to the managers in Virginia. To restrict the records merged when you

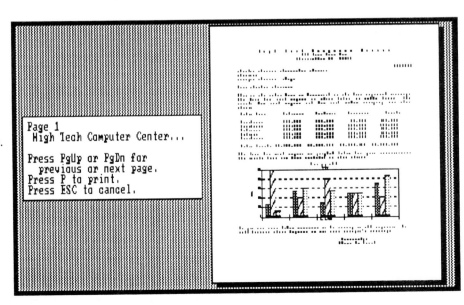

Figure 14.17

The Preview option in the Print menu can be used to determine that your charts appear the way you expect them to. The chart is displayed proportionally to the text.

print the form letter, you must make only these records visible in the database. Do this by making the following query on the database:

❑ **Press the Esc key to cancel the *Preview*.**

❑ **Select *MANAGERS.WDB* from the *Window* menu.**

❑ **Select *Query* from the *View* menu.**

❑ **Tab to the *State* field, enter VA, and press the Enter key.**

❑ **Choose *List* from the *View* menu. Three managers should now be visible.**

❑ **Select WORD1.WPS from the *Window* menu.**

You should now be back in the document window and ready to print your form letters. To print the form letters, you must choose the *Print Form Letters* option from the *Print* menu. This option will provide you with the dialog box shown in Figure 14.18. You must select the database from the dialog box and choose the *OK* button. Finally, you choose the *Print* button from the Print dialog box. Print your form letters now.

❑ **Select *Print Form Letters* from the *Print* menu.**

❑ **Select *MANAGERS.WDB* from the *Databases* list box.**

❑ **Press the Enter key.**

❑ **Select *Print* from the *Print* dialog box.**

Printing the Mailing Labels

Now assume that you will need mailing labels for your envelopes. To print mailing labels, you will need to create a new form. Start the form by selecting the *Create New File* option from the **File** menu.

❑ **Select *Create New File* from the *File* menu.**

❑ **Select *New Word Processor* from the applications screen.**

Since you already have the field placeholders in the form letter, the easiest way to create the mailing labels is to copy the the placeholders from your form letter. Do this now.

❑ **Choose the *Word1* file from the *Window* menu.**

❑ **Select the three lines that contain your mailing address.**

Figure 14.18

*The **Print Form Letters** option from the **Print** menu will provide a list box of all open databases. To merge the database with the form letter, you select the database that contains your data and choose the OK button.*

❑ **Choose** *Copy* **From the** *Edit* **menu.**

❑ **Choose the** *Word2* **file from the** *Window* **menu.**

❑ **Press the Enter key to complete the copy.**

Assume that you will be using labels that measure 1 inch by 2.5 inches set up as three across. This would give you 7.5 inches of labels (3 x 2.5). You must now remember that Works uses a default left margin of 1.3 inches and a right margin of 1.2 inches. This gives you 10 inches (7.5 + 1.3 + 1.2) for a page that is only 8.5 inches wide. To correct this, you should first change the *Page Setup & Margins* so the left and right margins are zero. Do this now.

❑ **Select** *Page Setup & Margins* **from the** *Print* **menu.**

❑ **Set the left margin to 0.**

❑ **Set the right margin to 0.**

❑ **Press the Enter key.**

Remember that you used a query to restrict the number of managers that received the letters. This time you want to print a mailing label for all managers. Before you print the labels, you will need to display all your records. Do this now.

❑ **Select** *MANAGERS.WDB* **from the** *Window* **menu.**

❑ **Choose** *Show all Records* **from the** *Select* **menu. You should now see all your records.**

❑ **Select** *WORD2.WPS* **from the** *Window* **menu.**

Now pull down the *Print* menu and select *Print Labels*.

❑ **Select** *Print Labels* **from the** *Print* **menu.**

You should get the *Print Labels* dialog box shown in Figure 14.19.

Make the following changes necessary to reflect the size and number of your labels and then print your labels:

❑ **Select** *MANAGERS.WDB* **as your database.**

❑ **Change** *Horizontal spacing* **to 2.5".**

❑ **Change** *Number of labels across page* **to 3.**

❑ **Select the** *Print* **button.**

❑ **Select** *Print* **from the** *Print* **dialog box.**

Figure 14.19

*The **Print Labels** option of the **Print** menu provides the labels dialog box. This box allows you set the size and number of labels across the page.*

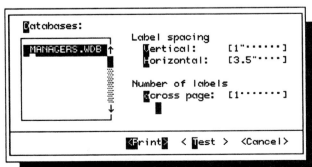

Conclusion

This completes your integration tutorial. You should save your two word processing documents before you exit Works. You will not need to save your database or spreadsheet, since no changes should have been made to them.

Hands on Practice

For this assignment, you will be using the files named HOP-14A1.WPS, HOP-14A2.WKS, and HOP-14A3.WDB. You will also be creating new word processing documents.

Exercise 1

Part 1

Create the document shown on the next page. To create this, document use the following requirements:

    ①   Use Insert Special and insert the Print Date here.

    ②   Enter this using data about yourself.

    ③   Copy this paragraph from the file named HOP-14A1.WPS.

    ④   Copy cells A1 through E7 from the spreadsheet named HOP-14A2.WKS.

    ⑤   Insert the chart named *Average* from the spreadsheet named HOP-14A2.WKS and insert it here.

    ⑥   Insert the chart named *Increase* from the spreadsheet named HOP-14A2.WKS and insert it here.

    ⑦   Query the database named HOP-14A3.WDB. Select all records that have Harrisonburg for the city, R2 for the zone, and between 1500 and 3500 square feet. Select all these records and copy them to here.

Part 2

Create a set of labels similar to the following for each of the records in the database named HOP-14A3.WDB. You should print the Contract number, Zone, City, and Appraisal price for each record. The labels are 1.5 inches high and 3 inches wide. There are two labels across. Print the labels sorted by city within state.

```
Contract: 10190                    Contract: 10678
Zone: B1   Harrisonburg           Zone: R1   Harrisonburg
Appraised: $35,000.00             Appraised: $37,900.00


Contract: 12222                    Contract: 12333
Zone: B2   Harrisonburg           Zone: B2   Augusta
Appraised: $27,800.00             Appraised: $250,000.00
```

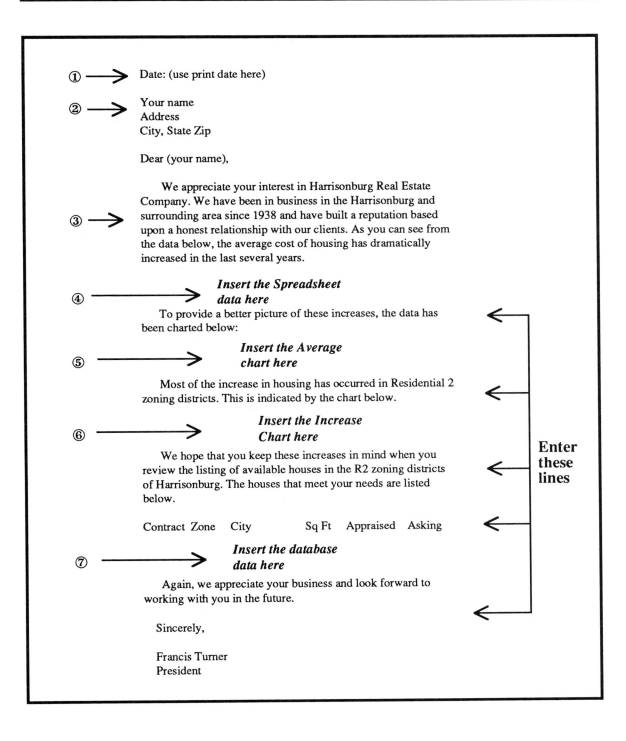

① → Date: (use print date here)

② → Your name
Address
City, State Zip

Dear (your name),

③ → We appreciate your interest in Harrisonburg Real Estate Company. We have been in business in the Harrisonburg and surrounding area since 1938 and have built a reputation based upon a honest relationship with our clients. As you can see from the data below, the average cost of housing has dramatically increased in the last several years.

④ → *Insert the Spreadsheet data here*

To provide a better picture of these increases, the data has been charted below:

⑤ → *Insert the Average chart here*

Most of the increase in housing has occurred in Residential 2 zoning districts. This is indicated by the chart below.

⑥ → *Insert the Increase Chart here*

We hope that you keep these increases in mind when you review the listing of available houses in the R2 zoning districts of Harrisonburg. The houses that meet your needs are listed below.

Contract Zone   City   Sq Ft   Appraised   Asking

⑦ → *Insert the database data here*

Again, we appreciate your business and look forward to working with you in the future.

Sincerely,

Francis Turner
President

Enter these lines

$\mathbf{A}$ ppendix

Telecommunications Concepts

You will find that it can be very helpful to have the ability to connect your computer to other systems so that you can communicate with other computers. This process is called **telecommunications**, since telephone lines are usually used to connect the computers together. One of the most powerful advantages of using telecommunications is the ability to connect your computer to many different kinds of computers, including other personal computers or even larger mainframe computers.

➢ *Using Your Computer as a Terminal to a Host Computer*

One of the most common ways in which you will use Microsoft Works to communicate is as a **terminal** or **remote computer**. When you use your personal computer as a terminal, it is acting as an input and output device to the other computer system. Normally, the other computer, which is often called the **host computer**, will be a larger, more sophisticated, mainframe computer. When you are connected to the host as a terminal, you will be able to run programs that are stored on the mainframe system and transfer information from the host to your personal computer. You can also transfer information from your PC to the host. This ability is very handy, since mainframes can store vast amounts of information that you can access when needed.

➢ *Communicating with Another Personal Computer*

The Microsoft Works software will also allow you to connect to another PC so you can transfer data from one machine to another. This peer-to-peer communications setup is most common when you want to transfer data from one PC to another but you cannot readily exchange diskettes between the systems due to either distance or incompatible diskette types. The use of telecommunications also allows you to exchange information between different kinds of computers (such as the IBM Personal Computer and the Apple Macintosh computer).

Telecommunications Hardware Requirements

Typically, computers are connected to one another through the use of telephone lines and will require several special pieces of equipment to operate correctly. Figure 1 provides an overview of most of the components required to utilize computer communications.

Figure 1

These are the typical components that are needed to send information between computers.

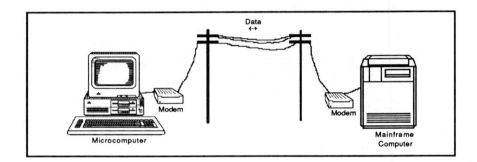

➤ *Using the Modem*

The computer stores data as a series of "bits," which are either "on" or "off." These digital bits are usually represented by a **1** when they are on and a **0** when off. By storing eight of these bits together, it is possible to store a character, or **byte**, of information.

Telephone lines, however, typically do not recognize these digital signals, since the phone system was designed to transmit voice frequencies which are **analog** in nature. You can see in Figure 2 that analog signals are transmitted in a continuous wave that varies with the frequency of the data. This is the same concept that we use when we talk and use high and low frequencies in our speech.

Figure 2

Digital signals must be converted to analog signals before transmitting.

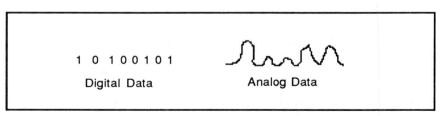

Figure 2 shows that the digital 1's and 0's sent by the computer are not compatible with the analog signal needed by the phone, so some conversion must be made between the two modes. This conversion is accomplished by the **modem**, which is used to translate the data signals from digital to analog or vice versa. When the modem translates from digital to analog, it is referred to as *modulation;* the translation from analog to digital is referred to as *demodulation.* These terms also provide the modem with its name, which is an acronym of these terms: **MOD**ulation **DEM**odulation.

Modems may be purchased either as an **external** modem or as an **internal** modem. An external modem is housed in a small separate box that is usually located next to your computer and connected to the computer via a plug called the serial port. The internal modem is installed inside the main unit of the machine.

Since a computer can only use digital data, you must have a modem on both sides of the communications link: one at the transmitting remote computer, and one at the host computer.

➤ The Serial Port

A computer **port** is special socket or plug that allows devices such as the modem or printer to be connected to the computer. The **serial** port is a special port that both transmits and receives data one bit at a time. When data is sent in this serial fashion, one bit of information is sent after another in a horizontal line. This serial port is often referred to as an **RS-232** serial port (sometimes called just a serial port) and normally has a 25-pin connector (this may also be a 9-pin connector on some computers) that is located on the back of the computer. These ports are displayed in Figure 3.

Figure 3

RS-232 serial ports can come in different sizes, but they work in the same way.

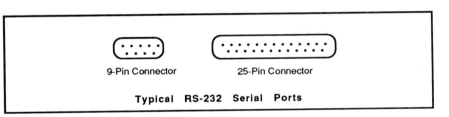

Figure 4

Serial transmission sends one bit at a time, while parallel sends eight bits or one character at a time.

There is usually one other type of port used on personal computer systems, called the **parallel** port. The parallel port gets its name from the bits of information that travel in a parallel fashion through the port. This port is used primarily for connecting the printer to the computer and is not used by the modem. The difference between serial and parallel transmission is shown in Figure 4.

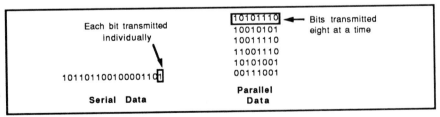

Telecommunications Software Requirements

In addition to the several hardware components required for communications, you will also need communications software. This software controls the data transmission from one computer to the other and provides the means to transfer files of data between computers. The Communications module of Microsoft Works does a good job in this area and can handle most requirements for computer communications.

➤ *The Function of Communications Software*

To better understand the functions performed by the communications software, consider the problems that can arise in our normal voice communications. When you talk to a friend over the phone, you are communicating in a manner similar to computer communications, except that you are the "host computer" and your friend is the "remote computer." You communicate by speaking words (in a language your friend understands), which consists of a series of syllables followed by a very short pause. These words are usually part of sentences, which are separated with a longer pause. Finally, if you do not include these pauses or if you talk too fast or too slow, your friend on the other end of the telephone line will have a difficult time understanding what you are saying. If for any reason your friend cannot understand your statements, he or she will ask you to repeat what you have said. These factors of transmission speed, message length, and error control are all present in computer communications and are handled by the communications software.

➤ *BAUD Rate (Transfer Speed)*

One of the most critical components of any communication is the speed at which the message is transmitted and received. This idea can be illustrated when you play a record too fast or too slow; the message is garbled and you probably will not understand all of what is said. This same thing happens with computers which use the **Baud Rate** to specify the speed at which data is to be sent and received. To avoid errors, both machines must send and receive data at the same speed. While each computer has a maximum speed at which it can operate, the modem is usually the constraining factor in that it operates at a lower speed than the computer. The modem speed or baud rate is used to define the number of bits that are transferred per second (bits per second, or **BPS**). Some of the more common rates include 300, 1,200, 2,400, 4,800, and 9,600 BPS. Usually, if your modem supports a higher BPS rate, it will also support the lower rates.

➤ *Setting the Baud Rate in Microsoft Works*

To set the BAUD rate in Microsoft Works, first open the telecommunications component of Works and then access the **Communications** option from the **Options** menu. This menu is shown in Figure 5.

➤ *Data Bits*

The **Data Bits** option, shown in Figure 5, specifies the number of digital bits that the host computer uses to denote a character. Typically, this value is either seven or eight bits and can be selected by tabbing to the Data Bits box and then using the arrow keys to scroll through the options. It is important that both the transmitting computer and the receiving computer use the same number of bits, so you need to find out how many bits the computer you are calling uses. Should you not have this information, try to communicate using the eight-bit option, which is most commonly used. If you see unreadable characters, try the seven-bit option.

Figure 5

The Communications Option box allows you to set the baud rate and several other options before you communicate with another computer.

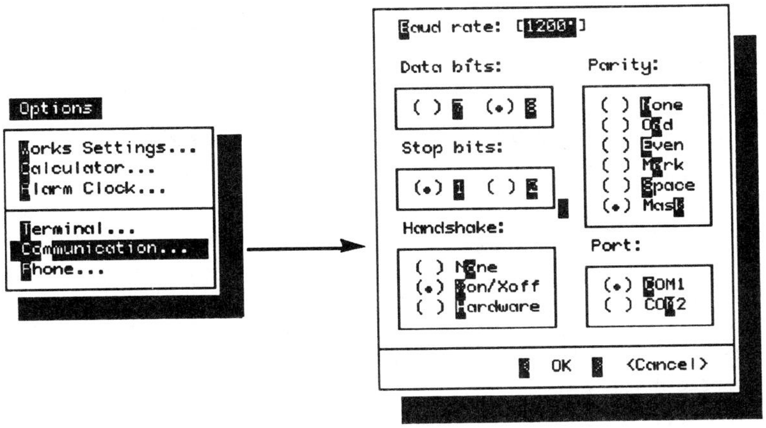

➤ Stop Bits

The next option displayed in the Communications dialog box specifies the number of **Stop Bits**. A stop bit acts like a pause in verbal communications in that it tells the receiving computer system that you have completed sending a specific character. Again, this parameter must be the same on both communicating computers; if you are uncertain as to the correct value, start with the stop bits set to 1.

➤ The Handshake Parameter

The fourth parameter that must be set defines the computer **Handshake**, which is a special character sent between the computers indicating that they are ready to send or receive data. This handshaking is most important when you are transmitting or receiving large segments of data.

The handshake concept is important, since most machines must perform some processing of the data as it is received. When the receiving computer is performing this processing, it would be possible for the sending machine to send too much data at one time and perhaps overload the receiving system, possibly resulting in the loss of some data. The automatic handshaking process avoids this problem by allowing the receiving machine to send a special signal to the sending machine instructing it to wait before more data is sent. When the receiving machine is again ready for more data, it notifies the transmitting system by sending a different signal. This automatic feature needs to be set the same for both systems; if you are uncertain as to the setting, try the XON/XOFF option.

➤ Establishing Parity

When we communicate with another person using verbal communications, we can easily ask for the message to be repeated if we do not understand something or if an error is made. This ability to check for errors is also required for computer communications, with the **Parity** system being one error-checking method available. Errors can occur when you send data across a telephone line, through the introduction of noise or static on the line. This static may then be interpreted as real data by the receiving computer, which would result in incorrect data. The parity system adds a given number of bits to each character sent, and when the character is received, the receiving computer checks these for the correct pattern. If the pattern is not correct, the receiving computer asks the sending computer to resend the message until the message is received correctly.

While the parity method does offer some protection against errors, many computers are now using more sophisticated methods that are automatic in their operation. For this reason, unless you know the parity setting for the computer you are communicating with, you should first try to communicate with parity set to the None position.

➢ *Specifying the Serial Port*

The **Port** specification is needed to identify which RS-232 serial communications port on the computer you will be using. While many computers are equipped with only one serial port, some computers have several. These ports are named as **COM1, COM2,** and **COM3,** depending on the number of ports the machine has. If you have only one serial port on your computer, it will likely be the COM1 port.

The Terminal Setup Screen

The Microsoft Works communications software allows you to specify certain characteristics of your computer to imitate a specific computer terminal. This process is known as **Terminal Emulation** and is very useful when you want to connect to a large computer that uses standard terminals of a specific type. The emulation process specifies such terminal characteristics as the clearing of the screen, positioning the cursor, and drawing lines. Since various terminal types operate differently, you will need to specify which kind of terminal you want Works to mimic. The choices of the **VT52** or the **ANSI** terminal type are found in the **Terminal** option of the **Options** menu and are illustrated in Figure 6. Ideally, you should find out from the computer center of the host computer what kind of terminal is used, however, in the absence of this information, you might try the ANSI specification first, as it is more commonly used.

The other options in this dialog box are normally set correctly; however, here are a couple of suggestions to try if you have problems:

Problem   *You connect to the host computer normally, but when you type, nothing shows on your screen.*
Answer: *The host computer needs the Local Echo option activated on your computer. Activate it in the Terminal option box.*

Problem: *Your screen does not display the very top line from the host computer; rather the Works menu shows on your computer.*
Answer: *Choose the Full Screen option shown in Figure 6. The Works menu will disappear, but you can call it up at any time by pressing the ALT key.*

Figure 6

Usually, you will set these options as shown here. If characters that you type do not appear on your screen, choose the Local Echo option.

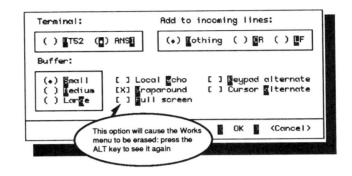

The Phone Setup Screen

Before you can communicate over a telephone line, you must first call and connect to the other computer system. The **Phone** option box of the **Options** menu will allow you to specify the phone number for the other computer system and some other setup commands for your modem. This will allow your modem to actually dial the other computer for you automatically. The Phone option box is shown in Figure 7.

Figure 7

Enter the host computer phone number in the Phone option box.

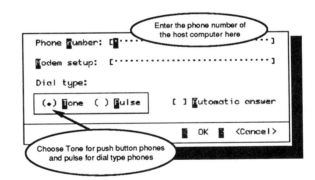

The phone number of the computer you want to call is entered in the **Phone Number** option box. The number should be entered using all the digits you would use if you were going to dial the number manually. You do not need to enter any hyphens or parentheses for the area code.

The **Modem Setup** option will allow you to specify special setup commands for your modem. These commands are specific to the type of modem you are using and are not required for normal modem dialing. See your modem instruction manual for a description of of these commands.

The **Dial Type** specifies the kind of telephone line you are using. The **Tone** option is used with the standard "Touch Tone" system, while the **Pulse** option refers to the older, rotary dialed phones.

The **Automatic Answer** option will set up your computer and modem to answer any incoming calls automatically. You might do this if you wanted to leave your machine on while you were away and let someone send you a file.

Saving the Communications Parameters

Once you have established all the parameters in the Options menu, you will want to save them as a file so that you do not have to enter them each time you decide to communicate. You can also save different files, each containing a different selection of options, for different computers that you usually communicate with. For example, you might have one file that you use to connect to the University system and another that is used to connect to a friend's computer.

To save the communications parameters that you have just entered, select the Save option under the File menu as you would to save a word processing file or spreadsheet. Works will then prompt you to enter a name for the file; just enter the first eight characters and Works will automatically enter the WCM extension to indicate it is a communications file.

Establishing Computer Communications

Once you have set up your machine with the communications parameters, you can establish the communications connection by using the **Connect** menu. This menu is shown in Figure 8.

Figure 8

The Connect menu is used to establish communications with another computer.

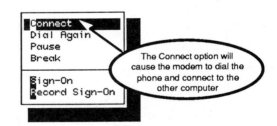

To establish a communication with another computer, select the **Connect** option from the **Connect** menu. Works will then check to see if there is a phone number in the Phone Number entry of the Phone dialog box and, if present, will cause this number to be dialed by your modem. This number will be displayed in the upper left corner of the computer screen while it is dialed. If there is no phone number in the entry, you must be directly connected to the computer by a cable or wire.

When the connection is made, a **CONNECT** message is displayed along with the BAUD rate that is being used. From this point on, you will be acting as a remote terminal on the computer system that you are connected to.

➢ Options in the Connect Menu

The **Dial Again** option will allow you to redial the number in case you get a busy signal the first time.

The **Pause** option will send a message to the sending or host machine to temporarily suspend sending data. When you are ready to receive data again, you can select **Pause** a second time. This option might be used when you are recording information to a diskette and need to change from one diskette to another.

The **Break** option will send a break signal to the host computer. This break is normally used to interrupt a program that is running on the host.

The **Sign-On** option allows you to **play back** a prerecorded sign-on sequence for the host computer, while the **Record Sign-On** option will record the sign-on sequence for play back at some future time.

Transferring Files Between Computers

One of the most useful benefits of communications is the ability to transfer files of information from one computer to another and thus easily share information between two computer users. This use of communications also uses the terms **host** and **remote computers** to identify each system.

When you transfer data between computers, you will *upload* or *download* data, depending on the direction of the transfer. When you *upload* data, you send data from the remote computer to the host, while *downloading* means you are transferring data from the host to the remote system. You may find that you want to download information when you want access to data or programs stored on a large mainframe or information service. There may also be times when you will need to use the power of the large mainframe to process data that is stored on your machine. In this case, you would need to upload the data.

This upload ability can be especially useful when developing a new program or taking programming courses that use the mainframe computer for processing. In this situation, you could create the program using Microsoft's word processor and then upload the file to the mainframe for testing. This would allow you to use all of the powerful word processing features for data entry and editing but still use the mainframe for actual program execution.

➤ *Preparing for File Transfer Using ASCII or TEXT Formats*

When you begin to transfer files from one computer to another, you will probably see the term "**ASCII files**" used. ASCII is an abbreviation for "American Standard Code for Information Interchange" and specifies a standard kind of file that can be used by many different computer systems. The ASCII format removes any special codes or control characters that are used by word processors and other software to align tabs, underline, change fonts, and so forth. If these codes were left in the file to be transferred, they could be interpreted differently by the other computer systems software, and unpredictable results could occur.

You can have Microsoft Works save files in the ASCII format by choosing the File menu and then selecting the **Text** option in the **Save As** dialog box. This save feature should be done in the Works module in which the document was created; for example, word processing documents should be saved in the TEXT format in the word processing module.

➤ *Downloading Files from the Host Computer with XMODEM*

To download or receive files from the host computer, you should already be connected to the host and somewhat familiar with the host operation. Most host computers that offer files for downloading will have a Help function that will describe the method that the host computer uses to download information.

Usually, this procedure will have you first specify the name or identification number of the file you want to download. The host will then ask you to choose the download method or protocol you would like to use. These protocols provide error checking to be sure the file is transferred correctly, and you will need to be sure to choose the one that is supported by Works, which is called **XMODEM**. After you have specified to the host that you would like to transfer the file using the XMODEM protocol, the host will wait for you to prepare the Works software on your computer to receive the file.

To instruct Works to receive a file using the XMODEM protocol, choose the **Transfer** menu and then select the **Receive File** option, as shown in Figure 9. When you highlight the Receive File option, you should see the statement "Receives file using XMODEM protocol" on the bottom left of your screen. Press Enter to begin the transfer.

Figure 9

Transfer files between two computers with the options in the Transfer menu.

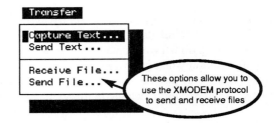

Works will next present you with a Save As dialog box in which you will need to specify the name under which the file will be saved. The file transfer will now proceed automatically with Works, updating you of the progress with a Transfer status box similar to Figure 10.

Figure 10

The Transfer file status box will keep you informed on the file transfer progress.

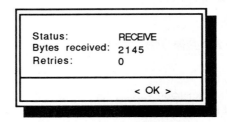

Works will notify you in the status box when the file transfer is complete; just press Enter to proceed. The file is now transferred to your computer and stored under the name you specified.

➤ *Uploading Files to the Host Computer Using XMODEM*

Uploading files to the host system works much the same as downloading, except that you will send files to the host rather than receive them. Again, you will first need to determine how the host system handles file uploads before continuing (you might want to check for help screens on the host, as many systems will have these to guide you). Once you have informed the host that you want to upload, you will need to tell it the file name and the protocol you will use, which will again be XMODEM. Next, select the **Send File** option from the Transfer menu that was illustrated in Figure 9. Works will now provide a list of all the files that are available so that you can select the file you want to transfer by first tabbing to the file box and using the arrow keys to select the file to upload. When you press Enter, the transfer will begin and the transfer status dialog should appear on your screen as shown in Figure 10, except that the word Send will replace Receive. When the transfer is complete, press the **Enter** key to finish the procedure.

The Ethical Use of Telecommunications

The ability to communicate between two computers is a powerful tool with which to distribute information quickly and accurately. It is possible, through the use of telecommunications, to access data and knowledge across town or across the country and therefore greatly enhance your ability to learn and advance. However, as with any powerful tool, it is possible to use computer communications in a fraudulent or even criminal manner. Many times, such efforts are started by individuals who just want to see if they can "break in" to another system and really do not mean to harm another individual's data. Other times, the intent is to try to steal or destroy data. Fortunately, such efforts, although widely publicized, are minimal and relatively easy to protect against. Further, there are now severe penalties to users who seek to break into other systems.

These concerns can be avoided through the ethical use of computers in general and telecommunications in particular. Simply put, ethical use means not attempting to break into other systems through fraudulent methods. These methods might include the use of another individual's password, copying a program from another for your own use, and the like. You should also be aware that the vast majority of host systems are very well equipped with security systems that can alert the authorities even as the unauthorized user is trying to gain access.

Conclusion

Telecommunications can open an entirely new world to the microcomputer user. Since you can access larger, more powerful computer systems, you conceivably have all the power of these larger systems at your fingertips. The larger systems normally have more information and more programs that you can access. Using telecommunications you can access many library systems to check on the availability of a book. You can also access financial information on any publicly held corporation or even shop through your computer. You can perform much of a research project sitting at your own microcomputer. In the future, this capability will dramatically expand and provide more information at your fingertips.

Telecommunications Self Test

1. Explain what the terms **host** and **remote** computer systems refer to.

2. What is meant by **downloading** and **uploading** a file?

3. What is the function of **a modem** in telecommunications?

4. What is the difference between **digital** and **analog** data?

5. Explain what each of the following refers to:

   a. BAUD rate

   b. Data bits

   c. Stop bits

   d. Handshake

   e. Parity

   f. Port

6. List the steps required to transfer a file from your Microcomputer to a host mainframe computer.

Index